Infectious Disease

ACP American College of Physicians®
Leading Internal Medicine, Improving Lives

Welcome to the Infectious Disease Section of MKSAP 18!

In these pages, you will find updated information on central nervous system infections, skin and soft tissue infections, community-acquired pneumonia, tick-borne diseases, urinary tract infections, *Mycobacterium tuberculosis* and nontuberculous mycobacterial infections, sexually transmitted infections, bioterrorism, travel medicine, infectious gastrointestinal syndromes, transplant-associated infections, HIV and AIDS, health care–associated infections, and other clinical challenges. All of these topics are uniquely focused on the needs of generalists and subspecialists *outside* of infectious disease.

The core content of MKSAP 18 has been developed as in previous editions—all essential information that is newly researched and written in 11 topic areas of internal medicine—created by dozens of leading generalists and subspecialists and guided by certification and recertification requirements, emerging knowledge in the field, and user feedback. MKSAP 18 also contains 1200 all-new peer-reviewed, psychometrically validated, multiple-choice questions (MCQs) for self-assessment and study, including 108 in Infectious Disease. MKSAP 18 continues to include *High Value Care* (HVC) recommendations, based on the concept of balancing clinical benefit with costs and harms, with associated MCQs illustrating these principles and HVC Key Points called out in the text. Internists practicing in the hospital setting can easily find comprehensive *Hospitalist*-focused content and MCQs, specially designated in blue and with the ⊞ symbol.

If you purchased MKSAP 18 Complete, you also have access to MKSAP 18 Digital, with additional tools allowing you to customize your learning experience. MKSAP Digital includes regular text updates with new, practice-changing information, 200 new self-assessment questions, and enhanced custom-quiz options. MKSAP Complete also includes more than 1200 electronic, adaptive learning–enhanced flashcards for quick review of important concepts, as well as an updated and enhanced version of Virtual Dx, MKSAP's image-based self-assessment tool. As before, MKSAP 18 Digital is optimized for use on your mobile devices, with iOS- and Android-based apps allowing you to sync between your apps and online account and submit for CME credits and MOC points online.

Please visit us at the MKSAP Resource Site (mksap.acponline.org) to find out how we can help you study, earn CME credit and MOC points, and stay up to date.

On behalf of the many internists who have offered their time and expertise to create the content for MKSAP 18 and the editorial staff who work to bring this material to you in the best possible way, we are honored that you have chosen to use MKSAP 18 and appreciate any feedback about the program you may have. Please feel free to send any comments to mksap_editors@acponline.org.

Sincerely,

Patrick C. Alguire, MD, FACP
Editor-in-Chief
Senior Vice President Emeritus
Medical Education Division
American College of Physicians

Infectious Disease

Committee

Patricia D. Brown, MD, FACP, Section Editor[1]
Professor of Medicine
Wayne State University School of Medicine
Associate Chief of Staff for Medicine
John D. Dingell VA Medical Center
Detroit, Michigan

Karen C. Bloch, MD, MPH, FACP[1]
Associate Professor
Department of Medicine and Health Policy
Division of Infectious Diseases
Vanderbilt University Medical Center
Nashville, Tennessee

Larry M. Bush, MD, FACP[2]
Affiliated Professor of Biomedical Sciences
Charles E. Schmidt College of Medicine
Florida Atlantic University
Boca Raton, Florida
Affiliated Associate Professor of Medicine
University of Miami-Miller School of Medicine
JFK Medical Center
Palm Beach County, Florida

Louise M. Dembry, MD, MS, MBA, FACP[2]
Professor of Medicine
Infectious Diseases and Epidemiology
Yale University School of Medicine
New Haven, Connecticut

Michael Frank, MD, FACP[1]
Professor of Medicine
Chief, Division of Infectious Diseases
Vice Chair for Education
Department of Medicine
Medical College of Wisconsin
Milwaukee, Wisconsin

Rodrigo Hasbun, MD, MPH[2]
Professor of Medicine
Department of Infectious Diseases
UT Health-McGovern Medical School
Houston, Texas

Fred A. Lopez, MD, MACP[2]
Richard Vial Professor
Vice Chair for Education
Department of Medicine
Louisiana State University Health Sciences Center
New Orleans, Louisiana

Jose A. Vazquez, MD, FACP[2]
Chief, Division of Infectious Diseases
Professor, Department of Medicine
Medical College of Georgia at Augusta University
Augusta, Georgia

Editor-in-Chief

Patrick C. Alguire, MD, FACP[2]
Senior Vice President Emeritus, Medical Education
American College of Physicians
Philadelphia, Pennsylvania

Deputy Editor

Davoren Chick, MD, FACP[2]
Senior Vice President, Medical Education
American College of Physicians
Philadelphia, Pennsylvania

Infectious Disease Reviewers
Susan C. Bleasdale, MD, FACP[2]
Beata C. Casanas, DO, FACP[2]
Manjit S. Dhillon, MBBS, FACP[1]
Dimitri M. Drekonja, MD, FACP[1]
Lisa A. Grohskopf, MD[1]
Muhammad Umar Khan, MBBS, FACP[1]
Felicia M. Lewis, MD, FACP[1]
Maricar F. Malinis, MD, FACP[2]
Zaw Min, MD, FACP[1]
George Samuel, MD[1]

Hospital Medicine Infectious Disease Reviewers

Ji Hoon Baang, MD, FACP[2]
Jeana Benwill, MD[1]

Infectious Disease ACP Editorial Staff

Linnea Donnarumma[1], Staff Editor
Margaret Wells[1], Director, Self-Assessment and Educational Programs
Becky Krumm[1], Managing Editor, Self-Assessment and Educational Programs

ACP Principal Staff

Davoren Chick, MD FACP[2]
Senior Vice President, Medical Education

Acknowledgments

The American College of Physicians (ACP) gratefully acknowledges the special contributions to the development and production of the 18th edition of the Medical Knowledge Self-Assessment Program® (MKSAP® 18) made by the following people:

Graphic Design: Barry Moshinski (Director, Graphic Services), Michael Ripca (Graphics Technical Administrator), and Jennifer Gropper (Graphic Designer).

Production/Systems: Dan Hoffmann (Director, Information Technology), Scott Hurd (Manager, Content Systems), Nell Kohl (Senior Architect), and Chris Patterson (Senior Architect).

MKSAP 18 Digital: Under the direction of Steven Spadt (Senior Vice President, Technology), the digital version of MKSAP 18 was developed within the ACP's Digital Products and Services Department, led by Brian Sweigard (Director, Digital Products and Services). Other members of the team included Dan Barron (Senior Web Application Developer/Architect), Chris Forrest (Senior Software Developer/Design Lead), Kathleen Hoover (Senior Web Developer), Kara Regis (Manager, User Interface Design and Development), Brad Lord (Senior Web Application Developer), and John McKnight (Senior Web Developer).

The College also wishes to acknowledge that many other persons, too numerous to mention, have contributed to the production of this program. Without their dedicated efforts, this program would not have been possible.

MKSAP Resource Site (mksap.acponline.org)

The MKSAP Resource Site (mksap.acponline.org) is a continually updated site that provides links to MKSAP 18 online answer sheets for print subscribers; access to MKSAP 18 Digital; Board Basics® e-book access instructions; information on Continuing Medical Education (CME), Maintenance of Certification (MOC), and international Continuing Professional Development (CPD) and MOC; errata; and other new information.

International MOC/CPD

For information and instructions on submission of international MOC/CPD, please go to the MKSAP Resource Site (mksap.acponline.org).

Continuing Medical Education

The American College of Physicians is accredited by the Accreditation Council for Continuing Medical Education (ACCME) to provide continuing medical education for physicians.

The American College of Physicians designates this enduring material, MKSAP 18, for a maximum of 275 *AMA PRA Category 1 Credits*™. Physicians should claim only the credit commensurate with the extent of their participation in the activity.

Up to 25 *AMA PRA Category 1 Credits*™ are available from December 31, 2018, to December 31, 2021, for the MKSAP 18 Infectious Disease section.

Learning Objectives

The learning objectives of MKSAP 18 are to:

- Close gaps between actual care in your practice and preferred standards of care, based on best evidence
- Diagnose disease states that are less common and sometimes overlooked and confusing
- Improve management of comorbid conditions that can complicate patient care
- Determine when to refer patients for surgery or care by subspecialists
- Pass the ABIM Certification Examination
- Pass the ABIM Maintenance of Certification Examination

Target Audience

- General internists and primary care physicians
- Subspecialists who need to remain up to date in internal medicine
- Residents preparing for the certifying examination in internal medicine
- Physicians preparing for maintenance of certification in internal medicine (recertification)

ABIM Maintenance of Certification

Check the MKSAP Resource Site (mksap.acponline.org) for the latest information on how MKSAP tests can be used to apply to the American Board of Internal Medicine (ABIM) for Maintenance of Certification (MOC) points following completion of the CME activity.

Successful completion of the CME activity, which includes participation in the evaluation component, enables the participant to earn up to 275 medical knowledge MOC points in the ABIM's MOC program. It is the CME activity provider's responsibility to submit participant completion information to ACCME for the purpose of granting MOC credit.

Earn Instantaneous CME Credits or MOC Points Online

Print subscribers can enter their answers online to earn instantaneous CME credits or MOC points. You can submit your answers using online answer sheets that are provided at mksap.acponline.org, where a record of your MKSAP 18 credits will be available. To earn CME credits or to apply for MOC points, you need to answer all of the questions in a test and earn a score of at least 50% correct (number of correct answers divided by the total number of questions). Please note that if you are applying for MOC points, you must also enter your birth date and ABIM candidate number.

Take either of the following approaches:

1. Use the printed answer sheet at the back of this book to record your answers. Go to mksap.acponline.org, access the appropriate online answer sheet, transcribe your answers, and submit your test for instantaneous CME credits or MOC points. There is no additional fee for this service.

2. Go to mksap.acponline.org, access the appropriate online answer sheet, directly enter your answers, and submit your test for instantaneous CME credits or MOC points. There is no additional fee for this service.

Earn CME Credits or MOC Points by Mail or Fax

Pay a $20 processing fee per answer sheet and submit the printed answer sheet at the back of this book by mail or fax, as instructed on the answer sheet. Make sure you calculate your score and enter your birth date and ABIM candidate number, and fax the answer sheet to 215-351-2799 or mail the answer sheet to Member and Customer Service, American College of Physicians, 190 N. Independence Mall West, Philadelphia, PA 19106-1572, using the courtesy envelope provided in your MKSAP 18 slipcase. You will need your 10-digit order number and 8-digit ACP ID number, which are printed on your packing slip. Please allow 4 to 6 weeks for your score report to be emailed back to you. Be sure to include your email address for a response.

If you do not have a 10-digit order number and 8-digit ACP ID number, or if you need help creating a user-name and password to access the MKSAP 18 online answer sheets, go to mksap.acponline.org or email custserv@acponline.org.

Disclosure Policy

It is the policy of the American College of Physicians (ACP) to ensure balance, independence, objectivity, and scientific rigor in all of its educational activities. To this end, and consistent with the policies of the ACP and the Accreditation Council for Continuing Medical Education (ACCME), contributors to all ACP continuing medical education activities are required to disclose all relevant financial relationships with any entity producing, marketing, re-selling, or distributing health care goods or services consumed by, or used on, patients. Contributors are required to use generic names in the discussion of therapeutic options and are required to identify any unapproved, off-label, or investigative use of commercial products or devices. Where a trade name is used, all available

trade names for the same product type are also included. If trade-name products manufactured by companies with whom contributors have relationships are discussed, contributors are asked to provide evidence-based citations in support of the discussion. The information is reviewed by the committee responsible for producing this text. If necessary, adjustments to topics or contributors' roles in content development are made to balance the discussion. Further, all readers of this text are asked to evaluate the content for evidence of commercial bias and send any relevant comments to mksap_editors@acponline.org so that future decisions about content and contributors can be made in light of this information.

Resolution of Conflicts

To resolve all conflicts of interest and influences of vested interests, ACP's content planners used best evidence and updated clinical care guidelines in developing content, when such evidence and guidelines were available. All content underwent review by peer reviewers not on the committee to ensure that the material was balanced and unbiased. Contributors' disclosure information can be found with the list of contributors' names and those of ACP principal staff listed in the beginning of this book.

Hospital-Based Medicine

For the convenience of subscribers who provide care in hospital settings, content that is specific to the hospital setting has been highlighted in blue. Hospital icons (🏥) highlight where the hospital-only content begins, continues over more than one page, and ends.

High Value Care Key Points

Key Points in the text that relate to High Value Care concepts (that is, concepts that discuss balancing clinical benefit with costs and harms) are designated by the HVC icon [**HVC**].

Educational Disclaimer

The editors and publisher of MKSAP 18 recognize that the development of new material offers many opportunities for error. Despite our best efforts, some errors may persist in print. Drug dosage schedules are, we believe, accurate and in accordance with current standards. Readers are advised, however, to ensure that the recommended dosages in MKSAP 18 concur with the information provided in the product information material. This is especially important in cases of new, infrequently used, or highly toxic drugs. Application of the information in MKSAP 18 remains the professional responsibility of the practitioner.

The primary purpose of MKSAP 18 is educational. Information presented, as well as publications, technologies, products, and/or services discussed, is intended to inform subscribers about the knowledge, techniques, and experiences of the contributors. A diversity of professional opinion exists, and the views of the contributors are their own and not those of the ACP. Inclusion of any material in the program does not constitute endorsement or recommendation by the ACP. The ACP does not warrant the safety, reliability, accuracy, completeness, or usefulness of and disclaims any and all liability for damages and claims that may result from the use of information, publications, technologies, products, and/or services discussed in this program.

Publisher's Information

Disclaimer Regarding Direct Purchases from Online Retailers

CME and/or MOC for MKSAP 18 is available only if you purchase the program directly from ACP. CME credits and MOC points cannot be awarded to those purchasers who have purchased the program from non-authorized sellers such as Amazon, eBay, or any other such online retailer.

Unauthorized Use of This Book Is Against the Law

MKSAP 18 ISBN: 978-1-938245-47-3
(Infectious Disease) ISBN: 978-1-938245-56-5

Printed in the United States of America.

For order information in the U.S. or Canada call 800-ACP-1915. All other countries call 215-351-2600, (Monday to Friday, 9 AM – 5 PM ET). Fax inquiries to 215-351-2799 or email to custserv@acponline.org.

Errata

Errata for MKSAP 18 will be available through the MKSAP Resource Site at mksap.acponline.org as new information becomes known to the editors.

Table of Contents

Infectious Disease High Value Care Recommendations

The American College of Physicians, in collaboration with multiple other organizations, is engaged in a worldwide initiative to promote the practice of High Value Care (HVC). The goals of the HVC initiative are to improve health care outcomes by providing care of proven benefit and reducing costs by avoiding unnecessary and even harmful interventions. The initiative comprises several programs that integrate the important concept of health care value (balancing clinical benefit with costs and harms) for a given intervention into a broad range of educational materials to address the needs of trainees, practicing physicians, and patients.

HVC content has been integrated into MKSAP 18 in several important ways. MKSAP 18 includes HVC-identified key points in the text, HVC-focused multiple choice questions, and, for subscribers to MKSAP Digital, an HVC custom quiz. From the text and questions, we have generated the following list of HVC recommendations that meet the definition below of high value care and bring us closer to our goal of improving patient outcomes while conserving finite resources.

High Value Care Recommendation: A recommendation to choose diagnostic and management strategies for patients in specific clinical situations that balance clinical benefit with cost and harms with the goal of improving patient outcomes.

Below are the High Value Care Recommendations for the Infectious Disease section of MKSAP 18.

- Blood cultures are not routinely indicated in patients with erysipelas and cellulitis.
- Primary treatment for abscesses, furuncles, and carbuncles is incision and drainage; mild infections do not require antibiotic therapy.
- Uninfected diabetic foot wounds should not be cultured or treated with antibiotics.
- Diagnostic studies to identify a causative organism are not routinely indicated in outpatients with community-acquired pneumonia.
- Patients with erythema migrans and a compatible exposure history do not require confirmatory laboratory testing for Lyme disease and should receive oral antibiotic therapy.

- No treatment is indicated for asymptomatic bacteriuria in otherwise healthy, nonpregnant patients (see Item 100).
- Urine culture is not recommended in women with uncomplicated cystitis.
- Indications for screening for and possibly treating asymptomatic bacteriuria include pregnancy and before an invasive urologic procedure (see Item 12).
- Follow-up urine cultures for acute pyelonephritis are only indicated in pregnant women.
- Acute, uncomplicated pyelonephritis can usually be managed with oral outpatient antimicrobial therapy (see Item 14).
- *Candida* isolated from the respiratory tract and urinary tract usually represents colonization; treatment is not indicated unless clinical infection is suspected.
- Test of cure is not recommended for *Chlamydia trachomatis* infection except in pregnancy.
- Test of cure in patients with *Neisseria gonorrhoeae* infection is recommended only when pharyngeal gonorrhea is treated with an alternate antibiotic regimen.
- The specificity of plain radiographs can confirm the diagnosis of osteomyelitis in most patients.
- Fluid replacement is the mainstay of treatment for travelers' diarrhea.
- Most healthy patients with watery diarrhea of less than 3 days' duration can be treated with supportive care and no antibiotic therapy or microscopic assessment.
- Most uncomplicated *Salmonella* infections in adults younger than 50 years resolve within 1 week and require only supportive care.
- Enterotoxigenic *Escherichia coli* infection is usually a self-limiting illness that resolves without treatment after approximately 4 days.
- Hand hygiene is the foundation of infection prevention.
- Catheter-associated asymptomatic bacteriuria generally does not require treatment.
- Antimicrobial- or antiseptic-coated catheters have not shown benefit for short-term or long-term bladder catheterization.
- Central venous catheters should be assessed daily for continued necessity and removed promptly when they are no longer needed (see Item 41).

Infectious Disease

Central Nervous System Infections

Meningitis

A positive Gram stain result for bacteria or yeast is seen in only 5% of patients with community-acquired meningitis. Meningitis with a negative Gram stain result is a diagnostic and management challenge because the differential diagnosis includes urgent treatable causes, such as bacterial or fungal meningitis. Bacterial cultures of cerebrospinal fluid (CSF) or blood are needed for antimicrobial sensitivity studies in suspected bacterial meningitis, but results are insufficiently timely to differentiate bacterial from viral meningitis. In situations of clinical uncertainty, rapid diagnostic techniques such as polymerase chain reaction (PCR) for common viruses and arboviral serologies can reduce use of clinically unhelpful cranial imaging, hospitalization, and antimicrobial therapy.

Viral Meningitis

Enteroviruses are the most common cause of viral meningitis, usually presenting between May and November in the Western Hemisphere, with symptoms including headache, fever, nuchal rigidity, photophobia, nausea, vomiting, myalgias, pharyngitis, maculopapular rash, and cough. Lymphocytic pleocytosis of the CSF with a normal glucose level and mildly elevated protein level is typical (Table 1). The diagnosis is confirmed by enterovirus PCR. Treatment is supportive with a benign clinical course.

Herpesviruses can cause meningitis year round and include herpes simplex virus (HSV) types 1 and 2, varicella-zoster virus (VZV), cytomegalovirus, Epstein-Barr virus, and human herpesvirus 6. Of the herpesviruses, HSV-2 is the most common cause of viral meningitis that can sometimes recur (recurrent benign lymphocytic meningitis, also called Mollaret meningitis). The CSF findings resemble enteroviral meningitis. Outcomes for HSV-2 meningitis are generally favorable without the need for acyclovir therapy.

VZV can cause encephalitis, aseptic meningitis, myelitis, and a vasculitis presenting as a stroke. Vesicular lesions are a clue to the diagnosis but may be absent (zoster sine herpete). VZV encephalitis and vasculitis may present with a hemorrhagic CSF. VZV may be present in the CSF without meningitis or encephalitis, and patients with primary varicella or zoster do not require lumbar puncture unless they have clinical signs of central nervous system (CNS) involvement. Immunocompromised and older adult patients are at higher risk of VZV meningitis and encephalitis. The diagnosis is confirmed by VZV PCR of the CSF, and therapy is parenteral acyclovir.

TABLE 1. Typical CSF Findings in Patients with Viral and Bacterial Meningitis

CSF Parameter	Viral Meningitis[a]	Bacterial Meningitis
Opening pressure	≤250 mm H_2O	200-500[b] mm H_2O
Leukocyte count	50-1000/μL (50-1000 × 10^6/L)	1000-5000/μL (1000-5000 × 10^6/L)[c]
Leukocyte predominance	Lymphocytes[d]	Neutrophils
Glucose level	>45 mg/dL (2.5 mmol/L)[e]	<40 mg/dL (2.2 mmol/L)[f]
Protein level	<200 mg/dL (2000 mg/L)	100-500 mg/dL (1000-5000 mg/L)
Gram stain	Negative	Positive in 60%-90%[g]
Culture	Negative	Positive in 70%-85%[h]

CSF = cerebrospinal fluid.

[a]Primarily nonpolio enteroviruses (echoviruses and coxsackieviruses) and West Nile virus between June and October; herpes simplex type 2 year round.

[b]Values exceeding 600 mm H_2O suggest the presence of cerebral edema, intracranial suppurative foci, or communicating hydrocephalus.

[c]Range may be <100/μL (100 × 10^6/L) to >10,000/μL (10,000 × 10^6/L).

[d]Neutrophil predominance occurs in 25% of viral meningitis cases, usually early in infection and more likely in young children with enteroviral infection.

[e]A mild hypoglycorrhachia (30-45 mg/dL [1.7-2.5 mmol/L]) can be seen in viral infections such as herpes simplex virus and West Nile virus.

[f]The CSF-to-plasma glucose ratio is ≤0.40 in most patients.

[g]The likelihood of a positive Gram stain correlates with the number of bacteria in the CSF.

[h]The yield of positive results is significantly reduced by previous administration of antimicrobial therapy.

CONT.

Mosquito-borne viruses such as West Nile virus (WNV), St. Louis encephalitis, and California encephalitis can cause meningitis or encephalitis between June and October in the Western Hemisphere. Neuroinvasive WNV may present with acute flaccid paralysis, which may lead to persistent weakness or death. The CSF formula resembles enteroviral meningitis. The diagnosis is made by serum or CSF serology (WNV IgM); WNV PCR of the CSF is insensitive. Treatment is supportive.

Acute HIV infection can present as aseptic meningitis associated with a mononucleosis-like syndrome with fever, rash, and myalgias.

Less common viral causes include mumps, lymphocytic choriomeningitis virus, parainfluenza, adenoviruses, influenza A and B, measles, rubella, poliovirus, rotavirus, and parvovirus B19.

KEY POINTS

- Enteroviruses are the most common cause of viral meningitis, usually presenting with symptoms of headache, fever, nuchal rigidity, photophobia, nausea, vomiting, myalgias, pharyngitis, maculopapular rash, and cough between May and November.
- Herpesviruses can cause meningitis year round; herpes simplex virus 2 is the most common cause and can recur.
- Neuroinvasive West Nile virus may present with acute flaccid paralysis, which may lead to persistent weakness or death.

Bacterial Meningitis

Bacterial meningitis usually presents with acute meningeal signs (fever, nuchal rigidity) and altered mental status. Since the introduction of conjugate vaccines, *Haemophilus influenzae* and *Neisseria meningitides* meningitis incidence has decreased, making *Streptococcus pneumoniae* the most common cause of community-acquired bacterial meningitis. *N. meningitides* serogroup B accounts for 40% of infections in the United States because the quadrivalent conjugate vaccine (ACYW-135) does not include serogroup B. Two FDA-approved vaccines that target serogroup B are available in the United States. *Streptococcus agalactiae* is now the third most common cause of bacterial meningitis in adults. *Listeria monocytogenes* is an uncommon cause of meningitis in adults; however, the risk increases in older adults and those with altered cell-mediated immunity.

Bacterial endocarditis caused by *S. pneumoniae* and *Staphylococcus aureus* can present as purulent meningitis. Clinical clues include a history of valvular disease, a new regurgitant murmur, embolic phenomena, or other stigmata of endocarditis. Injection drug use and hemodialysis are risk factors for *S. aureus*, and alcoholism is a risk factor for *S. pneumoniae* endocarditis. Patients may also present with stroke symptoms secondary to embolic infarction.

Lyme disease, caused by *Borrelia burgdorferi*, can present with a lymphocytic meningitis approximately 2 to 10 weeks after development of erythema migrans. Common clinical features include headache, photophobia, nausea, history of erythema migrans, tick bite in an endemic area, and facial paralysis, which can be unilateral or bilateral. Because the CSF formula resembles enteroviral meningitis, the "rule of 7s" was derived and validated to accurately classify a patient at low risk of having Lyme disease (headache duration <7 days, <70% CSF mononuclear cells, and absence of a seventh facial nerve palsy).

Treponema pallidum meningitis can occur in the secondary or tertiary phase of syphilis. Headache and meningismus are common, and the CSF usually shows a lymphocytic pleocytosis with an elevated protein level. In tertiary syphilis, neurosyphilis can be asymptomatic or symptomatic. Symptomatic neurosyphilis can present with primarily meningovascular (stroke presentation) or parenchymatous (tabes dorsalis, general paresis) features.

Leptospiral meningitis develops in the immune or second phase of the illness and is classically associated with uveitis, rash, conjunctival suffusion, lymphadenopathy, and hepatosplenomegaly. The CSF formula resembles enteroviral meningitis, and the diagnosis is established by CSF or urine culture or by serology.

Evaluation

All patients with suspected meningitis should undergo lumbar puncture. CSF findings characteristic of bacterial meningitis are provided in Table 1. A negative CSF Gram stain result is more common in patients with previous antibiotic therapy or in patients with *L. monocytogenes* or gram-negative bacilli (sensitivity <50%) infections. CSF latex agglutination tests for detecting bacterial antigens are no longer recommended because of low sensitivity (70%) and specificity, although they may play a role in patients with previous antibiotic therapy or culture-negative meningitis. Multiplex PCR assay for detection of *S. pneumoniae*, *N. meningitidis*, *H. influenzae*, and *L. monocytogenes* has high sensitivity (100%) and specificity (98%) and is increasingly available. If a head CT is indicated before lumbar puncture (focal neurologic findings, altered mental status, papilledema, new seizure, history of CNS disease, or immunocompromise), imaging should not delay empiric antibiotic therapy, which should be started after promptly obtaining blood cultures. See **Figure 1** for management of suspected bacterial meningitis.

Management

Intravenous antibiotic therapy should be started as soon as possible. If the CSF Gram stain result is negative, initial empiric antibiotic selection is based on age, local epidemiologic patterns of pneumococcal resistance, and the necessity for ampicillin coverage for *L. monocytogenes* (**Table 2**). Despite antibiotic therapy, mortality for bacterial meningitis remains approximately 25%. Adjunctive dexamethasone (10 mg every 6 hours for 4 days)

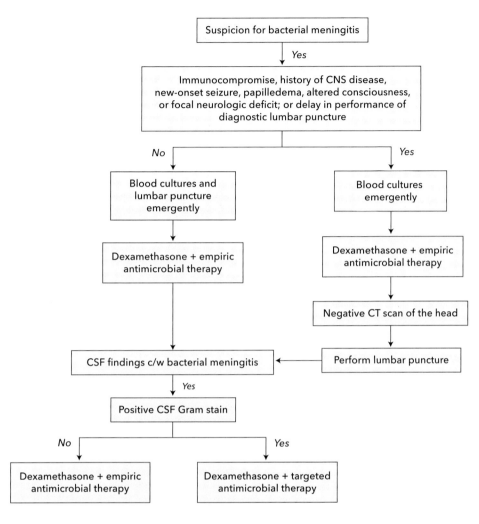

FIGURE 1. Management algorithm for adults suspected of having bacterial meningitis. CNS = central nervous system; c/w = consistent with; CSF = cerebrospinal fluid.

Adapted with permission from Tunkel AR, Hartman BJ, Kaplan SL, Kaufman BA, Roos KL, Scheld WM, et al. Practice guidelines for the management of bacterial meningitis. Clin Infect Dis. 2004;39:1267-84. [PMID: 15494903] Copyright 2004 Oxford University Press.

TABLE 2. Antibiotic Management of Bacterial Meningitis	
Clinical Characteristics	**Empiric Antibiotic Regimen**
Immunocompetent host age <50 y with community-acquired bacterial meningitis	IV ceftriaxone *or* cefotaxime plus IV vancomycin
Patient age >50 y or those with altered cell-mediated immunity	IV ampicillin (*Listeria* coverage) plus IV ceftriaxone *or* cefotaxime plus IV vancomycin
Allergies to β-lactams	IV moxifloxacin instead of cephalosporin
	IV trimethoprim-sulfamethoxazole instead of ampicillin
Hospital-acquired bacterial meningitis	IV vancomycin plus either IV ceftazidime, cefepime, or meropenem
Neurosurgical procedures	IV vancomycin plus either IV ceftazidime, cefepime, or meropenem
IV = intravenous.	

reduces morbidity and mortality in adults with pneumococcal meningitis and reduces the risk of neurologic sequelae in bacterial meningitis in developed countries; it should be given concomitantly with the first dose of antibiotic therapy. CONT.

KEY POINTS

- For diagnosis of bacterial meningitis, the cerebrospinal fluid Gram stain result is positive in 60% to 90% of infections; latex agglutination testing for bacterial antigens is not recommended because of low sensitivity and specificity.

- Intravenous antibiotic therapy and dexamethasone should be started as soon as possible when bacterial meningitis is suspected; selection of initial empiric antibiotics is based on age, local epidemiologic patterns of pneumococcal resistance, and the necessity for ampicillin coverage for *Listeria monocytogenes*.

- Adjunctive dexamethasone reduces morbidity and mortality in adults with pneumococcal meningitis and reduces the risk of neurologic sequelae in bacterial meningitis in developed countries.

Subacute and Chronic Meningitis

Subacute and chronic meningitis are defined by symptom duration between 5 and 30 days and more than 30 days, respectively. The most common infectious causes are *Mycobacterium tuberculosis* and fungi.

Tuberculous Meningitis

Mycobacterial tuberculosis meningitis classically presents as basilar meningitis with cranial neuropathies (particularly of cranial nerve VI), mental status changes, and the syndrome of inappropriate secretion of antidiuretic hormone. A history of tuberculosis exposure, an abnormal chest radiograph, a positive tuberculin skin test result, and a positive interferon-γ release assay result are suggestive but can be absent. CSF examination shows a lymphocytic pleocytosis (leukocyte count of 100-500/μL [100-500×10⁶/L]), elevated protein level, and hypoglycorrhachia. CSF acid-fast bacilli smear is insensitive, and culture results are positive in only 38% to 88% of patients. Culture sensitivity increases when lumbar punctures are performed serially for at least 3 days. Nucleic acid amplification testing should be performed when possible, especially when the acid-fast bacilli stain result is negative and suspicion is high, because it might increase diagnostic yield. Antituberculous therapy should be administered for 1 year, and adjunctive glucocorticoids should be given initially because of their association with improved outcomes.

Fungal Meningitis

Fungal pathogens, including *Cryptococcus neoformans*, *Coccidioides immitis*, *Histoplasma capsulatum*, and endemic mycoses, are a significant cause of subacute or chronic meningitis syndromes. Fungal meningitis is discussed in the Fungal Infections chapter.

Neurobrucellosis

Neurobrucellosis occurs in 4% to 11% of patients with brucellosis, which is endemic to countries in the Mediterranean, Middle East, and Central America. It may present with meningitis, meningoencephalitis, cranial neuropathies, myelopathy, radiculopathy, or stroke or as a brain abscess. The diagnosis is made by a positive culture or serologic test result for brucellosis in the CSF or blood. Treatment consists of combination antimicrobial therapy (such as ceftriaxone, rifampin, and doxycycline) for at least 6 months.

Parasitic Meningitis

Acute primary amebic meningoencephalitis caused by *Naegleria*, *Balamuthia*, and *Acanthamoeba* species is a fatal infection that clinically resembles bacterial meningitis. Freshwater exposure is a key historical clue. Examination of a fresh CSF sample can reveal motile trophozoites, but the Centers for Disease Control and Prevention should perform confirmatory testing by PCR. Treatment should include miltefosine.

Helminth infections causing eosinophilic meningitis include *Angiostrongylus cantonensis*, *Baylisascaris procyonis*,

Taenia solium (neurocysticercosis), *Schistosoma* species (schistosomiasis), and *Gnathostoma*. Neurocysticercosis is endemic in Mexico, South America, and Asia. It most commonly presents with seizures or hydrocephalus, and CT scan of the head shows multiple cysts or calcified lesions.

Noninfectious Causes

Medications such as NSAIDS, antibiotics, and intravenous immune globulin can occasionally cause aseptic meningitis. Meningeal involvement of leukemia, lymphoma, and metastatic carcinoma can also present as aseptic meningitis, with the CSF cytology showing atypical or immature cells and severe hypoglycorrhachia (<10 mg/dL [0.6 mmol/L]). Systemic lupus erythematosus, Behçet disease (recurrent oral and genital ulcers with iridocyclitis), Vogt-Koyanagi-Harada syndrome (uveomeningoencephalitis), and neurosarcoidosis can all present with aseptic meningitis. Finally, chemical meningitis can be seen after intrathecal injections, neurosurgical procedures, or spinal anesthesia.

KEY POINTS

- Tuberculous meningitis classically presents as basilar meningitis with cranial neuropathies, mental status changes, and the syndrome of inappropriate secretion of antidiuretic hormone; it should be treated with antituberculous therapy for 1 year along with initial adjunctive glucocorticoids.

- Freshwater exposure is a key historical clue in suspected acute primary amebic meningoencephalitis.

- Medications such as NSAIDS, antibiotics, and intravenous immune globulin can occasionally cause aseptic meningitis.

Health Care–Associated Meningitis and Ventriculitis

Health care–associated meningitis and ventriculitis, or nosocomial meningitis, can occur after head trauma or a neurosurgical procedure (craniotomy, lumbar puncture) or secondary to a device infection (for example, CSF shunt or drain, intrathecal pump, deep brain stimulator). Normal or abnormal CSF cell count, glucose level, and protein level do not reliably confirm or rule out infection in these patients. *Staphylococcus* species and enteric gram-negative bacteria are the most common causes, but up to 50% of infections can have negative culture results. The use of β-D-glucan and galactomannan CSF assays may aid in the diagnosis of health care–related fungal ventriculitis and meningitis. Empiric antimicrobial therapy is outlined in Table 2 and should be accompanied by device removal if present.

KEY POINT

- *Staphylococcus* species and enteric gram-negative bacteria are the most common causes of health care–associated meningitis and ventriculitis, but up to 50% of infections can have negative culture results.

Focal Central Nervous System Infections

Brain Abscesses

Brain abscesses can occur in immunocompetent or immuno-suppressed persons and are most commonly seen in men. Predisposing conditions in immunocompetent patients can be seen in **Table 3**. Brain abscesses are most commonly caused by anaerobes, aerobic and microaerophilic streptococci, and Enterobacteriaceae. Initial empiric therapy is guided by the likely predisposing condition and is outlined in **Table 4**. Aspiration of the brain abscess for culture is preferred for definitive diagnosis; surgical or stereotactic drainage should be performed if the abscess is large (>2.5 cm). Antibiotic therapy should be given for 4 to 8 weeks with follow-up cranial imaging to ensure resolution of the infection.

Immunosuppressed patients (those with HIV or AIDS, patients undergoing solid organ or bone marrow transplantation) are at risk for development of brain abscesses from several opportunistic infections. See HIV/AIDS and Infections in Transplant Recipients for further discussion.

KEY POINT

- Brain abscesses in immunocompetent patients are treated empirically based on the likely predisposing factor with surgical or stereotactic drainage of abscesses greater than 2.5 cm.

Cranial Abscess

Cranial epidural and subdural abscesses can arise from underlying osteomyelitis complicating paranasal sinusitis (Pott puffy tumor) or otitis media or after neurosurgical procedures or head trauma. Rarely, they may arise as a complication of bacterial meningitis. Cranial epidural abscesses are usually slow growing, presenting with subacute to chronic symptoms of headache, localized bone pain, and focal neurologic signs. In contrast, subdural empyema is a rapidly progressive infection

TABLE 3. Predisposing Conditions for Brain Abscess	
Condition	**Incidence**
Contiguous foci of infection such as sinusitis (frontal lobe) and otitis media (temporal lobe or cerebellum)	~50%
Hematogenous, sometimes with multiple abscesses (odontogenic resulting from viridans streptococci, endocarditis, injection drug use)	25%
Cryptogenic (most likely odontogenic)	15%
Neurosurgery or penetrating head trauma	10%

TABLE 4. Predisposing Conditions, Causative Agents, and Empiric Antimicrobial Therapy in Patients with Bacterial Brain Abscess		
Predisposing Condition	**Usual Causative Agents**	**Empiric Antimicrobial Therapy**
Otitis media or mastoiditis	Streptococci (aerobic or anaerobic), *Bacteroides* species, *Prevotella* species, Enterobacteriaceae	Metronidazole plus a third-generation cephalosporin[a]
Sinusitis	Streptococci, *Bacteroides* species, Enterobacteriaceae, *Staphylococcus aureus*, *Haemophilus* species	Metronidazole plus a third-generation cephalosporin[a,b]
Dental sepsis	Mixed *Fusobacterium*, *Prevotella*, and *Bacteroides* species; streptococci	Penicillin plus metronidazole
Penetrating trauma or after neurosurgery	*S. aureus*, streptococci, Enterobacteriaceae, *Clostridium* species	Vancomycin plus a third-generation cephalosporin[a,c]
Lung abscess, empyema, bronchiectasis	*Fusobacterium, Actinomyces, Bacteroides,* and *Prevotella* species; streptococci; *Nocardia* species	Penicillin plus metronidazole plus a sulfonamide[d]
Endocarditis	*S. aureus*, streptococci	Vancomycin plus gentamicin
Hematogenous spread from pelvic, intra-abdominal, or gynecologic infections	Enteric gram-negative bacteria, anaerobic bacteria	Metronidazole plus a third-generation cephalosporin[a,b,c]
Immunocompromised patients HIV-infected patients	*Listeria* species, fungal organisms (*Cryptococcus neoformans*), or parasitic or protozoal organisms (*Toxoplasma gondii*); *Aspergillus, Coccidioides,* and *Nocardia* species	Metronidazole plus a third-generation cephalosporin[a,b,c,d,e]; antifungal or antiparasitic agent

[a]Cefotaxime or ceftriaxone; the fourth-generation cephalosporin cefepime may also be used.

[b]Add vancomycin if infection caused by methicillin-resistant *Staphylococcus aureus* is suspected. Vancomycin can then be transitioned to antistaphylococcal β-lactam (oxacillin-nafcillin)-penicillin if methicillin-sensitive *S. aureus* is confirmed.

[c]Use ceftazidime or cefepime if infection caused by *Pseudomonas aeruginosa* is suspected. Meropenem can also be used for antipseudomonal coverage.

[d]Use trimethoprim-sulfamethoxazole if infection caused by *Nocardia* species is suspected.

[e]Use ampicillin if infection caused by *Listeria* species is suspected.

NOTE: If predisposing condition is unknown, empiric treatment should include vancomycin plus metronidazole and a third-generation cephalosporin.

with high mortality that represents a neurosurgical emergency. The CSF formula in both parameningeal infections shows neutrophilic pleocytosis and a very high protein level, frequently with negative Gram stain and culture results. Pathogen identification is best achieved by culture of the abscess obtained during surgical drainage.

KEY POINT

- In cranial epidural and subdural abscess, pathogen identification is best achieved by culture of the abscess obtained during surgical drainage.

 Spinal Epidural Abscess

Spinal epidural abscess most commonly results from hematogenous dissemination, with *S. aureus* accounting for approximately 50% of infections; streptococcus and gram-negative bacilli such as *Escherichia coli* are also implicated. Predisposing factors for bacteremia include endocarditis, injection drug use, long-term intravenous catheters (hemodialysis catheters, central lines), and urinary tract infection. Spinal epidural abscess can also occur after neurosurgical procedures (spinal fusion, epidural catheter placement) or paraspinal injection. Patients usually develop localized pain at the site of infection that later radiates down the spine. MRI is the imaging modality of choice to identify location and extent of the abscess. All patients should undergo a baseline laboratory evaluation, including erythrocyte sedimentation rate and C-reactive protein. Blood cultures should be obtained before starting antibiotics. Although the duration of antibiotic therapy lacks robust supporting data and must be determined on a case-by-case basis, at least 6 weeks of effective antimicrobial therapy is reasonable. Surgical drainage is indicated in patients with neurologic symptoms or signs (lower extremity weakness, numbness, bladder and bowel dysfunction). Follow-up MRI is not indicated unless the patient has persistent elevation of inflammatory markers, lack of clinical response, or new neurologic symptoms or signs. Tuberculosis (Pott disease) and brucellosis should be considered in patients with negative culture results and appropriate travel history and risk factors.

KEY POINT

- MRI is the imaging modality of choice to identify location and extent of a spinal epidural abscess, and blood cultures should be obtained before starting antibiotic therapy.

Encephalitis

Encephalitis is inflammation of the brain parenchyma. Possible encephalitis is defined by the presence of one major (altered consciousness for more than 24 hours) and two minor (fever, new-onset seizure, new-onset focal neurologic findings, CSF pleocytosis, and abnormal MRI or electroencephalographic findings) criteria from the International Encephalitis Consortium; probable or confirmed encephalitis requires one

major and at least three minor criteria. The causative agent is unknown in 37% to 70% of infections, depending on whether viral PCR is used and autoimmune causes are investigated. The most common known causes are viral (herpes simplex virus types 1 and 6, varicella-zoster virus, and West Nile virus) and autoimmune diseases.

Viral Encephalitis
Herpes Simplex Encephalitis

HSV-1 is the most common cause of sporadic encephalitis in the United States, requiring prompt identification and treatment with intravenous acyclovir. Factors associated with an adverse outcome include older age, abnormal Glasgow coma scale, and delay in starting antiviral therapy. HSV-1 encephalitis presents with fever, seizures, altered mental status, and focal neurologic deficits with unilateral temporal lobe edema, hemorrhage, or enhancement on imaging. Bilateral temporal lobe findings in the insula or cingulate are less commonly seen. The CSF formula usually shows lymphocytic pleocytosis, an elevated protein level, and a normal glucose level. The diagnosis is confirmed by HSV PCR of the CSF (98% sensitivity, 94% specificity). However, false-negative results have been reported; if HSV is suspected, a repeat PCR should be obtained within 1 week while continuing acyclovir therapy. Therapy duration for HSV encephalitis should be 14 to 21 days. Electroencephalography can be helpful in identifying the degree of cerebral dysfunction and specific area of the brain involved and in detecting subclinical seizure activity.

Human herpesvirus 6 can cause severe encephalitis in transplant recipients. Cytomegalovirus can cause encephalitis with periventricular enhancement on imaging in immunosuppressed patients (those with AIDS or after transplantation). Diagnosis is by PCR of the CSF for cytomegalovirus, and treatment is parenteral ganciclovir. Cytomegalovirus and Epstein-Barr virus can cause meningoencephalitis in young, immunocompetent patients presenting with infectious mononucleosis syndromes.

Varicella-Zoster Virus Encephalitis

Varicella-zoster virus (VZV) is a commonly underdiagnosed, treatable cause of encephalitis in adults. VZV can present with vasculopathy with a stroke, encephalitis, meningitis, radiculopathy, or myelitis. Patients can present without a vesicular rash, so a PCR of the CSF or a serum-to-CSF anti-VZV IgG should be ordered in all patients with encephalitis. Treatment with intravenous acyclovir for 10 to 14 days is recommended.

Arboviruses

Arboviral CNS infections in the United States are most commonly seen in summer or fall and include West Nile (WNV), Eastern and Western equine encephalitis, St. Louis encephalitis, Powassan, and La Crosse viruses. WNV is the most common cause of epidemic viral encephalitis in the United States. WNV can cause meningitis, encephalitis, acute flaccid paralysis (similar to poliomyelitis), neuropathy, and retinopathy.

CONT.

Older patients and those who have undergone transplantation or are immunosuppressed have a higher risk of death. WNV affects the thalamus and the basal ganglia; patients present with facial or arm tremors, parkinsonism, and myoclonus. Hypodense lesions or enhancements may be seen in the thalamus, basal ganglia, and midbrain on MRI of the brain. Diagnosis is confirmed by a positive WNV IgM in the CSF or serum; treatment is supportive.

HIV encephalitis is the cause of HIV-associated dementia in later stages of the untreated illness; it can also present as CD8 encephalitis, consisting of perivascular inflammation resulting from infiltration of CD8+ lymphocytes, which may occur as part of an immune reconstitution syndrome, in some cases associated with viral escape (low levels of detectable HIV RNA in CSF). **H**

KEY POINTS

- Herpes simplex virus 1 is the most common cause of sporadic encephalitis in the United States, presenting with fever, seizures, altered mental status, and focal neurologic deficits; prompt identification and treatment with intravenous acyclovir improves outcomes.
- Varicella-zoster virus (VZV) is a treatable form of encephalitis and may present without vesicular rash, so polymerase chain reaction of the cerebrospinal fluid (CSF) or a serum-to-CSF anti-VZV IgG should be ordered in all patients with encephalitis.
- West Nile virus is the most common cause of epidemic viral encephalitis in the United States.

Autoimmune Encephalitis

Autoimmune neurologic diseases can manifest as encephalitis, cerebellitis, dystonia, status epilepticus, cranial neuropathies, and myoclonus. Anti-*N*-methyl-D-aspartate receptor encephalitis is most common; it was initially described as a paraneoplastic syndrome affecting young women with ovarian teratomas, but it can be associated with other tumors (sex cord stromal tumors, small cell lung cancer) or occur without a tumor. Young women (<35 years) often present after viral-like illness with behavioral changes, headaches, and fever followed by altered mental status, seizures, abnormal movements, and autonomic instability. Treatment includes intravenous glucocorticoids, intravenous immune globulin, tumor removal (if present), and, in some cases, plasmapheresis and rituximab.

Prion Diseases of the Central Nervous System

Prions cause rare but relentlessly progressive and rapidly fatal neurodegenerative diseases characterized by dementia and ataxia. The cause of disease is an abnormally folded prion protein. In humans, prion diseases occur by three mechanisms: sporadic (spontaneous), familial (genetic), and acquired (infectious or transmissible). In patients of any age presenting with otherwise unexplained rapidly progressive dementia and ataxia, diagnosis of a prion disease should be considered (**Table 5**); the infectious forms are now rare (**Table 6**). Prion diseases have no known therapy.

Sporadic Creutzfeldt-Jakob Disease

Spontaneous (sporadic) disease is the most common form of Creutzfeldt-Jakob disease (CJD), with an incidence of 1 per million worldwide. No environmental risk factors are known. Clinical manifestations include rapidly progressive dementia, usually over 4 to 6 months. Ataxia, myoclonus, and pyramidal and extrapyramidal signs may be observed. Loss of vision is not uncommon, and patients become comatose before dying.

TABLE 5. Criteria for Diagnosis of Probable Prion Disease[a,b]
University of California, San Francisco Criteria (2007)[b]
Rapid cognitive decline
Two of the following signs or symptoms:
Myoclonus
Pyramidal/extrapyramidal dysfunction
Visual dysfunction
Cerebellar dysfunction
Akinetic mutism
Focal cortical signs (for example, neglect, aphasia, acalculia, apraxia)
Typical EEG and/or MRI
Other investigations should not suggest an alternative diagnosis
European MRI-CJD Consortium Criteria (2009)[b]
Progressive dementia
One of the following signs or symptoms:
Myoclonus
Pyramidal/extrapyramidal symptoms
Visual/cerebellar dysfunction
Akinetic mutism
AND
Either
Typical EEG
Elevated CSF protein 14-3-3 (with total disease duration <2 years)
OR
Typical MRI
Routine investigations should not suggest an alternative diagnosis

CJD = Creutzfeldt-Jakob disease; CSF = cerebrospinal fluid; EEG = electroencephalography.

[a]Definitive diagnosis requires neuropathologic confirmation.

[b]Fulfilling one criterion in all categories signifies a probable diagnosis.

TABLE 6. Human Transmissible Spongiform Encephalopathies

Disease Classification	Presentation
Acquired	
Idiopathic only (not environmental)	Sporadic fatal familial insomnia
	Sporadic CJD
Idiopathic/transmissible	Variant CJD (from BSE)
	Kuru
Inherited	Familial CJD
	GSS
	Fatal familial insomnia

BSE = bovine spongiform encephalopathy; CJD = Creutzfeldt-Jakob disease; GSS = Gerstmann-Sträussler-Scheinker syndrome.

The diagnosis can be made by clinical history and MRI; a cerebrospinal fluid analysis positive for either total Tau or 14-3-3 protein may also be useful.

Transmissible Prion Diseases

Variant CJD (vCJD) is the human form of bovine spongiform encephalopathy. It generally affects younger persons (age 15-50 years), frequently presenting with rapidly progressive neuropsychiatric manifestations (depression, withdrawal) and peripheral neuropathy, followed by cerebellar ataxia, involuntary movements, and cognitive decline over a 12-month period. Because vCJD can be transmitted through blood products and tissue, it is a serious public health concern worldwide. Probable vCJD is diagnosed by typical MRI findings ("hockey stick sign" in the posterior thalamus) and tonsil biopsy to detect scrapie-associated prion protein in a patient with a compatible clinical presentation (see Table 5).

Iatrogenic CJD is exceedingly rare, but transmission has been documented with contaminated cadaveric pituitary-derived human growth hormone and gonadotropin, dura mater, stereotactic electroencephalography needles, neurosurgical instruments, corneal transplants, medical instruments, implanted electroencephalography electrodes, and blood transfusions.

Familial Prion Disease

Many mutations have been associated with the prion protein gene. All are autosomally dominant. These include the gradually progressive Gerstmann-Sträussler-Scheinker syndrome and the rapidly progressive fatal familial insomnia.

KEY POINTS

- Prion disease should be included in the differential diagnosis of a patient of any age presenting with otherwise unexplained rapidly progressive dementia and ataxia.

- Spontaneous Creutzfeldt-Jakob disease is the most common form of prion disease and has no known risk factors.

Skin and Soft Tissue Infections

Introduction

Skin infections usually result from epidermal compromise that allows skin colonizers such as *Staphylococcus aureus* and *Streptococcus pyogenes* to become pathogenic. Predisposing conditions include vascular disease, immunodeficiency, neuropathy, previous cellulitis, obesity, skin trauma, tinea pedis, and lymphedema. Infections can be characterized by anatomic involvement and presence or absence of pus. Nonpurulent spreading skin infections include erysipelas, cellulitis, and necrotizing soft tissue infection; purulent skin infections refer to abscesses (**Figure 2**), furuncles, and carbuncles. Purulent skin infections are generally caused by staphylococci, including methicillin-resistant *Staphylococcus aureus* (MRSA); nonpurulent skin infections are usually caused by β-hemolytic streptococci. **Table 7** includes other skin pathogens and their associated risk factors for less common causes of skin infection. Complications of infections include systemic inflammatory response (as in severe cellulitis) or systemic toxin release (as in toxic shock syndrome).

Erysipelas and Cellulitis

Erysipelas refers to infection of the epidermis, upper dermis, and superficial lymphatics. Usually involving the face or lower extremities, this infection is brightly erythematous with distinct elevated borders and associated fever, lymphangitis, and regional lymphadenopathy (see MKSAP 18 Dermatology). Cellulitis refers to infection involving the deeper dermis and subcutaneous fat tissue. Inflammatory signs of infection are similar to erysipelas, but the area of involvement is less well demarcated.

Although the diagnosis of erysipelas or cellulitis is usually established clinically, approximately one third of patients are

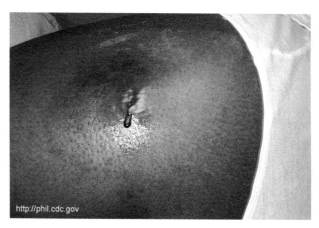

http://phil.cdc.gov

FIGURE 2. A cutaneous abscess draining purulent material is shown; it is caused by methicillin-resistant *Staphylococcus aureus* bacteria.

Image credit to the Centers for Disease Control and Prevention/Bruno Coignard, MD; Jeff Hageman, MHS.

TABLE 7. Skin Pathogens and Associated Risk Factors

Pathogen	Risk Factor	Comment
Aeromonas hydrophila	Contact with freshwater lakes, streams, rivers (including brackish water) Contact with leeches	Cellulitis nonspecific in clinical appearance; minor trauma to skin usually leads to inoculation of organism
Vibrio vulnificus, Vibrio parahaemolyticus	Contact with salt water or brackish water Contact with drippings from raw seafood Consumption of undercooked shellfish (particularly oysters) Liver cirrhosis or chronic liver disease	Cellulitis through direct inoculation into skin Ingestion leads to bacteremia with secondary skin infection Hallmark is hemorrhagic bullae in area of cellulitis lesion(s)
Erysipelothrix rhusiopathiae	Contact with saltwater marine life (can also infect freshwater fish)	Cellulitis usually involves the hand or arm, especially in those handling fish, shellfish, or, occasionally, poultry or meat contaminated with bacterium Causes erysipeloid disease
Pasteurella multocida	Contact primarily with cats and dogs	Cellulitis occurs as a result of cat scratch or bite
Capnocytophaga canimorsus	Contact primarily with dogs	Cellulitis and sepsis are present, particularly in patients with hyposplenism
Bacillus anthracis	Contact with infected animals or animal products. May be the result of bioterrorism	Edematous pruritic lesion with central eschar; spore-forming organism
Francisella tularensis	Contact with or bite from infected animal (particularly cats); arthropod bites (particularly ticks)	Ulceroglandular syndrome characterized by ulcerative lesion with central eschar and localized tender lymphadenopathy; constitutional symptoms often present
Burkholderia mallei	Contact with tissues or bodily fluids of infected mules or horses	Pustules with suppurative localized lymph nodes or ulcerative nodules at site of inoculation
Clostridium perfringens	Surgery or other significant trauma	Necrotizing infection, often referred to as clostridial myonecrosis or gas gangrene
Mycobacterium marinum	Contact with fresh water or salt water, including fish tanks and swimming pools	Lesion is often trauma associated and often involves the upper extremity; papular lesions become ulcerative at site of inoculation; ascending lymphatic spread can be seen ("sporotrichoid" appearance); systemic toxicity usually absent
Mycobacterium fortuitum	Exposure to freshwater footbaths/pedicures at nail salons, particularly after razor shaving; surgery	Furuncle(s); postoperative wound infection

misdiagnosed. Clinical mimics include contact or stasis dermatitis, lymphedema, erythema nodosum, deep venous thrombosis, thrombophlebitis, lipodermatosclerosis, erythromelalgia, trauma-related inflammation, and hypersensitivity reactions (see MKSAP 18 Dermatology). Blood culture results are positive in approximately 5% of patients with erysipelas and cellulitis and are not routinely indicated; however, cultures should be performed for those who are immunocompromised, exhibit severe sepsis, or have unusual precipitating circumstances, including immersion injury or animal bites. Culture of skin tissue aspirate or biopsy should also be considered for these patients. Radiographic imaging is not helpful for the diagnosis of erysipelas or cellulitis but may be helpful when a deeper necrotizing infection is suspected.

For immunocompetent patients with cellulitis or erysipelas who have no systemic signs or symptoms (mild infection),

empiric oral therapy directed against streptococci is recommended as outlined in **Table 8** (see MKSAP 18 Dermatology). Treatment duration for uncomplicated infection can be as short as 5 days but should be extended as necessary until the infection improves. In patients with systemic signs (moderate infection), intravenous treatment is recommended (see Table 8). Treating predisposing factors (such as tinea pedis, edema, and primary skin disorders) may decrease the risk for recurrent infection. Prophylactic antibiotics such as penicillin or erythromycin can be considered in patients with more than three episodes of cellulitis annually.

Patients who are immunocompromised, who have systemic inflammatory response syndrome and hypotension, or who have evidence of deeper necrotizing infection such as bullae and desquamation (severe infection) should receive urgent surgical evaluation for debridement. Initial empiric

TABLE 8.	Treatment of Skin Infections
Infection	**Treatment**
Erysipelas or cellulitis	Mild: Oral penicillin, amoxicillin, cephalexin, dicloxacillin, clindamycin
	Moderate: Intravenous penicillin, ceftriaxone, cefazolin, clindamycin
	Severe: Surgical assessment for possible necrotizing component and empiric intravenous vancomycin plus piperacillin-tazobactam, imipenem, or meropenem
Necrotizing fasciitis	Polymicrobial infection: Surgical assessment/debridement and combination therapy such as vancomycin plus piperacillin-tazobactam or imipenem or meropenem
	Streptococcus pyogenes or *Clostridium perfringens*: Surgical assessment/debridement and penicillin plus clindamycin
	Aeromonas hydrophila: Surgical assessment/debridement and ciprofloxacin plus doxycycline
	Vibrio vulnificus: Surgical assessment/debridement and ceftazidime, ceftriaxone, or cefotaxime plus doxycycline
Furuncle, carbuncle, or abscess	Mild: Incision and drainage
	Moderate: Incision and drainage plus empiric trimethoprim-sulfamethoxazole or doxycycline pending culture and susceptibilities
	Severe: Incision and drainage plus empiric vancomycin, daptomycin, linezolid, telavancin, or ceftaroline pending culture and susceptibilities

CONT.

broad-spectrum antibiotic therapy should be started (see Table 8); then treatment may be adjusted based on culture and sensitivity results from lesion-associated specimens.

KEY POINTS

HVC
- Blood cultures are positive in approximately 5% of patients with erysipelas and cellulitis and are not routinely indicated; however, cultures should be performed for those who are immunocompromised, exhibit severe sepsis, or have unusual precipitating circumstances, including immersion injury or animal bites.

- Patients with evidence of deeper necrotizing infection such as bullae and desquamation (severe infection) should receive urgent surgical evaluation for debridement and empiric broad-spectrum antibiotic therapy.

Necrotizing Fasciitis

Necrotizing soft tissue infections, which involve subdermal compartments including fascia and possibly muscle, are uncommon but potentially life threatening. In necrotizing fasciitis (NF), infection usually spreads along the superficial fascia. These infections may be monomicrobial or polymicrobial, consisting of a mixture of aerobic and anaerobic bacteria, and are often associated with the production of toxins. In monomicrobial infection, the classically associated pathogen is *Streptococcus pyogenes*; other potential organisms include *Staphylococcus aureus*, *Streptococcus agalactiae*, *Aeromonas hydrophila*, *Vibrio vulnificus*, and *Clostridium perfringens*.

NF characteristically occurs in the setting of previous skin trauma or infection and most commonly affects the extremities. Risk factors include diabetes mellitus, injection drug use, malignancy, immunosuppression, and liver disease. Patients with liver disease are at particular risk for infection with

V. vulnificus (**Figure 3**). Patients with diabetes are at risk for NF of the perineum, a polymicrobial infection known as Fournier gangrene that usually results from antecedent genitourinary, traumatic, or anorectal infection.

The initial presentation of NF resembles cellulitis before potentially rapid progression with edema, severe pain, hemorrhagic bullous lesions, skin necrosis, and local crepitus. Systemic toxicity manifests with fever, hypotension, tachycardia, mental status changes, and tachypnea. A hallmark of infection is "woody" induration appreciated by palpation of involved subcutaneous tissues. Necrosis of local nerves may result in anesthesia.

Laboratory study results are individually nonspecific. The Laboratory Risk Indicator for Necrotizing Fasciitis (LRINEC) score is derived from six variables that, when added together, are associated with an increased likelihood of necrotizing skin

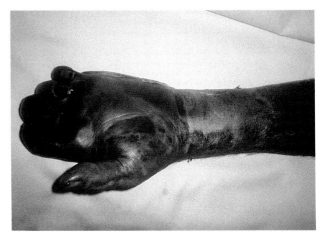

FIGURE 3. Bullous cellulitis characteristic of *Vibrio vulnificus* infection is shown in a patient with cirrhosis; cutaneous necrosis is also evident, most likely associated with disseminated intravascular coagulation.

CONT. infection: C-reactive protein level (>15 mg/dL [150 mg/L]), total leukocyte count (>15,000-25,000/µL [15-25 × 10⁹/L]), hemoglobin level (<11-13.5 g/dL [110-135 g/L]), sodium level (<135 mEq/L [135 mmol/L]), creatinine level (>1.6 mg/dL [141 µmol/L]), and glucose level (>180 mg/dL [10 mmol/L]). This tool was developed to improve diagnostic accuracy; the reported positive and negative predictive values are 92% and 96%, respectively. However, use of the score has not been prospectively validated in all clinical settings, so operative debridement should be pursued in patients with a high index of clinical suspicion for NF.

Plain radiographs and CT scans may demonstrate gas in soft tissues, but MRI with contrast is more sensitive and can help delineate anatomic involvement. Surgical exploration can confirm the diagnosis of NF. Blood culture(s) obtained before surgery and antibiotic administration or deep intraoperative specimen culture can establish the microbiologic cause.

In confirmed cases of NF, repeated surgical debridement is typically required. Pending culture results, empiric antibiotic treatment includes broad-spectrum coverage for aerobic and anaerobic organisms (including MRSA) and consists of vancomycin, daptomycin, or linezolid plus piperacillin-tazobactam, a carbapenem, ceftriaxone plus metronidazole, or a fluoroquinolone plus metronidazole. Some experts also recommend adding empiric clindamycin because of its suppression of toxin production by staphylococci and streptococci. See Table 8 for treatment of NF caused by *S. pyogenes*, *V. vulnificus*, *A. hydrophila*, or clostridial species. Antimicrobial discontinuation can be considered when the patient is afebrile and clinically stable, and surgical debridement is no longer required.

KEY POINTS

- Necrotizing fasciitis initially resembles cellulitis before rapid progression of subdermal infection manifesting with clinical signs of edema, "woody" induration, severe pain, hemorrhagic bullous lesions, skin necrosis, local crepitus, fever, hypotension, tachycardia, mental status changes, and tachypnea; necrosis of local nerves may result in anesthesia.

- In patients with suspected necrotizing fasciitis, MRI with contrast is more sensitive than plain radiography or CT and can help delineate anatomic involvement.

Purulent Skin Infections

Abscesses are erythematous, nodular, localized collections of pus within the dermis and subcutaneous fat. Furuncles (boils) are hair follicle–associated abscesses that extend into the dermis and subcutaneous tissue. These inflammatory nodules are typically seen on the face, neck, and axilla. Infection that extends subcutaneously to involve several furuncles is known as a carbuncle. This coalescence of abscesses can result in systemic signs of infection.

Primary treatment for abscesses, furuncles, and carbuncles is incision and drainage. Gram stain and culture should be obtained from the purulent drainage when antibiotic administration is planned. Mild lesions without systemic symptoms do not require antibiotic therapy after drainage. For patients with moderate infections who have systemic signs of infection, empiric treatment is recommended (see Table 8). Empiric treatment with parenteral therapy is also recommended in immunocompromised patients, patients with hypotension and systemic inflammatory response syndrome (severe infection), or patients in whom incision and drainage plus oral antibiotics fail. Treatment is adjusted based on sensitivities from culture of the purulent drainage.

If MRSA is the cause of multiple recurrences of purulent skin infection, decolonization with topical intranasal mupirocin and chlorhexidine washes should be considered. Other diagnoses such as hidradenitis suppurativa, pilonidal cysts, or a foreign body should be considered when no microbial cause is identified.

Newer antibiotics for skin and soft tissue infections caused by *Streptococcus* and *Staphylococcus* species (including MRSA) include tedizolid, oritavancin, and dalbavancin. Use of these antibiotics is recommended in consultation with infectious disease specialists.

KEY POINTS

- Primary treatment for abscesses, furuncles, and car- **HVC**
  buncles is incision and drainage; mild infections (without systemic symptoms) do not require antibiotic therapy.

- For moderate and severe purulent infections associated with systemic symptoms, Gram stain and culture should be performed on the purulent drainage followed by empiric oral antibiotic treatment for moderate infections and empiric intravenous antibiotics for severe infections.

Animal Bites

Bites from cats and dogs represent approximately 1% of emergency department visits in the United States; most wounds (about 80%) will not become infected. Cat bites are more likely to become infected because of deeper puncture wounds created by cats' sharp, slender teeth. The microbiology of infection depends on the microbiota of the animal's mouth and of the patient's skin. Mixed aerobes and anaerobes, including staphylococci, streptococci, *Bacteroides* species, *Porphyromonas* species, *Fusobacterium* species, and *Pasteurella* species, typically compose the bacteria in bite wounds. *Capnocytophaga canimorsus* is a common constituent of canine microbiota and can cause severe infections in patients with asplenia.

Wound management includes irrigation with sterile normal saline. Irrigation also allows for characterization of wound extent and dimensions; signs of inflammation and infection, including edema, erythema, pain, necrosis, lymphangitis, and pus; and local neurovascular involvement. Surgical evaluation for possible debridement and removal of foreign bodies is particularly important with hand bites. Culture of deep intraoperative tissue and antibiotic susceptibilities of isolated organisms allows for pathogen-directed therapy. Radiographs may demonstrate fracture, other bony involvement, or foreign bodies. Assessment for tetanus and rabies prophylaxis is essential. With the exception of facial wounds, primary wound closure is not generally pursued.

The decision to begin early antibiotic prophylaxis in the absence of clinical signs of infection is based on the severity of the wound and the immune status of the patient. Because of its activity against pathogens associated with animal bite wounds, a 3- to 5-day course of amoxicillin-clavulanate is recommended for patients who are immunosuppressed, including patients with cirrhosis and asplenia. Pre-emptive antibiotic therapy is also recommended for wounds with associated edema or lymphatic or venous insufficiency; crush injury; wounds involving a joint or bone; deep puncture wounds; or moderate to severe injuries, especially involving the face, genitalia, or hand. If a patient is allergic to penicillin, a combination of trimethoprim-sulfamethoxazole, or a fluoroquinolone, or doxycycline plus clindamycin or metronidazole can be used.

For clinically infected bite wounds, antibiotics are recommended after tissue wound cultures (and blood cultures, if systemic signs of infection are present) are obtained. For outpatient management of mildly infected wounds, oral antibiotics are recommended. The duration of antibiotic therapy is usually less than 2 weeks unless bone or joint involvement dictates a more prolonged course. Intravenous therapy is indicated for severe infections with systemic involvement, including sepsis; severe injuries, particularly those associated with tendon, nerve, vascular, or crush injuries; and hand infections. Intravenous antibiotic options include β-lactam or β-lactamase inhibitors (ampicillin-sulbactam, piperacillin-tazobactam), carbapenems (imipenem, meropenem, ertapenem), or ceftriaxone or a fluoroquinolone plus clindamycin or metronidazole. Empiric MRSA coverage may be included in patients with risk factors for MRSA infection (MRSA nasal colonization, recent hospitalization, recent antibiotic use, previous MRSA infection). Surgical consultation is usually obtained.

KEY POINTS

- Bite wound management includes irrigation with sterile normal saline; with the exception of facial wounds, primary closure is not generally pursued.

- Assessment for tetanus and rabies prophylaxis is essential in patients with animal bite wounds.

- Pre-emptive amoxicillin-clavulanate is recommended for patients who are immunosuppressed; wounds with associated edema or lymphatic or venous insufficiency; crush injury; wounds involving a joint or bone; deep puncture wounds; or moderate to severe injuries, especially involving the face, genitalia, or hand.

Human Bites

Intentional biting of others, self-inflicted wounds such as those occurring from fingernail biting, and clenched-fist injuries after a punch to another person's mouth are the most common causes of human bite wounds. These wounds are at risk for infection with human skin and mouth organisms. These organisms comprise aerobic organisms, including staphylococci, streptococci, and *Eikenella corrodens*, and anaerobic organisms, including *Peptostreptococcus, Fusobacterium*, and *Prevotella* species. Short-course prophylactic antibiotic therapy with amoxicillin-clavulanate is recommended for all human bites. The management of infected wounds is similar to that for animal bites, including empiric MRSA coverage in patients at increased risk for MRSA infection. Hand involvement warrants surgical evaluation. In addition to assessment for tetanus prophylaxis, evaluation for potential exposure to hepatitis B and C viruses, HIV, and other bodily fluid–transmitted pathogens is warranted.

KEY POINTS

- Short-course prophylactic antibiotic therapy with amoxicillin-clavulanate is recommended for all human bites.

- In addition to assessment for tetanus prophylaxis, evaluation of human bites for potential exposure to hepatitis B and C viruses, HIV, and other bodily fluid–transmitted pathogens is warranted.

Diabetic Foot Infections

Diabetic foot infections typically result after trauma in persons with vasculopathy, neuropathy, suboptimal glucose control, and immunologic deficits. Additional risk factors for infection include presence of an ulcer for greater than 1 month, recurrent ulcers, lower extremity amputation, kidney function impairment, walking barefoot, and a positive probe-to-bone test in the wound. Infection is diagnosed when pus or two or more inflammatory signs (warmth, induration, erythema, pain, and tenderness) are present.

Following debridement of overlying callous or necrotic tissue as necessary, infections should be classified according to severity and extent. Mild infections involve only skin and subcutaneous tissue with erythema confined to 2 cm beyond the ulcer. Moderate infections extend deeper than subcutaneous tissue (for example, abscess, fasciitis, and osteomyelitis), or the erythema is more extensive. Severe infections are associated with systemic signs such as fever, tachycardia, tachypnea, leukocytosis, and hypotension or metabolic complications such as acidosis, worsening kidney function, and hyperglycemia. The affected foot or limb should also be assessed for arterial ischemia, venous insufficiency, neuropathy, and biomechanical abnormalities such as Charcot arthropathy or hammer toe. Evidence of critical ischemia can be considered a proxy for severe infection.

Uninfected wounds should not be cultured or treated with antibiotics. Mild infections are typically caused by aerobic

CONT.

staphylococci (non-MRSA) and streptococci and can be empirically treated with a short course (7-14 days) of oral antibiotics, such as cephalexin, clindamycin, amoxicillin-clavulanate, or dicloxacillin. For mild infections with pus or MRSA risk factors (previous MRSA infection or colonization within the last year or high local prevalence), wound cultures should be obtained by curettage or biopsy of deep tissue before initiating antibiotics. Doxycycline or trimethoprim-sulfamethoxazole can also be used with a β-lactam antibiotic. For moderate and severe infections, polymicrobial coverage of staphylococci (including MRSA), streptococci, aerobic gram-negative bacilli, and anaerobes is recommended. Following deep-tissue culture, initial antibiotic regimens include β-lactam or β-lactamase inhibitors, carbapenems, or metronidazole plus a fluoroquinolone or third-generation cephalosporin in addition to an anti-MRSA agent (vancomycin, daptomycin, linezolid). Antibiotic choices are guided by culture results. Moderate to severe infections are usually treated with a longer course of antibiotics (2-4 weeks); if osteomyelitis is present, approximately 6 weeks of antibiotic therapy is administered after surgical debridement.

A positive probe-to-bone test in a diabetic foot wound is associated with increased risk for osteomyelitis. Surgical consultation is often pursued to evaluate the need for debridement, resection, amputation, or revascularization. Plain imaging is recommended for all patients with new foot infections to assess for soft tissue gas, foreign body, and bony involvement; additional imaging with ultrasonography (for abscess) or MRI (for bone involvement) is recommended when clinically indicated. CT with intravenous contrast or a labeled leukocyte scan combined with a radionuclide bone scan can be considered when MRI is not possible. Wound care, glycemic control, and off-loading areas of biomechanical stress are essential.

KEY POINTS

- Diabetic foot infection is diagnosed when pus or two or more inflammatory signs (warmth, induration, erythema, pain, and tenderness) are present.

HVC
- Uninfected diabetic foot wounds should not be cultured or treated with antibiotics.

- Deep-tissue culture (curettage or biopsy) is indicated before antibiotic therapy for moderate or severe infections and complicated mild infections (presence of pus or MRSA risk factors).

- Plain imaging is recommended for all patients with new diabetic foot infections; additional imaging with ultrasonography or MRI is recommended when abscess or bone involvement is suspected.

Toxic Shock Syndrome

S. aureus– and *S. pyogenes*–associated exotoxins result in cytokine production that can result in toxic shock syndrome (TSS) (**Table 9** and **Table 10**). Staphylococcal TSS is associated with tampon use, nasal packings, surgical wounds, skin ulcers,

TABLE 9. Diagnostic Criteria for Staphylococcal Toxic Shock Syndrome[a]

Fever >38.9 °C (102.0 °F)

Systolic blood pressure <90 mm Hg

Diffuse macular rash with subsequent desquamation, especially on palms and soles

Involvement of three or more of the following organ systems:

   Gastrointestinal (nausea, vomiting, diarrhea)

   Muscular (severe myalgia or fivefold or greater increase in serum creatine kinase level)

   Mucous membrane (hyperemia of the vagina, conjunctivae, or pharynx)

   Kidney (blood urea nitrogen or serum creatinine level at least twice the upper limit of normal)

   Liver (bilirubin, aspartate aminotransferase, or alanine aminotransferase concentration twice the upper limit of normal)

   Blood (platelet count <100,000/µL [100 × 10⁹/L])

   Central nervous system (disorientation without focal neurologic signs)

Negative results on serologic testing for Rocky Mountain spotted fever, leptospirosis, and measles; negative cerebrospinal fluid cultures for organisms other than *Staphylococcus aureus*

[a]Diagnosis is considered confirmed when fever, hypotension, and rash with involvement of three or more organ systems listed and negative serologic and cerebrospinal fluid results listed are all present.

Adapted with permission from Moreillon P, Que YA, Glauser MP. *Staphylococcus aureus*. In: Mandell GL, Dolin R, Bennett JE, eds. Principles and practice of infectious disease. 6th ed. Philadelphia, PA: Churchill Livingstone; 2005:2331. Copyright 2005, Elsevier.

TABLE 10. Diagnostic Criteria for Streptococcal Toxic Shock Syndrome[a]

Definite case

   Isolation of GABHS from a sterile site (blood, cerebrospinal fluid, operative wound)

Probable case

   Isolation of GABHS from a nonsterile site (throat, vagina, skin lesion)

Hypotension (systolic pressure ≤90 mm Hg)

The presence of ≥2 of the following findings:

   Kidney (acute kidney injury or failure)

   Liver (elevated aminotransferase concentrations)

   Skin (erythematous macular rash, soft tissue necrosis)

   Blood (coagulopathy, including thrombocytopenia and disseminated intravascular coagulation)

   Pulmonary (acute respiratory distress syndrome)

GABHS = group A β-hemolytic streptococci.

[a]A definite case is defined by the isolation of GABHS from a sterile site; hypotension with systolic blood pressure ≤90 mm Hg; plus the presence of two or more of the clinical findings listed.

CONT.

burns, catheters, and injection drug use. Streptococcal TSS is associated with skin and soft tissue infection, particularly NF. Bacteremia and mortality rates are higher with streptococcal than staphylococcal TSS. Source control typically requires surgical debridement. Antibiotics for streptococcal TSS consist of penicillin plus clindamycin, the latter added to eradicate the high inoculum of bacteria present and to suppress toxin production. If methicillin-susceptible *S. aureus* is the cause, nafcillin and clindamycin are recommended; for MRSA, vancomycin plus clindamycin or linezolid monotherapy is preferred. More studies are needed to establish the exact role of intravenous immune globulin in this setting, and it is not recommended in the most recent guidelines by the Infectious Diseases Society of America. H

KEY POINTS

- Source control for toxic shock syndrome typically requires surgical debridement.
- Streptococcal toxic shock syndrome is treated with penicillin and clindamycin.
- Infection with methicillin-susceptible *Staphylococcus aureus* is treated with nafcillin and clindamycin; linezolid monotherapy or vancomycin plus clindamycin is preferred for infection with methicillin-resistant *S. aureus*.

Community-Acquired Pneumonia

Epidemiology

Community-acquired pneumonia (CAP) is a leading cause of infection and hospitalization in the United States, associated with more than $10 billion annually in health care expenditures. The spectrum of illness due to CAP ranges from mild disease, with approximately 50% of patients managed in the ambulatory setting, to fatal infections. Rates of hospitalization increase with advanced age; the incidence of hospitalization for CAP among adults 80 years or older is 25 times higher than in adults younger than 50 years.

The definition of CAP has recently expanded to include some patients previously categorized as having health care–associated pneumonia (HCAP). This change was made because the microbiology and treatment of patients with CAP in long-term care facilities or who were hospitalized in the preceding 3 months do not differ substantially from that of community-dwelling patients with similar comorbidities. Practically, elimination of the HCAP classification simplifies treatment and has antibiotic stewardship implications, leading to a decrease in the use of unnecessarily broad antibiotics. Differentiating CAP from true hospital-acquired pneumonia (HAP) remains clinically meaningful (see Health Care–Associated Infections for HAP discussion).

Microbiology

CAP is usually caused by infection with a viral or bacterial pathogen; fungal or mycobacterial infections occur much less frequently. The probability of infection with a specific organism varies based on age, comorbidities, seasonality, and geography. Epidemiologic risk factors or conditions associated with specific pathogens are listed in **Table 11**. Because causative organisms have variable virulence, severity of illness, which influences site of care, is used to guide empiric antibiotic therapy (**Table 12**).

Streptococcus pneumoniae, previously considered the leading cause of CAP, accounts for only 5% to 15% of hospitalized cases in recent studies. This decrease in incidence at least partially results from the success of vaccination strategies. Conversely, rates of CAP caused by *Staphylococcus aureus* and Enterobacteriaceae are rising, even among patients without identifiable health care exposure. The CDC-EPIC trial, a recent multicenter study that performed prospective microbiologic and molecular testing on patients hospitalized with CAP, more frequently identified a single or multiple viruses rather than a bacterial pathogen in CAP infections requiring hospitalization (**Figure 4**). *S. pneumoniae* was the most common bacterial cause, although rhinovirus (9%) and influenza virus (6%) were higher in incidence. The significance of viral detection in CAP is unclear; an antecedent mild respiratory viral infection may increase the risk for a secondary bacterial infection. This phenomenon is well documented for postinfluenza CAP caused by *S. aureus*, *S. pneumoniae*, and *Streptococcus pyogenes*. Despite extensive laboratory investigation, no causative organism was identified in 62% of patients in the CDC-EPIC trial.

Atypical pneumonia refers to CAP caused by organisms not cultivatable on standard bacterial media, including viruses and fastidious bacteria such as *Legionella* species, *Mycoplasma*

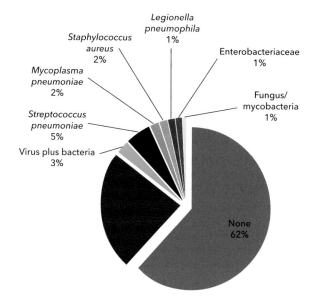

FIGURE 4. The chart depicts percentages of pathogens detected among hospitalized patients with community-acquired pneumonia in the CDC-EPIC Study.

Data from Jain S, Self WH, Wunderink RG, et al. Community-acquired pneumonia requiring hospitalization among U.S. adults. N Engl J Med. 2015;373:415-27.

TABLE 11.	Risk Factors for Pathogens Causing Community-Acquired Pneumonia
Risk Factor	**Common Pathogens**
Heavy alcohol use	*Streptococcus pneumoniae*, oral flora (aspiration), *Klebsiella pneumoniae*
COPD	*Haemophilus influenzae, S. pneumoniae, Moraxella catarrhalis, Legionella pneumophila, Pseudomonas aeruginosa*
Structural lung disease (bronchiectasis, cystic fibrosis)	*P. aeruginosa, Burkholderia cepacia, Stenotrophomonas maltophilia, Staphylococcus aureus*
Aspiration (seizures, neurologic impairment, loss of consciousness)	Oral anaerobes, Enterobacteriaceae
Age >65 years	Influenza virus, *S. pneumoniae*, rhinovirus
Post-viral illness	*S. aureus, Streptococcus pyogenes, S. pneumoniae*
Animal exposure	
Birds	*Chlamydophila psittaci, Histoplasma capsulatum, Cryptococcus neoformans*
Dogs	*Bordetella bronchiseptica*
Cats	*Pasteurella multocida*
Farm animals or domesticated pregnant animals	*Coxiella burnetii, Brucella* species
Horses	*Rhodococcus equi*
Rodent droppings	Hantavirus
Rabbits	*Francisella tularensis*
Hot tub exposure	*Legionella pneumoniae*, atypical mycobacteria (causing a hypersensitivity pneumonitis)
Geographic	
Eastern United States	*Histoplasma capsulatum, Blastomyces dermatitidis*
Southwest United States	Coccidioides
Southeast Asia	*Burkholderia pseudomallei*, SARS, avian influenza
Middle East	MERS
Late fall, winter, early spring (Western hemisphere)	Influenza virus, parainfluenza virus, rhinovirus

MERS = Middle East respiratory syndrome; SARS = severe acute respiratory syndrome.

CONT.

pneumoniae, and *Chlamydophila pneumoniae*. Respiratory viruses account for nearly all viral pneumonia infections, but less common pathogens include varicella-zoster virus or Hantavirus. *Legionella pneumophila* is a recognized cause of CAP requiring hospitalization or ICU admission. Legionellosis is associated with water exposure, including hot tubs and air conditioning units; however, infection may occur without an obvious source. A history of travel has been reported in approximately 10% of *Legionella* cases reported to the CDC.

CAP caused by anaerobic bacteria is uncommon, is primarily seen with aspiration, and is caused by microaerophilic oropharyngeal flora. Risk factors for aspiration pneumonia include decreased consciousness (alcohol or illicit substance use, seizures, stroke), poor dentition, gastroesophageal reflux, and vomiting. Zoonotic causes of CAP include *Coxiella burnetii* and *Francisella tularensis*. Mycobacterial or fungal causes of CAP should be considered in patients with immunocompromising conditions, epidemiologic risk factors for infection (such as incarceration, certain hobbies or occupations, and pertinent regional or foreign travel), or subacute presentations and in those who do not respond to conventional antibacterial treatment. **H**

KEY POINTS

- The definition of community-acquired pneumonia (CAP) has recently expanded to include some patients previously categorized as having health care–associated pneumonia because the microbiology and treatment of patients with CAP in long-term care facilities or who were hospitalized in the preceding 3 months do not differ substantially from that of community-dwelling patients with similar comorbidities.

- *Streptococcus pneumoniae* accounts for only 5% to 15% of community-acquired pneumonia (CAP) infections requiring hospitalization, whereas rates of CAP caused by *Staphylococcus aureus* and Enterobacteriaceae are rising, even among patients without identifiable health care exposure.

- The significance of viral detection in community-acquired pneumonia is unclear; however, an antecedent mild respiratory viral infection may increase the risk for a secondary bacterial infection.

TABLE 12. IDSA/ATS Recommendations for Empiric Antibiotics in Community-Acquired Pneumonia

Site of Treatment	Patient or Epidemiologic Considerations	Most Common Organisms	Regimens(s)
Outpatient	Healthy patient without antibiotics in preceding 3 months	*Streptococcus pneumoniae* *Mycoplasma* *Chlamydophila* Respiratory viruses	Macrolide OR Doxycycline
	Healthy patient from region with >25% macrolide resistance among *S. pneumoniae*	Same as above	Respiratory quinolone OR β-lactam plus a macrolide
	Comorbidities[a] or antibiotic use in preceding 3 months	Same as inpatient, non-ICU	Respiratory quinolone OR β-lactam plus a macrolide
Inpatient, non-ICU		*S. pneumoniae* *Mycoplasma* *Chlamydophila* *Haemophilus influenzae* *Legionella* Oral anaerobes Respiratory viruses	β-lactam plus a macrolide OR Respiratory quinolone
ICU treatment		*S. pneumoniae* *Staphylococcus aureus* *H. influenzae* *Legionella* Gram-negative bacilli	Parenteral β-lactam plus either azithromycin or a respiratory quinolone OR If penicillin allergic, a respiratory quinolone plus aztreonam
Any	Risk factor for *Pseudomonas* (see text)		Antipseudomonal β-lactam plus an antipseudomonal quinolone OR If penicillin allergic, a respiratory quinolone plus aztreonam
Any	Risk factor for CA-MRSA (see text)		Standard therapy PLUS vancomycin OR linezolid

CA-MRSA = community-acquired methicillin-resistant *Staphylococcus aureus*.

[a]Comorbidities include chronic heart, lung, liver, or kidney disease; diabetes mellitus; alcoholism; asplenia; malignancies; and immunosuppression.

Adapted with permission from Mandell LA, Wunderink RG, Anzueto A, Bartlett JG, Campbell GD, Dean NC, Dowell SF, File TM Jr, Musher DM, Niederman MS, Torres A, Whitney CG; Infectious Diseases Society of America; American Thoracic Society. Infectious Diseases Society of America/American Thoracic Society consensus guidelines on the management of community-acquired pneumonia in adults. Clin Infect Dis. 2007 Mar 1;44 Suppl 2:S27-72. [PMID: 17278083]

Diagnostic Evaluation

CAP should be suspected and chest imaging performed in any patient presenting with fever associated with cough, dyspnea, or chest pain. Symptoms may be subtle or absent in older adults or immunosuppressed patients, and clinicians should maintain a low threshold for pursuing radiographic studies in these populations. Posteroanterior and lateral chest radiography is recommended. In addition to confirming the diagnosis, radiographic patterns may provide clues to particular pathogens (**Table 13**) and guide clinical decisions regarding appropriate site of care. When plain radiographs are normal but suspicion for CAP remains high, chest radiography may be repeated after 24 hours; for patients at high risk (febrile neutropenia, risk for anthrax, or acute respiratory distress syndrome requiring intervention) with normal radiographs, chest CT should be pursued.

Routine laboratory studies are indicated to ascertain the severity of infection, determine the optimal site of care, and ensure appropriate antimicrobial dosing. HIV testing should

TABLE 13. Radiographic Patterns Associated with Specific Causes of Community-Acquired Pneumonia

Radiographic Appearance	Common Pathogens
Lobar pneumonia	*Streptococcus pneumoniae*
Right lower lobe pneumonia	Oral anaerobes (aspiration)
Lung abscess/cavitary lesion	Oral anaerobes, *Staphylococcus aureus*, *Klebsiella pneumoniae*, *Nocardia*, *Actinomyces*, *Rhodococcus*, mycobacteria, endemic fungi
Interstitial infiltrate	Atypical pathogens (*Legionella*, *Mycoplasma*, *Chlamydophila*), viruses
Pleural effusion/empyema	Oral anaerobes, anginosus-constellatus group streptococci, *S. aureus*, *S. pneumoniae*

be performed if indicated; a positive result expands the spectrum of potentially causative organisms. Procalcitonin level, if available as a point-of-care test, is insufficiently sensitive or specific to independently diagnose CAP or a microbiologic cause but may support a diagnosis along with other clinical findings. Rapid testing for influenza virus may assist in identifying patients who would benefit from oseltamivir and who require droplet precautions at hospital admission, but a positive test result does not exclude a concomitant bacterial pathogen.

Diagnostic studies to identify a causative organism are not routinely indicated in outpatients with CAP but should be considered in non-ICU hospitalized patients when this information would change therapy or allow treatment de-escalation. All patients with CAP who require admission to the ICU should undergo diagnostic evaluation in an attempt to confirm a microbial cause. Interpretation of sputum Gram stain and culture is hampered by the presence of oropharyngeal colonization, and growth may reflect nonpathogenic organisms. A good-quality sputum culture obtained before antibiotic initiation is suggestive or diagnostic in up to 80% of cases of pneumococcal pneumonia; sensitivity decreases after antibiotic therapy. Sputum Gram stain and culture are appropriate for patients admitted to the ICU, patients who did not respond to outpatient antibiotic therapy, patients with cavitary lung lesions, and patients with underlying structural lung disease. In these cases, consideration for mycobacterial or fungal causes may be necessary.

Blood culture results are positive in 20% to 25% of patients with pneumococcal pneumonia; fewer culture results are positive in patients with other bacterial causes. Pneumococcal urinary antigen testing is more than 70% sensitive, and results are not affected by antibiotic administration. *Legionella* urinary antigen test results are positive in most patients with *L. pneumophila* serotype 1 infection. However, the test does not detect other strains, and results can remain positive for prolonged periods after infection. Rapid antigen testing for

influenza virus on nasal swabs offers the advantage of point-of-care diagnosis but is less sensitive than polymerase chain reaction–based techniques. Respiratory viral panel results using nucleic acid amplification are positive in up to 40% of patients hospitalized with CAP; however, a positive result may reflect viral coinfection or antecedent predisposing infection rather than current clinical illness. Although these panels are less helpful in guiding decisions about discontinuing antibiotic therapy, a positive respiratory viral panel might have significant infection control implications among patients admitted to the hospital.

Additional testing is indicated only in select patients based on epidemiologic risk factors (see Table 11), clinical findings, or radiographic patterns (see Table 13). Fungal and acid-fast bacilli stains of sputum or fungal antigen testing can be performed. Serology for *Coxiella burnetii*, *Francisella tularensis*, *Legionella*, *Mycoplasma*, and *Chlamydophila*, using acute and convalescent sera, can document seroconversion or a fourfold increase in titers.

Patients with pleural effusions of unknown cause or those thicker than 1 cm should undergo thoracentesis to exclude concomitant empyema requiring drainage (see MKSAP 18 Pulmonary and Critical Care Medicine). Bronchoscopy with transbronchial biopsy should be considered in patients with an unrevealing noninvasive evaluation who do not respond to empiric therapy. ◪

KEY POINTS

- Diagnostic studies to identify a causative organism are **HVC** not routinely indicated in outpatients with community-acquired pneumonia (CAP) but should be considered in non-ICU hospitalized patients when this information would change management; diagnostic studies should be performed in all patients admitted to the ICU with CAP.

- For patients with pneumococcal pneumonia, a good-quality sputum culture obtained before antibiotic initiation is suggestive or diagnostic in up to 80% of cases; blood culture results are positive in 20% to 25% of cases; pneumococcal urinary antigen testing is more than 70% sensitive, and results are not affected by antibiotic administration.

- *Legionella* urinary antigen test results are positive in most patients with *L. pneumophila* serotype 1 infection, but it does not detect other strains, and results can remain positive for prolonged periods after infection.

Management
Site of Care
Ambulatory management is adequate for many patients with CAP. Multiple clinical prediction models are available to identify patients who would most benefit from hospital or ICU admission (**Table 14**), but complexity and lack of consensus limit their use. Although prediction rules may aid in

TABLE 14. Community-Acquired Pneumonia Clinical Decision Support Scoring Systems for Site of Care

Variable	PSI[a]	CURB-65[b]	IDSA/ATS Criteria[c]
Age	>50 years	≥65 years	
Comorbidities	Malignancy		
	Congestive heart failure		
	Cerebrovascular disease		
	Kidney disease		
	Liver disease		
Vital signs	Heart rate ≥125/min		
	Respiration rate ≥30/min	Respiration rate ≥30/min	Respiration rate ≥30/min
	Temperature <35 °C (95 °F) or ≥40 °C (104 °F)		Temperature <36 °C (96.8 °F)
	SBP <90 mm Hg	SBP <90 mm Hg or DBP ≤60 mm Hg	Hypotension requiring aggressive fluid resuscitation
Physical examination	Altered mentation	Confusion	Confusion or disorientation
Laboratory findings		BUN >20 mg/dL (7.1 mmol/L)	BUN ≥20 mg/dL (≥7.1 mmol/L)
			Leukocyte count <4000/µL (4 × 10⁹/L)
			Platelet count <100,000/µL (100 × 10⁹/L)
			P_{O_2}/F_{IO_2} ratio ≤250
Radiographic findings			Multilobar infiltrate

ATS = American Thoracic Society; BUN = blood urea nitrogen; CURB = Confusion, Urea, Respiration rate, Blood pressure; DBP = diastolic blood pressure; IDSA = Infectious Diseases Society of America; PSI = Pneumonia Severity Index; SBP = systolic blood pressure.

[a]PSI Step 1 Screen: If no factors are present, patient is assigned risk class I and can likely be managed as an outpatient. Patients with at least one risk factor are stratified by a more complex Step 2 scale (not shown) into risk class II-V.

[b]CURB-65 Score: Each variable present is assigned one point. Patients with a cumulative score of 0-1 are usually appropriate for outpatient treatment.

[c]IDSA/ATS ICU admission scale: Patients with a major criterion (either need for mechanical ventilation or septic shock requiring vasopressors) or ≥3 of the minor criteria are best managed in the ICU.

CONT.

site-of-care decisions, scores should not supersede clinical judgment.

The Pneumonia Severity Index (PSI) is a validated predictor of all-cause mortality at 30 days. The initial assessment determines the presence of 11 variables associated with adverse outcomes (see Table 14). Patients with no risk factors (severity risk class I) can typically be managed as outpatients. Those with at least one risk factor are stratified using a second scoring system into a risk classification between II and V based on a more complex point system that includes residence in a nursing home, abnormal laboratory test results, and radiographic findings.

The CURB-65 (Confusion, blood Urea nitrogen [BUN], Respiratory rate, Blood pressure, and age ≥65 years) score is a simplified, albeit slightly less predictive, tool for identifying patients at low risk. Thirty-day mortality among patients with a CURB-65 score of 0 or 1 was less than 3%, so ambulatory treatment is appropriate for most patients with scores less than 2. The modified CRB-65 omits BUN measurement and supports ambulatory clinical assessment; patients with a score of 1 or more warrant consideration for hospitalization.

Consensus guidelines by the Infectious Diseases Society of America and American Thoracic Society (IDSA/ATS) provide criteria to identify patients best managed in the ICU. The need for mechanical ventilation or vasopressor support to maintain blood pressure was considered a major criterion and mandated ICU admission. Minor criteria are listed in Table 14; the presence of three or more criteria suggests a higher mortality rate and necessitates ICU admission. **H**

KEY POINT

- A clinical prediction model (the Pneumonia Severity Index, CURB-65 or CRB-65, or Infectious Diseases Society of America/American Thoracic Society criteria) can be used to identify patients with community-acquired pneumonia who may require hospital or ICU admission.

Antimicrobial Therapy

IDSA/ATS guidelines for CAP treatment balance the need to effectively treat infection, often in the absence of an identified pathogen, with the competing imperative for judicious antibiotic use. Treatment recommendations are stratified by site of care (see Table 12). Since publication of these guidelines, studies have documented the changing microbiology of CAP in the United States and questioned the importance of empiric treatment for atypical bacteria. Updated CAP guidelines, which are scheduled to be published in 2018, are anticipated to address these issues.

Ambulatory empiric therapy for CAP is directed against *S. pneumoniae*, *Haemophilus influenzae*, and atypical bacteria, even though a significant proportion of patients with CAP infected with viral pathogens do not benefit from antibiotic therapy. In otherwise healthy patients, regimens include monotherapy with doxycycline or a macrolide (either azithromycin or clarithromycin). If local *S. pneumoniae* macrolide resistance is greater than 25%, a β-lactam plus a macrolide or a respiratory quinolone could be used instead. Respiratory quinolones include levofloxacin and moxifloxacin, which are active against *S. pneumoniae*; ciprofloxacin is not a respiratory quinolone because its activity against streptococcal species is limited.

For patients with significant comorbidities treated as outpatients, a respiratory quinolone or a β-lactam plus a macrolide is recommended. Options for oral β-lactams include high-dose amoxicillin; a second-generation cephalosporin is an alternative for patients allergic to penicillin. The risk of infection with drug-resistant *S. pneumoniae* is increased with antibiotic use in the preceding 3 months; these patients should be treated similarly to outpatients with comorbidities using an agent from a different class. Macrolides and quinolones may rarely induce fatal arrhythmias, and care should be used when these antibiotics are prescribed in conjunction with other medications that prolong the QTc interval. When macrolides and quinolones are contraindicated, doxycycline can be substituted for a macrolide and given in conjunction with a β-lactam.

Patients with more severe infections requiring hospitalization may be infected with a broader spectrum of bacterial pathogens, reflecting host susceptibility and organism virulence. Patients with CAP who warrant non-ICU hospital admission are most commonly infected with the organisms shown in Figure 1. Recommended empiric regimens include a parenteral β-lactam agent (a third-generation cephalosporin or ampicillin-sulbactam) plus a macrolide or a respiratory fluoroquinolone. Use of ampicillin-sulbactam or other penicillin-based antibiotics offers the advantage of increased anaerobic spectrum and should be considered when aspiration pneumonia is a concern. For patients allergic to β-lactams or those treated with a component of this regimen in the preceding 3 months, monotherapy with a respiratory quinolone is appropriate.

An area of controversy is whether empiric therapy for atypical bacterial infection confers an outcome advantage among hospitalized patients with CAP who do not require ICU care. The CAP-START study, a randomized controlled trial published in 2015, evaluated the two currently recommended regimens (a β-lactam plus a macrolide or a respiratory quinolone) compared with β-lactam monotherapy in this

population and found no significant difference in outcomes among the three groups. This result was not replicated in a second randomized trial or in several observational studies that found excess mortality associated with β-lactam monotherapy compared with standard therapy. Furthermore, several studies have shown a survival benefit for patients with bacteremic CAP caused by *S. pneumoniae* treated with combination β-lactam plus macrolide therapy; whether this benefit reflects a direct antimicrobial effect or the anti-inflammatory properties of azithromycin is uncertain.

The microbiology among patients with CAP requiring ICU care is shown in Table 12. In this population, monotherapy with a respiratory quinolone is contraindicated. Suggested regimens include coadministration of a parenteral β-lactam active against *S. pneumoniae* and a second agent active against *Legionella* species (either azithromycin or a quinolone). For patients with a history of immediate hypersensitivity reaction to β-lactam antibiotics, aztreonam, which is purely active against gram-negative bacteria, is an acceptable alternative if given with a respiratory quinolone to treat *S. pneumoniae* and atypical organisms.

Methicillin-resistant *S. aureus* (MRSA) is not adequately treated by the previously discussed empiric regimens, yet is increasingly recognized as causing CAP, particularly in critically ill patients. CAP caused by MRSA is associated with preceding influenza infection and injection drug use, although it may present in patients without any identifiable risk factors. Empiric therapy for MRSA should be considered in patients with one of these risk factors, a suspicious Gram stain (gram-positive cocci in clusters), conventional therapy failure, pleural-based lung nodules (suggesting septic pulmonary emboli), or cavitary lung lesions. Optimal treatment for MRSA CAP has not been defined, but options include vancomycin, linezolid, and ceftaroline. Notably, daptomycin binds to surfactant, resulting in negligible alveolar levels, and is therefore not effective in pulmonary infections.

Pseudomonas aeruginosa, a significant cause of HAP, can also cause CAP and is not adequately treated by standard empiric regimens. *Pseudomonas* should be considered in immunocompromised patients and in patients with underlying structural lung disease (bronchiectasis or cystic fibrosis) or medical conditions requiring repeated courses of antibiotics. When clinical concern for *Pseudomonas* is present, initial empiric therapy with two active agents is indicated. Options include an antipseudomonal β-lactam (piperacillin-tazobactam, cefepime, or meropenem) in conjunction with either a quinolone (levofloxacin or ciprofloxacin) or an aminoglycoside. If an aminoglycoside is chosen, a macrolide should be added for empiric coverage of atypical bacteria. Moxifloxacin, a respiratory quinolone with activity against *S. pneumoniae*, is relatively ineffective against *Pseudomonas* and should not be used for treatment when *Pseudomonas* is a concern. Inclusion of a quinolone in the empiric regimen is relatively contraindicated in patients who did not respond to previous courses of this drug.

Controversy exists over optimal management of hospitalized patients with CAP and a positive rapid viral test result.

Although respiratory viruses may cause severe CAP, a viral cause does not exclude a bacterial coinfection. *S. aureus*, *S. pneumoniae*, and *Streptococcus pyogenes* have all been associated with postinfluenza necrotizing CAP. Therefore, many authorities recommend continuing antibiotics for CAP even when a viral pathogen is identified.

For patients with uncomplicated CAP who demonstrate rapid defervescence and clinical improvement over the first 3 days, a 5-day course of therapy is adequate for cure. Exceptions include patients with cavitary disease or lung abscess, empyema, concomitant bacteremia, extrapulmonary infection, or ongoing instability, defined as persistent fever, abnormal vital signs, or hypoxia. Many authorities also recommend prolonged duration of antibiotics (at least 14 days) for CAP caused by *S. aureus* or Enterobacteriaceae; fungal or mycobacterial lung infections may require a more prolonged course of treatment.

KEY POINTS

- Ambulatory empiric therapy for community-acquired pneumonia in otherwise healthy patients includes monotherapy with doxycycline or a macrolide (either azithromycin or clarithromycin); if local *Streptococcus pneumoniae* macrolide resistance is greater than 25%, a β-lactam plus a macrolide or a respiratory quinolone could be used instead.

- Recommended empiric regimens for hospitalized non-ICU patients include a parenteral β-lactam agent (a third-generation cephalosporin or ampicillin-sulbactam) plus a macrolide; for patients allergic to β-lactams or those treated with a component of this regimen in the preceding 3 months, monotherapy with a respiratory quinolone is appropriate.

(Continued)

KEY POINTS *(continued)*

- Treatment regimens for patients with community-acquired pneumonia requiring ICU care include coadministration of a parenteral β-lactam active against *Streptococcus pneumoniae* and a second agent active against *Legionella* species.

Complications

CAP has a mortality rate of 10% to 12% among hospitalized patients. Survivors may experience significant morbidity, including prolonged hospitalization, protracted convalescence, and high rates of hospital readmission. Related complications include localized lung inflammation, secondary spread of infection, and toxicity related to treatment (**Table 15**).

Lack of response to antimicrobials raises consideration of a resistant or atypical organism, loculated infection (such as empyema), or an infection mimic (tumor, vasculitis, pulmonary embolism). Patients with significant pleural fluid collections should undergo diagnostic thoracentesis; chest tube drainage is indicated for empyema.

Severe CAP is often associated with a vigorous immune response resulting in acute respiratory distress syndrome. A recent meta-analysis found that for patients hospitalized for CAP, glucocorticoid administration was associated with significantly reduced mortality, reduced mechanical ventilation needs, and shorter hospital stay. Whether this glucocorticoid benefit extends to all hospitalized patients with CAP or is restricted to a subset at highest risk for acute respiratory distress syndrome has not been established; therefore, adjunctive glucocorticoids should not be routinely administered to all patients with severe CAP.

TABLE 15.	Complications of Community-Acquired Pneumonia	
Organ System	**Syndrome**	**Comments**
Pulmonary	Nonresolving pneumonia	Consider resistant infections, noninfectious causes
	Lung abscess	Prolonged course of antimicrobial treatment
	Empyema	Chest tube drainage of infected pleural fluid
	ARDS	Lung protective ventilation strategy indicated; glucocorticoids may decrease this complication
Neurologic	Delirium	May reflect hypoxemia, hypercarbia, or ICU stay
Hematologic	Leukopenia	May be related to sepsis, medication effect
	Thrombocytopenia	May be related to sepsis, medication effect
Cardiac	Acute coronary syndrome	Seen in 5%-10% of hospitalized patients
	Cardiac arrhythmias	Most commonly atrial fibrillation
Kidney	Acute kidney injury	May be related to hypoperfusion or medication effect
Endocrine	Adrenal insufficiency	Waterhouse-Friderichsen syndrome (acute adrenal necrosis), occurring in the setting of overwhelming bacterial infection/septic shock

ARDS = acute respiratory distress syndrome.

- Lack of response to antimicrobials in patients with community-acquired pneumonia raises consideration of a resistant or atypical organism, loculated infection, an infection mimic, or empyema.

- Patients hospitalized with community-acquired pneumonia experience significant morbidity and are at high risk for readmission.

Follow-up

For patients who do not require hospitalization, additional evaluation is only necessary in those who do not respond to empiric therapy within 3 days (of a standard 5-day course) or who develop new symptoms.

In contrast, readmission rates among hospitalized patients approach 20%. This population should have close outpatient follow-up to ensure clinical stability after therapy completion. Radiographic clearance often lags behind clinical response, so repeat imaging should be deferred at initial follow-up unless clinical improvement is slow or new symptoms have developed. Postobstructive pneumonia may be the presenting symptom of bronchial carcinoma, and repeat chest radiography in 2 to 3 months is recommended in patients at high risk (age >50 years or those with a significant smoking history) to document resolution.

HVC
- For patients who do not require hospitalization for community-acquired pneumonia, additional evaluation is only necessary in those who do not respond to empiric therapy within 3 days (of a 5-day course) or who develop new symptoms.

Tick-Borne Diseases

Lyme Disease

Lyme disease is the most common vector-borne infection in the United States. More than 30,000 new infections are reported annually, which likely represent only 10% of actual infections. More than 95% of infections in the United States occur in the northeastern, mid-Atlantic, and upper Midwest regions (**Figure 5**). These areas are endemic for the vector, *Ixodes scapularis* (the black-legged deer tick). The causative spirochete, *Borrelia burgdorferi*, is transmitted intradermally when a tick ingests a blood meal. In Europe, *Borrelia garinii* and *Borellia afzelii* cause Lyme disease, with *Ixodes ricinus* as the tick vector.

After a tick bite by *I. scapularis*, administration of a single dose (200 mg) of doxycycline may decrease the risk of subsequent Lyme disease development but should be considered only if (1) the tick is reliably identified as a black-legged deer tick; (2) attachment lasts 36 hours or longer; (3) antibiotics can

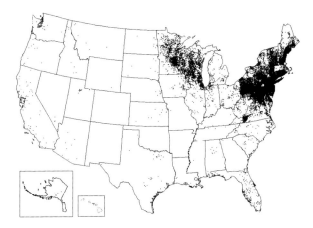

FIGURE 5. Lyme disease cases reported during 2016. Each dot represents the county of residence (not necessarily acquisition) for a confirmed case.

Reprinted with permission from "Reported Cases of Lyme Disease—United States 2016" (Washington, D.C.: Department of Health and Human Services, 2016), https://www.cdc.gov/lyme/resources/reportedcasesoflyme disease_2016.pdf.

be started less than 72 hours after tick removal; (4) prevalence of *B. burgdorferi* infection of ticks in the region exceeds 20%; and (5) doxycycline treatment is not contraindicated. Except for these selected situations, observation is recommended, with treatment given if suggestive symptoms occur.

The clinical manifestations, diagnostic testing, and treatment of Lyme disease vary according to the stage of infection (**Table 16**).

Early Localized Disease

Early localized disease presents within 4 weeks of infection. Most infected persons (70% to 80%) develop erythema migrans (EM), an annular skin lesion that often presents with central clearing (**Figure 6**). Systemic symptoms are variably present.

EM lesions are typically painless, nonpruritic, and circumferentially enlarging. Atypical presentations of EM, with confluent erythroderma, ulceration, or vesiculation, may confound the diagnosis. Local cutaneous reactions due to hypersensitivity to tick saliva may resemble EM but tend to occur earlier, are pruritic, and do not enlarge significantly after onset.

A patient with EM and a compatible exposure history does not require confirmatory laboratory testing. In fact, antibody testing in early localized disease is insensitive because seroconversion may be delayed for several weeks after onset of an EM lesion. Treatment is with an oral agent. Doxycycline offers the advantage of treating incubating *Anaplasma phagocytophilum*, which also is spread by black-legged ticks and can coinfect patients with Lyme disease.

Early Disseminated Disease

In the absence of treatment, hematogenous dissemination occurs in up to 60% of patients. Symptoms of early disseminated disease present weeks to months after infection. The most common manifestation is a flu-like illness characterized by fevers, arthralgia, myalgia, and lymphadenopathy and often

TABLE 16.	Clinical Manifestations, Diagnostic Testing, and Treatment of Lyme Disease by Stage of Infection			
Lyme Stage	**Onset after Infection**	**Clinical Findings**	**Laboratory Confirmation**	**Treatment[a]**
Early localized	≤4 wk	EM at site of tick attachment, fever, lymphadenopathy, myalgia	Not needed if EM present	Doxycycline, 100 mg PO BID × 10-21 d (first-line therapy) *or* Amoxicillin, 500 mg PO TID × 14-21 d *or* Cefuroxime axetil, 500 mg PO BID × 14-21 d
Early disseminated	2 wk-6 mo	Multiple sites of EM, flu-like syndrome, heart block, myocarditis, facial nerve palsy, meningitis, radiculitis	Not needed if EM is present; otherwise, two-tier serologic testing CSF testing for intrathecal antibody production if CNS involvement is a concern	1. First-degree block with PR interval ≥300 msec, second- or third-degree AV nodal block, myocarditis: IV penicillin or IV ceftriaxone × 28 d 2. First-degree AV block with PR interval <300 msec: oral treatment same as for early localized disease × 14-28 d 3. Meningitis: IV penicillin or IV ceftriaxone × 28 d 4. Other manifestations (including facial palsy): oral treatment the same as for early localized disease × 14-28 d
Late disseminated	≥6 mo	Recurrent large joint arthritis; neurologic symptoms (peripheral neuropathy, encephalopathy), or dermatologic symptoms (acrodermatitis chronica atrophicans)	Two-tier serologic testing	Initial rheumatologic treatment: same as for early localized but × 30 d Recurrent arthritis after initial treatment: IV ceftriaxone Neurologic disease: IV ceftriaxone × 28 d

AV = atrioventricular; BID = twice daily; CSF = cerebrospinal fluid; CNS = central nervous system; EM = erythema migrans; IV = intravenous; PO = by mouth; TID = three times daily.

[a]Doses are for adults with normal kidney function.

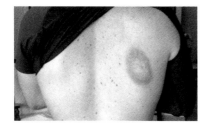

FIGURE 6. Erythema migrans lesion at site of tick attachment.

Figure courtesy of Dr. Karen Bloch.

associated with multiple concurrent EM lesions at sites distant from the original tick attachment.

Infection of cardiac tissue results in injury to the conduction system and atrioventricular (AV) nodal block. Progression to complete heart block can occur rapidly despite antibiotic treatment, so hospitalization is indicated for close monitoring of patients with severe cardiac involvement: symptomatic patients with dizziness, syncope, or dyspnea; asymptomatic patients with first-degree AV block and a PR interval of 300 milliseconds or greater; and patients with a higher-degree AV block. Permanent pacemaker placement is not necessary because the heart block is reversible.

Infection of neurologic tissue occurs in approximately 15% of untreated patients. Aseptic meningitis, facial palsy (unilateral or bilateral), and radiculopathy may be present in isolation or associated with skin, musculoskeletal, or cardiac findings. Lumbar puncture is indicated when central nervous system infection (such as neuroborreliosis) is suspected; cerebrospinal fluid lymphocytic pleocytosis supports the diagnosis (see Central Nervous System Infection).

When EM lesions are present, laboratory confirmation is unnecessary. In the absence of diagnostic skin findings, serologic diagnosis should be pursued through a two-tiered approach (**Figure 7**); the initial enzyme-linked immunosorbent assay (ELISA) is highly sensitive but lacks specificity and must be confirmed by a Western blot test. The C6 ELISA test detects antibody against a highly conserved bacterial epitope and may be more sensitive than traditional whole-cell sonicate ELISA, especially for the

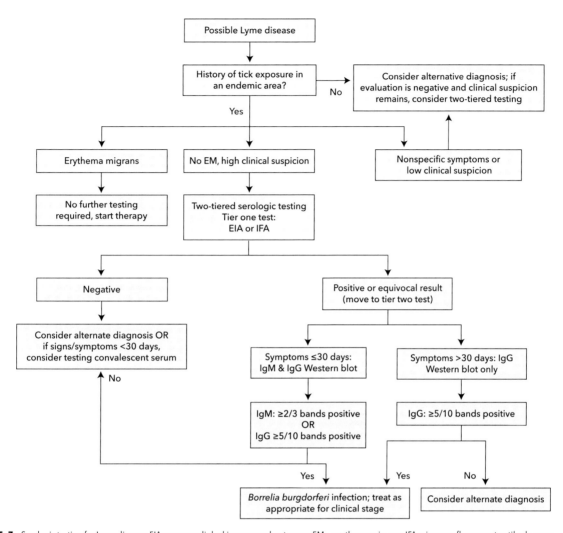

FIGURE 7. Serologic testing for Lyme disease. EIA = enzyme-linked immunosorbent assay; EM = erythema migrans; IFA = immunofluorescent antibody assay.

Adapted with permission from Moore A, Nelson C, Molins C, Mead P, Schriefer M. Current guidelines, common clinical pitfalls, and future directions for laboratory diagnosis of Lyme disease, United States. Emerg Infect Dis. 2016;22:1169. [PMID: 27314832] doi:10.3201/eid2207.151694

European strains *B. garinii* and *B. afzelii*, but, because of insufficient specificity, confirmatory Western blot testing is still required.

IgM antibody is detectable before IgG antibody in early infection; however, IgG antibody should be detectable after 30 days of symptoms. Because isolated IgM positivity is likely to be a false positive after the first month of symptoms, testing for IgM is not recommended after this time period. Antibodies may remain for years despite treatment; therefore, serial titers are not useful.

Late Disseminated Disease

Approximately 60% of untreated patients with Lyme disease develop a monoarticular or oligoarticular inflammatory arthritis as a late complication. The knee and other large joints are disproportionally affected. Even without antibiotic treatment, inflammation typically resolves over weeks to months but can have a relapsing-remitting pattern. In approximately 10% of untreated patients, arthritis persists (see MKSAP 18 Rheumatology). Late neurologic or skin findings (acrodermatitis chronica atrophicans and borrelial lymphocytoma) are rare in the United States but more frequent in European infections. Diagnosis is made with the two-tier serologic test. Treatment requires prolonged oral antibiotics; parenteral therapy is used when oral therapy is unsuccessful (see Table 16).

Post-Lyme Disease Syndrome

Post–Lyme disease syndrome has been reported in approximately 10% of patients after treatment of EM (**Table 17**). Although often erroneously called "chronic Lyme disease," studies have found no microbiologic evidence of chronic or latent infection after appropriate treatment. Symptoms include fatigue, arthralgia, myalgia, and impairment of memory or cognition that can last for years after treatment of the acute infection. Clinical trials have shown no benefit of prolonged antibiotic treatment for post–Lyme disease syndrome.

TABLE 17.	Definition of Post-Lyme Disease Syndrome
Inclusion Criteria	
Diagnosis of Lyme disease based on CDC case criteria (EM or positive serologic finding)	
Resolution or stabilization of the objective manifestations of Lyme disease after standard treatment	
Onset of at least one of the following within 6 months of Lyme disease diagnosis, with persistence for at least 6 months after antibiotic treatment, that is of sufficient severity to result in decreased level of functioning:	
1. Fatigue	
2. Widespread musculoskeletal pain	
3. Cognitive impairment	
Exclusion Criteria	
An untreated tick-borne coinfection (such as babesiosis)	
Ongoing symptoms attributable to Lyme disease (such as antibiotic-refractory Lyme arthritis)	
Symptoms of fatigue or musculoskeletal pains or a diagnosis of fibromyalgia or chronic fatigue syndrome predating the onset of Lyme disease	
An alternative diagnosis accounting for the symptoms	

CDC = Centers for Disease Control and Prevention; EM = erythema migrans.

Source: Wormser GP, Dattwyler RJ, Shapiro ED, Halperin JJ, Steere AC, Klempner MS, et al. The clinical assessment, treatment, and prevention of Lyme disease, human granulocytic anaplasmosis, and babesiosis: clinical practice guidelines by the Infectious Diseases Society of America. Clin Infect Dis. 2006;43:1089-134. [PMID: 17029130]

Evaluation for coinfection with another tick-borne pathogen or for a noninfectious cause is indicated; when no alternative diagnosis is found, treatment is symptomatic.

KEY POINTS

- The causative spirochete of Lyme disease may be transmitted when an infected *Ixodes scapularis* tick attaches for at least 36 hours.

HVC
- Early localized Lyme disease usually presents within 4 weeks of infection and is characterized by erythema migrans (EM) at the site of tick attachment; patients with EM and a compatible exposure history do not require confirmatory laboratory testing and should receive oral antibiotic therapy.

- Early disseminated Lyme disease can affect the cardiovascular and neurologic systems; the diagnosis should be confirmed through an enzyme-linked immunosorbent assay followed by confirmatory Western blot testing, with presumptive treatment depending on disease severity.

- Post–Lyme disease syndrome (fatigue, arthralgia, myalgia, and impairment of memory or cognition) can last for years, even after treatment of the acute infection; there is no role for prolonged antibiotics for this condition.

Babesiosis

Babesiosis is caused by the intraerythrocytic protozoan *Babesia microti*, which is spread by the black-legged deer tick. Because of the common vector, babesiosis occurs in areas of Lyme endemicity (see Figure 5), most frequently during summer months. In Europe, babesiosis is caused by several different *Babesia* species and is spread by the *I. ricinus* tick. Transfusion of infected blood products and rare congenital transmission also allows for year-round infection, which may occur outside endemic regions.

Clinical findings range from asymptomatic presentations (approximately 20%) to fatal disease (10%). Risk factors for severe disease include age older than 50 years, immunocompromise, or asplenia. Symptoms begin within 1 month after tick bite and within 6 months after transfusion of infected blood products. Symptoms are nonspecific and include fever (89%), fatigue (82%), chills (67%), headache (47%), myalgia (43%), and cough (28%). Physical examination may reveal jaundice, hepatomegaly, and splenomegaly, which rarely progresses to splenic rupture. The hallmark of babesiosis is hemolysis, with anemia almost invariably present. With severe disease, thrombocytopenia, elevated liver enzyme levels, and acute kidney injury are possible.

Babesiosis is diagnosed by visualization of the causative organism on thin blood smears, manifesting as intraerythrocytic ring forms similar to those seen in malaria or as tetrads resembling a Maltese cross (**Figure 8**). With low-level parasitemia, multiple smears may need to be examined, and the sensitivity of microscopy is low. Therefore, polymerase chain reaction or serology should be pursued if smear findings are negative but clinical suspicion of babesiosis is high.

Treatment depends on disease severity (**Table 18**). After treatment, patients should be monitored closely for relapse; if relapse occurs, prolonged therapy extending more than 2 weeks after clearance of parasitemia is necessary for cure.

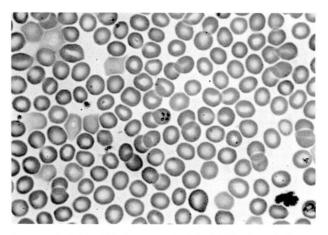

FIGURE 8. Peripheral blood smear showing babesiosis. The diagnosis of babesiosis is typically established by evaluation of a peripheral blood smear showing intraerythrocytic parasites. Occasionally, merozoites are arranged in tetrads, resembling a Maltese cross.

TABLE 18. Treatment for Babesiosis

Severity	Regimen
Asymptomatic, ≤3 months of parasitemia	Monitor for clearance; no treatment indicated
Asymptomatic, >3 months of parasitemia	Atovaquone plus azithromycin
Mild to moderate disease	Atovaquone plus azithromycin
Severe disease requiring ICU admission	Clindamycin plus quinine
Severe disease with >10% parasitemia, hemoglobin level <10 g/dL (100 g/L), ARDS, liver failure or kidney failure	Clindamycin plus quinine *and* Exchange transfusion

ARDS = acute respiratory distress syndrome.

KEY POINTS

- Babesiosis, an infection caused by an intraerythrocytic protozoan, presents with clinical findings ranging from asymptomatic infection to fatal disease; symptoms are usually nonspecific, but hemolytic anemia is a hallmark of disease.

- Diagnosis of babesiosis is by visualization of the organism on blood smear, serology, or polymerase chain reaction.

- Treatment of babesiosis depends on disease severity; atovaquone plus azithromycin are most appropriate for mild disease, whereas clindamycin plus quinine remains the regimen of choice for severe disease.

Southern Tick–Associated Rash Illness

Southern tick–associated rash illness (STARI) presents with EM lesions identical to those seen in Lyme disease but without clinical progression or complications. STARI is associated with *Amblyomma americanum*, also known as the Lone Star tick, and occurs in the southeastern, south-central, and eastern United States. No infectious cause has been confirmed. Therefore, diagnosis is based on clinical and geographic features. Because STARI and early-stage Lyme disease may be clinically indistinguishable, treatment with doxycycline is recommended.

KEY POINT

- Southern tick–associated rash illness may be clinically indistinguishable from early-stage Lyme disease, and thus treatment with doxycycline is recommended.

Human Monocytic Ehrlichiosis and Granulocytic Anaplasmosis

Human monocytic ehrlichiosis (HME) and human granulocytic anaplasmosis (HGA) are clinically similar illnesses spread by different tick vectors and caused by distinct bacterial pathogens. HME is caused by *Ehrlichia chaffeensis*, which is transmitted by the Lone Star tick, and occurs most commonly in the southeastern and south-central United States. HGA is caused by *Anaplasma phagocytophilum*, which is transmitted by *Ixodes* ticks, and occurs in areas of Lyme endemicity (see Figure 5).

These syndromes typically begin with a nonspecific febrile illness 1 to 2 weeks after a tick bite (**Table 19**). Rash is uncommon in contrast to Rocky Mountain spotted fever. Laboratory study abnormalities, including leukopenia, thrombocytopenia, and increased serum aminotransferase levels, are nonspecific.

The organisms causing HME and HGA replicate inside leukocytes and cause hallmark basophilic inclusion bodies called morulae (**Figure 9**). Serologic findings often are negative in acute illness; testing of a convalescent specimen 2 to 4 weeks after onset of symptoms is usually confirmatory. Polymerase chain reaction of whole blood at the time of acute illness may be diagnostic, particularly if performed before therapy. Doxycycline is the recommended treatment for both HME and HGA. Because delay in treatment is associated with increased mortality, empiric therapy should be started even in the absence of confirmatory testing.

KEY POINTS

- Human monocytic ehrlichiosis and human granulocytic anaplasmosis cause a nonspecific febrile illness beginning 1 to 2 weeks after a tick bite.

- Acute serologic findings are often negative in both human monocytic ehrlichiosis and human granulocytic anaplasmosis; polymerase chain reaction of whole blood at the time of acute illness may be diagnostic.

- Doxycycline is recommended for both human monocytic ehrlichiosis and human granulocytic anaplasmosis; empiric therapy should be started without awaiting results of confirmatory testing.

Rocky Mountain Spotted Fever

Rocky Mountain spotted fever (RMSF) is caused by *Rickettsia rickettsii* and transmitted by multiple tick vectors. It has been reported throughout the continental United States but occurs most frequently in the "RMSF belt" extending from North Carolina to Oklahoma.

Clinically, RMSF presents with nonspecific symptoms similar to those of HME and HGA (Table 19) but can progress to aseptic meningoencephalitis. The hallmark feature is a macular eruption around the ankles or wrists, with central spread and progression to petechiae or purpura (**Figure 10**). Lesions are found on the palms and soles in as many as 50% of patients; the face is generally spared. Purpura fulminans may occur and result in loss of digits or limbs. Although skin findings are ultimately noted in greater than 90% of patients with RMSF, the earliest macular rash occurs a median of 3 days after onset

TABLE 19. Comparison of Epidemiologic and Clinical Features of Human Monocytic Ehrlichiosis, Human Granulocytic Anaplasmosis, and Rocky Mountain Spotted Fever

Feature	HME	HGA	RMSF
Vector	Lone Star tick	Black-legged deer tick	American dog tick, brown dog tick, Rocky Mountain wood tick
Geography	Southeastern, mid-Atlantic, and south-central United States	Northeastern and upper Midwest United States	Throughout the United States[a]
Coinfection	Not reported; potential for coinfection with STARI or Heartland virus because of common vector	Lyme disease, babesiosis, Powassan virus, *Borrelia miyamotoi*	None
Incubation period	5-14 days	5-14 days	3-12 days
Presenting signs and symptoms	Fever, headache, myalgias, nausea, vomiting, diarrhea, conjunctival injection	Fever, headache, myalgias, chills	Fever, headache, chills, mylagia, nausea, abdominal pain, photophobia, aseptic meningitis
Cutaneous signs	Nonspecific rash in <30% of adults, with median onset 5 days after fever	Rash rare (<10%)	Maculopapular eruption in >90% of patients, progressing to petechia with involvement of palms and soles, edema; onset, median of 3 days after fever
Laboratory study abnormalities	Leukopenia, thrombocytopenia, increased serum aminotransferase levels, mild anemia	Leukopenia, thrombocytopenia, increased serum aminotransferase levels, mild anemia	Thrombocytopenia, increased serum aminotransferase levels, normal or slightly increased leukocyte count, hyponatremia
Diagnosis	Morulae in monocytes (<30%), acute and convalescent serologies, whole-blood PCR	Morulae in neutrophils (~50%), acute and convalescent serologies, whole-blood PCR	Acute and convalescent serologies, biopsy of skin with immunohistochemical analysis
Treatment	Doxycycline	Doxycycline	Doxycycline
Fatality	3%	<1%	5%-10%

HGA = human granulocytic anaplasmosis; HME = human monocytic ehrlichiosis; PCR = polymerase chain reaction; RMSF = Rocky Mountain spotted fever; STARI = Southern tick-associated rash illness.

[a]Two thirds of all patients with RMSF are infected in Arkansas, Missouri, North Carolina, Oklahoma, and Tennessee.

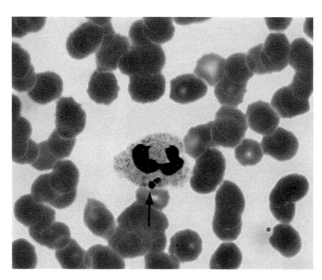

FIGURE 9. Morulae (*arrow*) appearing as basophilic inclusion bodies in leukocytes of a patient with ehrlichiosis.

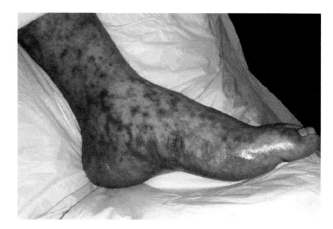

FIGURE 10. Petechial and purpuric skin eruption in a patient with late-stage Rocky Mountain spotted fever.

Reprinted with permission from Biggs HM, Behravesh CB, Bradley KK, Dahlgren FS, Drexler NA, Dumler JS, et al. Diagnosis and management of tickborne rickettsial diseases: Rocky Mountain spotted fever and other spotted fever group rickettsioses, ehrlichioses, and anaplasmosis - United States. MMWR Recomm Rep. 2016;65:1 44. [PMID: 27172113] doi:10.15585/mmwr.rr6502a1

of fever and thus may not be found at the first clinical presentation.

Immunohistochemical analysis of skin biopsy samples may be diagnostic. As with HME and HGA, acute serology is not sensitive, although testing convalescent serum may provide a retrospective diagnosis. Doxycycline should be given empirically when RMSF is clinically suspected because treatment delay is associated with more severe disease and increased mortality.

- Rocky Mountain spotted fever (RMSF) presents similarly to both human monocytic ehrlichiosis and human granulocytic anaplasmosis; the major differentiating feature of RMSF is the presence of a rash, but the rash may not appear until 3 days after onset of fever.

- Doxycycline should be given empirically when Rocky Mountain spotted fever is clinically suspected.

Urinary Tract Infections

Epidemiology and Microbiology

Community-acquired urinary tract infections (UTIs) account for approximately 8 million ambulatory visits and 1 million hospitalizations each year in the United States, making them one of the most common infections for which an antibiotic is prescribed in clinical practice. Another 1 million nosocomial UTIs are diagnosed annually, primarily indwelling urinary catheter–associated UTIs, accounting for an estimated 40% of all health care–associated infections (see Health Care–Associated Infections). Approximately half of all women experience a UTI by age 30 years; sexual activity is a major risk factor. Approximately 5% of otherwise healthy women who experience a UTI are at greater risk of developing future infections. Other UTI risk factors include structural and functional abnormalities, use of spermicidal agents and diaphragms, pregnancy, diabetes mellitus, obesity, urethral catheterization (or other urinary tract instrumentation), immunosuppression, and genetic factors.

UTIs are classified based on anatomic location as lower (cystitis), upper (pyelonephritis, perinephric abscess), or prostatitis. The term *uncomplicated* UTI refers to infections in nonpregnant women without structural or neurologic abnormalities or comorbidities. UTIs in men, pregnant women, and persons with foreign bodies (for example, indwelling catheters, calculi), kidney disease, immunocompromise, obstruction, urinary retention from neurologic disorders, health care–associated infections, or recent antibiotic use are considered to be *complicated*. Advanced age in the presence of other major comorbidities or with significant frailty may be considered a complicating factor in UTI, although age alone does not define a complicated versus uncomplicated infection. Designating an infection as complicated influences the choice and duration of antimicrobial therapy and extent of investigation. Nevertheless, the potential for uncomplicated UTIs to evolve into clinically severe disease should not be underestimated, nor should the urgency or seriousness of complicated UTIs be overstated.

Most infections occur by the ascending route. In 95% of these cases, UTIs are caused by a single bacterial species, mainly gram-negative aerobic bacilli originating from the bowel. Uropathogenic *Escherichia coli* accounts for 75% to 95% of UTIs in women. Less common urinary pathogens include other members of the Enterobacteriaceae family, streptococci (in particular *Streptococcus agalactiae*), enterococci, and staphylococci (most often *Staphylococcus saprophyticus*). UTIs occurring in hospitals and long-term care facilities frequently involve a more varied group of organisms (such as *Enterobacter*, *Providencia*, *Morganella*, *Citrobacter*, *Serratia*, and *Pseudomonas*). Isolation of *Staphylococcus aureus* from the urine may be related to instrumentation but should suggest the possibility of a hematogenous infection from a source outside the urinary tract.

- The term *uncomplicated* urinary tract infection refers to infections in nonpregnant women without structural or neurologic abnormalities or comorbidities.

- Designating an infection as complicated influences the choice and duration of antimicrobial therapy and extent of investigation.

- Urinary tract infections in men, pregnant women, and persons with foreign bodies, kidney disease, immunocompromise, obstruction, urinary retention from neurologic disorders, health care–associated infections, or recent antibiotic use are considered to be *complicated*.

Diagnosis

In persons with symptoms of UTI, diagnosis in the outpatient setting is based on a combination of clinical features, determining if the presumed infectious process is in the lower or upper urinary tract, and the findings of significant pyuria (≥10 leukocytes/µL) and bacteriuria (bacteria in the urine). Pyuria can be detected by urine dipstick, which relies on the presence of leukocyte esterase. Although the sensitivity and specificity of dipstick testing are high (about 75% and 85%, respectively), pyuria may result from urinary tract disorders other than infection. The presence of leukocyte casts supports a diagnosis of pyelonephritis. Microscopic or gross hematuria may be present with a UTI but may also be encountered with nephrolithiasis and tumors. A positive nitrite test result signifies the presence of gram-negative bacteria capable of converting nitrates into nitrites but is negative in UTI caused by nonconverting organisms (*Enterococcus*, *Staphylococcus*, or *Streptococcus* species).

Quantitative cultures of a midstream, clean-void urine sample are the most accurate way to demonstrate bacteriuria in patients with suspected UTI. Because the microbiology is predictable and treatment courses are short, culture is not recommended in women with uncomplicated cystitis. Urine cultures are indicated in pyelonephritis, complicated cystitis, and recurrent UTIs; additionally, they are recommended in patients with histories of multiple antibiotic allergies and in those in whom the presence of a resistant organism is suspected (such as recent antibiotic treatment, health care–associated infection, previous multidrug-resistant UTI). The growth of 10^5 colony-forming units (CFU)/mL of urine is considered significant bacteriuria; however, lower CFU counts support a diagnosis in those with UTI symptoms.

CONT.

In most adults, imaging studies are not required for diagnosis or treatment of UTIs. Imaging may be indicated when the diagnosis is unclear, when a structural abnormality or complication is suspected, or in patients with severe illness, immunocompromise, or lack of response to appropriate therapy. Ultrasonography can detect obstruction, whereas non-contrast helical CT is recommended for visualizing kidney stones. Although less sensitive than CT, kidney ultrasonography is less expensive, requires less radiation exposure, and can be used in pregnant women or if CT is unavailable. Contrast-enhanced CT (CT urography) is recommended when intrarenal or perinephric abscess is suspected.

KEY POINTS

- Quantitative cultures of a midstream, clean-void urine sample are the most accurate way to demonstrate bacteriuria in patients with suspected urinary tract infection.

HVC
- Urine culture is not recommended in women with uncomplicated cystitis but is indicated in pyelonephritis, complicated cystitis, recurrent urinary tract infections, patients with multiple antibiotic allergies, and in patients in whom a resistant organism is suspected.

Management

Asymptomatic Bacteriuria

Asymptomatic bacteriuria is defined as the presence of at least 10^5 CFU/mL of a uropathogen from two consecutive voided urine specimens in women or one specimen in men, or more than 10^2 CFU/mL of one bacterial species from a catheterized urine specimen in women or men, in all cases without local or systemic signs or symptoms of active infection. The prevalence of asymptomatic bacteriuria is as low as 1% to 5% in healthy premenopausal women (2%-10% in pregnant women) and nearly 100% in patients with long-term indwelling urinary catheters.

The presence of pyuria accompanying asymptomatic bacteriuria is not an indication for antimicrobial treatment. Although bacteriuria increases the risk of symptomatic UTI, treatment of asymptomatic bacteriuria neither decreases the frequency of symptomatic infections nor improves other outcomes. Inappropriate treatment of asymptomatic bacteriuria is a major driver of antimicrobial resistance, particularly in health care facilities. Treatment of asymptomatic bacteriuria is, however, indicated in pregnant women and in patients scheduled to undergo an invasive procedure involving the urinary tract.

KEY POINTS

HVC
- Inappropriate treatment of asymptomatic bacteriuria is a major driver of antimicrobial resistance, particularly in health care facilities.

- Treatment of asymptomatic bacteriuria is indicated in pregnant women and in patients scheduled to undergo an invasive procedure involving the urinary tract.

Cystitis

Recommended first-line antibiotic regimens for uncomplicated cystitis (urinary frequency and urgency, dysuria, and suprapubic discomfort) should consider the increased rate of antimicrobial resistance of *E. coli*, the efficacy and advantages of short-course therapies, and the potential adverse effects (of the ecology and on patients). Preferred agents include nitrofurantoin (5 days), trimethoprim-sulfamethoxazole (3 days), and fosfomycin (1 dose, but expensive and less efficacious).

In geographic areas where trimethoprim-sulfamethoxazole resistance exceeds 20%, an alternative agent should be selected. The FDA recently indicated that fluoroquinolones should be reserved for other serious bacterial infections; however, fluoroquinolones (3 days) and β-lactam agents (including amoxicillin-clavulanate, cefdinir, cefaclor, and cefpodoxime-proxetil, each 3-7 days) are considered acceptable alternative second-line therapies. β-Lactams are not preferred if other recommended agents are available because they are less effective in eradicating infection. During pregnancy, the safest antibiotics are amoxicillin-clavulanate, cephalosporins, and nitrofurantoin. Tetracyclines and fluoroquinolones are contraindicated, and trimethoprim-sulfamethoxazole can only be used safely during the second trimester. Extended-spectrum β-lactamase–producing strains of Enterobacteriaceae causing cystitis have increased in frequency, especially in patients with recent antimicrobial or health care–facility exposure. Because of the greater risk of resistant and polymicrobial infections, urine culture and susceptibility testing are indicated in all patients with complicated cystitis. Fluoroquinolones are the preferred choice pending results, although fosfomycin and nitrofurantoin are reasonable options. The recommended treatment duration is 7 to 10 days rather than a 3-day, short-course regimen but is much less well defined. Other than in pregnant women, test of cure is not indicated in those reporting resolution of symptoms.

KEY POINT

- Preferred agents for uncomplicated cystitis include nitrofurantoin (5 days), trimethoprim-sulfamethoxazole (3 days), and fosfomycin (1 day, but least preferred); fluoroquinolones should not be used as first-line therapy in cystitis.

Acute Pyelonephritis

Lower urinary tract symptoms (frequency, urgency, and dysuria) often precede the onset of fever, chills, flank pain, and at times nausea and vomiting, which characterize acute pyelonephritis. Infection can usually be managed in the outpatient setting with oral antibiotics. Hospitalization is advised for patients with hemodynamic instability, obstructive disease, pregnancy, complicating comorbidities, known pathogen resistance requiring parenteral antibiotic therapy, inability to tolerate oral medications, or lack of reliable home supervision and clinical follow-up.

CONT.

Every patient requires a urine culture with susceptibility testing obtained before initiation of empiric therapy. Fluoroquinolones (ciprofloxacin for 7 days or levofloxacin for 5 days for uncomplicated infections, 10-14 days in complicated infections) are the only oral agents recommended for empiric outpatient treatment, but an initial dose of a long-acting parenteral antibiotic (such as ceftriaxone, 1 g, or a once-daily aminoglycoside) should replace fluoroquinolones when local resistance rates exceed 10%. When a fluoroquinolone is contraindicated, trimethoprim-sulfamethoxazole twice daily for 14 days may be used after the pathogen is proven to be susceptible; trimethoprim-sulfamethoxazole should be avoided as initial empiric therapy because of the high level of *E. coli* resistance to this antibiotic in the community.

Depending on the risk of antimicrobial resistance and on recent antibiotic use, inpatient parenteral antimicrobial options include a fluoroquinolone, extended-spectrum cephalosporins (ceftriaxone or cefepime) or penicillins (piperacillin-tazobactam), or a carbapenem (meropenem, imipenem, or ertapenem). Again, fluoroquinolones are avoided for empiric therapy in severely ill patients with complicated pyelonephritis because of the increasing potential for resistance in *E. coli* and other aerobic gram-negative bacilli.

Therapy can be completed with active oral agents when an adequate clinical response has been observed. Patients with bacteremia do not require longer courses of treatment and may be converted to appropriate oral therapy when clinically stable.

Imaging studies are only necessary in patients with prolonged fever (>72 hours) or persistent bacteremia, in which complications such as obstruction or perinephric and intrarenal abscesses must be excluded. Routine follow-up urine cultures are only indicated in pregnant women. ▣

KEY POINTS

HVC • Every patient with acute pyelonephritis requires a urine culture with susceptibility testing obtained before initiation of empiric therapy; follow-up urine cultures are only indicated in pregnant women.

• It is prudent to avoid choosing a fluoroquinolone in severely ill patients with complicated pyelonephritis because of the increasing potential for resistance in *Escherichia coli* as well as other aerobic gram-negative bacilli.

Recurrent Urinary Tract Infections in Women

An estimated 25% to 30% of patients experience a second episode of infection within 6 months of their first UTI. *Relapsed* infections are those that recur within 2 weeks of completing antimicrobial therapy (5%-10% of cases) with the same organism (determined by repeat culture). Relapse suggests infection with a resistant strain of bacteria, incomplete treatment of an infection of the upper urinary tract, or a structural abnormality, including renal calculi. *Reinfection*, the most common type of recurrent UTI, is generally caused by a bacterial strain

separate from the original infection and presents more than 2 weeks after cessation of treatment for the previous infection. Symptomatic relapsed infection requires a urine culture. Assuming the organism is sensitive, patients are treated for infection of the upper urinary tract for 7 to 10 days with the same antibiotic as prescribed for the previous infection or, if bacterial resistance is discovered, an alternative agent. Likewise, the same first-line antimicrobial agent can be given for reinfections, although an alternative antibiotic should be used if the recurrence occurs within 6 months, particularly if the original agent was trimethoprim-sulfamethoxazole, because of the increased chance of resistance.

Strategies to prevent infection recurrence include avoidance of spermicide contraceptives, urination soon after intercourse, topical vaginal estrogens, ascorbic acid (vitamin C), and methenamine salts. Cranberry products have not been proven effective in controlled trials. Prophylactic daily antimicrobial agents have been found to reduce the risk of recurrences by nearly 95%; they are an option in women who have had three or more UTIs in the previous 12 months, or two or more in the previous 6 months, and have received no benefit from other prevention efforts. Prophylactic therapy should be considered in pregnant patients who have required treatment for cystitis or asymptomatic bacteriuria to prevent recurrence during pregnancy. Antibiotic complications and potential emergence of resistance must be considered. Approximately 50% of patients revert to previous recurrence patterns within 6 months of prophylaxis discontinuation. Recommended prophylactic antibiotics include nitrofurantoin, trimethoprim-sulfamethoxazole, trimethoprim, cephalexin, or fosfomycin. Fluoroquinolones are very effective but not recommended. Other options include postcoital antimicrobial prophylaxis and self-diagnosis with self-treatment.

KEY POINTS

• Reinfection is generally caused by a bacterial strain separate from the original infection and presents more than 2 weeks after cessation of treatment for the previous infection.

• Prophylactic daily antimicrobial therapy is an option in women who have had three or more urinary tract infections in the previous 12 months or two or more in the previous 6 months; other options include postcoital antimicrobial prophylaxis and self-diagnosis with self-treatment.

Acute Bacterial Prostatitis

Benign prostatic hyperplasia resulting in urinary obstruction and altered urine flow is the most common reason for the increased incidence of UTIs in men older than 60 years. Other risk factors include unprotected sexual intercourse, chronic indwelling urinary catheters, and transrectal prostate biopsy. Approximately 5% of men develop chronic prostatitis after acute infection.

CONT.

Presenting symptoms include sudden onset of fever, pelvic or perineal pain, urinary frequency and dysuria, and increasing obstructive symptoms. Acute bacterial prostatitis frequently presents as a severe systemic infection and is the most common cause of bacteremia in older men. Cautious digital rectal examination of the prostate reveals a boggy and tender gland. Urinalysis and culture are required to confirm the diagnosis. Although pyuria may be present for reasons other than infection, its absence strongly indicates no infection. Prostate-specific antigen test results may be elevated because of inflammation of the gland and should be avoided in the setting of presumed infection.

Hospitalized patients and those with severe infection require blood cultures. Gram-negative uropathogens account for about 80% of infections, two thirds of which are *E. coli*; *Proteus*, *Enterobacter*, *Serratia*, *Klebsiella*, and sometimes *Pseudomonas* and enterococcal species compose most of the other pathogens. In men 35 years or younger, sexually transmitted infections, including *Neisseria gonorrhoeae* and *Chlamydia trachomatis*, must be considered.

Fluoroquinolone antibiotics (ciprofloxacin, levofloxacin) are the preferred oral agents for treating acute bacterial prostatitis but should not be used if recent genitourinary instrumentation was performed, especially transrectal prostate biopsies, because most *E. coli* strains are now resistant to fluoroquinolones. Treatment duration is typically 4 weeks. Hospitalized patients should initially receive a broad-spectrum parenteral antibiotic, such as an extended-spectrum penicillin or cephalosporin, with the possible addition of an aminoglycoside. Imaging studies are not recommended unless a prostatic abscess is suspected clinically. **H**

KEY POINTS

- Gram-negative uropathogens account for about 80% of acute prostatitis infections; in men 35 years or younger, sexually transmitted infections, including *Neisseria gonorrhoeae* and *Chlamydia trachomatis*, must be considered.

- Fluoroquinolone antibiotics are the preferred oral agents for treating acute bacterial prostatitis but should not be used if recent genitourinary instrumentation was performed because most *E. coli* strains are now resistant to fluoroquinolones.

Mycobacterium tuberculosis Infection

Epidemiology

Tuberculosis is one of the oldest and most prevalent infectious diseases in the world. It remains one of the most common causes of death from an infectious disease worldwide. Although rates of *Mycobacterium tuberculosis* infection remain relatively low in North America, approximately one third of the world's population is infected with the bacteria. As of 2015, approximately 10 million new cases are reported each year throughout the world, and approximately 2 million deaths are documented each year, including 360,000 in persons infected with HIV. More than 60% of infections are reported from Southeast Asia, India, China, Micronesia, Russia, and sub-Saharan Africa. Multidrug-resistant tuberculosis (MDR-TB) accounts for 3.3% of new infections and 20% of relapsed infections. Extremely drug-resistant tuberculosis now accounts for approximately 10% of all MDR-TB infections worldwide. In 2015, 9557 tuberculosis infections were reported in the United States (3.0 per 100,000 persons). Most infections in the United States occur in foreign-born persons; however, other persons at high risk include those with alcoholism, urban poor, homeless persons, injection drug users, prison inmates, persons living in shelters, HIV-positive persons, and older adults.

Despite great strides worldwide in controlling *M. tuberculosis*, it remains a major global health concern. The burden of disease throughout the world and rapid travel from country to country ensures a steady stream of active tuberculosis cases in the United States.

KEY POINTS

- Most *Mycobacterium tuberculosis* infections in the United States occur in foreign-born persons; however, other persons at high risk include those with alcoholism, urban poor, homeless persons, injection drug users, prison inmates, persons living in shelters, HIV-positive persons, and older adults.

- Multidrug-resistant tuberculosis (MDR-TB) accounts for 3.3% of new infections and 20% of relapsed infections; extremely drug-resistant tuberculosis now accounts for approximately 10% of all MDR-TB infections worldwide.

Pathophysiology

Humans are the only known reservoir for *M. tuberculosis*, which is most commonly transmitted from person to person by aerosolized droplets. Although the droplets dry rapidly, the smallest droplets may remain suspended in the air for several hours. Persons who have visible acid-fast bacilli (AFB) on microscopy are the most likely to transmit infection. The most contagious patients are those with cavitary or laryngeal tuberculosis and those whose sputum contains a high bacterial load. After deposition in the respiratory tract, tubercular bacilli are ingested by alveolar macrophages that initiate an immunologic cascade eventually resulting in the development of classic caseating granulomas.

Most persons (>90%) who become infected with *M. tuberculosis* remain asymptomatic and develop latent tuberculosis. The risk of developing disease after infection depends primarily on endogenous factors such as the person's innate immune system, nonimmunologic defenses (alveolar macrophages, phagosome formation, phagocytosis), and the function of cell-mediated immunity. Specific risk factors for developing active tuberculosis among infected persons are shown in **Table 20**. The risk for developing active infection is approximately 5% in the first 2 years after infection and then 5% for the remainder of their life, assuming no cause of immunosuppression is present (see Table 20).

KEY POINTS

- Most persons who become infected with *Mycobacterium tuberculosis* remain asymptomatic and develop latent tuberculosis.

- Risk factors for developing active tuberculosis include immunosuppression, tumor necrosis factor-α inhibitors, injection drug use, silicosis, chronic kidney disease, diabetes mellitus, recent infection, and malnutrition.

Clinical Manifestations

Tuberculosis is classified as pulmonary, extrapulmonary, or both; the two main forms are primary and secondary tuberculosis. Primary tuberculosis occurs soon after the initial infection, most frequently in children and immunosuppressed persons. Often, the lesions heal spontaneously. Secondary or reactivation tuberculosis results from endogenous reactivation of a latent infection. Most cases of active tuberculosis are caused by reactivation of latent tuberculosis in the setting of immunosuppression. Seventy-five percent of secondary infections are pulmonary, except in those infected with HIV, in whom two thirds of patients have pulmonary and extrapulmonary infection.

 Frequent manifestations include fever, weight loss, productive cough (occasionally blood tinged), anorexia, malaise, and pleuritic chest pain. Patients may have a normal lung

TABLE 20.	Risk Factors for Acquiring *Mycobacterium tuberculosis*
Recent infection (<1 year)
Pulmonary fibrotic lesions
Malnutrition
Comorbidities
HIV infection
Silicosis
Chronic kidney disease
Diabetes mellitus
Injection drug use
Immunosuppressive therapy
Jejunoileal bypass
Solid organ transplantation
Tumor necrosis factor-α inhibitors
Head and neck cancer

examination or have crackles, rhonchi, or dullness to percussion. Hemoptysis occurs in 10% to 20% of patients with positive AFB smear results. In immunosuppressed patients, the infection may also disseminate into the bloodstream, producing miliary (disseminated) tuberculosis, which can result in a systemic inflammatory response syndrome, septic shock, and ultimately death if not diagnosed and treated early. Additionally, patients with disseminated infection may present with atypical clinical manifestations and chest radiographs. Extrapulmonary disease may be the result of hematogenous dissemination, can be seen in up to 30% of patients with active tuberculosis, and may involve almost any organ or organ system, including the pleura, lymph nodes, central nervous system, skeletal system, pericardium, larynx, peritoneum, and genitourinary system. **H**

KEY POINTS

- Clinical manifestations of tuberculosis include fever, weight loss, productive cough (occasionally blood tinged), anorexia, malaise, and pleuritic chest pain.

- In immunosuppressed patients, tuberculosis infection may disseminate to the bloodstream, which can result in a systemic inflammatory response syndrome, septic shock, and ultimately death if not treated early.

Diagnosis

The key to the diagnosis of tuberculosis is a high index of suspicion in patients at high risk.

Diagnosis of Latent Tuberculosis Infection

The goal of diagnosing latent tuberculosis infection (LTBI) is to identify and treat persons at increased risk for reactivation tuberculosis. Testing methods include interferon-γ release assay (IGRA) performed on a blood sample or tuberculin skin testing (TST). LTBI is diagnosed when an asymptomatic patient has a positive TST result or an IGRA with no clinical or radiographic manifestations of active tuberculosis.

The Centers for Disease Control and Prevention (CDC) recommends performing an IGRA rather than a TST in persons 5 years or older who are likely to have *M. tuberculosis* infection, have a low or intermediate risk of disease progression, have a history of bacillus Calmette-Guérin (BCG) vaccination, or are unlikely to return to have their TST result interpreted. IGRAs are in vitro assays that measure T-cell release of interferon-γ in response to stimulation with highly tuberculosis-specific antigens ESAT-6 and CFP-10 (QuantiFERON-TB Gold In-Tube and T-SPOT TB test). IGRAs are more specific than TST because they have less cross-reactivity resulting from BCG vaccination and sensitization by nontuberculous mycobacteria. Although not used to diagnose active tuberculosis, IGRAs appear to be at least as sensitive as the TST in patients with active tuberculosis.

TST has become the alternative diagnostic test if IGRA is not feasible or available. The purified protein derivative is injected intradermally and interpreted after 48 to 72 hours by measuring the transverse diameter of induration, not erythema. A positive result indicates delayed-type hypersensitivity response. The criteria for a positive TST result are based on the patient's risk factors for tuberculosis (**Table 21**). A false-negative TST result may occur in patients with recent tuberculosis infection, overwhelming active tuberculosis infection, recent viral infections, or severe immunocompromise (AIDS) and in those younger than 6 years. Patients with remote exposure to *M. tuberculosis* may initially have a negative TST result that can become positive several weeks later after a second TST, known as the "booster effect." The second test is recommended in health care workers 7 to 21 days after initial testing and should be performed on the opposite forearm; it is not required if IGRA is used. IGRAs are recommended in nearly all clinical settings in which TST is recommended; one exception is children younger than 5 years, for whom experts recommend both tests to increase specificity.

KEY POINTS

HVC
- The Centers for Disease Control and Prevention recommends performing an interferon-γ release assay instead of tuberculin skin testing in persons 5 years or older who are likely to have *Mycobacterium tuberculosis* infection, have a low or intermediate risk of disease progression, have a history of bacillus Calmette-Guérin vaccination, or are unlikely to return to have their tuberculin skin test interpreted.

- Latent tuberculosis infection is diagnosed when an asymptomatic patient has a positive tuberculin skin test or interferon-γ release assay result with no clinical or radiographic manifestations of active tuberculosis.

Diagnosis of Active Tuberculosis Infection

The CDC recommends AFB smear microscopy in all patients suspected of having active pulmonary tuberculosis. In vitro fluorescence microscopy of sputum is the preferred methodology. Testing three specimens is highly recommended because false-negative results from a single specimen are not uncommon. However, false-positive results are also not uncommon, thus a positive smear result requires mycobacterial culture confirmation. At least 3 mL of sputum should be submitted, although 5 to 10 mL is preferred. Serial specimens must be obtained at least 8 hours apart, and one must be an early morning specimen. Sputum induction is preferable to bronchoscopy as the sample methodology because of its greater sensitivity in patients who are unable to expectorate sputum.

The gold standard for diagnosis of active *M. tuberculosis* infection remains the mycobacterial culture. Whether AFB staining results are positive or negative, liquid and solid cultures should be performed for every specimen obtained. Liquid culture allows for faster growth and more rapid identification of organisms (2-4 weeks).

When a sputum smear result is positive for AFB, nucleic acid amplification testing (NAAT) is highly recommended to verify the organism. The positive predictive value of a NAAT on a smear-positive sputum sample is 95%. In patients with an intermediate to high level of suspicion for active disease who have a negative smear, the NAAT result will be positive in 65% of cases. If available, a NAAT assay that also detects for rifampin resistance is recommended for timely detection of rifampin resistance. Although the NAAT assays are quick and sensitive, mycobacterial cultures are still recommended for performance of in vitro susceptibilities to all antimicrobial agents. It is important to note that a negative NAAT result cannot be used to exclude pulmonary tuberculosis; NAAT can rapidly confirm the presence of *M. tuberculosis* in 50% to 80% of AFB smear-negative, culture-positive specimens. Moreover, NAAT can facilitate earlier decision making regarding whether to initiate tuberculosis therapy.

If signs of extrapulmonary infection are present, samples from those areas should be obtained and sent for AFB stain, mycobacterial culture, and histopathology. Histopathology may be beneficial by demonstrating caseating granulomas, which are suggestive for but not exclusive to or diagnostic of tuberculosis. In disseminated tuberculosis, blood cultures for mycobacteria using isolator methodology are helpful.

TABLE 21.	Interpretation of Tuberculin Skin Test Results		
Criteria for Tuberculin Positivity by Risk Group			
≥5 mm Induration	**≥10 mm Induration**		**≥15 mm Induration**
HIV-positive persons	Recent (<5 years) arrivals from high-prevalence countries		All others with no risk factors for TB
Recent contacts of persons with active TB	Injection drug users		
Persons with fibrotic changes on chest radiograph consistent with old TB	Residents or employees of high-risk congregate settings: prisons and jails, nursing homes and other long-term facilities for the elderly, hospitals and other health care facilities, residential facilities for patients with AIDS, homeless shelters		
Patients with organ transplants and other immunosuppressive conditions (receiving the equivalent of ≥15 mg/d of prednisone for >4 weeks)	Mycobacteriology laboratory personnel; persons with clinical conditions that put them at high risk for active disease (silicosis, diabetes mellitus, severe kidney disease, certain types of cancer, some intestinal conditions); children aged <4 years or exposed to adults in high-risk categories		
TB = tuberculosis infection.			

KEY POINTS

- The gold standard for the diagnosis of active *Mycobacterium tuberculosis* infection remains the mycobacterial culture; when a sputum smear result is positive for acid-fast bacilli, nucleic acid amplification testing is highly recommended to verify the organism.

- If signs of extrapulmonary tuberculosis infection are present, samples from those areas should be obtained and sent for acid-fast bacilli staining, mycobacterial culture, and histopathology.

Radiographic Procedures

The classic radiographic finding in pulmonary tuberculosis is that of upper lobe disease with air space disease and cavities. However, any radiographic pattern can be seen, from a "normal chest radiograph" or a solitary pulmonary nodule to diffuse alveolar infiltrates with acute respiratory distress syndrome.

Management

The primary goals of therapy include preventing additional morbidity, preventing mortality, and disrupting transmission of *M. tuberculosis* by eradicating the infection. When suitable antimicrobial therapy is administered and taken appropriately, clinical trials demonstrate clinical and microbiologic cure rates of approximately 95%. Therapy depends on several factors, including the classification of infection (latent versus active), pulmonary versus extrapulmonary infection, and patient adherence.

Treatment of Latent Tuberculosis

Patients who have a positive IGRA or a positive TST result should be evaluated for active disease with a full medical history, physical examination, and chest radiography. If no sign of active infection is present, all patients should be offered treatment for LTBI. CDC guidelines recommend four different treatment regimens (**Table 22**). Pyridoxine is recommended in

TABLE 22. Treatment Regimens for Latent Tuberculosis Infection

Drugs[a]	Duration	Dose[b]	Frequency	Total Doses
Isoniazid	9 months	5 mg/kg Maximum dose: 300 mg	Daily	270
		15 mg/kg Maximum dose: 900 mg	Twice weekly[c]	76
	6 months	5 mg/kg Maximum dose: 300 mg	Daily	180
		15 mg/kg Maximum dose: 900 mg	Twice weekly[c]	52
Isoniazid and rifapentine	3 months	Isoniazid[d]: 15 mg/kg rounded up to the nearest 50 or 100 mg; 900 mg maximum Rifapentine[d]: 10.0-14.0 kg: 300 mg 14.1-25.0 kg: 450 mg 25.1-32.0 kg: 600 mg 32.1-49.9 kg: 750 mg ≥50.0 kg: 900 mg maximum	Once weekly[e]	12
Rifampin	4 months	10 mg/kg Maximum dose: 600 mg	Daily	120

[a]Isoniazid is the preferred regimen, with therapy for 9 months preferable in patients with HIV and therapy for 6 months for patients without HIV and pulmonary lesions. CDC recommendations include isoniazid plus rifapentine in adults, in children aged 2-17 years, and in persons with HIV/AIDS taking antiretroviral therapy that does not interact with rifapentine. Rifampin is an option if other regimens cannot be used.

[b]Doses listed are for adults.

[c]Therapy may be either directly observed therapy (DOT) or self-administered therapy (SAT) in patients ≥2 years of age.

[d]Isoniazid is formulated in 100-mg and 300-mg tablets. Rifapentine is formulated in 150-mg tablets in blister packs that should be kept sealed until use.

[e]May be provided by DOT or SAT. Factors that should be considered when choosing between DOT and SAT include local practice, patient attributes and preferences, and risk of progression to severe disease. Use of concomitant latent tuberculosis infection treatment and antiretroviral agents should be guided by clinicians experienced in the management of both conditions.

Recommendations from the Centers for Disease Control and Prevention. Latent tuberculosis infection: a guide for primary health care providers. Treatment of latent TB infection. Table 2. Choosing the most effective LTBI treatment regimen. www.cdc.gov/tb/publications/ltbi/treatment.htm#2. Accessed October 15, 2017; and Borisov AS, Bamrah Morris S, Njie GJ, Winston CA, Burton D, Goldberg S, et al. Update of recommendations for use of once-weekly isoniazid-rifapentine regimen to treat latent mycobacterium tuberculosis infection. MMWR Morb Mortal Wkly Rep. 2018;67:723-726. [PMID: 29953429] doi:10.15585/mmwr.mm6725a5 patients who will receive isoniazid and are at risk for peripheral neuropathy (diabetes mellitus, chronic kidney disease, malnutrition, HIV, and alcoholism). Baseline and monthly monitoring of liver chemistry tests are not routinely required unless patients are at risk for hepatotoxicity (HIV infection, chronic hepatitis B or C, alcohol abuse, pregnancy, concurrent hepatotoxic drugs, or underlying liver disease).

In pregnant women with LTBI, a 6- to 9-month regimen of isoniazid plus pyridoxine may be offered; however, some experts prefer to defer therapy until after delivery, unless the patient is at high risk of developing active infection owing to immunocompromise, including HIV infection.

KEY POINTS

- Patients with a positive interferon-γ release assay or tuberculin skin test result should be evaluated for active disease; if no sign of active infection is present, patients should be offered treatment for latent tuberculosis infection.

- Recommended treatment regimens for latent tuberculosis infection are isoniazid (daily or twice weekly) for 9 or 6 months, isoniazid plus rifapentine weekly for 3 months, or rifampin daily for 4 months.

Treatment of Active Tuberculosis

When active tuberculosis is verified, in vitro susceptibility testing of the initial isolate should be done for the first-line agents (isoniazid, rifampin, pyrazinamide, and ethambutol). This becomes increasingly important because of the advent of multidrug-resistant and extensively drug-resistant tuberculosis. If rifampin resistance has been detected during NAAT assessment, in vitro susceptibilities to first-line and second-line agents should be performed (**Table 23**).

The American Thoracic Society/CDC guidelines published in 2016 recommend 6 to 9 months of treatment in patients with drug-susceptible active tuberculosis. A four-drug regimen is given daily for 2 months, followed by a continuation phase of isoniazid plus rifampin daily, usually for 4 months (**Table 24**).

Directly observed therapy, generally through the local health department, is recommended for the treatment of active tuberculosis. Sputum specimens should be evaluated at 1- and 2-month intervals to assess for efficacy. In addition, clinical assessment and laboratory testing (complete blood count, liver chemistry testing, hepatitis serology) should be performed before initiating therapy.

It is essential to advise the patient of the possible adverse effect profiles of the various medications (see Table 23). In several studies, approximately 15% to 25% of patients receiving the four-drug regimen experienced some type of adverse effect. Most adverse effects are mild, and therapy may be continued; up to 15% are severe enough that therapy must be discontinued temporarily. If a hypersensitivity reaction is observed, then all four drugs should be discontinued and rechallenged sequentially to determine the cause.

KEY POINTS

- Directly observed therapy is recommended for the treatment of active tuberculosis.

- American Thoracic Society/Centers for Disease Control and Prevention guidelines recommend 6 to 9 months of treatment in patients with drug-susceptible active tuberculosis; a four-drug regimen is given daily for 2 months, followed by a continuation phase of isoniazid plus rifampin daily, usually for 4 months.

Drug-Resistant Tuberculosis

M. tuberculosis resistance to individual drugs arises by spontaneous point mutations. Depending on the resistance, the regimen must be altered. In isoniazid-resistant tuberculosis, the regimen of isoniazid, rifampin, and ethambutol can be safely administered for 6 months, although some experts would add a fluoroquinolone. In those with isoniazid- and rifampin-resistant tuberculosis (MDR-TB), experts agree that a five-drug regimen depending on the susceptibility of the isolate should be provided for 4 months, followed by a four-drug regimen for an additional 12 to 18 months (see Table 23). Consultation with an expert in the event of MDR-TB is required.

Tuberculosis in patients with HIV infection may be complicated by immune reconstitution inflammatory syndrome. Although the general recommendations for treatment are the same, antiretroviral therapy should be initiated within 2 weeks for patients with a CD4 cell count less than 50/µL and by 8 to 12 weeks for those with CD4 cell counts of 50/µL or more. An exception is HIV-positive patients with tuberculous meningitis, in whom antiretroviral therapy should not be initiated during the first 8 weeks of tuberculosis therapy regardless of the CD4 cell count to avoid increased morbidity because of immune reconstitution inflammatory syndrome.

KEY POINTS

- In patients with multidrug-resistant tuberculosis, experts agree that a five-drug regimen should be provided for 4 months, followed by a four-drug regimen for an additional 12 to 18 months.

- Tuberculosis in patients with HIV infection may be complicated by immune reconstitution inflammatory syndrome, and antiretroviral therapy initiation should be delayed to prevent this occurrence.

Tumor Necrosis Factor Antagonist and Tuberculosis

Patients being treated with a tumor necrosis factor inhibitor (such as infliximab, etanercept, adalimumab, or certolizumab) have been reported to have an increased risk of reactivation to active infection or death from disseminated disease. It is recommended that these patients be evaluated for active or latent tuberculosis by performing chest radiography and simultaneous TST or IGRA. All patients should receive treatment for LTBI if identified, although LTBI treatment does not completely

TABLE 23. Antituberculous Drugs

Agent	Adverse Effects	Notes
First-Line Medications		
Isoniazid	Rash; liver enzyme elevation; hepatitis; peripheral neuropathy; lupus-like syndrome	Hepatitis risk increases with age and alcohol consumption. Pyridoxine may prevent peripheral neuropathy. Adjust for kidney injury.
Pyrazinamide	Hepatitis; rash; GI upset; hyperuricemia	May make glucose control more difficult in patients with diabetes. Adjust for kidney injury.
Rifampin	Hepatitis; rash; GI upset	Contraindicated or should be used with caution when administered with protease inhibitors and nonnucleoside reverse transcriptase inhibitors. Do not administer to patients also taking saquinavir/ritonavir. Colors body fluids orange.
Rifabutin	Rash; hepatitis; thrombocytopenia; severe arthralgia; uveitis; leukopenia	Dose adjustment required if taken with protease inhibitors or nonnucleoside reverse transcriptase inhibitors. Monitor for decreased antiretroviral activity and for rifabutin toxicity.
Rifapentine	Similar to rifampin	Contraindicated in patients who are HIV positive (unacceptable rate of failure/relapse).
Ethambutol	Optic neuritis; rash	Baseline and periodic tests of visual acuity and color vision. Patients are advised to call immediately if visual acuity or color vision changes. Adjust for kidney injury.
Second-Line Medications[a]		
Streptomycin	Auditory, vestibular, and kidney toxicity	Avoid or reduce dose in adults >59 years. Monitor hearing and kidney function test results. Adjust for kidney injury.
Cycloserine	Psychosis; convulsions; depression; headaches; rash; drug interactions	Pyridoxine may decrease CNS adverse effects. Measure drug serum levels.
Capreomycin	Kidney, vestibular, and auditory toxicity	Monitor hearing and kidney function test results. Adjust for kidney injury.
Ethionamide	GI upset; hepatotoxicity; hypersensitivity	May cause hypothyroidism.
Kanamycin and amikacin	Auditory, vestibular, and kidney toxicity	Not approved by the FDA for TB treatment. Monitor vestibular, hearing, and kidney function.
Levofloxacin, moxifloxacin	GI upset; dizziness; hypersensitivity; drug interactions	Not approved by the FDA for TB treatment. Should not be used in children.
Para-aminosalicylic acid	GI upset; hypersensitivity; hepatotoxicity	May cause hypothyroidism, especially if used with ethionamide. Measure liver enzyme levels.
Bedaquiline	Nausea, joint pain, headache, elevated aminotransferase levels, hemoptysis, prolonged QT interval	FDA-approved oral agent for MDR pulmonary TB treatment indicated for combination therapy when other alternatives are not available. Novel mechanism of action inhibits mycobacterial adenosine triphosphate synthase. Should be given as directly observed therapy.

CNS = central nervous system; GI = gastrointestinal; MDR = multidrug resistant; TB = tuberculosis.

[a]Use these drugs in consultation with a clinician experienced in the management of drug-resistant TB.

eliminate risk for active mycobacterial infection in this population.

- All patients diagnosed with latent tuberculosis who are being treated with a tumor necrosis factor inhibitor should receive treatment to reduce risk of reactivation and death from disseminated disease.

Prevention

From the public health perspective, the best way to prevent tuberculosis is to diagnose, isolate, and treat infection rapidly until patients are considered noncontagious and the disease is cured. In the hospital, this means having a high index of suspicion for *M. tuberculosis* in high-risk groups and initiating immediate airborne isolation in negative pressure rooms (airborne infection isolation rooms) until the diagnosis can be excluded.

Recent CDC guidelines recommend criteria to determine that a patient is no longer contagious and a possible public health threat. These include appropriate antimicrobial therapy for at least 2 weeks, clinical improvement of signs and symptoms, and three negative sputum smears collected at least 8 hours apart, with one being an early-morning specimen. Patients with negative smear results are less contagious, although they may still have tuberculosis.

TABLE 24. Preferred Treatment Regimens for Active Tuberculosis

Treatment Phase	Regimen	Comments
Initial	Daily INH, RIF, PZA, and EMB[a] for 56 doses (8 wk) *or*	Alternative regimens available at https://www.cdc.gov/tb/topic/treatment/tbdisease.htm
	DOT 5 d/wk for 90 doses (18 wk)	DOT should be used when medications are administered less than 7 d/wk
		Pyridoxine 25-50 mg/d is given to all patients at risk for neuropathy[b]; 100 mg/d for patients with peripheral neuropathy
Continuation	INH and RIF 7 d/wk for 126 doses (18 wk) *or*	Based on expert opinion, patients with cavitation on the initial chest radiograph and positive cultures at completion of 2 months of therapy should receive a 7-month (31-wk) continuation phase
	DOT 5 d/wk for 90 doses (18 wk)	

DOT = directly observed therapy; EMB = ethambutol; INH = isoniazid; PZA = pyrazinamide; RIF = rifampin.

[a]EMB can be discontinued if drug susceptibility studies demonstrate susceptibility to first-line drugs.

[b]Pregnant women; breastfeeding infants; persons with HIV; patients with diabetes, alcoholism, malnutrition, or chronic kidney disease; patients of advanced age.

Recommendations from the Centers for Disease Control and Prevention. Tuberculosis. Treatment for TB disease. Table 1. Basic TB disease treatment regimens. Available at www.cdc.gov/tb/topic/treatment/tbdisease.htm. Accessed August 27, 2014.

The BCG vaccination is a live-attenuated vaccine derived from an attenuated strain of *Mycobacterium bovis*. It has been in use for more than 90 years throughout the world, although it is not routinely used in the United States. It is recommended for use at birth in countries with high rates of *M. tuberculosis*. In several international studies, the BCG vaccine has been shown to be effective in preventing severe infection, including meningitis in children. However, the efficacy in adults has not been established. CDC guidelines do not recommend the vaccine in the United States; however, the World Health Organization still recommends its use in high-prevalence areas.

KEY POINT

- Guidelines for determining a patient with tuberculosis is no longer contagious include appropriate antimicrobial therapy for at least 2 weeks, clinical improvement in signs and symptoms, and three negative sputum smears collected at least 8 hours apart.

Nontuberculous Mycobacterial Infections

Nontuberculous mycobacteria (NTM) comprise species other than *Mycobacterium tuberculosis* complex and *Mycobacterium leprae*. NTM are often divided into slow and rapid growers (**Table 25**). These organisms are found in surface water, soil, domestic and wild animals, milk, and food products. Additionally, they can be colonizers, particularly in the airways of persons with chronic lung disease. They can cause a spectrum of infections (**Table 26**).

Risk factors for NTM infections include immunocompromise, chronic lung disease, and postoperative status. Health

TABLE 25. Classification of Common Nontuberculous Mycobacteria

Slow-growing Mycobacteria
M. kansasii
M. marinum
M. gordonae
M. scrofulaceum
M. avium complex
M. ulcerans
M. xenopi
Rapidly Growing Mycobacteria
M. abscessus
M. chelonae
M. fortuitum

care-associated *Mycobacterium chimaera* infections have been documented worldwide in association with heater-cooler units used during cardiac surgery.

NTM diagnosis is difficult because a positive culture result from a nonsterile site (such as the lung) without other evidence of disease may reflect colonization rather than infection. However, when recovered from a normally sterile site, active infection is very likely. Because antibiotic susceptibility of species vary, it is important to identify organisms to species level. American Thoracic Society (ATS) guidelines recommend fulfillment of clinical, radiologic, and microbiologic criteria to diagnose an NTM pulmonary infection. Most NTM infections require treatment with two to four antimicrobials; ATS guidelines should be used to guide therapy.

TABLE 26.	Diseases Caused by Nontuberculous Mycobacteria		
Clinical Disease	**More Common**	**Less Common**	**Infection Risks**
Pulmonary	MAC M. kansasii M. abscessus	M. fortuitum M. xenopi M. malmoense M. szulgai M. simiae M. asiaticum	Older persons with or without underlying lung disease; cystic fibrosis
Lymphadenitis	MAC	M. abscessus M. fortuitum M. scrofulaceum M. malmoense	Children
Skin and soft tissue	M. marinum M. ulcerans M. abscessus	MAC M. kansasii	Direct inoculation
Catheter-related bloodstream infections	Rapidly growing mycobacteria	MAC M. kansasii	Long-term catheterization
Disseminated	MAC M. kansasii (in persons with AIDS and CD4 cell count <100/μL)	Rapidly growing mycobacteria	Immunocompromise, especially persons with AIDS or those taking tumor necrosis factor-α inhibitors

MAC = Mycobacterium avium complex.

KEY POINTS

- Risk factors for nontuberculous mycobacteria infections include immunocompromise, chronic lung disease, and postoperative status; additionally, health care–associated *Mycobacterium chimaera* infections have been documented in association with heater-cooler units used during cardiac surgery.

- Because antibiotic susceptibility of nontuberculous mycobacteria species varies, it is important to identify organisms to species level.

Mycobacterium avium Complex Infection

Mycobacterium avium complex is the most common cause of chronic lung infection worldwide. Cavitary lung disease is seen classically in white, middle-aged, or older adult men, especially those with underlying lung disease, such as COPD, cystic fibrosis, or interstitial lung disease. Disseminated infection is seen predominantly in patients with HIV with CD4 cell counts less than 50/μL. The clinical presentation often consists of fever, night sweats, weight loss, and gastrointestinal symptoms.

Mycobacterium kansasii

M. kansasii infection mimics pulmonary tuberculosis with cavitary lung disease. Predisposing conditions include underlying lung disease, alcoholism, cancer, and immunocompromised status.

Rapidly Growing Mycobacteria

Rapidly growing NTM have been implicated in NTM outbreaks. The most common rapidly growing mycobacterial species include *M. abscessus*, *M. chelonae*, and *M. fortuitum*. Of these, *M. abscessus* is most frequently identified and one of the most difficult to treat. These mycobacteria are associated with chronic, nonhealing ulcers unresponsive to appropriate empiric antibiotic therapy for typical skin and soft tissue infections.

KEY POINTS

- *Mycobacterium avium* complex is the most common cause of chronic lung infection worldwide, causing cavitary lung disease.

- *Mycobacterium abscessus*, *Mycobacterium chelonae*, and *Mycobacterium fortuitum* can produce lung disease, adenitis, skin and soft tissue infections, surgical site infections, and prosthetic device infections.

Fungal Infections

The incidence of fungal infection is increasing because of the increased recognition of these infections and an increase in the population at risk worldwide. According to a recent analysis by the Prospective Antifungal Therapy Alliance, the most commonly encountered infections in North America were caused by *Candida* species (73%) followed by *Aspergillus* species (14.8%), other yeast (such as *Cryptococcus* species; 6.2%), and mucormycetes (including *Rhizopus* species and *Mucor* species; 1.7%).

Systemic Candidiasis

Candida species are the fourth most commonly isolated organisms in bloodstream infections and are associated with a mortality rate of 30% to 40%. Risk factors for systemic candidiasis are listed in **Table 27**.

Manifestations of candidiasis depend on the organ involved. Candidemia can present as an isolated fever or septic shock. Signs and symptoms of focal infection depend on the site involved (abscess or peritonitis in the peritoneum, empyema in the pleural cavity, or pyelonephritis in the kidneys). Other forms of invasive infection include meningitis, osteomyelitis, septic arthritis, and endocarditis. Although often found in the respiratory tract, *Candida* species rarely cause infections there and are likely the result of colonization. The presence of yeast in the urinary tract (for example, because of the presence of an indwelling catheter) may represent colonization (most commonly) or true infection.

Diagnosis of invasive candidiasis is challenging because only 40% to 60% of patients with infection have positive blood culture results, and cultures can take days to demonstrate growth. Recognizing risk factors (see Table 27) for candidiasis is thus essential to avoid delays in initiating antifungal therapy and resultant increased mortality. The T2 magnetic resonance assay of whole blood provides rapid (within hours) diagnosis of culture-negative invasive candidal infections and can be performed on blood samples even after initiation of antifungal therapy. The β-D-glucan assay also can be used to diagnose invasive candidiasis in patients with negative blood culture results. These assays should be obtained when a patient at high risk (see Table 27) receiving antimicrobial agents is not responding to therapy.

When the *Candida* genus is identified from a sterile site (blood or tissue), specific species identification is necessary. Although more than 160 species of *Candida* are known, fewer than 15 produce disease in humans. Additionally, several species (such as *C. glabrata* and *C. krusei*) have intrinsic resistance to antifungal agents, especially the azoles, and their proper identification guides therapy.

Treatment of candidemia and invasive candidiasis should include an echinocandin (caspofungin, micafungin, or anidulafungin) and removal of intravascular devices (if possible). However, because of poor penetration of echinocandins into the central nervous system (CNS) and the eye, patients with these infections should be treated with an azole or amphotericin B. Additional treatment of candidal endophthalmitis varies depending on the extent of disease (chorioretinitis with or without macular involvement, vitreous involvement). All patients initially given amphotericin B or an echinocandin may be de-escalated to an oral azole (fluconazole or voriconazole) if the *Candida* species is susceptible and the gastrointestinal tract is functional. Duration of antifungal therapy for candidemia should be 14 days from the first negative blood culture result in patients with uncomplicated candidemia or 14 to 42 days in patients with invasive candidal infections. **H**

KEY POINTS

- *Candida* species are the fourth most commonly isolated organisms in bloodstream infections and are associated with a 30% to 40% mortality rate.

- Because only 40% to 60% of patients with invasive candidal infection have positive blood culture results, recognizing risk factors of candidiasis is essential to avoid delays in initiating effective antifungal therapy.

- The T2 magnetic resonance assay of whole blood may provide a rapid diagnosis of culture-negative invasive candidal infections.

- *Candida* species isolated from the respiratory tract and from the urinary tract usually represent colonization; treatment is not indicated unless clinical infection is suspected. **HVC**

- Treatment of candidemia and invasive candidiasis should include an echinocandin (caspofungin, micafungin, or anidulafungin) and removal of intravascular devices (if possible); central nervous system and ocular infections require amphotericin B or an azole.

TABLE 27.	Risk Factors for Systemic Candidiasis
Central venous catheters	
Broad-spectrum antimicrobial agents	
Neutropenia	
ICU stay for more than 3 days	
Total parenteral nutrition	
General surgery (especially of the gastrointestinal tract)	
Burns	
Trauma	
Mechanical ventilation for more than 3 days	
Transplantation (bone marrow/solid organ)	
Hemodialysis-associated catheters	
Severe acute pancreatitis	

Aspergillosis and Aspergilloma

Aspergillus is ubiquitous in the environment. The most common species are *A. fumigatus*, *A. flavus*, *A. niger*, and the amphotericin-resistant *A. terreus*. *Aspergillus* produces disease after inhalation of airborne spores (90%) and only occasionally by traumatic skin inoculation. Of all the fungi, *Aspergillus* is notable for the diverse settings in which it can occur and the various clinical manifestations it can produce.

Invasive pulmonary aspergillosis, the most serious form of *Aspergillus* infection, most often occurs in immunosuppressed patients who are neutropenic or are hematopoietic stem cell transplant recipients (**Table 28**). This type of aspergillosis usually begins in the respiratory tract and then enters the circulatory system (angioinvasion). This is followed by the formation of a fungus-septic emboli complex with subsequent hematogenous dissemination. The most common manifestation of angioinvasive disease is pulmonary aspergillosis (60%), but sinusitis, brain abscess, endocarditis, disseminated infection, and osteomyelitis also may occur. Timely diagnosis of invasive aspergillosis is essential to decrease morbidity and mortality, but symptoms and signs are nonspecific (**Table 29**), and blood culture results are generally negative. Therefore, bronchoscopy, bronchoalveolar lavage, and, if possible, tissue biopsy are often necessary to establish a definitive diagnosis. Early CT of the chest in patients with suspected invasive pulmonary aspergillosis—with typical findings suggestive of septic emboli (nodules, often with a "halo sign") (**Figure 11**), thromboembolic pulmonary infarction (wedge-shaped peripheral densities), or necrosis with cavitation and a crescent sign—and the serum galactomannan assay can be useful in establishing a presumptive diagnosis of invasive infection, especially in neutropenic patients and hematopoietic stem cell transplant recipients, in whom the assay has a sensitivity of approximately 80%. First-line treatment of invasive aspergillosis is with a triazole (voriconazole, posaconazole, or isavuconazole); amphotericin B deoxycholate or liposomal amphotericin B can be used for amphotericin-sensitive *Aspergillus* species if triazoles are not available. When possible, reversal of immunosuppression improves treatment response.

Other forms of *Aspergillus* infection occur in different clinical settings. Chronic necrotizing aspergillosis is a semi-invasive indolent form of infection that does not disseminate and occurs in patients who have lesser degrees of immunosuppression (such as those who take chronic glucocorticoids or those who have intrinsic immune defects) or chronic pulmonary disease. Treatment is similar to that for invasive pulmonary aspergillosis.

Allergic bronchopulmonary aspergillosis results from a hypersensitivity overreaction to *Aspergillus* species colonizing the respiratory tract; this disorder is seen primarily in patients with cystic fibrosis and occasionally in those with asthma (see MKSAP 18 Pulmonary and Critical Care Medicine for more information). Because allergic bronchopulmonary aspergillosis represents a hypersensitivity response, systemic glucocorticoids are the mainstay of treatment (sometimes supplemented by antifungal therapy with an azole). H

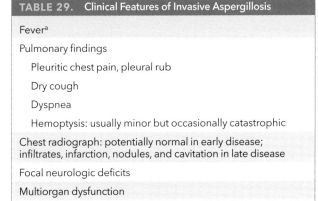

TABLE 28. Risk Factors for Invasive Aspergillosis	
Major	**Minor**
Neutropenia	COPD treated with glucocorticoids
Graft-versus-host disease	Cirrhosis
Cytomegalovirus infection/ reactivation	Burns
Hematopoietic stem cell transplantation	Solid organ malignancies
Solid organ transplantation	Immunosuppressants
Systemic glucocorticoids (>1 mg/ kg/d) or inhaled steroids	Cyclosporine
Hematologic malignancies	Methotrexate
	Azathioprine
	Cyclophosphamide
	Advanced HIV with CD4 cell count <50/µL (50 × 10⁶/L)
	Injection drug use (rare)
	Gram-negative bacterial pneumonia

TABLE 29. Clinical Features of Invasive Aspergillosis
Fever[a]
Pulmonary findings
Pleuritic chest pain, pleural rub
Dry cough
Dyspnea
Hemoptysis: usually minor but occasionally catastrophic
Chest radiograph: potentially normal in early disease; infiltrates, infarction, nodules, and cavitation in late disease
Focal neurologic deficits
Multiorgan dysfunction
Hemorrhagic skin lesions

[a]Frequently the only feature present.

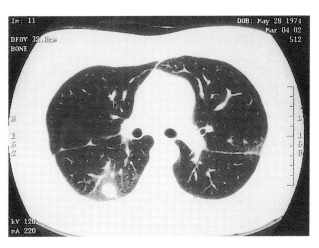

FIGURE 11. CT scan showing typical findings suggestive of septic emboli. Note the nodule with a "halo sign," which is a surrounding area of low attenuation that reflects hemorrhage into the tissues surrounding the fungus.

Pulmonary aspergillomas (fungus balls consisting of hyphae, mucus, and cellular debris) may form in patients with pre-existing cavities, such as old tuberculosis cavities and in bullae of patients with COPD; the presence of significant hemoptysis is a potential complication. In the absence of associated symptoms or hemoptysis, pulmonary aspergillomas may not require therapy; however, in the setting of significant bleeding, surgical resection or embolization may be necessary. Antifungal therapy is typically not effective against pulmonary aspergillomas, and its role in aspergilloma treatment is unclear.

KEY POINTS

- *Aspergillus* species produce disease after inhalation of airborne spores (90% of affected patients).

- *Aspergillus* infection can manifest in various ways, including invasive pulmonary aspergillosis, chronic necrotizing pulmonary aspergillosis, allergic bronchopulmonary aspergillosis, and aspergillomas.

- Tissue biopsy is frequently necessary to establish a definitive diagnosis of invasive aspergillosis; however, early chest CT and the serum galactomannan assay can be useful in establishing a presumptive diagnosis in patients at high risk of infection.

- First-line treatment of invasive or chronic pulmonary *Aspergillus* infection is with a triazole, such as voriconazole, posaconazole, or isavuconazole; liposomal amphotericin B can be used as an alternative in sensitive species and if triazoles are not available.

Cryptococcosis

Cryptococcus is an encapsulated yeast that is ubiquitous in the environment. Although cryptococcal infection can occur in healthy persons, most infected patients have advanced immune suppression, such as AIDS, neutropenia, or organ transplantation. *C. neoformans* is the most commonly identified species, but *C. gattii* is seen with increased frequency in the Pacific Northwest region of North America and has been associated with severe and recalcitrant infection. Pathogenesis of cryptococcosis involves inhalation of spores into the respiratory tract, followed by dissemination into susceptible tissues, especially the CNS.

Cryptococcal infection most commonly manifests in the CNS, and cryptococcosis is the most common cause of fungal meningitis worldwide. Clinical manifestations are listed in **Table 30**, and indicators of a poor prognosis in cryptococcal meningitis are provided in **Table 31**. Because patients with cryptococcosis-related increased intracranial pressure (ICP) may develop sudden blindness, deafness, or coma, initial opening pressure should be documented during lumbar puncture. Cerebrospinal fluid analysis is essential to diagnose CNS involvement; classic findings include an increased leukocyte count (mainly lymphocytes), an increased protein

TABLE 30. Clinical Features of Cryptococcosis
Signs and Symptoms of Meningeal Infection (% Affected)
Fever (60%-90%)
Headache (80%-90%)
Nausea/vomiting (~50%)
Meningism (30%)
Altered mental status (20%-30%)
Extrameningeal Infection Sites
Lung
Bone marrow
Skin
Prostate (cryptic source)

TABLE 31. Indicators of Poor Prognosis in Cryptococcal Meningitis
Altered mental state
Visual abnormalities
CSF leukocyte count less than 20/µL (20 × 10⁶/L)
CSF cryptococcal antigen assay greater than 1:10,000
No previous antiretroviral therapy in those with HIV infection
CSF = cerebrospinal fluid.

level, a low to normal glucose level, and the presence of cryptococcal antigen. Serum cryptococcal antigen also is positive in greater than 95% of infected patients; occasionally, blood culture results are positive and thus indicate disseminated disease.

Many symptoms of increased ICP may be improved by cerebrospinal fluid removal through daily lumbar puncture or insertion of a shunt. Aggressive reduction of ICP reduces early morbidity and mortality. Amphotericin B plus flucytosine is the treatment of choice and is effective in more than 90% of patients. HIV-infected patients require maintenance antifungal therapy until they have maintained their CD4 cell counts above 100/µL (100 × 10⁶/L) for a minimum of 3 months and have a suppressed viral load.

KEY POINTS

- In patients with suspected cryptococcal infection, cerebrospinal fluid (CSF) analysis is necessary, as is documentation of the CSF opening pressure; CSF and serum cryptococcal antigen are both highly sensitive for identifying infection.

- Amphotericin B plus flucytosine is effective in more than 90% of patients; for those with elevated intracranial pressure (ICP), cerebrospinal fluid removal through daily lumbar puncture or insertion of a shunt can reduce ICP and thus early morbidity and mortality.

Histoplasmosis

Histoplasma capsulatum is responsible for one of the most common endemic mycoses in the world. Acquired by inhalation of airborne conidia, this organism primarily produces asymptomatic pulmonary infection. It is distributed along the Mississippi River Valley (Ohio, Missouri, Indiana, Mississippi) in the United States, in Central and South America, in the Caribbean, and in regions of Africa, Australia, and India.

Histoplasmosis most commonly presents with acute respiratory symptoms. Other presentations, in declining order of frequency, include asymptomatic infection, disseminated infection, chronic pulmonary symptoms, rheumatologic symptoms, pericarditis, and sclerosing mediastinitis.

The *Histoplasma* urinary antigen assay has a sensitivity and specificity of greater than 85% in acute and disseminated infection but less than 50% in chronic infection. Identification of the fungus by tissue culture can be a lengthy process but is indicated for clinically suspected cases in which the urinary antigen assay result is negative.

Asymptomatic and mild pulmonary histoplasmosis typically resolves without treatment. Antifungal therapy is recommended for more severe or disseminated disease. Itraconazole is the agent of choice; duration of therapy is 6 to 12 weeks for acute infection and as long as 12 months for chronic cavitary pulmonary infection. For severe lung disease and disseminated infection, liposomal amphotericin B should be used initially, followed by de-escalation to oral itraconazole for an additional 12 weeks.

KEY POINTS

- *Histoplasma* urinary antigen assay has a sensitivity and specificity of greater than 85% in acute and disseminated infection but less than 50% in chronic infection.
- Itraconazole is the antifungal agent of choice for most patients with histoplasmosis; liposomal amphotericin B should be used initially for those with severe lung disease and disseminated infection.

Coccidioidomycosis

Coccidioides is a dimorphic fungus that exists as a mold in the environment. There are two species: *C. immitis* refers to isolates from California, and *C. posadasii* refers to isolates from all other endemic areas, including Arizona, New Mexico, western Texas, northern Mexico, and parts of Central and South America. In endemic areas, the annual risk of infection is approximately 3% for most persons, although the risk of infection (and dissemination) is greater in those who are pregnant, younger than 5 years or older than 50 years, or of African, Filipino (and possibly other Asian), and Native American ancestry.

Infection is usually acquired by inhalation of aerosolized arthroconidia. Once inhaled, the fungus begins its dimorphic change in the lungs and becomes a yeast cell. Several clinical syndromes are seen in coccidioidomycosis and may manifest as acute or chronic pulmonary infection, as cutaneous infection (~40%), as meningitis (~33%), or as musculoskeletal infection.

Diagnosis is straightforward in endemic areas and usually is based on clinical manifestations and confirmatory testing by a mycologic culture of affected tissue, histopathologic evaluation of tissue, serology for *Coccidioides* antibodies, or urinary antigen testing.

Fluconazole is the first-line treatment for symptomatic infection. In patients with meningitis, fluconazole is continued for life. In patients who do not respond to azoles, intrathecal amphotericin B may be an alternative.

KEY POINTS

- The diagnosis of coccidioidomycosis should be suspected clinically in endemic areas and may be confirmed by a mycologic culture of affected tissues, histopathologic evaluation of tissue, serology for *Coccidioides* antibodies, or urinary antigen testing.
- Fluconazole is first-line treatment for symptomatic coccidioidomycosis infection.

Blastomycosis

Blastomyces dermatitidis is a dimorphic, round, budding yeast; daughter cells form a bud with a broad base. Blastomycosis affects immunocompetent hosts. In the United States, blastomycosis is found primarily along the Mississippi and Ohio River valleys but can be found as far north as Wisconsin and Minnesota and as far south as Florida. As with most dimorphic yeast, infection occurs by inhalation of conidia and manifests initially as a primary pulmonary infection (acute or chronic pneumonia). Occasionally, a chest radiograph shows a spiculated nodular appearance that may be mistaken for lung cancer. Rarely, dissemination occurs and produces extrapulmonary disease (osteomyelitis, genitourinary infection, or CNS infection).

Diagnosis of blastomycosis can be made by direct fungal stain of clinical specimens (sputum, tissue, or purulent material) and confirmed by culture or serology for *Blastomyces* antibodies. Urinary antigen testing is also available. The preferred treatment for mild to moderate infection is itraconazole for 6 to 12 months. Liposomal amphotericin B is recommended for CNS, severe pulmonary, and disseminated infections.

KEY POINTS

- Blastomycosis occurs by inhalation of *Blastomyces dermatitidis* conidia and manifests initially as a primary pulmonary infection; diagnosis is made by direct fungal stain of clinical specimens and confirmed by culture, urinary antigen testing, or serology for *Blastomyces* antibodies.
- The preferred treatment for mild to moderate infection is itraconazole, with liposomal amphotericin B used for central nervous system and disseminated infection.

Sporotrichosis

Sporothrix schenckii is a dimorphic fungus found most often in soil, living plants, or plant debris. Although found worldwide, most reported infections are from North and South America and Japan. Infection can occur after direct contact with plants, such as roses and sphagnum moss. Direct inoculation of the organism into the skin or subcutaneous tissue manifests as fixed, "plaque-like" cutaneous sporotrichosis or as lymphocutaneous sporotrichosis presenting as papular lesions along lymphatic channels proximal to the inoculation site. Extracutaneous infection (osteoarticular, pulmonary, ocular, or disseminated) can occur in immunocompromised hosts.

Diagnosis requires culture of the organism from affected tissues. Treatment is with itraconazole and should extend for 2 to 4 weeks after lesions have resolved.

KEY POINTS

- Sporotrichosis is an infection of cutaneous and lymphocutaneous tissues and usually is caused by direct contact with plants; extracutaneous infection can occur in immunocompromised hosts.
- Itraconazole is the preferred treatment for cutaneous and lymphocutaneous sporotrichosis.

Mucormycosis

Mucormycosis (formerly zygomycosis) is the third most frequent cause of invasive fungal infections in immunocompromised hosts but is rarely seen in immunocompetent hosts. Particularly at risk are patients with neutropenia, diabetes mellitus, and acidosis. The most common mucormycetes are *Rhizopus arrhizus* and *Mucor* species. These fungi are commonly found in the environment on decaying organic debris, including fruit, bread, and soil.

Infection is acute and rapidly fatal, even with early diagnosis and treatment. Major blood vessels are invaded, with ensuing ischemia, necrosis, and infarction of adjacent tissues. Mucormycosis has five major clinical forms: (1) rhinocerebral; (2) pulmonary; (3) abdominal, pelvic, gastric, gastrointestinal; (4) primary cutaneous; and (5) disseminated.

Because laboratory studies are nonspecific, diagnosis relies on a high index of suspicion in a host with appropriate risk factors and evidence of tissue invasion, including the characteristic appearance of broad, nonseptate hyphae with acute-angle branches. Serologic tests and blood cultures offer no diagnostic benefit.

Treatment requires reversal of any predisposing condition, extensive surgical removal of affected tissue, and early antifungal therapy. Initial treatment is high-dose liposomal amphotericin B, with later de-escalation to posaconazole or isavuconazole. If amphotericin B is not tolerated, initial therapy with one of the azoles is warranted. Mortality rates remain as high as 60% to 80%, even with therapy.

KEY POINTS

- Mucormycosis is acute and rapidly fatal, even with early diagnosis and treatment.
- Because laboratory studies are nonspecific, diagnosis relies on a high index of suspicion; serologic tests and blood cultures offer no diagnostic benefit.
- Treatment requires reversal of any predisposing condition, extensive surgical removal of affected tissue, and initial antifungal therapy with high-dose liposomal amphotericin B.

Sexually Transmitted Infections

Introduction

Sexually transmitted infections (STIs) occur most commonly in adolescents, young adults, and men who have sex with men (MSM), but STIs affect all demographics. Most infections are asymptomatic, so it is imperative that a detailed sexual history, including sexual practices, be obtained to understand individual risk. STI risk factors include a new partner, more than one current partner, a partner with an STI, or a partner who has concurrent partners. Particularly high-risk populations include persons attending STI clinics and MSM.

Unrecognized or inadequately treated upper genitourinary tract infection is a preventable cause of infertility in women. Evidence-based guidelines for the evaluation and management of STIs are available from the World Health Organization and the Centers for Disease Control and Prevention (CDC); the CDC guidelines are recommended for use in the United States. Any patient diagnosed with an STI should be evaluated for other STIs, including HIV, and receive risk reduction counseling.

Chlamydia trachomatis Infection

Chlamydia trachomatis is the most commonly reported bacterial STI in the United States, and incidence has increased steadily over the past two decades. Screening of all sexually active women younger than 25 years is recommended. Women aged 25 years and older should be screened if they have STI risk factors. The U.S. Preventive Services Task Force (USPSTF) concluded that evidence is insufficient to support routine screening in men; the CDC recommends screening men in settings or populations with high prevalence or burden of disease (MSM, STI clinics).

Nucleic acid amplification testing (NAAT) is preferred for screening and diagnosis. First-catch urine (for men and women) and endocervical (for women) or urethral (for men) swabs can be used. NAAT of urine samples for *C. trachomatis* and *Neisseria gonorrhoeae* has been shown to have a sensitivity and specificity nearly identical to tests obtained from urethral and endocervical samples. In addition to cervicitis and urethritis, chlamydia may cause oropharyngeal and rectal infection, and these sites should be evaluated based on history of sexual practices. Although commercially available,

NAAT may not be FDA cleared for testing extragenital sites; laboratories can provide this testing if they have confirmed internal criteria for validity of test results.

Treatment of clinical syndromes caused by *C. trachomatis* is outlined in **Table 32**. Test of cure is not recommended,

TABLE 32. Treatment of *Chlamydia trachomatis* and *Neisseria gonorrhoeae* Infections and Their Complications

Clinical Syndrome	Preferred Regimen	Alternate Regimen
Cervicitis and urethritis (empiric therapy)	Ceftriaxone, 250 mg IM single dose, plus azithromycin, 1 g PO single dose (preferred), or doxycycline[a], 100 mg PO twice daily for 7 d (only if azithromycin cannot be used)	Cefixime, 400 mg PO single dose, plus azithromycin, 1 g PO single dose (preferred), or doxycycline, 100 mg PO twice daily for 7 d
Chlamydia cervicitis, urethritis, or proctitis	Azithromycin, 1 g PO single dose, or doxycycline, 100 mg PO twice daily for 7 d (21 d if *C. trachomatis* LGV serovars suspected or confirmed)	Erythromycin base, 500 mg PO four times daily, or erythromycin ethylsuccinate, 800 mg PO four times daily, or levofloxacin, 500 mg PO daily, or ofloxacin, 300 mg PO twice daily for 7 d
Gonococcal cervicitis, urethritis, or proctitis and pharyngeal infection[b]	Ceftriaxone, 250 mg IM single dose, plus azithromycin, 1 g PO single dose (preferred), or doxycycline, 100 mg PO twice daily for 7 d (only if azithromycin cannot be used)	Cefixime[c], 400 mg PO single dose, plus azithromycin, 1 g PO single dose (preferred), or doxycycline, 100 mg PO twice daily for 7 d Test of cure 2 weeks after treatment for pharyngeal gonorrhea treated with an alternate regimen
Disseminated gonococcal infection[d]	Ceftriaxone, 1 g IM or IV every 24 h, plus azithromycin, 1 g PO single dose	Cefotaxime, 1 g IV every 8 h, or ceftizoxime[e], 1 g IV every 8 h, plus azithromycin, 1 g PO single dose
Pelvic inflammatory disease		
Parenteral therapy[f]	Cefotetan, 2 g IV every 12 h, or cefoxitin, 2 g IV every 6 h, plus doxycycline, 100 mg IV or PO every 12 h OR Clindamycin, 900 mg IV every 8 h, plus gentamicin, 2 mg/kg IV loading dose followed by 1.5 mg/kg IV every 8 hours or a single daily dose of 3-5 mg/kg/d	Ampicillin-sulbactam, 3 g IV every 6 h, plus doxycycline, 100 mg IV or PO every 12 h
Oral/IM therapy	Ceftriaxone, 250 mg IM single dose, plus doxycycline, 100 mg PO twice daily for 14 d, with or without metronidazole, 500 mg PO twice daily for 14 d, or cefoxitin, 2 g IM single dose, with probenecid, 1 g PO, plus doxycycline, 100 mg PO every 12 h for 14 d, with or without metronidazole, 500 mg PO twice daily for 14 d	
Epididymitis	Ceftriaxone, 250 mg IM single dose, plus doxycycline, 100 mg PO twice daily for 10 d if infection most likely due to chlamydia/gonorrhea Ceftriaxone, 250 mg IM single dose, plus levofloxacin, 500 mg PO once daily, or ofloxacin, 300 mg PO twice daily for 10 d if infection might be caused by chlamydia/gonorrhea and enteric organisms (insertive anal intercourse) Levofloxacin, 500 mg PO once daily, or ofloxacin, 300 mg PO twice daily, for 10 d if infection most likely caused by enteric organisms	

IM = intramuscularly; IV = intravenously; LGV = lymphogranuloma venereum; PO = orally.

[a]Doxycyline should be avoided or used with caution in pregnant patients.

[b]Treatment for possible chlamydial infection is recommended for all patients diagnosed with gonorrhea. Currently recommended treatment regimens for gonorrhea provide this coverage.

[c]Cefixime should be used only if ceftriaxone is unavailable because oral cephalosporin resistance to *N. gonorrhoeae* has been increasingly reported.

[d]For arthritis-dermatitis syndrome, parenteral therapy should be used until 24 to 48 hours after substantial clinical improvement and then switched to an oral therapy based on susceptibility results for a total of 7 to 10 days of treatment. Parenteral therapy is required for the entire course of treatment for meningitis (10 to 14 days) and endocarditis (at least 28 days).

[e]Not available in the United States.

[f]Patients can be switched to oral therapy within 24 to 48 hours of clinical improvement using doxycycline, 100 mg PO twice daily, with or without metronidazole, 500 mg PO twice daily, to complete a total of 14 days of therapy.

except in pregnancy. Because of the high risk of repeat infection, men and women should be retested after 3 months or the next time they are seen for medical care.

KEY POINTS

- First-catch urine (or genital swab) nucleic acid amplification testing is the preferred screening and diagnostic method for *Chlamydia trachomatis* infection.

HVC • Test of cure is not recommended in patients with *Chlamydia trachomatis* infection except in pregnancy; however, patients should be retested for possible repeat infection after 3 months or at their next medical visit.

Neisseria gonorrhoeae Infection

The incidence of *N. gonorrhoeae* infection has been increasing since 2013, with rates of infection increasing more rapidly among men than women. Persons aged 20 to 24 years are at highest risk. In addition to cervicitis, urethritis, pharyngitis, and rectal infection, disseminated gonococcal infection (presenting as arthritis-dermatitis syndrome) can occur (see MKSAP 18 Rheumatology). Infection can be asymptomatic, especially in women, so screening is recommended for women younger than 25 years and those 25 years and older with STI risk factors. The USPSTF does not recommend screening for men; the CDC recommends screening men at high risk, as for *C. trachomatis*.

For screening and diagnosis, NAAT is preferred. Men and women can be screened using a first-catch urine sample; endocervical and urethral swabs may also be used. NAAT availability for samples from extragenital sites is limited, and physicians should determine what testing is available from their preferred laboratory. In patients with disseminated gonococcal infection (arthritis-dermatitis, endocarditis, or meningitis), all *N. gonorrhoeae* isolates should be tested for antimicrobial susceptibility. Patients with suspected disseminated gonococcal infection should have cultures performed on blood, joint fluid (if arthritis is present), purulent skin lesions (if present), and cerebrospinal fluid (if meningitis is suspected); however, culture yield is not high, so NAAT from all potential sites of exposure (genital, pharyngeal, rectal) should be obtained.

Treatment of *N. gonorrhoeae* is outlined in Table 32. Because of the increasing prevalence of antimicrobial resistance among *N. gonorrhoeae* isolates in the United States, cephalosporins are the only antimicrobial class recommended. Previously, the rationale for combination therapy was to treat concomitant *C. trachomatis* infection; the current rationale is based on increased efficacy of combination therapy. In the United States, *N. gonorrhoeae* isolates are more likely to be susceptible to azithromycin than doxycycline, and azithromycin can be given as a single dose. Doxycycline should only be used in the setting of macrolide allergy. In patients with an allergy precluding use of cephalosporins, oral gemifloxacin or parenteral gentamicin plus oral azithromycin is an option;

however, the dose of azithromycin is higher, which is associated with a high incidence of gastrointestinal intolerance. ◨

Test of cure is only recommended 2 weeks after therapy when pharyngeal gonorrhea is treated with an alternate antibiotic regimen. Patients with infections caused by *N. gonorrhoeae* who do not respond to treatment should have repeat testing with NAAT and culture so that susceptibility data can be obtained; consultation with an expert in the management of these infections should be sought.

KEY POINTS

- Screening for *Neisseria gonorrhoeae* infection is recommended for women younger than 25 years and those 25 years and older with risk factors (new partner, more than one partner, a partner with an STI, or a partner who has concurrent partners).

- First-catch urine (or genital swab) sample nucleic acid amplification testing is the preferred screening and diagnostic method for *Neisseria gonorrhoeae* infection.

- Parenteral ceftriaxone with oral azithromycin is the preferred regimen for the treatment of *Neisseria gonorrhoeae* infection.

- Test of cure in patients with *Neisseria gonorrhoeae* **HVC** infection is recommended 2 weeks after therapy only when pharyngeal gonorrhea is treated with an alternate antibiotic regimen.

Clinical Syndromes

Cervicitis

Women with cervicitis may present with vaginal discharge and intermenstrual bleeding, but many are asymptomatic. The major diagnostic criteria are (1) visualization of mucopurulent discharge from the cervical os or on a swab obtained from the endocervical canal and (2) eliciting bleeding by passing a swab into the cervical os; cervicitis should be considered in women with either of these findings. *N. gonorrhoeae* and *C. trachomatis* are the most commonly isolated pathogens; however, many cases are enigmatic. The role of *Mycoplasma genitalium* is still unclear; herpes simplex virus is occasionally implicated. Noninfectious causes (for example, chemical irritation from douching) should be sought. Patients should be tested for *N. gonorrhoeae* and *C. trachomatis* with NAAT; evaluation for bacterial vaginosis and trichomoniasis should also be performed (see MKSAP 18 General Internal Medicine).

Pelvic Inflammatory Disease

Unrecognized pelvic inflammatory disease (PID) may result in long-term sequelae, including infertility, chronic pelvic pain, and ectopic pregnancy. Symptoms include lower abdominal pain, vaginal discharge, intermenstrual bleeding or bleeding after intercourse, and dyspareunia. Some women have fever and other signs of systemic toxicity, but this is uncommon.

The diagnostic accuracy of clinical examination is poor; however, because of the potential consequences of untreated infection, clinical findings with a high sensitivity for PID should be used. The presence of uterine tenderness, adnexal tenderness, or cervical motion tenderness is sufficient to make a clinical diagnosis of PID, especially if accompanied by mucopurulent cervical discharge.

PID is believed to be polymicrobial; however, testing only for *N. gonorrhoeae* and *C. trachomatis* is indicated. Most women can be managed in the ambulatory setting with oral antibiotics (see Table 32). Indications for hospitalization include inability to exclude a surgical emergency such as appendicitis, pregnancy, severe systemic toxicity, tubo-ovarian abscess, inability to tolerate oral antibiotics, and failure of initial outpatient management.

H Urethritis

Men with urethritis present with dysuria, urethral pruritus, and discharge. Mucopurulent discharge may be the only symptom and is clinically diagnostic. *N. gonorrhoeae*, *C. trachomatis*, and *M. genitalium* are common causes of urethritis; *Trichomonas* may also be causative. The role of other *Mycoplasma* and *Ureaplasma* species is uncertain at present. A first-catch urine sample should be tested for *N. gonorrhoeae* and *C. trachomatis* by NAAT for diagnosis and for public reporting purposes; FDA-approved tests for *M. genitalium* are not yet available. Microscopic examination of a urethral sample that reveals more than 2 leukocytes per high-powered field has a high positive predictive value for infectious urethritis, but the negative predictive value is poor. A positive leukocyte esterase test result or a microscopic examination with 10 or more leukocytes on a first-void urine specimen is also diagnostic for infectious urethritis. This testing is not required if mucoid, mucopurulent, or purulent urethral discharge is demonstrated on examination. H

Epididymitis

Men with epididymitis present with unilateral pain and swelling in the epididymis; the testes may also be inflamed (epididymo-orchitis). Testicular torsion must be excluded in men with symptoms of sudden onset. *N. gonorrhoeae* and *C. trachomatis* are likely causes in younger, sexually active men. Older men and men who practice insertive anal intercourse may be infected with enteric gram-negative organisms such as *Escherichia coli*. NAAT for STI pathogens should be performed on first-catch urine, and a urine culture should be obtained. See MKSAP 18 General Internal Medicine for further information.

Anorectal Infections

Patients who present with anorectal pain, rectal discharge, or tenesmus should be questioned regarding sexual practices. In addition to receptive anal intercourse, infection may occur in women as a result of autoinoculation from vaginal discharge. Causes include *C. trachomatis*, *N.*

gonorrhoeae, syphilis, and herpes simplex virus (HSV). Infections caused by the lymphogranuloma venereum (LGV) serovars (L1, L2, or L3) of *C. trachomatis* had previously been rarely described in the United States, but they are increasingly reported as a cause of proctitis and proctocolitis, mainly among MSM.

Diagnostic evaluation should include NAAT for *C. trachomatis*, *N. gonorrhoeae*, and HSV as well as serologic testing for syphilis (dark-field examination should be performed if available). Additional molecular testing is required to identify LGV serovars of *C. trachomatis*, but it is not widely available commercially; LGV serovars of *C. trachomatis* will be detected by currently available NAATs.

KEY POINTS

- *Chlamydia trachomatis* and *Neisseria gonorrhoeae* are the primary causative organisms in cervicitis, pelvic inflammatory disease, urethritis, epididymitis, and anorectal infections, although other organisms may also be implicated.

- The two major diagnostic criteria of cervicitis are visualization of mucopurulent discharge from the cervical os or on a swab obtained from the endocervical canal or eliciting bleeding by passing a swab into the cervical os.

- The presence of uterine tenderness, adnexal tenderness, or cervical motion tenderness is sufficient to make a clinical diagnosis of pelvic inflammatory disease, especially if accompanied by mucopurulent cervical discharge.

- *Neisseria gonorrhoeae* and *Chlamydia trachomatis* are likely causes of epididymitis in younger, sexually active men; older men and men who practice insertive anal intercourse may be infected with enteric gram-negative organisms such as *Escherichia coli*.

Treatment

Treatment of the clinical syndromes discussed previously is outlined in Table 32. Symptomatic patients evaluated in urgent care centers or emergency departments and others who may not be able to return for follow-up should be treated empirically based on clinical syndrome. Diagnostic testing should still be obtained because STIs are reportable and test results will be informative if the infection fails to respond to empiric therapy.

Patients should abstain from sexual contact for 7 days after completion of therapy and until all sexual partners have been treated. Sexual partners in the previous 60 days, or the most recent partner if greater than 60 days, should be referred for evaluation and treatment. Although independent evaluation and testing of sexual partners is preferred, most states have provisions for providing empiric antibiotic therapy prescriptions to the patient for their partners (expedited partner therapy, or EPT).

- Diagnostic testing should be performed even if empiric therapy will be provided to patients unlikely to return for follow-up care, because *Neisseria gonorrhoeae* and *Chlamydia trachomatis* infections are reportable, and because test results will be informative if the infection fails to respond to therapy.

- Most states have provisions for providing empiric antibiotic therapy prescriptions for sexual partners (expedited partner therapy, or EPT).

Genital Ulcers

Herpes Simplex Virus

The epidemiology of HSV genital ulcer disease is changing; in some populations, such as young heterosexual women and MSM, HSV-1 is now a more common cause of symptomatic primary infection than HSV-2. Although the clinical manifestations of primary infection by HSV-1 and HSV-2 are indistinguishable, HSV-1 is less likely than HSV-2 to cause symptomatic recurrent ulcers and subclinical shedding. Differentiation between the two viral subtypes is important in counseling patients regarding the natural history of their infection.

Primary infection presents as multiple painful lesions that begin as erythematous papules, progress to vesicles, then ulcerate, crust, and eventually heal within 2 to 3 weeks (**Figure 12**). Primary infection is often accompanied by significant systemic symptoms. Tender inguinal lymphadenopathy may be present.

Although the clinical manifestations of primary infection are quite characteristic, the viral cause and HSV subtype should be confirmed. NAAT, such as polymerase chain reaction, for HSV-1 and HSV-2 is preferred; other methodologies are far less sensitive. Testing is performed by obtaining a swab from the ulcer base; if only vesicles are present, a vesicle must be unroofed to obtain cells from the ulcer base. The swab must be placed in viral transport medium, so the appropriate sample collection kit must be used. Type-specific serologic testing is not advised for the diagnosis of symptomatic ulcer disease because patients can be seropositive for HSV-1 or HSV-2 yet have genital ulcers from another cause. Potential roles for serologic testing include testing a sexual partner when evaluating the potential benefits of long-term suppressive therapy because a partner who is already infected would not be at risk for transmission. The CDC recommends considering HSV serologic testing in persons who present for STI evaluation, MSM, and persons with HIV infection. Serologic screening in the general population is not recommended.

Antiviral therapy for primary infection has been shown to decrease time to resolution of symptoms, lesion healing, and viral shedding. Antiviral regimens appropriate for treatment of primary infection are outlined in **Table 33**.

Recurrent genital HSV infections are less severe, and symptom duration, time to lesion healing, and duration of viral shedding are reduced. Many patients will experience prodromal itching, burning, or tingling before ulcers appear. Atypical presentations such as fissures and excoriations may occur. Recurrent infection can be managed with either episodic self-start therapy (initiated within 24 hours of symptoms) or long-term suppressive therapy (see Table 33). Long-term suppressive therapy should be considered for persons with frequent recurrences and should be discussed with all patients because this strategy has been shown to decrease the risk of transmission to sexual partners. Laboratory monitoring is not required for patients undergoing long-term suppressive therapy; however, the continued need for therapy should be reviewed annually. Length of time since last recurrence and potential benefits of continued suppression in preventing

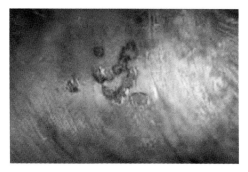

FIGURE 12. Penile lesions seen in herpes simplex virus (HSV) type 2. Patients with genital HSV infection initially have painful lesions that begin as vesicles and progress to ulcers on an erythematous base.

TABLE 33. Treatment of Herpes Simplex Virus Genital Infections

Clinical Syndrome	Recommended Regimen[a]
Primary infection[b]	Acyclovir, 400 mg three times daily, *or* acyclovir, 200 mg five times daily, *or* famciclovir, 250 mg three times daily, *or* valacyclovir, 1 g twice daily; all regimens for 7-10 days
Recurrent infection	Acyclovir, 400 mg three times daily for 5 days, *or* acyclovir, 800 mg twice daily for 5 days, *or* acyclovir, 800 mg three times daily for 2 days, *or* famciclovir, 125 mg twice daily for 5 days, *or* famciclovir, 1 g twice daily for 1 day, *or* famciclovir, 500 mg once followed by 250 mg twice daily for 2 days, *or* valacyclovir, 500 mg twice daily for 3 days, *or* valacyclovir, 1 g once daily for 5 days
Suppressive therapy	Acyclovir, 400 mg twice daily, *or* famciclovir, 250 mg twice daily, *or* valacyclovir, 500 mg daily[c], *or* valacyclovir, 1 g daily

[a]All regimens are given orally; topical preparations are not recommended for treatment of genital herpes simplex virus.

[b]Therapy can be extended if healing is incomplete after 10 days of treatment.

[c]The 500-mg dose of valacyclovir may be less effective than the 1-g dose in patients who have very frequent recurrences (≥10 episodes per year).

CONT.

transmission to sexual partners are factors that can inform the decision to stop suppressive therapy.

Patients should be counseled regarding the natural history of infection and informed that asymptomatic viral shedding is the most common source of HSV transmission to sexual partners. Condoms and abstinence from sexual activity when lesions are present can reduce the risk of transmission. Suppressive therapy to reduce risk of transmission should be discussed. Men and women should be counseled about the risks of neonatal HSV infection. Women should be advised to inform their obstetric provider and pediatrician of HSV infection in themselves or their sexual partner if they become pregnant. ▢

KEY POINTS

- Viral cause and herpes simplex virus subtype in primary infection should be confirmed by nucleic acid amplification testing, such as polymerase chain reaction, using a swab obtained from the ulcer base.

- The Centers for Disease Control and Prevention recommend considering herpes simplex virus serologic testing in persons who present for sexually transmitted infection evaluation, men who have sex with men, and persons with HIV infection; screening in the general population is not recommended.

- Long-term suppressive therapy of recurrent herpes simplex virus infection may be preferred over self-start episodic therapy because of decreased risk of transmission to sexual partners.

Syphilis

The incidence of primary and secondary syphilis has been increasing in the United States since 2000. The USPSTF recommends screening nonpregnant adolescents and adults at high risk of infection. Persons at risk include MSM and commercial sex workers and those with HIV infection, multiple sex partners, and previous syphilis. In 2015, the CDC issued a clinical advisory regarding the increasing incidence of ocular syphilis.

Primary syphilis presents as a painless genital ulcer (chancre) with a raised regular border that demonstrates firm induration on palpation (**Figure 13**). Several chancres may be present and may occur in the oral cavity. Regional lymphadenopathy may be present. The diagnosis of primary syphilis can be made on the basis of dark-field examination of material from a suspect lesion. Serologic test results may be negative in early primary infection. Even in the absence of treatment, lesions heal spontaneously in 3 to 6 weeks.

The most common manifestation of secondary syphilis is rash. Various morphologies are described; involvement of the palms and soles is characteristic. In intertriginous areas, papules may coalesce to form condyloma lata (plaque-like lesions). Mucous patches (superficial erosions on mucosal surfaces) may occur in the oral cavity and moist genital regions and are

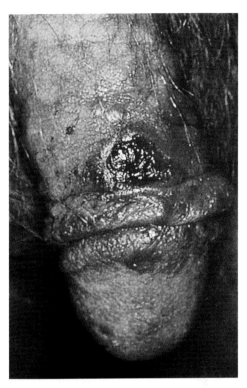

FIGURE 13. The primary ulcerative lesion (chancre) in patients with syphilis develops approximately 3 weeks after infection occurs, has a clean appearance with heaped-up borders, and is indurated and usually painless. It is often unrecognized.

highly infectious. Prominent systemic symptoms and generalized lymphadenopathy are common. Uveitis and neurosyphilis (meningitis) can occur. Secondary syphilis manifestations can also resolve without treatment, followed by latent infection (a positive serologic test result without clinical manifestations). If latent infection is of less than 12 months' duration, it is termed early latent; if greater than 12 months' duration, it is late latent. Practically, these determinations can be made only if past serology results are available. Otherwise, patients are considered to have syphilis of unknown duration.

Tertiary syphilis is rarely seen in the United States, although neurologic disease still occurs. Spinal fluid examination should be sought in any patient with unexplained neurologic symptoms and serologic evidence of syphilis as well as in those who do not demonstrate an appropriate serologic response to syphilis treatment.

Diagnosis of secondary and tertiary syphilis relies on serologic testing. Many laboratories use the "reverse" serologic testing strategy, starting with an automated enzyme immunoassay followed by a nonspecific test (rapid plasma reagin or Venereal Disease Research Lab test). Patients with a positive enzyme immunoassay result but negative rapid plasma reagin or Venereal Disease Research Lab test result should have a second specific treponemal antibody test to confirm the result. Those with a confirmed positive result and no history of syphilis treatment should be offered treatment for syphilis of unknown duration.

CONT.

Syphilis treatment is outlined in **Table 34**. Sexual partners of those with primary, secondary, or early latent syphilis exposed in the preceding 90 days should be treated regardless of serologic results.

KEY POINTS

- Primary syphilis presents as a painless genital ulcer (chancre) with a raised regular border that demonstrates firm induration on palpation; lesions heal spontaneously in 3 to 6 weeks even without treatment.

- The most common manifestation of secondary syphilis is rash, with characteristic involvement of the palms and soles; in intertriginous areas, papules may coalesce to form condyloma lata (plaque-like lesions), and mucous patches (superficial erosions on mucosal surfaces) may occur in the oral cavity and moist genital regions and are highly infectious.

- Diagnosis of secondary and tertiary syphilis relies on serologic testing; patients with a positive enzyme immunoassay result and positive rapid plasma reagin or Venereal Disease Research Lab test result and no history of syphilis treatment should be offered treatment for syphilis of unknown duration.

Chancroid and Lymphogranuloma Venereum

With the exception of proctitis or proctocolitis caused by the LGV serovars of *C. trachomatis*, these two STIs are rarely seen in the United States. The clinical presentation and evaluation are outlined in **Table 35**, and treatment is outlined in **Table 36**.

Genital Warts

Genital warts have a variety of appearances, including papular or pedunculated lesions (**Figure 14**). Larger, verrucous, exophytic lesions can occur. Most are asymptomatic; however, large lesions may cause irritation or pain depending on their location. Nononcogenic types of human papillomavirus (HPV) are responsible for most lesions. Oncogenic subtypes less commonly cause genital warts. HPV infection can be diagnosed based on the presence of lesions with a consistent morphologic appearance. Specific testing for HPV is not recommended for diagnosis.

Warts will often resolve without therapy, but treatment is indicated for symptomatic warts or if the cosmetic appearance of the warts is causing psychological distress. Patients should be counseled that successful treatment may not eliminate the risk of transmission. Therapy includes patient-applied

---

TABLE 34. Treatment of Syphilis

Stage	Recommended Regimen[a]	Alternate Regimen for Penicillin-Allergic Patients
Primary and secondary	Benzathine penicillin G, 2.4 million units IM single dose	Doxycycline, 100 mg PO twice daily, *or* tetracycline, 500 mg PO four times daily, for 14 days
Early latent	Benzathine penicillin G, 2.4 million units IM single dose	Doxycycline, 100 mg PO twice daily, *or* tetracycline, 500 mg PO four times daily, for 14 days
Late latent or syphilis of unknown duration	Benzathine penicillin G, 2.4 million units IM at 1-week intervals for 3 doses	Doxycycline, 100 mg PO twice daily, *or* tetracycline, 500 mg PO four times daily, for 28 days
Neurosyphilis	Aqueous crystalline penicillin G, 18-24 million units daily given as 3-4 million units IV every 4 hours or by continuous infusion for 10-14 days, *or* procaine penicillin, 2.4 million units IM daily, plus probenecid, 500 mg PO four times daily, both for 10-14 days	Ceftriaxone, 2 g IM or IV daily for 10-14 days[b]

IM = intramuscularly; IV = intravenously; PO = orally.

[a]Penicillin is the only effective antimicrobial agent for treatment of syphilis at any stage in pregnancy; therefore, pregnant penicillin-allergic patients should be desensitized and treated with the appropriate penicillin regimen as outlined above.

[b]Limited data are available to support the use of this alternate regimen, and the possibility of cross-reaction in penicillin-allergic patients must be considered. In patients who cannot take ceftriaxone, penicillin desensitization is recommended.

TABLE 35. Clinical Presentation and Diagnosis of Chancroid and Lymphogranuloma Venereum

Clinical Entity	Causative Agent	Presentation	Diagnosis
Chancroid	*Haemophilus ducreyi*	Painful genital ulcer; tender inguinal lymph nodes, which often suppurate	Culture is difficult; consider diagnosis if painful ulcer with tender and suppurative regional lymphadenopathy, no evidence of syphilis by dark-field examination or serology, and negative HSV PCR or HSV culture
LGV	L1, L2, and L3 serovars of *Chlamydia trachomatis*	Painless genital papule or ulcer with unilateral tender inguinal lymphadenopathy	NAAT for *C. trachomatis*; does not distinguish the serovars, so diagnosis is made based on clinical and epidemiologic findings

HSV = herpes simplex virus; LGV = lymphogranuloma venereum; NAAT = nucleic acid amplification test; PCR = polymerase chain reaction.

TABLE 36. Treatment of Chancroid and Lymphogranuloma Venereum

Clinical Entity	Recommended Regimen
Chancroid	Azithromycin, 1 g PO single dose, *or* ceftriaxone, 250 mg IM single dose, *or* ciprofloxacin, 500 mg PO twice daily for 3 days, *or* erythromycin base, 500 mg PO three times daily for 7 days
Lymphogranuloma venereum	Doxycycline[a], 100 mg PO twice daily for 21 days (preferred), *or* erythromycin base, 500 mg PO four times daily for 21 days (alternate)

IM = intramuscularly; PO = orally.

[a]Doxycyline should be avoided or used with caution in pregnant patients.

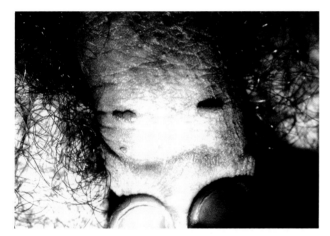

FIGURE 14. Genital warts caused by human papillomavirus infection are typically flesh colored and exophytic; pedunculated lesions often occur.

or physician-administered modalities. Patient-applied therapies include imiquimod, podofilox, and sinecatechins; provider-administered therapies include trichloroacetic acid or bichloroacetic acid, cryotherapy with liquid nitrogen or cryoprobe, or surgical removal. The modality chosen depends on size, number, and location of warts; patient preference; and provider experience. No evidence indicates superiority of any of the modalities recommended. Ulcerated or pigmented warts and those that fail to respond to or worsen after therapy should be biopsied to exclude a cancerous lesion.

KEY POINT

- Nononcogenic types of human papillomavirus are responsible for most genital warts, which often resolve without therapy.

Osteomyelitis

Osteomyelitis occurs as a result of hematogenous dissemination or contiguous spread of bacteria. Hematogenous osteomyelitis in adults most commonly affects vertebral bodies,

although involvement of other sites has been described, particularly in persons who inject drugs. Contiguous-spread osteomyelitis may arise from direct contamination (fracture, joint replacement, orthopedic implant), wounds (pressure sores, diabetic foot ulcers), or adjacent soft tissue infection. Population-based studies suggest that the incidence of osteomyelitis among adults is increasing in the United States, most likely because of the increasing prevalence of diabetes mellitus. Osteomyelitis can be difficult to diagnose, can cause indolent infections that persist for prolonged periods, and requires long-term antibiotic treatment; thus, the economic impact of this infection is substantial.

Clinical Manifestations

Osteomyelitis frequently presents as subacute or chronic pain over the affected region of bone. If osteomyelitis has resulted from direct contamination of a wound, the wound may fail to heal or may reopen after healing. Spontaneously opening wounds accompanied by drainage (sinus tracts) are a late manifestation of infection. Underlying osteomyelitis should be considered when chronic wounds, such as pressure ulcers, do not respond to appropriate therapy. Fever and other systemic manifestations of infection are not common but are more likely in patients with acute hematogenously disseminated infection. Clinical findings in patients with diabetes-associated foot ulcer osteomyelitis and vertebral osteomyelitis are discussed separately.

KEY POINTS

- Osteomyelitis frequently presents as subacute to chronic pain over the affected region of bone; fever and other systemic manifestations of infection are uncommon.
- Underlying osteomyelitis should be considered when chronic wounds, such as pressure ulcers, do not respond to appropriate therapy.

Diagnosis

Laboratory and Imaging Studies

Laboratory studies are nondiagnostic for osteomyelitis. Elevated inflammatory markers, such as erythrocyte sedimentation rate or C-reactive protein level, increase the pretest probability of infection and can be useful in monitoring therapeutic response; normal inflammatory markers alone are insufficient to exclude the diagnosis. Except in acute hematogenous osteomyelitis, leukocytosis is uncommon; in chronic osteomyelitis, anemia may be present. Blood culture results are rarely positive, except in patients with hematogenous osteomyelitis (such as vertebral osteomyelitis). Blood cultures should be obtained when hematogenous osteomyelitis is suspected or in patients with systemic manifestations of sepsis.

Plain radiography is not adequately sensitive to exclude a diagnosis of osteomyelitis, but it is recommended during

CONT.

initial evaluation because of the relatively low cost. The specificity of plain radiography is sufficient to confirm the diagnosis in most patients. If a plain radiograph is not diagnostic, MRI, with and without intravenous contrast, is preferred. If MRI cannot be obtained because of specific contraindications, CT with intravenous contrast is an alternative. Nuclear medicine studies are less sensitive and specific for osteomyelitis but can be used when neither CT with contrast nor MRI are possible after review with the consulting radiologist. H

KEY POINTS

- Laboratory studies are nondiagnostic for osteomyelitis; blood culture results are rarely positive, except in patients with hematogenous osteomyelitis.

HVC
- The specificity of plain radiographs is sufficient to confirm the diagnosis in most patients; if plain radiographs do not positively identify osteomyelitis, MRI, with and without intravenous contrast, is the preferred imaging modality.

Bone Biopsy

Obtaining biopsy material for culture and pathologic examination is essential to the evaluation of suspected osteomyelitis. Confirming the presence of a pathogen maximizes the chance that the chosen antibiotic therapy will be successful. Specimens may be obtained at surgery or by image-guided biopsy. A bone biopsy is generally not required in persons with positive blood culture results. A possible exception is injection drug users because they have frequent bacteremias, and the organism in the blood culture may not represent the pathogen in the bone. In culture-negative disease, additional testing of biopsy material with nucleic acid amplification techniques, such as broad-range 16S ribosomal RNA gene amplification, may yield the causative organism, although these techniques will not provide information regarding antimicrobial susceptibilities. H

KEY POINT

- Obtaining biopsy material for culture and pathologic examination is essential to the evaluation of suspected osteomyelitis.

Treatment

Antibiotic therapy for osteomyelitis should be based on results of susceptibility testing from bone or blood culture isolates and knowledge of antibiotic levels achievable in bone for the selected agent. Unless systemic signs of sepsis or concomitant soft tissue infection or bacteremia are present, empiric antibiotics should be withheld until a bone biopsy is obtained. Surgical debridement is indicated if bone necrosis is extensive. Orthopedic hardware should be removed, if possible, to increase the chance of therapeutic success. Parenteral antimicrobial agents are usually chosen initially, but highly bioavailable oral agents with good bone penetration, such as

fluoroquinolones, may be considered. Rifampin should be used in combination with another antistaphylococcal agent to manage *Staphylococcus aureus* infections in the setting of orthopedic hardware if the hardware cannot be removed. Little evidence is available to guide recommendations on duration of therapy; 4 to 6 weeks of antibiotics is considered sufficient for acute infections, whereas longer courses may be required for chronic infections. In some circumstances, especially when hardware cannot be removed, indefinite suppressive therapy may be required. Patients should be informed about the risk of relapse and told that relapse can occur many years after therapy completion. H

KEY POINTS

- Unless systemic signs of sepsis or concomitant soft tissue infection or bacteremia are present, empiric antibiotics should be withheld in suspected osteomyelitis until a bone biopsy is obtained.

- Surgical debridement is indicated for osteomyelitis if bone necrosis is extensive.

- Generally, 4 to 6 weeks of antibiotic therapy is sufficient for acute osteomyelitis; longer courses are required for chronic infections.

Evaluation and Management of Osteomyelitis in Diabetic Foot Ulcers

The incidence of diabetic foot infection is increasing with the increasing prevalence of diabetes mellitus both in the United States and worldwide (see MKSAP 18 Dermatology). These infections are the most frequent diabetes-related complication necessitating hospitalization, cause significant morbidity (especially limb amputation), and are associated with increased mortality. Nonhealing ulcers become colonized with bacteria, after which infection may develop with contiguous spread to bone.

A diagnosis of osteomyelitis should be considered when a diabetic foot ulcer is deep (presence of exposed bone), large (>2 cm in diameter), or chronic (nonhealing after 6 weeks of standard care). Up to two thirds of affected patients do not have leukocytosis or elevated inflammatory markers. A probe-to-bone test (sterile probe inserted into the ulcer base to evaluate for contact with a hard or gritty surface representing bone or joint capsule) should be performed. In a clinically infected ulcer (presence of pus), the positive predictive value of the probe-to-bone test is high; in a noninfected ulcer, the negative predictive value is high. Imaging options are as described for other causes of osteomyelitis. All patients with a new diabetic foot infection should have plain radiography to assess for bony abnormalities, soft tissue gas, and foreign bodies.

Bone samples for histologic confirmation of diagnosis and for culture can be obtained during bone debridement; if debridement is not required, a bone biopsy should be

CONT.

obtained. *S. aureus* and streptococcal species account for most osteomyelitis complicating diabetic foot ulcers; gram-negative organisms are found in as many as 25% of infections. Anaerobes are much less common. Infections may be polymicrobial.

Although deep sinus-tract tissue cultures can be obtained, the correlation with bone biopsy samples is variable, and bone biopsy remains the recommended modality for microbiologic diagnosis. Recent evidence shows that patients treated with antibiotics chosen on the basis of bone culture results have a better outcome than those treated without these results. If infected but viable bone is present, a 4- to 6-week course of parenteral or oral antibiotic therapy is recommended, as it is for other forms of osteomyelitis. Prolonged oral therapy is indicated if there is residual necrotic bone.

Indications for amputation include persistent sepsis, inability to tolerate antibiotic therapy, progressive bone destruction despite appropriate therapy, or bone destruction that compromises the mechanical integrity of the foot. The patient may also choose amputation over prolonged antibiotic therapy. Hyperbaric oxygen therapy, growth factors, and topical negative-pressure therapy have insufficient evidence of benefit to recommend their use. However, limb salvage may be possible far more often than previously thought when treatment is directed by a dedicated multidisciplinary team consisting of a foot surgeon, a vascular surgeon, an internist, an infectious diseases specialist, nurses, and a physical therapist. H

KEY POINTS

- Osteomyelitis should be considered when a diabetic foot ulcer is deep (presence of exposed bone), large (>2 cm in diameter), or chronic (nonhealing after 6 weeks of standard care).

- Bone samples for diagnosis and guidance of antimicrobial therapy should be obtained in patients with osteomyelitis during bone debridement or by bone biopsy.

- If infected but viable bone is present in patients with diabetes mellitus–associated osteomyelitis, a 4- to 6-week course of antibiotic therapy is recommended; prolonged oral therapy is indicated for patients with residual necrotic bone.

H Evaluation and Management of Vertebral Osteomyelitis

Except when resulting from surgical instrumentation, vertebral osteomyelitis is almost exclusively secondary to hematogenous dissemination. Risk factors for vertebral osteomyelitis include older age, immunocompromise, indwelling catheters, hemodialysis, and injection drug use. Infection occurs in the intervertebral disk space and then spreads to the adjacent vertebral bodies (spondylodiskitis). The lumbar spine is most frequently involved, followed by the thoracic and then the cervical spine. Most infections are due to *S. aureus*, but *S. lugdunensis* is increasingly implicated. Persistent bacteremia with other coagulase-negative staphylococci in patients treated with hemodialysis and those with intravascular devices may obviate the need for biopsy. Enterobacteriaceae, *Pseudomonas aeruginosa* (especially in persons who inject drugs), and *Candida* species also may cause vertebral osteomyelitis.

New-onset back or neck pain or progressive worsening of chronic pain that is unresponsive to conservative management should raise concern for vertebral osteomyelitis, especially when accompanied by elevated levels of inflammatory markers, neurologic findings, or unexplained fever. Neurologic findings can include sensory loss, weakness, or radiculopathy and are reported in up to one third of patients. Point tenderness is present in as few as one third of patients. Delay in diagnosis is common; in a third of patients, pain is initially attributed to degenerative disease.

As with other forms of osteomyelitis, MRI is the preferred imaging modality. Blood cultures should be performed in all patients. Testing for *Mycobacterium tuberculosis* infection (with tuberculin skin testing or an interferon-γ release assay), fungal blood cultures, and serologic tests for *Brucella* species are appropriate for patients at risk for these pathogens (see *Mycobacterium tuberculosis* Infection, Fungal Infections, and Travel Medicine). A positive *Brucella* serologic result in the correct epidemiologic setting is considered diagnostic, and biopsy is not needed. Otherwise, image-guided biopsy has a diagnostic yield of approximately 60% and should be used in patients with negative blood culture results. A second biopsy should be obtained if the first is not diagnostic. Nucleic acid amplification techniques can increase biopsy yield; specimens should also be sent for pathologic examination. Open biopsy or percutaneous endoscopic diskectomy and drainage may be considered if the microbiologic diagnosis remains elusive after a second image-guided biopsy attempt.

Patients with neurologic compromise or evidence of spinal instability should undergo evaluation for immediate surgical intervention. Patients with complications, such as severe sepsis, progressive neurologic deficit, spinal instability, or epidural abscess, should receive empiric antibiotic therapy. Otherwise, initiation of antibiotic therapy for uncomplicated vertebral osteomyelitis is based on culture results. Parenteral therapy is generally recommended, especially for *S. aureus*. However, oral agents with high bioavailability and good bone penetration (such as fluoroquinolones) may be used, especially for Enterobacteriaceae. The duration of antibiotic therapy for vertebral osteomyelitis is typically 6 weeks. Patients should be followed clinically for improvement in symptoms, and inflammatory markers can be monitored. Repeat imaging, especially MRI, should be reserved for patients who do not respond clinically; worsening of imaging findings in patients with a satisfactory clinical response is well described. H

- New-onset back or neck pain or progressive worsening of chronic pain that is unresponsive to conservative management should raise concern for vertebral osteomyelitis, especially when accompanied by elevated inflammatory markers, neurologic findings, or unexplained fever.

- The diagnostic evaluation of vertebral osteomyelitis should include blood cultures for all patients; testing for *Mycobacterium tuberculosis* infection, fungal blood cultures, and serologic tests for *Brucella* species are appropriate for patients at risk for these pathogens.

- Parenteral antibiotic therapy chosen on the basis of culture results is recommended for uncomplicated vertebral osteomyelitis, although oral agents with high bioavailability and good bone penetration also can be used; duration of treatment is 6 weeks.

Fever of Unknown Origin

Introduction

The classic definition of fever of unknown origin (FUO) has changed over time (including removing the requirement for in-hospital evaluation), and three categories have been added: health care–associated, neutropenic, and HIV-associated (**Table 37**). Diagnostic advances have revealed a spectrum of diseases causing FUO, with origins more rapidly identifiable for many cases.

Causes

The differential diagnosis of FUO includes more than 200 diseases, although most adult cases are attributed to one of several dozen causes. Common causes of FUO include infections, neoplasm or malignancy, rheumatologic or inflammatory disorders, and miscellaneous causes (see Table 37).

Evaluation

Many FUO occurrences are atypical presentations of common diseases. A careful history and physical examination should be performed and repeated intermittently during the period of evaluation. The history should include procedures, surgeries, presence of foreign bodies or implants, immunosuppression, travel, animal and other exposures (including hobbies), dietary habits, and medications (including over-the-counter medications). The degree and pattern of fever is not specific and not diagnostic in most instances.

TABLE 37. Categories and Common Causes of Fever of Unknown Origin

Category	Definition	Common Causes
Classic	Temperature >38.3 °C (100.9 °F) for at least 3 weeks with at least 1 week of in-hospital investigation[a] *or* Temperature >38.3 °C (100.9 °F) for at least 3 weeks that remains undiagnosed after 2 visits in the ambulatory setting[b] or 3 days in the hospital	Infection (endocarditis, tuberculosis [extrapulmonary/disseminated], abscess, endemic mycoses), neoplasm (leukemia, lymphoma, renal cell carcinoma, hepatocellular carcinoma), connective tissue disease (adult-onset Still disease, polymyalgia rheumatica, vasculitis, systemic lupus erythematosus, giant cell arteritis), endocrine disorder (hyperthyroidism, subacute thyroiditis), genetic (familial Mediterranean fever), or miscellaneous (drug fever, factitious fever)
Health care–associated	Temperature >38.3 °C (100.9 °F) in patients hospitalized ≥3 days (without fever or evidence of potential infection at the time of admission) and negative evaluation for at least 3 days	Drug fever, septic thrombophlebitis, deep venous thrombosis/pulmonary embolism, sinusitis in the setting of a nasogastric tube, chronic sinusitis without a nasogastric tube, postoperative abscess, *Clostridium difficile* infection, device- or procedure-related endocarditis
Neutropenic	Temperature >38.3 °C (100.9 °F) and neutrophil count <500/μL (0.5 × 10^9/L) for >3 days and negative evaluation after 48 hours	Bacteremia, opportunistic fungal infections (aspergillosis, candidiasis; more common than bacteremia after 7 days), drug fever, deep venous thrombosis/pulmonary embolism, underlying malignancy, allograft rejection in transplant; undocumented in 40%-60% of cases
HIV-associated	Temperature >38.3 °C (100.9 °F) for >3 weeks (outpatients) or >3 days (inpatients) in patients with confirmed HIV infection	Primary HIV infection, opportunistic infections (cytomegalovirus, cryptococcosis, tuberculosis, atypical mycobacteria, toxoplasmosis, *Pneumocystis jirovecii* pneumonia), lymphoma, immune reconstitution inflammatory syndrome

[a]Original definition of fever of unknown origin.

[b]Ambulatory setting is the preferred venue for evaluation and treatment.

Initial testing for the evaluation of classic FUO includes complete blood count with differential, electrolyte levels, kidney and liver function tests (hepatitis serology if results are abnormal), lactate dehydrogenase level, urinalysis or microscopy and urine culture, erythrocyte sedimentation rate, C-reactive protein, antinuclear antibodies, rheumatoid factor, HIV testing, cytomegalovirus polymerase chain reaction testing, blood cultures (three sets, each set obtained at least several hours apart), tuberculosis testing, and chest radiography (or chest CT). Q-fever serology should be considered if risk factors exist, and mycobacterial blood cultures should be obtained in HIV-positive patients with CD4 cell counts of 50/µL or less.

If initial tests do not suggest a cause, abdominal or pelvic CT may be considered to evaluate for intra-abdominal abscess or lymphoproliferative disorders. Liver, lymph node, and temporal artery biopsies have a diagnostic yield of about 35%, particularly when performed when infection is unlikely. Posterior cervical, supraclavicular, infraclavicular, epitrochlear, hilar, mediastinal, and mesenteric lymph node biopsies are more likely to provide a diagnosis than that of other lymph nodes. Bone marrow biopsy can be helpful when leukopenia or thrombocytopenia is present.

A definitive diagnosis is lacking in up to half of patients after extensive evaluation. FUO lasting more than 1 year is unlikely to be caused by infection or malignancy. Undiagnosed FUO is generally associated with a benign long-term course, particularly when fever is not associated with weight loss or other signs of underlying serious disease.

KEY POINTS

- The classic definition of fever of unknown origin no longer requires inpatient evaluation and has been expanded to include health care–associated, neutropenic, and HIV-associated designations.

- In patients with fever of unknown origin, a careful history and physical examination should be performed, including past procedures or surgeries, presence of foreign bodies or implants, immunosuppression, travel, animal or other exposures, dietary habits, and medications.

- A definitive diagnosis is lacking in up to half of patients with fever of unknown origin after extensive evaluation, but duration of more than 1 year is unlikely to be caused by infection or malignancy.

Primary Immunodeficiencies
Introduction

Primary immunodeficiency disorders often present during childhood, but milder heritable forms may not manifest until adulthood. Primary immunodeficiency should be considered when patients present with frequent infections or infections with unusual organisms. The specific microbiology is often a clue to which arm of the immune system is affected (**Table 38**).

TABLE 38. Properties of Selected Primary Immunodeficiency Disorders

	Common Infections and Pathogens	Diagnostic Testing	Treatment
Selective IgA deficiency	Sinopulmonary infections: *Streptococcus pneumoniae* *Haemophilus influenzae* Diarrhea/malabsorption: *Giardia lamblia*	Undetectable (severe deficiency) or low (partial deficiency) IgA level with normal IgG and IgM levels	Vaccination against *S. pneumoniae* Prophylactic antibiotics are controversial
Common variable immunodeficiency	Sinopulmonary infections: *S. pneumoniae* *H. influenzae* *Mycoplasma pneumoniae* Respiratory viruses Diarrhea: Norovirus *Campylobacter* *G. lamblia* Urethritis: *Mycoplasma* *Ureaplasma*	IgG level and either IgA or IgM ≤2 standard deviations below the mean PLUS impaired humoral response to vaccination	Immune globulin replacement therapy Immunization with inactivated vaccines Prophylactic antibiotics are controversial
Complement deficiency	Early components (C2-C4): Similar to CVID Late components (C5-C9): Recurrent infections with *Neisseria gonorrhoeae* or *Neisseria meningitidis*	Decreased level of total hemolytic complement (CH$_{50}$)	Same as CVID for C2-C4 complement deficiency Quadrivalent meningococcal conjugate and serogroup B meningococcal vaccines for C5-C9 complement deficiency

CVID = common variable immunodeficiency.

Diagnosis of primary immunodeficiency allows directed therapy, targeted immunization, and optimized empiric treatment of secondary infections.

Selective IgA Deficiency

Although most patients with selective IgA deficiency (SIgAD) remain asymptomatic, it is the most common primary antibody deficiency. IgA provides mucosal immunity; therefore, patients with SIgAD are susceptible to infections of the respiratory tract and, less frequently, gastrointestinal tract. Sinopulmonary infections are the most common presenting manifestation, particularly with encapsulated bacteria (see Table 38). Anaphylaxis to blood products may occur because of the presence of anti-IgA antibodies. Testing for anti-IgA antibodies should be considered in patients with severe SIgAD or history of reaction to blood products or intravenous immune globulin infusion.

KEY POINT

- Patients with selective IgA deficiency may be asymptomatic, present with sinopulmonary or gastrointestinal tract infections, or experience anaphylaxis to blood products.

Common Variable Immunodeficiency

Common variable immunodeficiency (CVID) is a heterogenous syndrome associated with decreased quantitative immunoglobulin levels and impaired humoral response to antigens. Impaired humoral response can be tested by measuring specific antibody production before and after immunization with tetanus and pneumococcal polysaccharide vaccines. Diagnosis is usually delayed until adolescence or adulthood, although a history of recurrent infection throughout childhood may often be elicited.

CVID increases risk of infections of the upper and lower respiratory tracts caused by encapsulated bacteria, *Mycoplasma* species, and respiratory viruses. Gastrointestinal infections typically present with acute diarrhea caused by common enteropathogenic viruses or bacteria. Chronic diarrhea with malabsorption suggests giardiasis or chronic norovirus infection, an increasingly recognized pathogen in this population. Additionally, patients with CVID are at increased risk of autoimmune disease, inflammatory bowel disease, granulomatous disease (noncaseating granulomas in the lymphoid or solid organs), bronchiectasis, and malignancy.

Pooled immune globulin replacement therapy for CVID is performed through intravenous infusions or subcutaneous injections. Passive replacement is associated with lower rates of infections and hospitalizations. Immunization is only partially effective because of impaired vaccination response; live vaccines should be avoided. The role of prophylactic antibiotics is controversial because they can predispose patients to infection with more resistant organisms.

KEY POINTS

- Patients with common variable immunodeficiency can experience recurrent infections and are at increased risk of noninfectious complications, including autoimmune disease, inflammatory bowel disease, granulomatous disease, bronchiectasis, and malignancy.
- Live vaccines should be avoided in persons with common variable immunodeficiency.

Abnormalities in the Complement System

Infections and other antigenic stimuli trigger an inflammatory reaction through the classical, alternative, or lectin pathway of the complement cascade system. The result is formation of the membrane attack complex, which adheres to pathogens to facilitate immune detection and destruction.

Complement deficiencies can be divided into deficiencies in early or activating components (C2, C3, C4) and late or terminal components (C5-C9). Early component deficiency, especially C4, is associated with increased rates of systemic lupus erythematosus and increased risk of infection with encapsulated organisms. Patients with early complement deficiency present similarly to patients with CVID, with recurrent sinopulmonary infections. Terminal complement protein defects lead to an inability to form the membrane attack complex and typically present with recurrent infections of *Neisseria* species, particularly meningococcal meningitis. *N. meningitidis* infection in this population tends to be less severe than in immunocompetent persons, perhaps owing to uncommon serogroups. A personal or family history of recurrent *Neisseria* infections is an indication to test the total hemolytic complement (CH_{50}) level because any defect in the classical complement pathway will result in a low total level.

KEY POINTS

- Early component complement deficiency is associated with an increased rate of systemic lupus erythematosus and risk of infection with encapsulated organisms; terminal complement defects can result in recurrent *Neisseria* infections.
- Any defect in the classical complement pathway will result in low total hemolytic complement (CH_{50}) level.

Bioterrorism
Introduction

Unusually severe illness, rapid increase in disease incidence, atypical clinical presentation, and uncommon geographic, temporal, or demographic clustering of disease outbreaks suggest a bioterrorism attack. Bioterrorism agents are classified (**Table 39**) according to ease of dissemination, mortality rate, potential for public panic and social disruption, and need for special action for public health preparedness.

Anthrax

Anthrax infection is caused by *Bacillus anthracis* spores (**Figure 15** panel A and Figure 15 panel B). Spores may be spread by aerosolization or in the mail, with infection following inhalation; any case of inhalation anthrax must be considered potential bioterrorism. Infection may also occur by cutaneous contact, with a characteristic black eschar forming (Figure 15 panel C), or by ingestion. Person-to-person transmission does not occur.

The clinical presentation of inhalational anthrax includes malaise, myalgia, fever, cough, dyspnea, and substernal chest discomfort. Meningitis occurs in up to 50% of persons. Rapid clinical deterioration leads to shock and death. Diagnosis is made by culture or polymerase chain reaction (PCR) of blood, tissues, or fluid samples. Radiographic imaging reveals a widened mediastinum (Figure 15 panel D).

Treatment is outlined in **Table 40**. Toxin-neutralizing human monoclonal antibodies and anthrax immune globulin are approved for treatment and prevention of inhalation anthrax in conjunction with antibiotics. Postexposure prophylaxis consists of a fluoroquinolone or doxycycline in conjunction with vaccination.

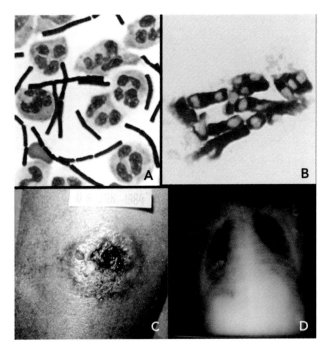

FIGURE 15. *A*, "box-car"-shaped, gram-positive *Bacillus anthracis* bacilli in the cerebrospinal fluid of the index case of inhalational anthrax resulting from bioterrorism in the United States; *B*, terminal and subterminal spores of *B. anthracis*; *C*, black eschar lesion of cutaneous anthrax; *D*, chest radiograph of a patient with anthrax showing a widened mediastinum caused by hemorrhagic lymphadenopathy.

KEY POINTS

- Any case of inhalation anthrax should be considered potential bioterrorism.
- Patients with inhalational anthrax infection present with malaise, myalgia, fever, cough, dyspnea, and substernal chest discomfort; radiographic imaging reveals a widened mediastinum.

Smallpox (Variola)

Routine smallpox vaccination ceased in 1980, after the World Health Organization declared the disease eradicated, leaving much of the world's population without immunity. Following inhalation, multiplication in regional lymph nodes results in viremia.

Secondary viremia occurs 1 week later, accompanied by fever, systemic symptoms, and rash, beginning with lesions on the oral mucosa and face and then the arms, legs, hands and feet, and to a lesser extent the trunk. Lesions evolve synchronously (same stage of maturation on any one area of the body) from macules to papules to vesicles to pustules before eventually crusting (**Figure 16**). Patients remain contagious until all scabs and crusts are shed. Mortality ranges from 15% to 50%.

Treatment is listed in Table 40. The oral antiviral agent tecovirimat was approved in 2018 for the treatment of smallpox in the event of a potential outbreak. Vaccination within

TABLE 39.	Potential Agents of Bioterrorism	
Class A[a]	**Class B**[b]	**Class C**[c]
Anthrax	Q fever	Emerging infectious diseases
Botulism	Brucellosis	
Plague	Glanders	Nipah virus
Smallpox	Melioidosis	Hantavirus
Tularemia	Viral encephalitis	
Viral hemorrhagic fever	Typhus fever	
	Ricin toxin	
	Staphylococcal enterotoxin B	
	Psittacosis	
	Foodborne illness	
	Waterborne illness	

[a]Greatest potential for use in an attack, easy dissemination, high mortality, and profound public health implications.

[b]Less easily spread, fewer illnesses and deaths, fewer public health preparation measures required.

[c]Potential to be engineered for future mass dissemination and significant mortality.

TABLE 40. Class A Bioterrorism Agents

Disease—Agent	Incubation Period	Clinical Features	Treatment	Prophylaxis
Anthrax—*Bacillus anthracis*	1-60 days	Inhalational: febrile respiratory distress Cutaneous: necrotic eschar Gastrointestinal: distention, peritonitis	Ciprofloxacin, levofloxacin, moxifloxacin, or doxycycline plus one or two additional agents[a] for 60 days Consider raxibacumab, obiltoxaximab, or intravenous anthrax immune globulin	Ciprofloxacin, levofloxacin, moxifloxacin, or doxycycline Amoxicillin if penicillin-sensitive strain
Smallpox virus—variola virus	7-17 days	Fever followed by pustular cutaneous rash (face, followed by upper extremities, lower extremities, and trunk)	Tecovirimat	Vaccine if exposure occurred in the previous 7 days
Plague—*Yersinia pestis*	1-6 days	Fulminant pneumonia and sepsis	Streptomycin or gentamicin for 7 to 10 days Alternatives: doxycycline or levofloxacin if aminoglycosides contraindicated	Doxycycline or levofloxacin for 7 days
Botulism—*Clostridium botulinum*	2 hours to 8 days	Cranial nerve palsies and descending flaccid paralysis	Antitoxin and supportive care	Antibotulinum antitoxin (equine serum heptavalent botulism toxin)
Tularemia—*Francisella tularensis*	3-5 days	Fever, respiratory distress, and sepsis	Streptomycin or gentamicin (severe disease) for 7 to 14 days Doxycycline or ciprofloxacin (nonsevere disease) for 14 days	Doxycycline or ciprofloxacin
Viral hemorrhagic fevers—Ebola and Marburg viruses	Variable	Hemorrhage and multiorgan failure	Supportive care	None available

[a]Penicillin, ampicillin, imipenem, meropenem, clindamycin, linezolid, rifampin, vancomycin, or clarithromycin.

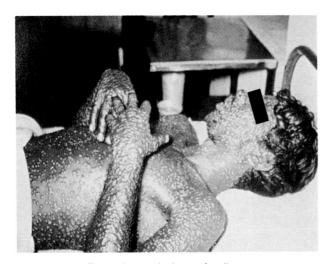

FIGURE 16. Diffuse synchronous skin lesions of smallpox.

7 days of potential exposure is effective in preventing or lessening disease severity and should be provided to close contacts. Intravenous vaccinia immune globulin is indicated in certain vaccinia-related complications or when vaccination is contraindicated.

KEY POINT

• Smallpox viremia results in fever and systemic symptoms, followed by lesions on the oral mucosa, then the face, and then the arms, legs, hands and feet, and to a lesser extent the trunk.

Plague

Primary pneumonic plague occurs after *Yersinia pestis* (**Figure 17**) exposure through infectious aerosols and person-to-person transmission through respiratory droplets, which are likely scenarios for bioterrorism. Patients with suspected pneumonic plague require droplet precautions.

Bubonic plague is characterized by lymphadenopathy (buboes), fever, rigors, and headache. Chest radiographs are nonspecific. Gram stain and cultures of sputum and blood (performed using the highest level biosafety procedures) are often diagnostic.

Untreated, pneumonic plague is uniformly fatal. Treatment is outlined in Table 40. Asymptomatic persons exposed to aerosolized *Y. pestis* and close contacts of infected patients within the previous 7 days warrant postexposure

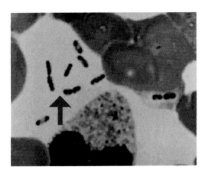

FIGURE 17. This Wright-Giemsa stain shows *Yersinia pestis*, a gram-negative coccobacillus with a "safety-pin" appearance (bipolar staining pattern).

prophylaxis. The available vaccine is ineffective at protecting against pneumonic plague. A live attenuated vaccine with protection from respiratory challenge is under investigation.

KEY POINTS

- Primary pneumonic plague occurs after *Yersinia pestis* exposure through infectious aerosols and person-to-person transmission through respiratory droplets, which are likely scenarios for bioterrorism.

- Asymptomatic persons exposed to aerosolized *Yersinia pestis* and close contacts of infected patients within the previous 7 days warrant postexposure prophylaxis with levofloxacin or doxycycline.

Botulism

Botulism may spread in a bioterrorism attack through inhalation or ingestion of botulinum neurotoxin after deliberate aerosol release or purposeful food contamination. Patients present with symmetric, descending flaccid paralysis with prominent bulbar signs (the "4 Ds": diplopia, dysarthria, dysphonia, and dysphagia), which may progress to respiratory failure. Patients remain afebrile and mental status remains normal, but nausea, abdominal pain, and dry mouth often accompany the paralysis. Autonomic dysfunction may also occur.

Diagnosis depends on identifying the toxin from serum, vomitus, stool, gastric contents, or foods. Organism isolation is rare. Treatment is supportive (see Table 40). Antitoxin should be obtained from the Centers for Disease Control and Prevention and administered promptly but will not reverse existent paralysis. Antibiotics are not useful.

KEY POINT

- Botulism treatment includes supportive care and early administration of antitoxin, although this will not reverse existent paralysis.

Tularemia

Francisella tularensis transmission to humans occurs by vectors, direct animal contact, and inhalation; person-to-person

spread does not occur. Abrupt onset of fever and respiratory symptoms follow inhalation of even a small inoculum of organisms. Chest radiographs demonstrate infiltrates, hilar lymphadenopathy, and pleural effusions.

Rapid diagnosis relies on serologic, immunohistochemical, and PCR testing; culture of tissues and fluids is low yield and potentially dangerous to laboratory personnel. Treatment is noted in Table 40. Death occurs in less than 4% of treated patients, with mortality rates reaching 30% in untreated pneumonic or typhoidal tularemia. No vaccine is available.

KEY POINT

- Patients with tularemia experience abrupt onset of fever and respiratory symptoms, and chest radiographs demonstrate infiltrates, hilar lymphadenopathy, and pleural effusions.

Viral Hemorrhagic Fever

The Ebola and Marburg viruses are the most likely to be used as biologic weapons. In endemic areas, spread to humans occurs by vectors, contact with bodily fluids, or fomites. Aerosolization is a likely mode of terrorist dissemination. Symptoms of fever, headache, myalgia, abdominal pain, diarrhea, and unexplained bleeding and bruising appear 2 to 21 days after exposure. Disease progression results in maculopapular rash, hemorrhagic diathesis, shock, and multiorgan failure. Mortality rates can reach 90%. Persons are contagious only after symptom onset, but virus may spread by sexual contact in semen for weeks to months after recovery.

Depending on the stage of infection, diagnosis may be confirmed by virus detection in blood or other bodily fluids and tissues, antigen and antibody assays, and PCR. Exposed persons are monitored during the 21-day incubation period, with prompt isolation if symptoms develop. Treatment is supportive (see Table 40). Vaccine and antiviral medications are under development.

KEY POINT

- Symptoms of viral hemorrhagic fever include fever, headache, myalgia, abdominal pain, diarrhea, and unexplained bleeding and bruising, appearing 2 to 21 days after exposure; disease progression results in maculopapular rash, hemorrhagic diathesis, shock, and multiorgan failure.

Travel Medicine
Introduction

Pretravel consultation should occur no less than 4 to 6 weeks before departure. Regularly updated information by country is available on the Centers for Disease Control and Prevention (CDC) and World Health Organization (WHO) websites (http://www.cdc.gov/travel and http://www.who.int/ith).

Travel-related illnesses (mostly febrile, diarrheal, respiratory, and cutaneous infections) are reported in 20% to 60% of returning travelers; many of these are vaccine preventable. Required and recommended pretravel immunizations are listed in **Table 41**. Potentially severe travel-associated infections are listed in **Table 42**, the most significant of which are reviewed here.

Malaria

Malaria is transmitted to humans by the female *Anopheles* mosquito. It is the most common cause of febrile illness in returning travelers, particularly from sub-Saharan Africa and large parts of Asia. Preventive measures include limiting outdoor exposure between dusk and dawn, using insecticide-impregnated bed nets and insect repellents containing 20% N-diethyl-3-methylbensamide (DEET), and using antimalarial chemoprophylaxis.

Incubation periods vary by species and range from 1 week to 3 months in semi-immune persons or those taking inadequate prophylaxis. Symptoms include fever (characteristically paroxysms in 48- or 72-hour cycles), headache, myalgia, and gastrointestinal symptoms. More severe disease occurs with hyperparasitemia (5%-10% parasitized erythrocytes) leading to adherence in small blood vessels causing infarcts, capillary leakage, and multiorgan system dysfunction. Serious disease primarily occurs with *Plasmodium falciparum*; manifestations include mental status alterations, seizures, hepatic failure, disseminated intravascular coagulation, brisk intravascular hemolysis, metabolic acidosis, kidney disease, hemoglobinuria, and hypoglycemia. Subsequently, patients may develop anemia, thrombocytopenia, splenomegaly, and elevated aminotransferase levels. See **Table 43** for specific features of the five *Plasmodium* species.

Diagnosis is made by identification of malarial parasites on the peripheral blood smear. Morphologic features help determine the specific species. Rapid tests that detect malaria antigens are available but may lack sensitivity and specificity. Polymerase chain reaction (PCR) and serologic assays exist, although each has limitations.

It is critical to identify *P. falciparum* and *P. knowlesi* because of their potential for severe infection. The onset of malarial symptoms shortly after returning from travel to endemic zones, such as Africa, and recognition of a high level of parasitemia and distinctive morphologic characteristics (**Figure 18**) should raise suspicion for *P. falciparum* infection. *P. knowlesi* is an emerging human pathogen found in South and Southeast Asia; high levels of parasitemia may occur, and examination of the peripheral blood smear reveals all stages of the parasite.

Malarial chemoprophylaxis and treatment depend on possible drug resistance and individual contraindications to specific medications (**Table 44** on page 61 and **Table 45** on page 62). Additional detailed information about malaria is provided in the CDC Yellow Book (https://wwwnc.cdc.gov/travel/yellowbook/2018/infectious-diseases-related-to-travel/malaria) or by calling the CDC malaria hotline (855-856-4713).

KEY POINTS

- Malaria is the most common cause of febrile illness in returning travelers; symptoms include fever, headache, myalgia, and gastrointestinal symptoms.

- The onset of malarial symptoms shortly after returning from travel to endemic zones, such as Africa, and recognition of a high level of parasitemia and distinctive morphologic characteristics should raise suspicion for *Plasmodium falciparum* infection.

Typhoid (Enteric) Fever

Salmonella typhi and *Salmonella paratyphi* (A, B, and C) cause prolonged febrile and often serious infection (typhoid fever). Infection is acquired by consuming food or water contaminated by organisms shed in the stool of infected humans.

TABLE 41. Immunizations for Travel[a]
Recommended According to Destination, Itinerary, and Purpose of Travel
Hepatitis A[b]: 1 month before travel, booster at 6-18 months
Hepatitis B[b]: 0, 1 month, 6 months; accelerated schedule: 0, 1 week, 3 weeks, and 12 months (combination vaccine with hepatitis A available)
Typhoid[c]: Live-attenuated oral vaccine (Ty21a); 0, 2 days, 4 days, 6 days; capsular Vi polysaccharide intramuscular vaccine; 1 dose (preferred for immunocompromised persons)
Cholera: Live oral, 10 days before travel; killed oral, whole-cell-B subunit; 0, 1 week (available outside the United States)
Rabies: Inactivated; 0, 7 days, 21-28 days
Japanese encephalitis: Inactivated; 0, 28 days
Tick-borne encephalitis: Inactivated; 0, 1-3 months, 9-12 months (not available in the United States)
Required for Certain Destinations
Yellow fever: Live attenuated; 1 dose
Meningococcal: Quadrivalent conjugate (MenACWY) or polysaccharide (MPSV4); 1 dose; travel to Saudi Arabia during the Hajj
Meningococcal B (MenB); 2 or 3 doses; high-risk groups

[a]All patients being evaluated for travel should receive or be up to date with all scheduled immunizations, including influenza, pneumococcal, tetanus-diphtheria-pertussis, polio, varicella, and zoster vaccines. See MKSAP 18 General Internal Medicine for routine adult immunization recommendations.

[b]If not received as part of routine scheduled immunizations. If the vaccine series was completed as part of scheduled immunization, repeat immunization is not required.

[c]Oral vaccine should not be administered within 24 hours of the antimalarial drug mefloquine because of the potential to decrease the vaccine's immunogenicity; patients must not take any antibiotic for at least 72 hours before receiving the vaccine.

Data from the Centers for Disease Control and Prevention. CDC Yellow Book 2018: Health Information for International Travel. New York: Oxford University Press; 2017. Available online at https://wwwnc.cdc.gov/travel/yellowbook/2018/.

TABLE 42. Travel-Associated Infections

Condition	Clinical Clues
Febrile Illnesses	
Malaria	Paroxysmal fever (every 48 or 72 hours, depending on the species and may be continuous with *Plasmodium falciparum*), intraerythrocytic parasites, thrombocytopenia
Dengue fever	Acute onset of fever with chills, biphasic fever pattern ("saddleback"), frontal headache, lumbosacral pain, extensor surface petechiae
Chikungunya fever	Fever (abrupt onset up to 40 °C [104 °F] with rigors with recrudescent episodes), rash, and small joint polyarthritis
Zika virus	Mosquito exposure in endemic areas; nonspecific symptoms of fever, rash, joint pain, and/or conjunctivitis (asymptomatic in up to 80% of persons)
Typhoid fever	Prolonged fever, pulse-temperature dissociation, diarrhea or constipation, faint salmon-colored macules on the abdomen and trunk ("rose spots")
Rickettsial infection	Tick or flea exposure, maculopapular or petechial rash, eschar, lymphadenopathy, fever
Coxiella infection (Q fever)	Animal contact, self-limited febrile illness common, atypical pneumonia, elevated aminotransferase levels
Yellow fever	Abrupt fever with periods of remission, bradycardia, jaundice, kidney injury, hemorrhage
Viral hepatitis	High fever initially, then low-grade fever, fatigue and anorexia, hepatomegaly, dark urine, clay-colored stools
Mononucleosis syndrome (cytomegalovirus and Epstein-Barr virus)	Sore throat, fever, cervical lymphadenopathy, splenomegaly, atypical lymphocytes, elevated aminotransferase levels
Brucellosis	Zoonotic exposure, waxing and waning (undulant) fever, arthralgia, hepatosplenomegaly, depression
Leptospirosis	Conjunctival suffusion (erythema without inflammatory exudates), calf and lumbar spine muscle tenderness, aseptic meningitis, jaundice, kidney failure, acute high remittent fever in initial septicemic phase with brief decline before second immune phase
Lyme disease	Flu-like syndrome, target skin lesions (erythema migrans) may be accompanied by fever, arthralgias, bilateral Bell palsy
Histoplasmosis	Nonproductive cough, chest pain, fever
Legionellosis	Pneumonia, diarrhea, dry cough, progressive dyspnea, lymphopenia, thrombocytopenia, elevated aminotransferase and lactate dehydrogenase levels
Novel coronaviruses (severe acute respiratory syndrome [SARS], Middle East respiratory syndrome [MERS-CoV])	Flu-like syndrome prodrome, diarrhea, dry cough with progressive dyspnea, lymphopenia, thrombocytopenia, elevated lactate dehydrogenase levels
Japanese encephalitis	High fever, altered mentation, cranial nerve palsies
Hemorrhagic fever viruses (Ebola, Marburg, and Lassa)	Fever, malaise, myalgia, vomiting, diarrhea, coagulation disorders, and bleeding
Rabies	Paresthesias or pain at wound site, fever, nausea and vomiting, hydrophobia, delirium, agitation
Travelers' Diarrhea	
Bacterial agents: *Escherichia coli*, *Campylobacter* species, *Salmonella* species, *Vibrio* species, *Shigella* species	Abrupt onset, crampy diarrhea, blood in stools
Viral agents: rotavirus, norovirus	Closed setting (such as cruise ship or classroom) acquisition, vomiting, diarrhea, short duration
Protozoa: *Cryptosporidium* species, microsporidia, *Giardia* species, *Entamoeba histolytica*, and *Isospora* species	Gradual onset, progressive and prolonged diarrhea, foul-smelling and greasy stools, mucus or visible blood in stools

Travel to South, East, and Southeast Asia (Indian subcontinent) and portions of sub-Saharan Africa pose the greatest risk of infection. Unlike other nontyphoidal *Salmonella* (see Infectious Gastrointestinal Syndromes), the causative agents of enteric fever are human-only pathogens. Oral and parenteral vaccines (see Table 41) afford temporary protective immunity in 50% to 80% of recipients.

The gradual onset of fever with headache, arthralgia, myalgia, pharyngitis, and anorexia follows a 1- to 2-week incubation period. Abdominal pain and tenderness can be

TABLE 43. Characteristics of *Plasmodium* Species

Characteristics	P. vivax	P. ovale	P. malariae	P. falciparum	P. knowlesi
Incubation period	10-30 days	10-20 days	15-35 days	8-25 days	Indeterminate
Geographic distribution	Tropical and temperate zones	West Africa and Southeast Asia	Tropical zones	Tropical and temperate zones	South and Southeast Asia
Parasitemia	Low	Low	Very low	High	Can be high
Risk for disease severity	Low risk	Low risk	Very low risk	High risk	High risk
Disease relapse risk	Yes	Yes	Yes	No	No
Chloroquine resistance	Yes	No	Rare	Yes	No

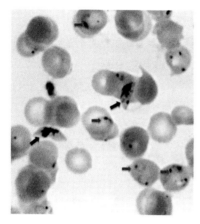

FIGURE 18. Thin, often multiple rings (*blue arrows*) on the inner surface of young and old erythrocytes as well as banana-shaped gametocytes (*black arrows*) are distinctive morphologic characteristics of *Plasmodium falciparum* species.

accompanied by early-onset diarrhea, which may spontaneously resolve or become severe late in disease. One fifth of patients have constipation at diagnosis. In untreated illness, temperature progressively increases and may remain elevated (up to 40 °C [104 °F]) for 4 to 8 weeks. A pulse-temperature dissociation (relative bradycardia) and prostration are common. During the second week of illness, discrete, blanching, 1- to 4-mm salmon-colored macules, known as rose spots (**Figure 19**, on page 63) develop in crops on the chest and abdomen in about 20% of patients. Moderate hepatosplenomegaly, leukopenia, anemia, thrombocytopenia, and elevated aminotransferase levels are common. Secondary bacteremia may cause pyogenic complications such as empyema, muscle abscess, and endovascular infections. Intestinal hemorrhage or perforation may occur 2 to 3 weeks after infection onset. Encephalopathy occurs in more severe cases.

Invasion of the gallbladder by typhoid bacilli may result in a long-term carrier state with shedding of organisms in the stool for more than 1 year. Those with gallstones and chronic biliary disease are at greatest risk.

Diagnosis is made through isolation of *S. typhi* or *S. para-typhi* from blood, stool, urine, or bone marrow; isolation success declines after the first week of illness. Rapid serologic tests are available to distinguish *Salmonella enterica* serotype *typhi* antibodies.

Antibiotic treatment decreases mortality and shortens the duration of fever. The emergence of antibiotic resistance in many geographic areas necessitates that in vitro susceptibility testing be performed on all clinical isolates. Ceftriaxone, fluoroquinolones, and azithromycin are preferred treatments. Dexamethasone has been shown to decrease mortality in severe illness, such as in patients with shock and encephalopathy. A 28-day course of ciprofloxacin is effective in eradicating chronic carriage, although cholecystectomy may be needed in cases of cholelithiasis.

KEY POINTS

- Typhoid fever commonly presents with fever, headache, arthralgia, myalgia, pharyngitis, anorexia, abdominal pain with early-onset diarrhea, pulse-temperature dissociation (relative bradycardia), and prostration.

- Ceftriaxone, fluoroquinolones, and azithromycin are preferred treatments for typhoid fever; dexamethasone decreases mortality in severe disease, such as patients with shock and encephalopathy.

Travelers' Diarrhea

The most common travel-associated infection is diarrhea, defined by the sudden onset of three or more loose or watery stools per day with at least one additional gastrointestinal or systemic clinical sign or symptom (fever, cramps, nausea, abdominal pain, or blood in the stools). Risk factors, including geographic location (greatest in South and Southeast Asia, sub-Saharan Africa, the Middle East, and Latin America), type and duration of travel, and host characteristics, contribute to the 30% to 60% occurrence rate.

Most travelers' diarrhea episodes occur within the first 2 weeks of travel. Episodes are usually self-limited, lasting approximately 4 days; however, life-threatening volume depletion or severe colitis with systemic manifestations can occur. Some travelers develop chronic diarrhea or a postinfective irritable bowel syndrome.

TABLE 44.	Antimalarial Chemoprophylaxis Regimens		
Drug	**Dose**	**Time of Prophylaxis Initiation (before Travel)**	**Time of Prophylaxis Discontinuation (after Returning)**
For endemic areas with chloroquine-resistant *Plasmodium falciparum*			
Atovaquone/proguanil[a]	250 mg/100 mg once daily	1-2 days	7 days
Mefloquine	250 mg once weekly	1-2 weeks	4 weeks
Doxycycline[a]	100 mg once daily	1-2 days	4 weeks
For endemic areas with chloroquine and mefloquine-resistant *P. falciparum*[b]			
Atovaquone/proguanil	250 mg/100 mg once daily	1-2 days	7 days
Doxycycline	100 mg once daily	1-2 days	4 weeks
For endemic areas with chloroquine-sensitive *P. falciparum*			
Chloroquine	500 mg once weekly	1-2 weeks	4 weeks
Hydroxychloroquine	400 mg once weekly	1-2 weeks	4 weeks
Atovaquone/proguanil	250/100 mg once daily	1-2 days	7 days
Mefloquine	250 mg once weekly	2 weeks	4 weeks
Doxycycline	100 mg once daily	1-2 days	4 weeks
Primaquine	26.3 mg once daily	1-2 days	1 week
For endemic areas with *Plasmodium vivax*			
Primaquine[c]	52.6 mg once daily	1-2 days	1 week
Chloroquine	500 mg once weekly	1-2 days	4 weeks
Hydroxychloroquine	400 mg once weekly	1-2 days	4 weeks
Atovaquone/proguanil	250/100 mg once daily	1-2 days	7 days
Mefloquine	250 mg once weekly	2 weeks	4 weeks
Doxycycline	100 mg once daily	1-2 days	4 weeks
Prophylaxis for relapse due to *P. vivax* or *Plasmodium ovale*			
Primaquine	52.6 mg once daily	As soon as possible	2 weeks

[a]Should not be used in pregnant women.

[b]Borders of Thailand with Cambodia and Myanmar (Burma).

[c]Contraindicated in persons with severe forms of glucose-6-phosphate dehydrogenase deficiency or methemoglobin reductase deficiency; should not be administered to pregnant women.

Recommendations from the Centers for Disease Control and Prevention. CDC Yellow Book 2018: Health Information for International Travel. New York: Oxford University Press; 2017. Available online at https://wwwnc.cdc.gov/travel/yellowbook/2018/infectious-diseases-related-to-travel/malaria.

Enterotoxigenic *Escherichia coli* is the most common causative agent (see Table 42). Younger age, use of gastric acid–reducing medications, abnormal gastrointestinal motility or altered anatomy, O blood type, and other genetic factors increase risk. Immunocompromised travelers may experience more serious and protracted illness with typical pathogens and are more prone to infection with opportunistic infectious agents. Chronic gastrointestinal conditions (such as inflammatory bowel disease) do not increase risk of infection but do predispose travelers to more severe symptoms.

Pretravel advice includes avoiding consumption of tap water (through drinks, ice, or when brushing teeth), undercooked meats, unpasteurized dairy products, and fruits that are not peeled just before eating. Water disinfection can be accomplished by boiling for 3 minutes or by chemical means using chlorine and iodine. Two drops of sodium hypochlorite (bleach) or five drops of tincture of iodine per liter of water are equally effective. Commercial water filters are not as dependable.

Antimicrobial prophylaxis for travelers' diarrhea is effective but is generally not recommended because of the potential for adverse effects. Prophylaxis should be considered in persons with coexisting inflammatory bowel disease, immunocompromised states (including advanced HIV), and comorbidities that would be adversely affected by significant dehydration. Bismuth subsalicylate can be used to prevent diarrhea, but the doses required are inconvenient and can lead to salicylate toxicity. Probiotics have not been proven

TABLE 45. Malaria Treatment Regimens[a]	
Drug	**Dose and Duration**
Non-*falciparum* Species[b]	
Chloroquine phosphate (500 mg)	1000 mg, then 500 mg at 6, 24, and 48 h
Hydroxychloroquine (400 mg)	800 mg, then 400 mg at 6, 24, and 48 h
***Plasmodium falciparum* or Species Not Identified**	
Acquired in chloroquine-sensitive area	
Chloroquine phosphate (500 mg) or Hydroxychloroquine (400 mg)	Same as for non-*falciparum* species
Acquired in chloroquine-resistant area	
Atovaquone-proguanil (250 mg/100 mg)	4 tabs daily (or 2 tabs twice/d) for 3 d
Artemether-lumefantrine[c] (20 mg/120 mg)	4 tabs at 0, 8, 24, 36, 48, and 60 h
Quinine sulfate (325 mg) plus one of the following:	2 tabs (650 mg) three times/d for 3 or 7 d[d]
Doxycycline (100 mg)	100 mg twice/d for 7 d
Tetracycline (250 mg)	250 mg four times/d for 7 d
Clindamycin (300 mg)	20 mg base/kg/d divided three times/d for 7 d
Mefloquine[e] (250 mg)	3 tabs (750 mg), then 2 tabs (500 mg) in 6-12 h
Acquired in mefloquine-resistant area[f]	
Atovaquone-proguanil or Quinine sulfate plus doxycycline or tetracycline or clindamycin	Same as above
Relapse prevention (infection *with Plasmodium vivax* or *Plasmodium ovale*)	
Primaquine phosphate[g] (15 mg)	2 tabs daily for 14 d
Treatment in pregnant women	
Chloroquine-sensitive species: Chloroquine phosphate (500 mg)	Same as above
P. vivax and *P. ovale* relapse prevention: Chloroquine phosphate (500 mg)	Once weekly until after delivery
Chloroquine-resistant *P. falciparum*[h]: Quinine sulfate plus clindamycin or mefloquine	Same as above
Treatment of severe disease (acquired in all malarial areas)	
Quinidine gluconate	Initial 10 mg/kg IV over 1-2 h, then 0.02 mg/kg/min continuous IV for at least 24 h until parasitemia ≤1% and oral medications can be tolerated
Artesunate[i] (parenteral)	2.4 mg/kg IV at 0, 12, 24, and 48 h

IV = intravenous.

[a]Patients who develop malaria while receiving prophylaxis should be treated with a different drug regimen.

[b]*P. vivax* acquired in Papua New Guinea or Indonesia should be considered chloroquine resistant.

[c]Artemisin-based combination therapies (ACTs) are the most rapid and effective therapies and active against all malarial species. Artemether-lumefantrine is the only approved ACT in the United States.

[d]Seven-day duration is indicated if infection was acquired in Southeast Asia.

[e]Increased risk of neuropsychiatric reactions; not recommended for *P. falciparum* infection acquired in Southeast Asia because of drug resistance.

[f]Found on the eastern border of Myanmar (Burma) and adjacent parts of China, Laos, and Thailand; western border of Thailand and adjacent parts of Cambodia and Laos; and southern Vietnam.

[g]Confirm absence of glucose-6-phosphate dehydrogenase deficiency in patient. Not indicated in pregnant women.

[h]Atovaquone-proguanil and artemether-lumefantrine are generally not recommended for use in pregnant women. Doxycycline and tetracycline are not indicated in pregnancy.

[i]Available in the United States from the CDC under an investigational new drug protocol; www.CDC.gov/malaria (call 770-448-7100).

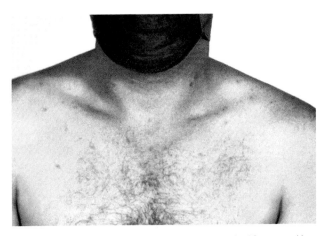

FIGURE 19. Rose spots on the chest of a patient with typhoid fever caused by the bacterium *Salmonella typhi*.

Reproduced from the CDC Public Health Image Library.

effective in the prevention of travelers' diarrhea and are not recommended.

Fluid replacement is the mainstay of treatment. Antimicrobials reduce the duration of diarrhea by 1 to 2 days but are recommended only in severe disease (**Table 46**). Self-treatment with a fluoroquinolone, azithromycin (preferred in South and Southeast Asia), or rifaximin is usually sufficient. Bismuth subsalicylate in large doses can be beneficial in decreasing the frequency and duration of diarrhea in milder cases. Antimotility drugs such as loperamide and diphenoxylate should only be given in conjunction with antimicrobial

therapy but should not be used in cases of dysentery or bloody diarrhea because of increased risk of colitis and colonic perforation.

KEY POINTS

- Fluid replacement is the mainstay of treatment for travelers' diarrhea; fluoroquinolones, azithromycin (preferred in South and Southeast Asia), and rifaximin reduce the duration of diarrhea by 1 to 2 days but are recommended only in severe disease.

- Antimicrobial prophylaxis for travelers' diarrhea is generally not recommended; however, prophylaxis should be considered in persons with coexisting inflammatory bowel disease, immunocompromised states (including advanced HIV), and comorbidities that would be adversely affected by significant dehydration.

HVC

Dengue Fever, Chikungunya, and Zika

Arboviruses are spread by arthropod vectors. Mosquitoes spread most travel-related arboviral diseases. Some arboviruses, such as yellow fever, are endemic throughout the tropics, and several countries require proof of vaccination before allowing entry by travelers. Other viruses, such as Japanese encephalitis, have more restricted geographic areas. The dengue fever, chikungunya, and Zika arboviruses are all spread by *Aedes* species mosquitoes and will be discussed here (**Table 47**).

Dengue fever is the most prevalent arthropod-borne viral infection in the world. Endemic areas include Southeast Asia, the South Pacific, South and Central America, and the Caribbean. The incubation period is 4 to 7 days. Patients may be asymptomatic or present with an acute febrile illness associated with frontal headache, retro-orbital pain, myalgia, and arthralgia, with or without minor spontaneous bleeding. Gastrointestinal or respiratory symptoms may predominate. Severe lumbosacral pain is characteristic. As the fever abates, a macular or

TABLE 46.	Oral Treatment and Prophylaxis for Travelers' Diarrhea
Agent	**Regimen**
Treatment	
Bismuth subsalicylate	1 oz every 30 min for 8 doses
Norfloxacin	400 mg twice daily for 3 d
Ciprofloxacin	500 mg twice daily for 3 d
Ofloxacin	200 mg twice daily for 3 d
Levofloxacin	500 mg once daily for 3 d
Azithromycin	1000 mg, single dose
Rifaximin	200 mg three times daily for 3 d
Prophylaxis	
Bismuth subsalicylate	Two tablets chewed 4 times daily
Norfloxacin	400 mg daily[a]
Ciprofloxacin	500 mg daily[a]
Rifaximin	200 mg once or twice daily[a]

[a]Chemoprophylaxis is recommended for no more than 2 to 3 weeks (the duration studied in trials and a period short enough to minimize the risk for antimicrobial-associated adverse effects).

Source: Hill DR, Ericsson CD, Pearson RD, Keystone JS, Freedman DO, Kozarsky PE, et al; Infectious Diseases Society of America. The practice of travel medicine: guidelines by the Infectious Diseases Society of America. Clin Infect Dis. 2006;43: 1499-539. [PMID: 17109284]

TABLE 47.	Important Clinical Distinguishing Features of Arbovirus Infection		
Clinical Finding	**Dengue**	**Chikungunya**	**Zika**
Fever	+++	+++	++
Myalgia	++	+	+
Arthralgia	+	+++	++
Headache	++	++	+
Conjunctivitis	−	−	++
Rash	+	++	+++
Bleeding	++	−	−
Shock	+	−	−

+++ = always; ++ = common; + = rare; − = almost never

scarlatiniform rash, which spares the palms and soles, may develop and evolve into areas of petechiae on extensor surfaces (**Figure 20**). Fever resolves after 5 to 7 days; however, some patients experience a second febrile period (saddleback pattern). A prolonged period of severe fatigue may follow. In patients with severe infection, life-threatening hemorrhage (dengue hemorrhagic fever) or shock may ensue, with liver failure, encephalopathy, and myocardial damage. This syndrome appears to be related to previous infection of a different serotype and is unlikely in travelers who have not had dengue fever previously. Abnormal laboratory findings include leukopenia, thrombocytopenia, and elevated serum aminotransferase levels.

Diagnosis of dengue fever is based on clinical suspicion in a patient who traveled to an endemic area and presents with fever and other typical signs, symptoms, and abnormal laboratory findings. Diagnosis is confirmed by serology (IgM and IgG) or reverse transcriptase PCR. Therapy is supportive. No licensed dengue vaccine is available in the United States, although clinical trials are ongoing. A live attenuated tetravalent vaccine, CYD-TDV, which is recommended for use only in persons previously infected by dengue virus, is available in several countries outside the United States.

Historically, chikungunya virus was limited to Southeast Asia and Africa but has recently emerged in the Americas, with outbreaks in Central and South America and the Caribbean. No vaccine is available. Symptoms resemble dengue fever, including abrupt onset of fever (≥39.0 °C [102.2 °F]) and severe bilateral and symmetrical polyarthralgia, often involving the hands and feet. A maculopapular rash on the limbs and trunk is common. Rarely, central nervous system, ophthalmologic, hepatic, and kidney manifestations are present. Abnormal laboratory findings include lymphopenia, thrombocytopenia, and elevated aminotransferase levels. Definitive diagnosis relies on serologic assays or detection of viral RNA by reverse transcriptase PCR testing. Disease is generally self-limited, resolving in 7 to 10 days. However, some patients may experience relapsing and chronic rheumatologic

symptoms for months or even years. Symptomatic treatment includes NSAIDs and aspirin avoidance (risk of bleeding complications and potential risk of Reye syndrome in children).

Before the 2015 Zika virus epidemic in Central and South America, human infection occurred chiefly in Africa, Southeast Asia, and the Pacific Islands. More than 5600 infections have been reported in the United States since the epidemic, of which greater than 225 are presumed to be from local transmission (Florida and Texas) and 55 acquired by sexual or laboratory transmission. This flavivirus is closely related to dengue, yellow fever, and Japanese encephalitis viruses. Intrauterine and perinatal maternal-fetal spread and sexual transmission from an infected male partner are other less common modes of transmission. An estimated 18% of those infected demonstrate clinical symptoms, which are similar to dengue and chikungunya virus infections, with the additional finding of conjunctivitis in most Zika infections. Most patients recover uneventfully after a mild illness lasting about 1 week, but some develop Guillain-Barré syndrome. Of most concern are risks to fetal development in pregnant women infected with Zika, including microcephaly, other severe brain and eye defects, and impaired growth and fetal loss. Women who are pregnant must be advised against travel to areas where Zika virus is known to be present. Likewise, women and men who are planning to conceive in the near future should consider avoiding nonessential travel to areas with risk of Zika infection; it is recommended couples wait to conceive until at least 3 months (for men) or 8 weeks (for women) after the last possible Zika virus exposure or from the onset of symptoms or diagnosis. Those not planning to conceive should use condoms for all forms of sexual activity together with their chosen birth control method or abstain from sex if Zika virus transmission is a concern. All pregnant women should be assessed for possible Zika exposure, and those who return from areas with outbreaks should be screened for evidence of infection. Reverse transcriptase PCR testing on serum and urine is used for diagnostic evaluation during the initial 2 weeks after illness onset. Thereafter, IgM antibody detection is used. Virus-specific plaque reduction neutralization tests can discriminate between Zika virus and cross-reacting antibodies against related flaviviruses. Because the epidemiology of Zika infection in the United States is still evolving, women who are pregnant and those who are planning to conceive should consult the CDC website for the most updated information when considering travel. No specific medications are available for treating Zika virus. Active vaccine development is ongoing.

KEY POINTS

- Dengue fever typically presents with acute febrile illness, frontal headache, retro-orbital pain, myalgia, and arthralgia, with or without minor spontaneous bleeding; gastrointestinal or respiratory symptoms may predominate, and severe lumbosacral pain is characteristic.

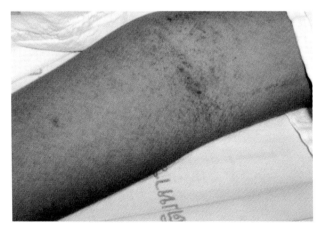

FIGURE 20. Petechial rash following application of blood pressure cuff constituting a positive "tourniquet test" that supports the presence of microvascular fragility compatible with dengue fever.

(Continued)

- Symptoms of chikungunya resemble dengue fever, including abrupt onset of fever (≥39.0 °C [102.2 °F]) and severe bilateral and symmetrical polyarthralgia, often involving the hands and feet; a maculopapular rash on the limbs and trunk is common.

- Of most concern in Zika virus infection is the risk to fetal development in infected pregnant women, including microcephaly, other severe brain and eye defects, impaired growth, and fetal loss.

Hepatitis Virus Infections

Hepatitis A virus (HAV) infection is acquired through ingestion of food and water contaminated with fecal waste from another infected human in geographic areas with poor sanitation practices. Travel to Central and South America, Mexico, South Asia, and Africa poses the greatest risk of infection (for further information, see MKSAP 18 Gastroenterology and Hepatology).

Hepatitis A vaccination is recommended for persons traveling to developing countries who are not already immune (see Table 41). Protective antibody titers develop within 2 to 4 weeks in almost 100% of healthy recipients. A booster dose is given 6 to 12 months after the initial injection and provides protection for at least 10 years. Serum immune globulin is indicated for persons aged 12 months or younger and for those who decline vaccination or are allergic to its components. It has also been recommended for immunocompromised persons (who are less responsive to hepatitis A vaccine) and patients with chronic liver disease. Concurrent administration of hepatitis A vaccine and immune globulin is no longer recommended for those planning to depart within 2 weeks.

The risk for travel-associated acquisition of hepatitis B virus (HBV) is low. Previously unvaccinated persons traveling as health care workers, seeking medical care, or likely to engage in sexual activity with local residents in countries where HBV is prevalent warrant pretravel vaccination. Persons with insufficient time before travel to receive the standard three-dose/6-month vaccination series can complete an accelerated vaccination schedule (0, 7, and 21-30 days); these persons require a booster dose at 12 months to ensure long-term protection. A combined hepatitis A/B vaccine is also available for this rapid three-dose schedule.

No vaccine prevents hepatitis C virus infection, and immune globulin offers no protection (see MKSAP 18 Gastroenterology and Hepatology).

KEY POINTS

- Protective hepatitis A antibody titers develop within 2 to 4 weeks following vaccination in almost 100% of healthy recipients; concurrent administration of hepatitis A vaccine and immune globulin is no longer recommended for those planning to depart within 2 weeks.

(Continued)

- Persons with insufficient time before travel to receive the standard three-dose/6-month hepatitis B vaccination series can complete an accelerated vaccination schedule (0, 7, and 21-30 days), which is also available in a combined hepatitis A/B vaccine; these persons require a booster dose at 12 months to ensure long-term protection.

Rickettsial Infection

Rickettsial infections occur worldwide. They usually belong to the typhus or spotted fever groups and are transmitted by small vectors (fleas, lice, mites, and ticks). Outbreaks have been associated with war and natural disasters and are promoted by suboptimal hygiene conditions and tick infestation. *Rickettsia typhi* is prevalent in tropical and subtropical areas. *Rickettsia prowazeki* is the only rickettsial species transmitted by human body lice and has a worldwide distribution.

Fever is the most common presenting symptom; African tick typhus (*Rickettsia africae*) is second only to malaria as the cause of febrile illness in those who have journeyed to Africa, especially South Africa. Clinical presentation also includes headache, malaise, conjunctivitis, and pharyngitis often accompanied by a maculopapular, vesicular, or petechial rash. Following the bite of an infected tick or mite, an eschar with regional lymphadenopathy develops at the site of inoculation with *R. africae*, *Rickettsia conorii*, and *Orientia tsutsugamushi*. Endothelial damage in the microcirculation leads to increased vascular permeability and is the hallmark of rickettsial infections, with extensive vasculitic-appearing lesions. Severe complications may include shock, meningoencephalitis, and significant damage to the kidneys, lungs, liver, and gastrointestinal tract. Recrudescent attacks designated Brill-Zinsser disease are known to occur months and even years later.

Diagnosis is confirmed by PCR, immunohistochemical analysis of tissue samples, or culture during the acute stage of illness before antibiotics are initiated. Confirmatory serologic assays often do not detect antibodies until the convalescent phase of illness, limiting their utility with acute disease. When clinical suspicion is high, empiric therapy is warranted. The treatment of choice for all rickettsial infections is doxycycline for 7 to 10 days.

KEY POINTS

- Rickettsial infections occur worldwide, with clinical presentation including fever, headache, malaise, conjunctivitis, and pharyngitis often accompanied by a maculopapular, vesicular, or petechial rash.

- The treatment of choice for all rickettsial infections is doxycycline for 7 to 10 days.

Brucellosis

Human brucellosis may follow ingestion of unpasteurized dairy products or undercooked meat, by direct contact with fluids from infected animals through skin wounds or mucous membranes, or by inhalation of contaminated aerosols. *Brucella* is present in animal reservoirs worldwide, but the highest prevalence is found in the Mediterranean countries, Balkans, Persian Gulf, Middle East, and Central and South America. *Brucella melitensis* (from sheep and goats) has the highest pathogenicity and is the leading cause of human brucellosis.

After a variable incubation period, patients develop fever, myalgia, arthralgia, fatigue, headache, and night sweats. Focal infection may occur, commonly affecting the central nervous system and osteoarticular, cardiovascular, and genitourinary systems. Depression is frequent. Hepatosplenomegaly and lymphadenopathy may be apparent on physical examination with granuloma formation in reticuloendothelial tissues and organs. Disease relapse and chronic infection may occur owing to persistent foci of infection or inadequate antibiotic treatment.

Diagnosis relies on isolating the organism from cultures of blood, bone marrow, other body fluids, or tissue. The serum agglutination test is the most widely used available serologic test. An initial elevated titer of 1:160 or greater or demonstration of a fourfold increase from acute to convalescent titers is considered diagnostic. The Rose Bengal slide agglutination test, if available, is a convenient, simple, rapid, and sensitive point-of-care screening test.

The treatment of choice for uncomplicated brucellosis is a combination of doxycycline, rifampin, and streptomycin (or gentamicin), often given for several weeks. Neurobrucellosis requires several months of combined ceftriaxone, doxycycline, and rifampin.

KEY POINT

- The treatment of choice for uncomplicated brucellosis is a combination of doxycycline, rifampin, and streptomycin (or gentamicin), often given for several weeks; neurobrucellosis requires several months of combined ceftriaxone, doxycycline, and rifampin.

Infectious Gastrointestinal Syndromes

Overview

Diarrhea, defined as three or more unformed stools daily or a quantity greater than 250 grams daily, is a major public health concern. Diarrhea lasting less than 14 days is considered acute, 14 to 30 days is persistent, and longer than 30 days is chronic. Acute infectious diarrheal presentations include acute gastroenteritis, with associated fever, nausea, vomiting, flatulence,

tenesmus, and crampy abdominal pain. Chronic infectious diarrhea is most likely due to parasites. Not all diarrheal presentations are infectious, such as inflammatory bowel disease, endocrine disorders, celiac disease, irritable bowel syndrome, and medication-induced diarrhea.

Patients with mucoid or bloody diarrhea, fever, significant abdominal cramping, or suspected sepsis and those who are immunocompromised or require hospitalization should have diagnostic assessment of their stool to guide antimicrobial use. Additional areas of concern include symptoms that persist for longer than 1 week or outbreak settings where day-care participants, institutional residents, health care providers, or food handlers are involved. Increasingly more available, rapid multiplex molecular gastrointestinal assays that identify common bacterial, parasitic, and viral pathogens from a single stool sample are generally more sensitive than historical stool culture and microscopy with special stains. (**Table 48**). Isolates from culture, however, can provide antibiotic susceptibilities and strain-typing information in outbreak situations that are not available from culture-independent diagnostic assays.

Most healthy patients with watery diarrhea of less than 3 days' duration can be treated with supportive care and no antibiotic therapy or diagnostic assessment. When acute diarrhea is debilitating (moderate or severe) and associated with travel, antibiotic therapy with a fluoroquinolone, azithromycin, or rifaximin is recommended. If a patient has dysentery with visible mucus or blood in the stool and a temperature less than 37.8 °C (100 °F), then microbiologic assessment is recommended to guide therapy. When severe debilitating disease is present with temperatures of 38.4 °C (101.1 °F) or greater, microbiologic assessment should be considered, followed by empiric azithromycin treatment (see Table 48). Antimotility agents, such as loperamide, are discouraged in patients with inflammatory diarrhea (fever, abdominal pain, bloody stools) or *Clostridium difficile*-associated infection.

KEY POINTS

- Patients with mucoid or bloody diarrhea, fever, significant abdominal cramping, or suspected sepsis and those who are immunocompromised or require hospitalization should have diagnostic assessment of their stool to guide antimicrobial use; rapid multiplex molecular gastrointestinal assays that identify common bacterial, parasitic, and viral pathogens in stool specimens are generally more sensitive than historical stool culture and microscopy with special stains.

- Most healthy patients with watery diarrhea of less than 3 days' duration can be treated with supportive care and no antibiotic therapy or microscopic assessment; when the illness is debilitating and associated with travel, antibiotic therapy with a fluoroquinolone, azithromycin, or rifaximin is recommended. **HVC**

TABLE 48. Causative Agents, Clinical Presentation, and Management of Infectious Diarrhea

Agent	Clinical Findings	Diagnosis[a]	Antimicrobial Treatment[b]
Bacterial Agent			
Campylobacter	Fevers, chills, diarrhea (watery or bloody), crampy abdominal pain; postinfection Guillain-Barré syndrome, IBS, or reactive arthritis	Standard stool culture or NAAT	Azithromycin; ciprofloxacin (alternative)
Shigella	Dysentery (fevers, abdominal cramps, tenesmus, bloody/mucous-filled stools); postinfection HUS, reactive arthritis or IBS	Routine stool culture or NAAT; blood cultures (with severe disease)	Fluoroquinolone (ciprofloxacin) or azithromycin or ceftriaxone
Salmonella	Fever, chills, diarrhea (watery or bloody), cramps, myalgia; bacteremia in 10%-25% of patients; postinfection reactive arthritis	Routine stool culture or NAAT; blood cultures (moderate to severe disease); bone marrow and duodenal fluid cultures may also be helpful when enteric fever suspected	Mild: none Underlying disease or severe illness: fluoroquinolone (ciprofloxacin) and/or parenteral third-generation cephalosporin
EHEC/STEC, including *Escherichia coli* O157:H7	Bloody stools in >80% of patients; fever often absent or low grade; may be associated with HUS	Stool culture with specialized media and immunoassay for Shiga toxin or NAAT	None
ETEC (travelers' diarrhea)	Nonbloody, watery stools; constitutional symptoms rare	None—usually a clinical diagnosis	Fluoroquinolone, azithromycin, or rifaximin
Yersinia	Fever, diarrhea, right lower quadrant pain (may mimic appendicitis); pharyngitis; postinfection reactive arthritis and erythema nodosum	Stool culture with specialized media (or culture of other involved sites); NAAT	Trimethoprim-sulfamethoxazole Alternatives: a fluoroquinolone (ciprofloxacin) or a third-generation cephalosporin (such as cefotaxime or ceftriaxone) Severe extraintestinal disease: requires a longer treatment duration, including intravenous agents (such as a third-generation cephalosporin)
Vibrio (not *V. cholerae*)	Bloody stools (>25% of patients), fever, vomiting (>50% of patients)	Stool culture with specialized media (blood culture with suspected invasive disease)	Usually no treatment unless invasive Fluoroquinolone (ciprofloxacin), azithromycin, or doxycycline if treating gastrointestinal illness Doxycycline plus ceftriaxone for invasive infection
Clostridium difficile	Diarrhea, fever, abdominal pain/cramping, colonic distention (including toxic megacolon in severe disease), leukocytosis, sepsis; gross blood uncommon	Stool NAAT alone or stool EIA toxin test as part of stepwise approach, including NAAT plus toxin, or GDH plus toxin, or GDH plus toxin followed by NAAT when results are discordant	Nonsevere: oral vancomycin or oral fidaxomicin; if neither is available, oral metronidazole Severe: oral vancomycin or fidaxomicin Fulminant: oral vancomycin, IV metronidazole, and (possibly) vancomycin enema
Viral			
Norovirus	Watery, noninflammatory diarrhea and fever; vomiting in >50% of patients; short incubation period and high attack rate	NAAT, particularly for outbreak investigations	None
Parasitic			
Giardia	Watery diarrhea, abdominal cramping, nausea, steatorrhea, flatulence, weight loss; fever uncommon; postinfection lactose intolerance	EIA or NAAT preferred; stool microscopy for ova and parasites	Tinidazole, nitazoxanide, or metronidazole
Cryptosporidium	Watery diarrhea; abdominal cramping; malaise; weight loss	Modified acid-fast stain; immunoassays; NAAT	Nitazoxanide Effective antiretroviral therapy in patients with HIV infection
Amebiasis	Dysentery, abdominal pain, fever, weight loss	Stool microscopy for ova and parasites; stool antigen immunoassay; NAAT; serologic antibodies	Tinidazole or metronidazole followed by paromomycin or diloxanide
Cyclospora	Watery diarrhea, bloating, flatulence, weight loss, nausea, anorexia	Modified acid-fast stain; fluorescence microscopy; NAAT	Trimethoprim-sulfamethoxazole

EHEC = enterohemorrhagic *E. coli*; EIA = enzyme immunoassay; ETEC = enterotoxigenic *E. coli*; GDH = glutamate dehydrogenase; HUS = hemolytic uremic syndrome; IBS = irritable bowel syndrome; IV = intravenous; NAAT = nucleic acid amplification test; STEC = Shiga toxin-producing *E. coli*.

[a]Multiplex molecular assays are becoming increasingly available for identification of bacterial, parasitic, and viral gastrointestinal pathogens.

[b]Empiric treatment, with the final choice of the antimicrobial agent to use guided by in vitro susceptibility testing.

Campylobacter Infection

Campylobacter species–associated gastroenteritis is usually foodborne, often secondary to consumption of inadequately cooked poultry. The incubation period is several days, and symptoms typically include diarrhea (visibly bloody in <15% of patients), crampy abdominal pain, and fever. Stool culture can confirm the diagnosis, and blood cultures can identify extraintestinal disease. Diarrhea usually resolves spontaneously without antibiotics. Patients who have severe disease (bloody stools, bacteremia, high fever, or prolonged [>1 week] symptoms) or are immunocompromised should receive antibiotic therapy. When indicated, macrolide therapy is preferred empirically because of increasing fluoroquinolone resistance. Possible post–*Campylobacter* infection complications include irritable bowel syndrome, reactive arthritis, and Guillain-Barré syndrome.

KEY POINT

- *Campylobacter* infection-associated diarrhea usually resolves spontaneously without antibiotic therapy; macrolides are the preferred empiric treatment for those who have severe disease or are immunocompromised.

Shigella Infection

Shigella infection is more commonly spread from person to person than by consumption of contaminated food or water. Fewer than 100 bacteria can cause infection, and the incubation period is approximately 3 days. Patients typically present with crampy abdominal pain, tenesmus, small-volume bloody and/or mucoid diarrhea, high fever, and (possibly) vomiting. More serious complications include bacteremia, seizures, and intestinal obstruction and perforation. Potential postinfectious sequelae include hemolytic uremic syndrome, reactive arthritis, and irritable bowel syndrome. Routine stool culture or molecular testing will establish the diagnosis. Invasive disease in patients with severe infection can also be established with blood cultures. Treatment with antibiotic agents is recommended for those with severe illness (that is, those who require hospitalization, have invasive disease, or have complications of infection) and those who are immunocompromised. Public health officials may also recommend treatment when outbreaks occur. Antibiotic susceptibilities should be obtained to determine treatment because of increasing resistance rates against the quinolones.

KEY POINT

- In patients with *Shigella* infection, treatment with antibiotic agents is recommended for those with severe illness (that is, those who require hospitalization, have invasive disease, or have complications of infection) and those who are immunocompromised.

Salmonella Infection

Salmonella infection can be typhoidal (serotypes Paratyphi or Typhi) or nontyphoidal. The typhoidal types cause enteric fever, a syndrome consisting of fever, abdominal pain, rash, hepatosplenomegaly, and relative bradycardia. This type of infection is uncommon in the United States, with most affected persons traveling to endemic areas and ingesting contaminated water or food. In contrast, nontyphoidal *Salmonella* serotypes are the most common bacterial cause of foodborne illness in the United States.

Nontyphoidal *Salmonella* infection usually results from ingesting fecally contaminated water or food of animal origin, including poultry, beef, eggs, and milk. Contact with infected animals (including pet reptiles, turtles, and snakes; farm animals; amphibians; and rodents) is a much less common mode of transmission. The incubation period is usually less than 3 days, and symptoms typically include crampy abdominal pain, fever, diarrhea (not usually visibly bloody), headache, nausea, and vomiting. Diagnosis can be made by stool culture or molecular testing. Illness is usually self-limited, although bacteremia with extraintestinal infection (involving vascular endothelium, joints, or meninges) may occur; *Salmonella* osteomyelitis also can occur and is classically associated with sickle cell disease. Severe invasive disease is more likely in infants, older adults, patients with cell-mediated immunodeficiency, and patients with hypochlorhydria. Reactive arthritis is a potential postinfection complication.

Most uncomplicated *Salmonella* infections in adults younger than 50 years resolve within 1 week and require only supportive care. Antibiotic agents are typically reserved for patients with more serious illness (including severe diarrhea requiring hospitalization, bacteremia, or high fever or sepsis) and those at high risk for severe complicated invasive disease (including infants, patients 50 years and older, or those with prosthetic materials, significant atherosclerotic disease, or immunocompromising conditions [such as HIV infection]). When empiric treatment is indicated, fluoroquinolones (such as levofloxacin or ciprofloxacin) are most likely to be effective, but azithromycin, trimethoprim-sulfamethoxazole, and amoxicillin also are potentially active agents. A fluoroquinolone, third-generation cephalosporin (such as ceftriaxone), or both are often initiated as empiric therapy for patients with severe disease requiring hospitalization. Local antibiotic susceptibilities of *Salmonella* should dictate choice of empiric therapy.

KEY POINTS

- Nontyphoidal *Salmonella* serotypes are the most common bacterial cause of foodborne illness in the United States; diagnosis is made by stool culture or molecular testing, and the illness is usually self-limited, although bacteremia with extraintestinal infection may occur.

(Continued)

• Most uncomplicated *Salmonella* infections in adults younger than 50 years resolve within 1 week and require only supportive care; when empiric treatment is indicated for those with more severe or invasive disease, fluoroquinolones (such as levofloxacin or ciprofloxacin) are most likely to be effective.

Escherichia coli Infection

Although *Escherichia coli* are normal inhabitants of the intestinal microbiome, some strains become enteropathogenic by using different mechanisms of infection (**Table 49**).

Enterotoxigenic *E. coli* infection (ETEC) is the most common cause of travelers' diarrhea. ETEC results from ingestion of water or food contaminated with stool and has an incubation period of 1 to 3 days. Enterotoxins cause watery diarrhea with associated abdominal cramping, nausea, and low-grade or no fever. Usually self-limiting, the illness resolves after approximately 4 days. Hydration and empiric antibiotic therapy with fluoroquinolones, azithromycin, or rifaximin are recommended in travelers with ETEC when symptoms restrict activities.

Enterohemorrhagic *E. coli* (EHEC) strains, such as -0157:H7 and -0104:H4, produce a Shiga-like toxin that can cause hemorrhagic colitis. EHEC bacteria are found in cow intestines and are transmitted by ingestion of undercooked hamburgers or fecally contaminated food (such as spinach, lettuce, fruit, milk, and flour) and water;

fecal-oral transmission through exposure to infected animals at petting zoos is also possible. The incubation period is 3 to 4 days, and patients typically have visibly bloody diarrhea, crampy abdominal pain, and no fever, the latter a distinguishing feature from other causes of bloody diarrhea. Alerting the laboratory about the symptoms is recommended so that appropriate media, antigen testing, and Shiga toxin assays can be performed. Hemolytic uremic syndrome is found in less than 10% of patients infected with EHEC and manifests as microangiopathic hemolytic anemia, thrombocytopenia, and kidney injury. Treatment of EHEC infection is primarily supportive; antibiotics and antimotility agents may increase the risk of developing hemolytic uremic syndrome and do not appear to shorten the duration of infection.

• Enterotoxigenic *Escherichia coli* infection is usually a self-limiting illness that resolves without treatment after approximately 4 days; hydration and empiric antibiotic therapy with fluoroquinolones, azithromycin, or rifaximin are recommended in travelers when symptoms restrict activities.

• Enterohemorrhagic *Escherichia coli* strains produce a Shiga-like toxin that can cause hemorrhagic colitis; treatment is primarily supportive because antibiotics and antimotility agents may increase the risk of developing hemolytic uremic syndrome and do not appear to shorten the duration of infection.

Yersinia Infection

Most diarrheal illness due to *Yersinia* species is caused by *Yersinia enterocolitica*, usually after ingestion of contaminated food, particularly undercooked pork. Patients with iron overload states, including hemochromatosis, are at increased risk for infection (including bacteremia) owing to the siderophilic characteristics of *Yersinia* species. The incubation period is approximately 5 days, and patients typically have fever, abdominal pain, diarrhea (possibly bloody), and (sometimes) nausea and emesis at presentation. The organism has tropism for lymphoid tissue (including tonsillar tissue and mesenteric lymph nodes), which results in pharyngitis or right lower-quadrant pain mimicking appendicitis. Postinfection complications include erythema nodosum and reactive arthritis. The diagnosis is confirmed by molecular testing of stool or by culture of stool, blood, a throat swab, or infected tissue; the testing laboratory should be alerted when *Yersinia enterocolitica* infection is suspected so that optimal media and enrichment conditions are applied. When treatment is indicated, trimethoprim-sulfamethoxazole (first choice) or a fluoroquinolone (such as ciprofloxacin) or a third-generation cephalosporin is recommended.

TABLE 49. Diarrheagenic Strains of *Escherichia coli*		
Strain	**Epidemiology**	**Clinical Findings**
Enteroaggregative *E. coli* (EAEC)	Diarrhea in travelers, young children, and patients with HIV infection	Watery diarrhea, fever typically absent
Enteroinvasive *E. coli* (EIEC)	All ages, primarily in developing countries	Inflammatory diarrhea (dysentery) with fever, abdominal pain
Enteropathogenic *E. coli* (EPEC)	Sporadic, occasionally persistent diarrhea in young children	Nausea, vomiting, malnutrition (when chronic)
Enterotoxigenic *E. coli* (ETEC)	Diarrhea in travelers, foodborne outbreaks	Watery diarrhea, fever typically absent or low grade
Shiga toxin-producing *E. coli* (STEC)	Foodborne outbreaks (associated with beef and other contaminated food), person-to-person, and zoonotic transmission	Bloody stools, progression to hemolytic uremic syndrome, fever typically absent

- Most diarrheal illness due to *Yersinia* species is caused by *Yersinia enterocolitica*, usually after ingestion of contaminated food, particularly undercooked pork; the diagnosis is confirmed by molecular testing of stool or by culture of stool, blood, a throat swab, or infected tissue.
- When treatment is indicated, trimethoprim-sulfamethoxazole (first choice) or either a fluoroquinolone (such as ciprofloxacin) or a third-generation cephalosporin is recommended.

Vibrio Infection

In the United States, *Vibrio parahaemolyticus* is the most common *Vibrio* species to cause gastrointestinal illness, usually after consumption of contaminated or undercooked oysters and other shellfish. The incubation period is approximately 1 day; infected patients typically report diarrhea (not commonly bloody), fever, nausea or emesis, and crampy abdominal pain at presentation. *V. parahaemolyticus* can cause septicemia in patients who have liver disease, which may lead to secondary necrotizing skin infections. Severe noninvasive gastrointestinal illness can be treated with doxycycline, although fluoroquinolones and macrolides also can be used. Patients with septicemia require more aggressive combination therapy, typically with doxycycline plus ceftriaxone.

- *Vibrio parahaemolyticus* can cause septicemia and necrotizing skin infections in patients who have liver disease.
- Severe noninvasive *Vibrio parahaemolyticus* gastrointestinal illness is treated with doxycycline, although fluoroquinolones and macrolides also can be used.

[H] *Clostridium difficile* Infection

Clostridium difficile is the leading cause of hospital-acquired infectious diarrhea and results from fecal-oral transmission. The number of these infections reported in the United States has increased significantly since the year 2000, owing in large part to the emergence of a hypervirulent strain. Risk factors for infection include exposure to antibiotic and chemotherapeutic agents, older age, presence of inflammatory bowel disease, gastrointestinal surgery, and (possibly) gastric acid suppression with proton pump inhibitors. Antibiotic stewardship is paramount in reducing incidence of infection, and hand washing with soap and water is the gold standard for infection control; alcohol-based gels do not eliminate spores.

Asymptomatic colonization can occur; for those with pathologic infection, the incubation period can be as long as 6 weeks after perturbation of the intestinal flora with antibiotic agents. Community-acquired infections without previous exposure to health care settings, antibiotic agents, or both have been increasingly reported.

Clostridium difficile produces both an enterotoxin (toxin A) and a cytotoxin (toxin B) that are pathogenic. Symptomatic patients typically have watery diarrhea (rarely bloody), crampy abdominal pain, malaise, and sometimes nausea and fever. Abnormal laboratory study findings are nonspecific but can include leukocytosis, an elevated creatinine level, and hypoalbuminemia. Radiographic imaging, also nonspecific, may demonstrate colonic wall thickening, mucosal edema, fat stranding, and megacolon. Colonoscopy, although not a routine diagnostic modality, may visualize pseudomembranes associated with infection.

Diagnosis is usually established by testing unformed stools from persons not taking laxatives who have unexplained new-onset diarrhea occurring three or more times daily. Although highly specific and rapid, enzyme immunoassay (EIA) testing for presence of toxin A or B lacks sensitivity. EIA testing for presence of glutamate dehydrogenase, an antigenic protein present in all *C. difficile* isolates, is quite sensitive but lacks specificity. Nucleic acid amplification testing (NAAT) for *C. difficile* toxin genes is rapid, highly sensitive, and specific. If NAAT is not used as a stand-alone technique, then combining EIA tests for glutamate dehydrogenase plus toxin (discordant results require polymerase chain reaction testing for resolution) or NAAT plus toxin can be performed.

In all infected patients, the antibiotic agent associated with the infection should be stopped if possible. Treatment is otherwise dictated by severity of disease (**Table 50**). Severe disease is supported clinically by a leukocyte count of 15,000/µL (15×10^9/L) or greater or a serum creatinine level greater than 1.5 mg/dL (133 µmol/L). Oral vancomycin or fidaxomicin for 10 days is recommended. Fulminant disease is defined as severe *C. difficile* infection with associated shock, ileus, toxic megacolon, ICU admission, elevated serum lactate level, hypotension, altered mental status, or organ failure. Higher-dose oral or nasogastric vancomycin, intravenous metronidazole, and (possibly) vancomycin enema (when ileus is present) are recommended. Patients with

TABLE 50.	Treatment of *Clostridium difficile* Infection[a]
Severity of Disease	**Treatment**
Nonsevere	Vancomycin, 125 mg four times daily PO × 10 d *or*
	Fidaxomicin, 200 mg twice daily PO × 10 d
	If neither of these agents is available, metronidazole, 500 mg three times daily PO × 10 d
Severe	Vancomycin, 125 mg four times daily PO × 10 d *or*
	Fidaxomicin, 200 mg twice daily PO × 10 d
Fulminant	Vancomycin, 500 mg four times daily PO *or*
	NGT plus metronidazole, 500 mg every 8 h IV
	When ileus is present, consideration of vancomycin PR

IV = intravenously; NGT = by nasogastric tube; PO = by mouth; PR = per rectum.

[a]Initial presentation.

CONT.

fulminant disease warrant surgical evaluation. For nonsevere disease, defined as *C. difficile* infection that is neither severe nor fulminant, oral vancomycin or fidaxomicin for 10 days is recommended. If neither of these agents is available, oral metronidazole for 10 days can be used.

Recurrent infection is reported in as many as 25% of patients, and treatment recommendations are found in **Table 51**. Studies have shown that fecal microbiota transplantation is effective in the management of patients with multiple recurrences. Retesting stool for *C. difficile* after treatment for evidence of cure in patients who have no symptoms is not recommended. **H**

KEY POINTS

HVC
- *Clostridium difficile* is the leading cause of hospital-acquired infectious diarrhea; antibiotic stewardship is paramount in reducing incidence of infection, and hand washing with soap and water is important to eliminate spores.

- Testing unformed stools usually establishes the diagnosis; nucleic acid amplification testing for *Clostridium difficile* toxin genes is rapid, highly sensitive, and specific; enzyme immunoassay testing for presence of toxin A or B is highly specific and rapid but lacks sensitivity, and enzyme immunoassay testing for presence of glutamate dehydrogenase is quite sensitive but lacks specificity.

- Treatment of an initial *Clostridium difficile* infection is dictated by severity of disease, with nonsevere disease treated with oral vancomycin or fidaxomicin (or with oral metronidazole if neither of these drugs is available), severe disease treated with oral vancomycin or fidaxomicin, and fulminant disease treated with higher-dose oral vancomycin, intravenous metronidazole, and (when ileus is present) vancomycin enema.

TABLE 51.	Treatment of Recurrent *Clostridium difficile* Infection
First recurrence	Vancomycin, 125 mg four times daily PO × 10 d, if metronidazole used for initial episode *or*
	Prolonged tapered and pulsed vancomycin if standard regimen was used for initial episode (that is, vancomycin, 125 mg four times daily PO × 10 d, then 125 mg twice daily PO × 7 d, then 125 mg every 2 or 3 d PO for 2-8 wk) *or*
	Fidaxomicin, 200 mg twice daily PO × 10 d, if vancomycin was used for the initial episode
Second or subsequent recurrence	Prolonged tapered and pulsed vancomycin PO (see above) *or*
	Vancomycin, 125 mg four times daily PO × 10 d, followed by rifaximin, 400 mg three times daily PO × 20 d *or*
	Fidaxomicin, 200 mg twice daily PO × 10 d *or*
	Fecal microbiota transplantation (after two recurrences treated with appropriate antibiotics)
PO = by mouth.	

Viral Gastroenteritis

Viruses are responsible for acute gastroenteritis in most patients. Rotavirus infects young children, and noroviruses, which are estimated to cause more than 50% of foodborne gastroenteritis in the United States, affect all ages. Norovirus outbreaks on cruise ships and in schools and other institutionalized settings are well documented. Transmission from person to person is primarily fecal-oral. Highly contagious infection can develop after ingestion of fewer than 100 viral particles. The incubation period is typically less than 2 days, and infected patients typically have watery diarrhea, nausea, vomiting, and fever at presentation. Infection is usually self-limited and requires supportive care because of the lack of effective antiviral agents. Diagnostic molecular testing is available. Viral shedding persists for as long as 2 weeks after symptom resolution, which contributes to its high infectivity.

KEY POINT

- Noroviruses cause more than 50% of foodborne gastroenteritis in the United States; the incubation period is typically less than 2 days; viral shedding persists as long as 2 weeks after symptom resolution, which contributes to high infectivity.

Parasitic Infection

Parasitic infection should be considered in patients with persistent or chronic diarrhea. Immunosuppressed persons are at increased risk for more chronic and severe infection.

Giardia lamblia Infection

Giardia lamblia is the most common parasitic pathogen in the United States. Cysts from infected animals are excreted in stool into reservoirs of natural fresh water, and subsequent ingestion of contaminated water (or food) can lead to human infection. Secondary spread from person to person via fecal-oral transmission is also possible because cysts may be excreted for many months. Persons at risk for infection include international outdoor travelers, children in day-care centers, immunocompromised hosts (particularly those with humoral immunodeficiency), and persons engaged in sexual activity that includes oral-anal contact. The incubation period ranges from 1 to 3 weeks. More than half of infected patients are asymptomatic. Symptomatic patients typically report watery diarrhea that is fatty and foul smelling, flatulence, bloating, nausea, and crampy abdominal pain; fever is uncommon. Symptoms can last for several weeks until spontaneously resolving; chronic infection may develop, particularly in persons with hypogammaglobulinemia. EIA and molecular testing of stool is more sensitive than stool microscopy for confirming the diagnosis. Treatment is recommended for symptomatic patients; metronidazole, tinidazole, or nitazoxanide can be used. Postinfection lactose intolerance is common and may be mistaken for recurrent or resistant *Giardia* infection.

- More than half of patients infected with *Giardia lamblia* are asymptomatic; treatment with metronidazole, tinidazole, or nitazoxanide can be used.

- Postinfection lactose intolerance is common and may be mistaken for recurrent or resistant *Giardia* infection.

Cryptosporidium Infection

Cryptosporidium species can infect humans and other mammals. Infection occurs through consumption of fecally contaminated water or food or through close person-to-person or animal-to-person transmission. Municipal water supplies and swimming pools can be a source of infection because the thick-walled oocysts are chlorine resistant and can evade filtration. This parasite is highly infectious; ingestion of fewer than 50 oocysts may result in infection. The incubation period is 7 days. Although some infected patients will be asymptomatic, symptomatic patients typically report watery diarrhea, crampy abdominal pain, nausea, vomiting, malaise, fever, dehydration, and weight loss. Symptoms usually last less than 2 weeks before spontaneously resolving in immunocompetent hosts. Immunocompromised patients, in particular patients with AIDS, can develop serious and prolonged infection. Diagnosis can be established microscopically by visualization of oocysts with modified acid-fast staining, molecular testing, and enzyme or direct fluorescent immunoassay testing. Treatment for immunocompetent patients usually consists of supportive care. When antimicrobial agents are considered for severe or prolonged infection, nitazoxanide is recommended. In HIV-infected patients, antiretroviral therapy is most effective in resolving infection. Nitazoxanide also can be considered when supportive care does not result in symptom resolution.

- The diagnosis of *Cryptosporidium* infection can be established microscopically by visualization of oocysts using modified acid-fast staining, polymerase chain reaction testing, and enzyme immunoassay or direct fluorescent antibody testing.

- Treatment of *Cryptosporidium* infection consists of supportive care for most immunocompetent hosts; nitazoxanide is recommended for severe or prolonged infection or if supportive care does not resolve symptoms; antiretroviral therapy is most effective in resolving infection in HIV-infected patients.

Amebiasis

Entamoeba histolytica is the parasitic organism responsible for amebiasis. In the United States, most infections are diagnosed in travelers returning from visits to unsanitary tropical or developing countries, immigrants from these areas, persons in institutionalized settings, or those who practice oral-anal sex. Amebiasis is highly infectious, with ingestion of only a small number of infective cysts in contaminated water or food needed for infection. The incubation period is 2 to 4 weeks. Most infections are asymptomatic, but some patients develop diarrhea with visible blood, mucus, or both and associated abdominal pain, fever, and weight loss. Colonic perforation, peritonitis, and death may complicate more fulminant infections. Risk factors for severe infection in adults include immunodeficiency. Diagnosis can be established microscopically by visualization of cysts or trophozoites, immunoassay testing, molecular testing, and serologic antibody testing, although the latter technique does not distinguish current from remote infection. Treatment is recommended for all infected patients. In symptomatic patients, treatment with metronidazole or tinidazole is recommended initially for parasitic clearance followed by an intraluminal amebicide, such as paromomycin or diloxanide, for cyst clearance. In asymptomatic infections, an intraluminal agent for eradication of cysts is recommended.

- Treatment is recommended for all patients with amebiasis; for symptomatic patients, treatment with metronidazole or tinidazole is recommended initially for parasitic clearance followed by an intraluminal amebicide for cyst clearance, and for asymptomatic patients, an intraluminal agent for eradication of cysts is recommended.

Cyclospora Infection

Cyclospora infections are typically acquired after consumption of food or water that is fecally contaminated with *Cyclospora* oocysts. In the United States, most of these infections have been traced to imported fresh produce from tropical areas or have occurred in persons who have traveled to areas of endemicity. The incubation period is approximately 1 week. Infected patients typically report watery diarrhea, decreased appetite, weight loss, crampy abdominal pain, bloating, flatulence, nausea, fatigue, and (sometimes) fever. Symptoms can last for several weeks and may be more pronounced in HIV-infected patients. Diagnosis is typically established microscopically by visualization of oocysts with modified acid-fast staining, microscopy with ultraviolet fluorescence, or molecular testing. Trimethoprim-sulfamethoxazole is recommended for treatment of symptomatic infection.

- *Cyclospora* infection is typically diagnosed microscopically by visualization of oocysts with modified acid-fast staining, microscopy with ultraviolet fluorescence, or molecular testing; trimethoprim-sulfamethoxazole is recommended for treatment of symptomatic infection.

Infections in Transplant Recipients

Introduction

Despite improvements in immunosuppression and antimicrobial therapy, infection remains a significant cause of morbidity and mortality after solid organ transplantation (SOT) and hematopoietic stem cell transplantation (HSCT). Infection is the most common cause of death in the first year after SOT. Additionally, the interaction of the immune system and infection goes both ways; although immune suppression to prevent rejection increases risk of infection, infection also raises the risk of rejection.

The occurrence of SOT and HSCT procedures continues to increase, as do long-term survival rates owing to improved management of rejection and decreased complications. With more patients living longer after transplantation, awareness of principles involved in the recognition and prevention of infection in transplant recipients remains important for physicians who are not transplant specialists.

Antirejection Drugs in Transplant Recipients

Success after transplantation depends on modulating the immune system to prevent organ rejection in SOT and to minimize graft-versus-host disease (GVHD) in allogeneic HSCT. Antirejection regimens involve multiple agents (**Table 52**) with

TABLE 52. Immunosuppressive Agents Used in Transplantation	
Class	**Agents**
Glucocorticoids	Prednisone, others
Cytotoxic agents (DNA synthesis inhibitors, antimetabolites)	Mycophenolate mofetil
	Mycophenolate sodium
	Azathioprine
	Methotrexate
	Cyclophosphamide
Calcineurin pathway inhibitors	Cyclosporine
	Tacrolimus
mTOR inhibitors	Sirolimus (rapamycin)
	Everolimus
Lymphocyte-depleting antibodies	
Polyclonal	Antithymocyte globulins
Monoclonal	Muromonab (anti-CD3)
	Basiliximab (anti-IL-2 receptor)
	Daclizumab (anti-IL-2 receptor)
	Rituximab (anti-CD20)
	Alemtuzumab (anti-CD52)

IL-2 = interleukin-2; mTOR = mammalian target of rapamycin.

different mechanisms of action, which are chosen to minimize overlapping toxicities. After SOT, an induction and maintenance strategy is applied; immunosuppression is most intensive in the early period after transplantation and often includes lymphocyte depletion therapy. Immunosuppression may require intensification later for episodes of rejection, and this may again increase the risk of infection.

Glucocorticoids have historically been the cornerstone of antirejection therapy, but steroid-sparing or minimizing regimens are increasingly being used to avoid the toxicities of long-term therapy. Tacrolimus, cyclosporine, or sirolimus are the cornerstones, usually with mycophenolate or, less commonly, azathioprine. Drug interactions are common with these agents, and many drugs can affect antirejection medication levels. Monitoring is important to balance adequate immunosuppression with toxicity.

KEY POINT

- Glucocorticoid-sparing or minimizing regimens (with tacrolimus, cyclosporine, or sirolimus) are increasingly used to avoid the toxicities of long-term steroid therapy.

Posttransplantation Infections

Timeline and Type of Transplant

Infection may occur at any time after transplantation, but periods of highest immunosuppression, usually within the first few months after transplantation, carry the highest likelihood. Risk for infection is also affected by pre-existing conditions (such as diabetes mellitus, cirrhosis, or neutropenia) and by colonization with resistant organisms (such as *Burkholderia* in cystic fibrosis).

The risk of specific infections varies depending on the time frame after transplantation. **Table 53** shows the typical timeline of risk for specific infections after SOT. However, the timeline restarts when treating episodes of rejection, and infection risk in the late period depends on the level of immunosuppression required. Knowledge of the risk timeline and effect of the immunosuppression level can be helpful in recognizing likely infections and in preventing infections through targeted prophylaxis. In the first month after SOT, infections are similar to those seen in other hospitalized postsurgical patients, including a risk of resistant bacteria, and most often involve the lungs, urinary tract, and surgical sites. The middle period usually encompasses the most intensive immunosuppression, with significant risk for viral (such as cytomegalovirus) and fungal (such as *Pneumocystis*) infections owing to defects in cell-mediated immunity. If immunosuppression can be de-escalated during the late period, risk for opportunistic infections decreases overall, but patients remain at risk for certain viral infections and have increased risk for community-acquired bacterial infections.

Additional general considerations include the higher likelihood of infections to disseminate after transplantation and the subtle or atypical presentation of infection because of

TABLE 53. Timeline of Common Infections after Solid Organ Transplantation

Early Period (<1 Month after Transplantation)	Middle Period (1-6 Months after Transplantation)	Late Period (>6 Months after Transplantation)[a]
Staphylococcus aureus infection (including methicillin-resistant)	Cytomegalovirus infection	Epstein-Barr virus (including PTLD) infection
	Epstein-Barr virus (including PTLD) infection	Varicella-zoster virus infection
Nosocomial gram-negative bacterial infection	Herpes simplex virus infection	Community-acquired pneumonia
Clostridium difficile colitis	Varicella-zoster virus infection	Urinary tract infections
Candida infection	Polyoma BK virus infection	Polyoma BK virus infection
Aspergillus infection	Pneumocystis jirovecii infection	Cytomegalovirus infection
Surgical site infections	Toxoplasma, Trypanosoma, Strongyloides	
Nosocomial pneumonia	Listeria infection	
Catheter-related bacteremia	Nocardia infection	
Urinary tract infections	Tuberculosis reactivation	
	Fungal infections, including Cryptococcus	

PTLD = posttransplant lymphoproliferative disorder.

[a]For opportunistic infections in the late period, risk depends on level of immunosuppression. Infections such as Pneumocystis and other fungi, Listeria, and Nocardia can be seen in the late period in patients with higher immunosuppression.

changed anatomy after transplantation. Immunosuppressive drugs may also contribute to altered presentation because of reduction in fever and other inflammatory responses making the usual signs and symptoms of infection less prominent. Noninfectious complications such as GVHD or malignancy may also be confused with infection. For some infections, the risk strongly depends on donor and recipient characteristics. Standard donor and recipient pretransplantation testing includes serologies for cytomegalovirus; Epstein-Barr virus; varicella-zoster virus; HIV; hepatitis B, C, and E viruses; syphilis; toxoplasmosis; and Strongyloides, Leishmania, and Trypanosoma if from an endemic area and interferon-γ release assay for latent tuberculosis infection.

Risk after HSCT is much greater for allogeneic than autologous transplantation because of the myeloablative conditioning regimen. After allogeneic HSCT, patients undergo a prolonged period of intense neutropenia, putting them at risk for bacterial infections, Candida and mold infections, and herpes simplex and other virus reactivation. This is followed by a prolonged period of impaired cell-mediated and humoral immunity because of immunosuppression to reduce GVHD.

Development of chronic GVHD can also increase risk for infections caused by immune system effects and breakdowns in mucosal and other barriers. Infections in this later period are similar to those in the later period after SOT. **Figure 21** shows the timeline of risk for specific infection after allogeneic HSCT.

KEY POINTS

- Infection may occur at any time after transplantation but is most likely at periods of highest immunosuppression; the risk for specific organisms varies depending on the time frame after transplantation.

- Infection risk is much greater after allogeneic than autologous hematopoietic stem cell transplantation because of myeloablative conditioning with a prolonged period of neutropenia and immunosuppression given to reduce graft-versus-host disease.

Specific Posttransplantation Infections
Viral Infections

Cytomegalovirus is the most significant viral infection after transplantation, with risk for infection depending on donor and recipient serology. After SOT, the risk for cytomegalovirus is highest (>50%) for donor-positive/recipient-negative, intermediate (15%-20%) for recipient-positive, and lowest for donor-negative/recipient-negative transplantations. Risk is also significantly increased with use of lymphocyte-depleting agents. Comparatively, after allogeneic HSCT, the risk of cytomegalovirus is highest for donor-negative/recipient-positive transplantations. Cytomegalovirus is an immunomodulatory virus, and active cytomegalovirus infection after transplantation is associated with increased rates of rejection and GVHD, as well as increases in other opportunistic infections and posttransplant lymphoproliferative disorder (PTLD). Cytomegalovirus often presents as a nonspecific viral syndrome with fever and cytopenias. Specific organ disease owing to cytomegalovirus includes pneumonitis (more common in HSCT than SOT), encephalitis, hepatitis, and other gastrointestinal sites. Although cytomegalovirus can cause disease anywhere in the gastrointestinal tract, colitis is the most common gastrointestinal disease after SOT, whereas esophagitis is more common after HSCT. Definitive diagnosis of organ disease depends on demonstration of cytomegalovirus in biopsy, although presumptive diagnosis can be made based on cytomegalovirus viremia, demonstrated by quantitative nucleic acid amplification testing, in the appropriate clinical setting.

Epstein-Barr virus is most significant for its relationship to PTLD resulting from B-cell proliferation; PTLD should be suspected in any patient in the middle or late period presenting with lymphadenopathy or an extranodal mass, often with fever. Treatment of PTLD involves rituximab and decreasing immunosuppression. Reactivation of herpes simplex virus is especially common after HSCT and can be reduced with acyclovir prophylaxis (if the patient is not already receiving an agent for cytomegalovirus). Patients with chronic hepatitis B

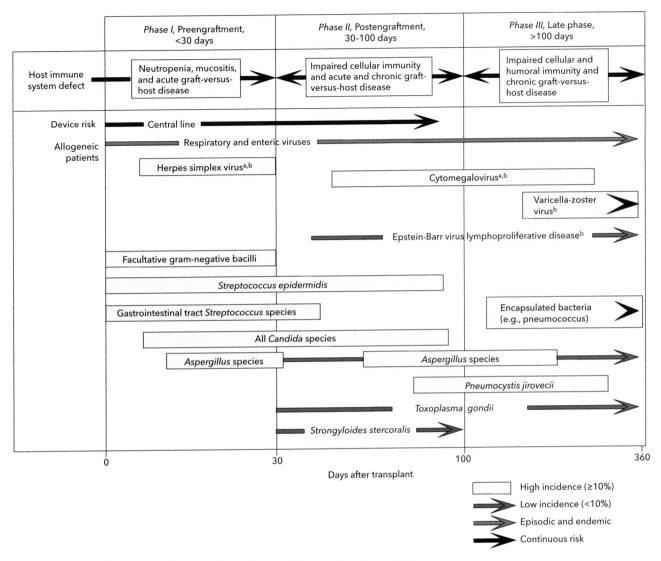

FIGURE 21. Phases of opportunistic infections in allogeneic hematopoietic stem cell transplant recipients.

[a]Without standard prophylaxis.

[b]Primarily among persons who are seropositive before transplantation.

Reprinted with permission from CDC, Infectious Diseases Society of America, and the American Society of Blood and Marrow Transplantation. Guidelines for preventing opportunistic infections among hematopoietic stem cell transplant recipients. Recommendations of CDC, the Infectious Diseases Society of America, and the American Society of Blood and Marrow Transplantation. Cytotherapy. 2001;3(1):41-54. PMID: 12028843

can have flares of disease if not taking suppressive therapy. Polyoma BK virus can cause a nephropathy in the middle or late period after transplantation.

Bacterial Infections

Bacterial infections are common in the early period after SOT and during neutropenia after HSCT. These are often typical nosocomial infections, including resistant organisms such as methicillin-resistant staphylococci, vancomycin-resistant enterococci, and multidrug-resistant gram-negative organisms. *Clostridium difficile* colitis is common, especially with the extensive antibiotic use that accompanies transplantation. *Mycobacterium tuberculosis* can reactivate with the immunosuppression of transplantation and may present with an

atypical pattern on chest radiography or with extrapulmonary disease. Related to persistently low antibody levels, encapsulated organisms such as *Streptococcus pneumoniae* remain common even late after HSCT. ▣

Fungal Infections

Fungal infections are most common in the middle period after SOT but may also occur late, especially in the setting of rejection or cytomegalovirus infection. The most common fungal infection without prophylaxis is *Pneumocystis* pneumonia, which is typically a more aggressive pneumonia in patients after transplantation than in those with AIDS. Cryptococcosis usually presents as subacute meningitis with fever, headache, mental status changes, and lymphocytic pleocytosis in cerebrospinal fluid, although skin and other organ involvement may also occur; cryptococcal antigen testing is key to diagnosis. Histoplasmosis may also occur in geographically endemic areas and is more likely to present with disseminated disease after transplantation. Mucocutaneous candidiasis is common after SOT and HSCT. Invasive *Candida* infections and candidemia can be seen, especially in the neutropenic phase after HSCT, as can aspergillosis and other invasive molds, such as *Mucor*. The risk for invasive fungal infection after HSCT is also increased in later periods by the use of immunosuppressive agents for GVHD. In SOT, pulmonary aspergillosis is most common after lung transplantation.

Protozoa and Helminths

Toxoplasma gondii is a protozoan that can reactivate with immunosuppression after transplantation, usually causing encephalitis with fever, headache, and focal neurologic deficits and with multiple ring-enhancing brain lesions on imaging. *Strongyloides* can cause a hyperinfection syndrome with significant immunosuppression (especially glucocorticoid use), often with secondary pneumonia and gram-negative bacteremia. Reactivation of *Trypanosoma* or *Leishmania* can also occur after transplantation, if the recipient or donor were from an endemic area.

KEY POINTS

- Cytomegalovirus is the most significant viral infection after transplantation and may present as a nonspecific viral syndrome with fever and cytopenias or with specific organ disease, including pneumonitis, encephalitis, esophagitis, and colitis.

- *Clostridium difficile* colitis is common after transplantation, complicating the extensive antibiotic use that accompanies transplantation.

- *Mycobacterium tuberculosis* can reactivate with the immunosuppression of transplantation and may present with an atypical pattern on chest radiography or with extrapulmonary disease.

- *Pneumocystis* pneumonia is the most common fungal infection without prophylaxis; it is typically a more aggressive pneumonia in patients after transplantation than in those with AIDS.

Prevention of Infections in Transplant Recipients

Prevention is preferred over treatment strategies for most common infections after transplantation because most opportunistic infections have devastating effects and the cost and toxicity of prophylaxis and immunization are relatively low. Recommended immunizations for SOT and HSCT are shown in **Table 54**. Most immunizations are safe in patients after transplantation except for live virus vaccines, which should be avoided after transplantation.

Trimethoprim-sulfamethoxazole is one of the most important prophylactic medications after transplantation. Used to prevent *Pneumocystis*, it may also reduce toxoplasmosis and certain bacteria, including *Listeria* and agents causing urinary tract infections. Trimethoprim-sulfamethoxazole is usually given up to 1 year after transplantation and often longer if immunosuppression cannot be adequately reduced.

Antifungal prophylaxis is indicated during the early months after HSCT and may need to be extended in the setting of GVHD. Coverage should include *Candida* and *Aspergillus*, typically with posaconazole or voriconazole.

Strategies to reduce the effects of cytomegalovirus remain important and include primary prophylaxis, usually with valganciclovir, or regular monitoring for active cytomegalovirus replication by quantitative nucleic acid amplification testing and institution of pre-emptive therapy based on results. Monitoring and pre-emptive therapy is more often used after HSCT, partially because of increased concerns for neutropenia as an adverse effect of prophylaxis and because prophylaxis was not found to be superior to pre-emptive therapy in a randomized controlled trial. The potential role of letermovir, a new antiviral agent without the hematologic toxicity of ganciclovir, is being studied for cytomegalovirus prophylaxis. For SOT, prophylaxis with valganciclovir is preferred for patients at high risk (donor-positive/recipient-negative, those receiving lymphocyte-depleting agents, lung transplants) and is usually given for at least 3 to 6 months.

KEY POINTS

- Prophylaxis and immunization are preferred over treating active infections after transplantation; live virus vaccines should not be given after transplantation. **HVC**

- Monitoring by quantitative nucleic acid amplification testing for active cytomegalovirus replication and institution of pre-emptive therapy based on results is preferred to ganciclovir primary prophylaxis of cytomegalovirus infection after hematopoietic stem cell transplantation.

Health Care-Associated Infections   H

Epidemiology

Health care–associated infections (HCAI) have been linked to indwelling medical devices, prosthetic devices and materials, surgery, invasive procedures, transmission of organisms between patients and health care personnel, and environmental factors. Four percent of hospitalized patients acquire at least one HCAI, costing the U.S. health care system an estimated $28 billion to $45 billion annually. HCAIs include pneumonia and surgical site infections (21.8% each), gastrointestinal infections (17.1%), urinary tract infections (12.9%; 67.7%

TABLE 54. Immunization Recommendations for Adult Recipients of Transplants[a]

Immunization	Recommendations for Solid Organ Transplantation	Recommendations for Hematopoietic Stem Cell Transplantation[b]
Pneumococcal	Before transplantation: PCV13 followed 8 weeks later by PPSV23	3-6 months after transplantation: 3-4 doses of PCV13
	After transplantation: PCV13 (if not administered pretransplantation) 2-6 months after transplantation; 1 dose PPSV23 at least 8 weeks after PCV13 and 5 years after any previous PPSV23	12 months after transplantation: 1 dose of PPSV23
Influenza (inactivated only)	Annually	Annually
Tdap	Before transplantation: complete series, including Tdap booster	6 months after transplantation: 3 doses Tdap
MMR	Contraindicated after transplantation	24 months after transplantation: 1-2 doses, only if no GVHD or immune suppression
Inactivated polio	Before transplantation: complete series	6-12 months after transplantation: 3 doses
Haemophilus influenzae type B	No recommendation	6-12 months after transplantation: 3 doses
Meningococcal	Per recommendations for nontransplant patients	6 months after transplantation: both quadrivalent conjugate vaccine and serogroup B vaccine
Hepatitis B	Before transplantation: complete series if not already immune	6-12 months after transplantation: 3 doses if indications for nontransplant patients are met
Hepatitis A	Before transplantation: complete series if not already immune	Per recommendations for nontransplant patients
Varicella-zoster virus		
Live attenuated vaccine	>4 weeks before transplantation: varicella if not immune	>4 weeks before transplantation: varicella if not immune
	>4 weeks before transplantation: zoster if same indications as nontransplant patients are met	24 months after transplantation: 2 doses varicella if seronegative and only if no GVHD or immunosuppression
	Both contraindicated after transplantation	
Recombinant adjuvanted zoster vaccine	Theoretically safe, but data in severely immunocompromised patients not yet available; no recommendations after transplantation	Theoretically safe, but data in severely immunocompromised patients not yet available; no recommendations after transplantation
	Should be given before transplantation if possible	Should be given before transplantation if possible
Human papillomavirus	Before transplantation: per recommendations for nontransplant patients	Per recommendations for nontransplant patients

GVHD = graft-versus-host disease; MMR = measles, mumps, and rubella vaccine; PCV13 = 13-valent pneumococcal conjugate vaccine; PPSV23 = 23-valent pneumococcal polysaccharide vaccine; Tdap = tetanus, diphtheria, and acellular pertussis vaccine.

[a]See MKSAP 18 General Internal Medicine for more information on vaccination recommendations and schedules.

[b]For multiple-dose immunizations, the time period between doses is generally 1-2 months.

associated with catheters), and primary bloodstream infection (9.9%; 84% associated with central venous catheters).

Elimination of HCAIs remains important for the U.S. health care system. Sixty-five percent to 70% of catheter-associated bloodstream and urinary tract infections and 55% of ventilator-associated pneumonias and surgical site infections are preventable. Progress toward elimination varies by type of infection. Central line–associated bloodstream infections decreased by 50% and surgical site infections by 17% between 2008 and 2014; rates of catheter-associated urinary tract infections showed little change between 2009 and 2014. **H**

KEY POINT

- Approximately 65% to 70% of catheter-associated bloodstream and urinary tract infections and 55% of ventilator-associated pneumonias and surgical site infections are preventable.

Prevention

Hand hygiene is the foundation of infection prevention, but adherence has been reported as less than 50%. Most facilities have improved in the last decade, with some facilities showing sustained improvement to 90% adherence. Hand hygiene should be performed at least before and after every patient contact. The World Health Organization's five key hand hygiene moments are commonly used to define hand hygiene opportunities: before touching a patient, before clean or aseptic procedures, after body fluid exposure risk, after touching a patient, and after touching patient surroundings. Hand hygiene should include all surfaces of the hands up to the wrists, between fingers, and the fingertips. Alcohol-based hand rubs are generally preferred to soap and water hand disinfection, except when hands are visibly soiled, when personnel come in direct contact with blood or body fluids, or after contact with a patient with *Clostridium difficile* infection or his or her environment.

Standard precautions should be practiced for every patient to protect health care personnel from exposure to bloodborne pathogens. Blood and all body fluids except sweat are potentially infectious, regardless of the patient's presumed or known infection status. Personal protective equipment (gloves, gown, mask, and eye protection) are barriers protecting health care personnel from exposure to blood and body fluids. Protective equipment should be removed in the following order: 1) gloves, careful not to contaminate hands; 2) goggles/face shields; 3) gown, pull away from neck and shoulders, turn inside out to discard; 4) mask/respirator by grasping bottom then top ties/elastic. This process should be followed by hand hygiene. Transmission-based precautions (airborne, contact, droplet) are performed in addition to standard precautions to prevent transmission of epidemiologically significant organisms (**Table 55**).

Additional preventive measures include careful and judicious device use, safe injection practices (one needle, one syringe, only one time), aseptic technique for invasive procedures and surgery, and a clean environment and patient equipment. HCAI prevention "bundles" comprise three to five evidence-based processes of care that, when performed together, consistently have a greater impact on decreasing HCAIs than individual components performed inconsistently. **H**

KEY POINT

- Hand hygiene is the foundation of infection prevention; the World Health Organization has identified five key hand hygiene moments (before touching a patient, before clean or aseptic procedure, after body fluid exposure risk, after touching a patient, and after touching patient surroundings).

HVC

Catheter-Associated Urinary Tract Infections

Catheter-associated urinary tract infections (CAUTIs) are the most common device-associated HCAI, and 17% to 69% may be preventable. Urinary catheters are used in 15% to 25% of hospitalized patients in the United States, compelling efforts to establish appropriateness criteria for catheter use. Adverse outcomes related to CAUTI include pyelonephritis, perinephric abscess, and bacteremia (<5%). *Escherichia coli* is the most common CAUTI pathogen, followed by *Pseudomonas aeruginosa*, *Klebsiella pneumoniae/Klebsiella oxytoca*, *Candida* species, and *Enterococcus* species; antibiotic resistance among these pathogens is increasing.

Duration of catheterization is the primary modifiable risk factor for CAUTI; each day of catheterization increases the risk of CAUTI. Nonadherence to aseptic technique (for example, opening a closed system) and insertion by a less experienced operator also increase the risk. Other risk factors for CAUTI include female sex, age older than 50 years, diabetes mellitus, severe or nonsurgical underlying illness, and serum creatinine level greater than 2.0 mg/dL (176.8 µmol/L). Appropriate indications for indwelling urinary catheters are listed in **Table 56**. Management of urinary incontinence using external catheters is preferred when feasible. Provision of care in the ICU is not itself an indication for a catheter.

Diagnosis
Patients with an indwelling urethral or suprapubic catheter (or catheter removed in the 48 hours before symptom onset) or

TABLE 55.	Transmission-Based Precautions[a]		
Precaution Type	**Indications**	**Precaution**	**Examples**
Airborne	Organisms transmitted from respiratory tract by small droplet nuclei (≤5 microns) that travel long distances on air currents	Airborne infection isolation room (negative-pressure room); HCP wear fit-tested N95 respirator	Chickenpox (plus contact precautions), tuberculosis, measles
Contact	Organisms transmitted by direct or indirect contact	Single room; gloves and gown for HCP entering room	Multidrug-resistant organisms (such as MRSA, VRE, ESBL-producing gram-negative organisms), *Clostridium difficile*, rotavirus
Droplet	Organisms transmitted from respiratory tract by large droplet nuclei (>5 microns) that travel less than 3 feet on air currents	Single room; HCP wear face or surgical mask when within 3 feet of patient	Influenza, *Bordetella pertussis*, *Neisseria meningitidis* for first 24 hours of therapy, mumps

ESBL = extended-spectrum β-lactamase; HCP = health care personnel; MRSA = methicillin-resistant *Staphylococcus aureus*; VRE = vancomycin-resistant enterococci.

[a]Some organisms and infections require a combination of transmission-based precautions (adenovirus: contact and droplet; disseminated varicella-zoster virus: airborne and contact).

TABLE 56. Appropriate Indications for Use of Indwelling Urinary Catheters

Indication
Management of acute urinary retention without bladder outlet obstruction
Management of acute urinary retention with bladder outlet obstruction not related to infection or trauma
Management of chronic urinary retention with bladder outlet obstruction when ISC is not feasible
Management of stage III or IV or unstageable pressure ulcers that cannot be kept clear of urinary incontinence despite other urinary management strategies (e.g., barrier creams, absorbent pads, prompted toileting, non-indwelling catheters)
Hourly measurement of urine volume required to provide treatment
Daily measurement of urine volume required to provide treatment when it cannot be assessed by other volume (e.g., daily weighing, physical examination) and urine collection (e.g., urinal, bedside commode, bedpan, external catheter, ISC) strategies
Collection of a single 24-hour urine sample needed for diagnostic test that cannot be obtained by other urine collection strategies
Reduction in instances of acute, severe pain with movement when other urine management strategies are difficult
Improvement in comfort when urine collection by catheter addresses patient and family goals in a dying patient
Management of gross hematuria with blood clots in urine
Management of clinical condition for which ISC or external catheter is appropriate but placement is difficult or bladder emptying is inadequate for the patient with non-indwelling strategies

ISC = intermittent straight catheterization.

CONT. using intermittent catheterization who have signs and symptoms compatible with urinary tract infection (UTI; see Urinary Tract Infections for information), no other identifiable infection source, and ≥10^3 colony-forming units/mL of one or more bacterial species in a urine specimen are diagnosed with a CAUTI. Catheter-associated asymptomatic bacteriuria (≥10^3 colony-forming units/mL without urinary tract signs or symptoms) is common and generally does not require treatment. 🄷

KEY POINT

HVC • Catheter-associated asymptomatic bacteriuria (≥10^3 colony-forming units/mL without urinary tract signs or symptoms) is common and generally does not require treatment.

🄷 Treatment

A urinalysis and urine culture should always be obtained before initiating antimicrobial treatment to determine if antimicrobial resistance is present and to guide definitive therapy. CAUTI management includes removing the urinary catheter (and only replacing if still needed). Removal is strongly recommended for catheters in place for 2 or more weeks because

biofilm on the catheter makes it difficult to eradicate bacteriuria or funguria and may lead to antimicrobial resistance. Therapy should always be adjusted to the narrowest coverage spectrum possible based on culture results. Treatment is given for 7 days if symptoms resolve promptly and longer (10-14 days) for patients with delayed response. Candiduria in a patient with a catheter almost always represents colonization and rarely requires treatment. *Candida* CAUTI is considered when significant candiduria persists despite catheter removal or replacement and the patient is symptomatic. CAUTIs caused by *Candida* species requiring treatment should be treated for 14 days. 🄷

KEY POINTS

• Catheter-associated urinary tract infection management includes catheter removal, with replacement only if still necessary. **HVC**

• Candiduria in a patient with a catheter almost always represents colonization and rarely requires treatment. **HVC**

Prevention 🄷

Key prevention strategies include appropriately limiting urinary catheter use (see Table 56) and considering other options associated with lower infection risk (intermittent straight catheterization, external catheters) when urine collection is necessary (**Table 57**). Most studies have not shown definitive benefit of antimicrobial- or antiseptic-coated catheters for short- (<14 days) or long-term catheterization; these catheters are more expensive and, in some cases (such as nitrofurazone-coated catheters), cause more patient discomfort. 🄷

KEY POINT

• Antimicrobial- or antiseptic-coated catheters have not shown benefit for short-term or long-term catheterization, are more expensive, and, in some cases, cause more patient discomfort. **HVC**

Surgical Site Infections

Surgical site infections (SSIs) account for 23% of HCAIs. The overall risk of developing an SSI after surgery is 1.9%. Wound class affects the risk of infection, with clean wounds having less than a 2% risk of infection, clean contaminated wounds having less than a 10% risk, and contaminated wounds having a 20% risk. Most infections occur within 30 days after surgery or within 90 days after surgery with implants; however, infections can manifest beyond these ranges. Risk factors include patient-related, procedure-related, and postoperative factors (**Table 58**). The patient's skin and gastrointestinal or female genital tracts are major sources of organisms causing infection, depending on the type of surgery. The time during which the surgical site is open represents the period of greatest risk. Common SSI pathogens are *Staphylococcus aureus* (23%), coagulase-negative staphylococci (17%), enterococci (7%), *Escherichia coli* (5%), and

TABLE 57.	Prevention of Catheter-Associated Urinary Tract Infection
Period	**Preventive Measures**
Before catheterization	Avoid catheterization whenever possible
	Insert catheter only for appropriate indications
	Consider alternatives, such as condom catheters and intermittent catheterization
At time of catheter insertion	Ensure that only properly trained persons insert and maintain catheters
	Adhere to hand hygiene practices and standard (or appropriate isolation) precautions according to CDC HICPAC/WHO guidelines
	Use proper aseptic techniques and sterile equipment when inserting the catheter (acute care setting)
After catheter insertion	Promote early catheter removal whenever possible
	Secure the catheter
	Use aseptic technique when handling the catheter, including for sample collection from the designated port (not collecting bag)
	Maintain a closed drainage system
	Avoid unnecessary system disconnections
	Maintain unobstructed urine flow
	Keep the collecting bag below the level of the bladder and off the floor
	Empty the collecting bag regularly, using a separate collecting container for each patient

CDC = Centers for Disease Control and Prevention; HICPAC = Healthcare Infection Control Practices Advisory Committee; WHO = World Health Organization.

TABLE 58.	Mitigation of Risk Factors for Surgical Site Infection
Risk Factor	**Intervention**
Hyperglycemia	Maintain blood glucose level ≤180 mg/dL (10 mmol/L) during first 48 hours after surgery
Immunosuppression	Reduce doses of immunosuppressive agents
Tobacco use	Cease 30 days before surgery
Obesity	Weight loss
Malnutrition	Optimize nutritional status before surgery
S. aureus nasal carriage	For cardiovascular and orthopedic surgeries, test for nasal carriage 1-2 weeks before
	If positive, decolonize using intranasal 2% mupirocin ointment with or without chlorhexidine body wash
Skin preparation	Shower the night before (soap or an antiseptic)
	Use an alcohol-based chlorhexidine scrub at incision site
Hair removal	Do not shave site of incision
	If hair must be removed, it should be clipped as close to time of incision as possible
Hypothermia and hypovolemia	Maintain perioperative normothermia (temperature >36 °C [96.8 °F]) and adequate volume replacement to ensure maximum tissue oxygen delivery
	2 °C (3.6 °F) decrease in body temperature associated with threefold increase in surgical site infection
Incision dressing	Primarily closed incision covered with sterile dressing for 24-48 hours

Pseudomonas aeruginosa (5%). Exogenous sources of organisms (surgical personnel, surgical instruments, environment) are less common causes of SSIs, usually identified when a cluster of infections is present.

KEY POINT

- Most surgical site infections occur within 30 days after surgery or within 90 days after surgery with implants.

Diagnosis

Clinical signs and symptoms vary by site and type of infection as well as by implicated organism (for example, some are more likely to cause purulence). Inflammatory changes at the surgical site (pain or tenderness, warmth, swelling, erythema) and purulent drainage suggest a superficial incisional infection. Deep incisional SSIs have more extensive tenderness expanding outside the area of erythema and more systemic signs, such as fever and leukocytosis. Wound dehiscence suggests a deep incisional SSI unless the wound or drainage is culture negative. Organ and deep-space SSIs are associated with more

systemic signs and local symptoms related to a deep abscess or infected fluid collection. In cases of suspected organ or deep-space SSIs, CT is helpful to localize the infection and determine the best approach to drainage of the fluid or abscess for culture and treatment. When an SSI is suspected, drainage, purulent fluid, and infected tissue should be obtained for culture. Deep-tissue or wound cultures are preferable to superficial wound swab cultures that are likely to reflect skin or wound colonization and not necessarily yield the causative pathogen.

KEY POINT

- Deep tissue, drainage, and purulent fluid should be obtained for culture in surgical site infections; superficial wound swab cultures are likely to reflect skin or wound colonization rather than the causative pathogen.

Treatment

SSI treatment requires debridement of necrotic tissue, drainage of abscesses or infected fluid, and specific antimicrobial therapy

CONT.

for organ or deep-space and deep incisional infections. Repeat debridement or drainage may be required to control and resolve the infection even with appropriate antimicrobial therapy. When an SSI involves an implant, removal of the implant is preferred, followed by a prolonged course of antibiotics (6-8 weeks). Superficial incisional infections can usually be managed with oral antibiotics without tissue debridement. The choice of antimicrobial agent is guided by culture results; duration of treatment varies by anatomic site and by depth of infection. ◧

KEY POINT

- Surgical site infection treatment requires debridement of necrotic tissue, drainage of abscesses or infected fluid, and specific antimicrobial therapy for organ or deep-space and deep incisional infections.

Prevention

Prevention is divided into preoperative, intraoperative, and postoperative measures (see Table 58). Modifiable host factors should be optimized before surgery. If antibiotic prophylaxis is indicated, select the correct agent, dose, and time for administration (60 minutes before incision, 2 hours before incision for vancomycin or fluoroquinolones), and redose during surgery based on surgery duration and antibiotic half-life. Continuing antibiotics postoperatively does not decrease SSI incidence, even in cases of intraoperative spillage of gastrointestinal contents or presence of wound drains. ◧

KEY POINT

- Optimizing modifiable risk factors before surgery (hyperglycemia control, reduction of immunosuppressive agents, cessation of tobacco use, weight loss) can help prevent surgical site infections.

Central Line-Associated Bloodstream Infections

Central line–associated bloodstream infections (CLABSIs), associated with all types of central venous catheters (CVCs), are the most preventable HCAI. In the United States, CVC rates are 55% in ICU patients and 24% in non-ICU patients. Pathogens associated with CLABSIs include coagulase-negative staphylococci (20.5%), *S. aureus* (12.3%), *Enterococcus faecalis* (8.8%), non-albicans *Candida* species (8.1%), *Klebsiella pneumoniae* or *oxytoca* (7.9%), *Enterococcus faecium* (7%), and *Candida albicans* (6.5%). Antimicrobial resistance is a problem for many of these pathogens. CLABSI risk factors include prolonged hospitalization before catheterization, neutropenia, and reduced nurse-to-patient ratio in the ICU. Additional risk factors (modifiable) are shown in **Table 59**.

Diagnosis

CLABSI is suspected when a patient with a CVC has bacteremia not resulting from infection at another site. Two

TABLE 59. Mitigation of Risk Factors for Central Line-Associated Bloodstream Infections

Modifiable (Extrinsic) Risk Factor	Intervention
Prolonged catheterization	Daily review of continued need for CVC
	Discontinue as soon as practical
Multiple CVCs (increases risk 3.4-fold)	Minimize the number of CVCs as much as practical
Multilumen CVC	Use a catheter with the minimum number of lumens needed
Femoral vein catheterization; particularly in obese patients	Use subclavian site when possible
	Use ultrasonographic guidance for internal jugular catheter insertion
	Remove femoral vein CVCs as soon as practical, relocate to another site (e.g., subclavian, internal jugular vein) when possible
Heavy microbial colonization at insertion site and catheter hub	Chlorhexidine skin antisepsis at time of insertion
	Chlorhexidine-impregnated dressing
	Daily chlorhexidine bathing of patients in ICU
	Minimize catheter access
	Hand hygiene before manipulation of IV system; use aseptic technique for all IV access
	Disinfect catheter hub and needleless connectors ("scrub the hub") before accessing
Lack of maximal sterile barriers for insertion and breaks in aseptic technique	Follow CVC insertion bundle
Emergent insertion	When adherence to aseptic technique cannot be ensured, replace CVC as soon as possible (at least within 48 hours) to a new site
Total parenteral nutrition	Consider other options for delivering nutrition when possible

CVC = central venous catheter; IV = intravenous.

sets of peripheral blood cultures (20 mL blood/set) should be obtained from different sites before starting antibiotics. Blood cultures drawn directly from CVCs have a higher rate of false positivity and should be avoided; they may falsely identify a CLABSI and lead to unnecessary antibiotic therapy. ◧

KEY POINT

- A central line-associated bloodstream infection should be suspected when a patient with a central venous catheter has bacteremia not resulting from infection at another site.

Treatment

Infected CVCs should be removed. CVC removal is particularly important for *S. aureus*, *P. aeruginosa*, and *Candida* species infections. The duration of therapy for most cases of uncomplicated non–*S. aureus* CLABSI is 7 to 14 days (**Table 60**). *S. aureus* CLABSI is usually treated for at least 4 weeks; however, shorter-term therapy may be considered in select patients who have immediate catheter removal with resolution of fever and bacteremia within 72 hours of starting appropriate therapy and who have no implanted prosthetic devices, no evidence of endocarditis by echocardiography (preferably transesophageal), no evidence of suppurative thrombophlebitis, no evidence of metastatic infection, and neither diabetes mellitus nor immunosuppression. Bacteremia clearance should be confirmed with follow-up blood cultures. If bacteremia persists after CVC removal and appropriate antimicrobial therapy, evaluation for a deeper source of infection, including endocarditis, should be performed. All patients with candidemia should be evaluated by an ophthalmologist to rule out the presence of candida endophthalmitis within 1 to 2 weeks. **H**

KEY POINT

- The duration of therapy for most cases of uncomplicated non-*Staphylococcus aureus* central line–associated bloodstream infection is 7 to 14 days, although *S. aureus* infection is usually treated for at least 4 weeks.

Prevention

CVCs should be inserted only by experienced personnel using the insertion bundle of hand hygiene, chlorhexidine skin antisepsis of the insertion site using recommended application methods and contact time, maximal barrier precautions (mask, cap, gown, sterile gloves, large sterile drape covering patient), and optimal catheter site selection (subclavian site preferred, avoid femoral site). See Table 59 for further modifiable factors to prevent CLABSI. Insertion bundles, checklists, and staff education have significantly reduced CLABSIs. If CLABSI rates remain high despite adherence to these strategies, patient chlorhexidine bathing and antimicrobial-impregnated catheters (silver-sulfadiazine–chlorhexidine, minocycline-rifampin) may be considered. Routine CVC exchange or replacement or administration of systemic antimicrobial prophylaxis at time of insertion or during CVC use should be avoided.

Staphylococcus aureus Bacteremia

S. aureus is a leading cause of hospital-acquired bacteremia. Endocarditis and vertebral osteomyelitis are two important complications of *S. aureus* bacteremia, although they are less likely when the infection is hospital acquired. The source of bacteremia and possible metastatic infection should be determined, starting with a detailed history and examination. All patients should undergo evaluation for endocarditis with echocardiography, preferably transesophageal. Source control with removal or drainage of any focus of infection is important for treatment success. Blood cultures should be repeated every 2 to 4 days until results are negative to document clearance.

Bacteremia caused by methicillin-sensitive *S. aureus* (MSSA) should be treated with a penicillinase-resistant semisynthetic penicillin (such as oxacillin) or first-generation cephalosporin (such as cefazolin) at maximal doses. Vancomycin should be avoided in patients with MSSA who are not allergic to β-lactam antibiotics. Vancomycin is associated with higher rates of relapse and microbiologic failure in the treatment of MSSA bacteremia.

For methicillin-resistant *S. aureus* (MRSA) bacteremia, vancomycin and daptomycin are the preferred antibiotics. Vancomycin trough concentrations of 15 to 20 µg/mL are recommended; however, these concentrations increase the risk of nephrotoxicity, and kidney function should be closely monitored. Patients with concomitant *S. aureus* pneumonia should not receive daptomycin because it is inactivated by surfactant. The clinical and microbiologic response (clearance of bacteremia) determines whether to continue vancomycin or change to daptomycin when the MRSA isolate has a vancomycin

TABLE 60.	Management of Central Venous Catheter-Related Bloodstream Infection Based on Pathogen[a]
Organism	**Treatment**
Uncomplicated[b]	
Coagulase-negative staphylococci	Remove catheter, antimicrobial therapy for 5-7 days
	If catheter is not removed, systemic antimicrobials and antimicrobial lock treatment[c] for 10-14 days
Staphylococcus aureus (no active malignancy or immunosuppression)	Remove catheter, antimicrobials for ≥14 days (usually 4 weeks)
Enterococcus species	Remove catheter, antimicrobials for 7-14 days
Gram-negative bacilli	Remove catheter, antimicrobials for 7-14 days
Candida species	Remove catheter, antifungal agent for 14 additional days after first negative blood culture
Complicated	
Suppurative thrombophlebitis, endocarditis, osteomyelitis, other site of metastatic or deep-seated infection	Remove catheter, antimicrobials for 4-6 weeks (6-8 weeks for osteomyelitis)

[a]Short-term catheters.

[b]Bloodstream infection and fever resolve in 72 hours, no intravascular hardware, no endocarditis or suppurative thrombophlebitis.

[c]Antimicrobial solution (such as vancomycin) instilled into the lumen of a catheter and removed after a specified period of time.

CONT.
minimum inhibitory concentration of ≤2 µg/mL. Persistent bacteremia may be the result of slow bactericidal activity of vancomycin, inadequate dosing, poor tissue penetration, or inadequate source control. Higher-dose daptomycin (8-10 mg/kg/d) is sometimes used if bacteremia persists despite adequate source control. Vancomycin should not be used when the isolate has a minimum inhibitory concentration greater than 2 µg/mL; daptomycin is an acceptable alternative if the isolate is susceptible. The median time to clearance of MRSA bacteremia is 7 to 9 days.

Bacteremia that persists beyond 72 hours of starting appropriate antibiotic treatment suggests a complicated *S. aureus* infection and requires additional evaluation and a longer course of antibiotics (4-6 weeks). Management of persistent MSSA and MRSA bacteremia also includes a thorough search for and removal of all foci of infection, including surgical debridement of infected wounds and abscess drainage. A new focus of infection may develop with persistent bacteremia and should always be considered in the evaluation of persistent bacteremia. Combination antimicrobial agents (for example, a β-lactam and aminoglycoside, vancomycin and rifampin) have not been shown to improve outcomes and should not be used. H

KEY POINTS

- Bacteremia caused by methicillin-sensitive *Staphylococcus aureus* (MSSA) should be treated with a penicillinase-resistant semisynthetic penicillin or first-generation cephalosporin at maximal doses; vancomycin should be avoided in patients who are not allergic to β-lactam antibiotics because it is associated with higher rates of relapse and microbiologic failure in the treatment of MSSA bacteremia.

- Vancomycin and daptomycin are the preferred antibiotics for methicillin-resistant *Staphylococcus aureus* bacteremia, although patients with concomitant *S. aureus* pneumonia should not receive daptomycin because it is inactivated by surfactant.

H Hospital-Acquired Pneumonia and Ventilator-Associated Pneumonia

Hospital-acquired pneumonia (HAP) is pneumonia developing more than 48 hours after hospitalization. Ventilator-associated pneumonia (VAP) is pneumonia developing 48 hours after endotracheal intubation; it occurs in 10% of patients undergoing ventilation. Half of patients with HAP develop serious complications, including respiratory failure, pleural effusion, septic shock, empyema, and kidney injury. Mechanical ventilation increases the risk of pneumonia 6-fold to 21-fold. HAP and VAP risk factors include age older than 70 years, recent abdominal or thoracic surgery, immunosuppression, and underlying chronic lung disease. Modifiable risk factors are listed in **Table 61**.

TABLE 61. Mitigation of Risk Factors for Ventilator-Associated Pneumonia	
Risk Factor	**Intervention**
Mechanical ventilation	Consider noninvasive, positive-pressure ventilation
Sedation	Minimize
	Intermittent infusions or daily interruption and daily assessment of readiness for extubation
Supine position	Risk highest for patients receiving enteral nutrition
	Elevate head of bed 30°-45°
Oropharyngeal colonization	Daily oral care; oral care with chlorhexidine may be beneficial in some patients
Physical conditioning	Facilitate early mobility (speeds extubation)
Reintubation	Consider noninvasive, positive-pressure ventilation

HAP and VAP are most commonly caused by bacteria, but viral and fungal pathogens should be considered in immunocompromised patients. The main risk factor for MRSA, antibiotic-resistant *Pseudomonas*, or other antibiotic-resistant pathogens is intravenous antibiotic use within the past 90 days. Additional risk factors for multidrug-resistant pathogens associated with VAP are septic shock at the time of VAP, acute respiratory distress syndrome preceding VAP, 5 or more days of hospitalization before VAP, and acute kidney replacement therapy before VAP.

Diagnosis

Diagnosis relies on a combination of clinical, radiographic, and microbiologic findings. A new lung infiltrate on imaging plus clinical findings, including new-onset fever (temperature >38 °C [100.4 °F]), leukocytosis or leukopenia, purulent sputum, and decline in oxygenation, suggest pneumonia. Noninvasive sampling (endotracheal aspiration) with semiquantitative sputum cultures (heavy, moderate, light, and no growth) are suggested for diagnosing VAP. Clinical findings without radiographic support suggest tracheobronchitis, which does not require antibiotic treatment. H

KEY POINT

- The diagnosis of hospital-acquired and ventilator-associated pneumonia are suggested by a new lung infiltrate on imaging plus clinical findings, including new-onset fever, leukocytosis or leukopenia, purulent sputum, and decline in oxygenation.

Treatment

Therapy for suspected HAP should be based on respiratory sample culture results; a specimen from the lower respiratory tract should be obtained before starting antimicrobial therapy. However, inability to obtain a specimen should not delay therapy initiation for VAP, and empiric antimicrobial therapy

CONT.

should be instituted for patients with VAP pending results of noninvasive sampling with semiquantitative cultures and based on local VAP antibiograms, if available.

Empiric VAP regimens should include coverage for *S. aureus*, *P. aeruginosa*, and other gram-negative bacilli. An agent active against MRSA (vancomycin, linezolid) should be included for patients with MRSA risk factors or those in a unit with MRSA prevalence greater than 10% to 20% or unknown. Two antipseudomonal agents of different classes are recommended for empiric regimens only for patients with risk factors for resistance, with structural lung disease (bronchiectasis, cystic fibrosis), or in a unit with greater than 10% resistance to an agent being considered for monotherapy. Similar regimens are recommended for patients with HAP who are treated empirically. Antimicrobial coverage for oral anaerobes may be considered in patients with witnessed aspiration events or recent surgery. Cephalosporins should be avoided as monotherapy in settings where extended-spectrum β-lactamase (ESBL)–producing gram-negative organisms (such as *Klebsiella pneumoniae*) are prevalent; consider a carbapenem instead. VAP caused by gram-negative organisms sensitive only to aminoglycosides or colistin may be treated with a combination of systemic and aerosolized antibiotics.

Microbiologic results should be reviewed at 48 to 72 hours, and all patients should be re-evaluated for clinical improvement. Antimicrobial therapy should be de-escalated (to narrow-spectrum or oral therapy) based on microbiologic results and clinical stabilization or discontinued if the diagnosis of pneumonia is in doubt. Patients who do not improve within 72 hours of appropriate therapy should undergo investigation for infectious complications, an alternate diagnosis, or another site of infection. HAP and VAP should be treated for 7 days or less.

KEY POINT

- Empiric ventilator-associated pneumonia regimens should include coverage for *Staphylococcus aureus*, *Pseudomonas aeruginosa*, and other gram-negative bacilli; an agent active against methicillin-resistant *S. aureus* (MRSA) should be included for patients with MRSA risk factors or where MRSA prevalence exceeds 10% (or is unknown); similar regimens are recommended for empiric hospital-acquired pneumonia treatment.

Prevention

Commonly used ventilator bundles include subglottic suctioning, peptic ulcer disease and deep venous thrombosis prophylaxis, and avoiding gastric overdistention. Use of ventilator bundles has been shown to decrease VAP rates by 71%. Additional interventions are listed in Table 61.

KEY POINT

HVC

- In patients receiving mechanical ventilation, the head of the bed should be elevated 30° to 45°; a supine position, particularly in patients receiving enteral nutrition, increases the risk for developing ventilator-associated pneumonia.

Hospital-Acquired Infections Caused by Multidrug-Resistant Organisms

Antimicrobial resistance has been noted in nearly all bacterial pathogens. Multidrug-resistant organisms (MDROs) are most prevalent in health care settings (highest incidence in long-term acute care hospitals) but are also observed in the community. Seven of the 15 MDROs deemed urgent threats are predominantly health care associated. Nearly half of *S. aureus* HCAIs in the United States are methicillin resistant, 30% of enterococci are vancomycin resistant, 18% of Enterobacteriaceae produce ESBL and are resistant to all β-lactam antibiotics, 4% of Enterobacteriaceae are resistant to carbapenems, and 16% of *P. aeruginosa* and about half of *Acinetobacter* species are multidrug resistant. *Clostridium difficile* is not technically an MDRO, but it is a problematic pathogen in health care settings.

MDRO infections are difficult to treat, with mortality rates up to four times higher than infections caused by antibiotic-sensitive strains. Limiting transmission of MDROs in health care settings requires full adherence to hand hygiene protocols, contact precautions, and cleaning and disinfecting of the environment and patient care equipment. More than half of hospitalized patients receive antibiotics, a major risk for acquiring an antibiotic-resistant organism and *C. difficile* infection. Judicious use of antimicrobial agents is increasingly important to combat the rise of MDROs and emergence of untreatable infections.

KEY POINTS

- Multidrug-resistant organisms (MDROs) are most prevalent in health care settings (highest incidence in long-term acute care hospitals) but are also observed in the community.

HVC

- Limiting emergence and transmission of multidrug-resistant organisms in health care settings requires full adherence to hand hygiene protocols, contact precautions, cleaning and disinfecting of the environment and equipment, and judicious use of antimicrobial agents.

HIV/AIDS

HIV is a retrovirus that infects CD4 lymphocytes, among other cell types. Depletion of CD4 T-helper cells results in impairment of cell-mediated immunity and increasing risk for opportunistic infections. This chapter will focus on HIV-1. Infection with HIV-2 primarily occurs in parts of Africa and remains rare in the United States; HIV-2 generally is a less progressive disease with less immunocompromise and lower risk of opportunistic infections. Current testing for HIV infection detects HIV-1 and HIV-2 antibodies (see Screening and Diagnosis).

Epidemiology and Prevention

HIV infection remains a significant global health concern despite being a treatable disease. Many persons living with HIV infection are not aware of their status because they have never been tested; others have been diagnosed but are not receiving care. Those with undiagnosed or untreated infection are responsible for most new infections. Diagnosis and successful treatment are crucial for personal and public health.

HIV transmission occurs through sexual contact or exposure to other body fluids (**Table 62**). Reducing transmission can be accomplished by using barrier methods, such as condoms during sexual contact, and through clean syringe services programs (needle exchange programs) for injection drug users. Universal blood donor testing has all but eliminated infection through blood transfusion in the United States, with current risk estimated to be one in 2 million.

HIV treatment has extraordinary potential to reduce new infections in addition to benefiting the treated person. Successful treatment is associated with significant reductions in HIV transmission. Although reducing viral load to an undetectable level in blood does not prove absence of virus in semen or vaginal fluid, the rate of transmission from a sexual partner with undetectable blood viral load has been demonstrated to be close to zero, at a level the Centers for Disease Control and Prevention (CDC) called "effectively no risk" in a September 2017 statement, leading to the slogan "Undetectable = Untransmissable" ("U=U"). In what is known as the "treatment cascade," steps of medical care necessary to achieve successful viral suppression consist of testing and diagnosing infected persons, linking them to health care for counseling and treatment, keeping them in a treatment program, and ensuring antiretroviral and other treatment adherence. Each step along this continuum of care is a potential obstacle to successful management of HIV on a personal and public health level. Even high-income countries, such as the United States, have poor rates of retention in care and adherence to medication. One study estimated that the undiagnosed and not-in-care groups with HIV infection were responsible for 91.5% of HIV transmissions in the United States in 2009.

In 2014, the Joint United Nations Programme on HIV/AIDS (UNAIDS) launched its "90-90-90" program of ambitious goals for reducing new HIV infection worldwide. These goals include that by 2020, 90% of HIV-infected persons will have been diagnosed, 90% of those diagnosed will be receiving treatment, and 90% of those receiving treatment will have successful viral suppression. Achieving such goals will require considerable resource commitment but, if achieved, will also dramatically reduce transmission and new HIV infections.

Postexposure prophylaxis antiretroviral therapy has been used successfully for many years in uninfected persons to prevent infection after occupational and nonoccupational HIV exposure. Prophylaxis should be started as soon as possible after exposure; it is not recommended if more than 72 hours have passed. A three-drug regimen is given for 4 weeks; the preferred regimen is tenofovir disoproxil fumarate and emtricitabine plus either raltegravir or dolutegravir. HIV testing of the exposed person should be conducted at baseline and at 4 to 6 weeks and 3 months after exposure. **Figure 22** shows an algorithm for evaluation of possible HIV exposure.

Pre-exposure prophylaxis (PrEP) with antiretroviral medication is recommended in select persons at high risk for exposure to HIV to reduce the risk of infection. A two-drug combination of tenofovir disoproxil fumarate and emtricitabine, taken once daily, is FDA approved for HIV PrEP; it has been shown to be effective in reducing infection in heterosexual couples, men who have sex with men, and injection drug users. Effectiveness is greater than 90% in those with proven adherence. Patients should also be counseled on the need to continue barrier precautions, on medication toxicity, and on continued risk for other sexually transmitted infections (STIs). Testing should be performed for HIV, hepatitis B virus (HBV), kidney function, and pregnancy before PrEP initiation; monitoring for HIV, other STIs, and pregnancy every 3 months and performing kidney function assessment every 6 months are also recommended during PrEP therapy. Persons taking PrEP who test positive for HIV should have a third drug (either ritonavir-boosted darunavir or dolutegravir) added to the two-drug PrEP regimen pending results of HIV RNA and viral resistance testing. The evidence is conflicting concerning potentially increased high-risk behavior and incidence of other STIs in PrEP users during therapy. PrEP has also been calculated to have favorable cost effectiveness, well below that for other accepted preventive health measures.

TABLE 62.	Risk of HIV-1 Transmission per Single Exposure
Exposure	**Risk (%)**
Occupational—needlestick	0.23
Occupational—mucous membrane	0.09
Needle-sharing injection drug use	0.63
Receptive anal intercourse	1.4
Receptive vaginal intercourse	0.08
Insertive anal intercourse	0.11
Insertive vaginal intercourse	0.04
Oral sex	0.01

KEY POINTS

- Although reducing viral load to an undetectable level in blood does not equal absence of virus in semen or vaginal fluid, the rate of transmission from a sexual partner with undetectable blood viral load is exceedingly low, with reductions in risk greater than 95%.

- Postexposure prophylaxis with a three-drug regimen (tenofovir disoproxil fumarate and emtricitabine plus either raltegravir or dolutegravir) should be started as soon as possible after HIV exposure; it is not recommended if more than 72 hours have passed.

(Continued)

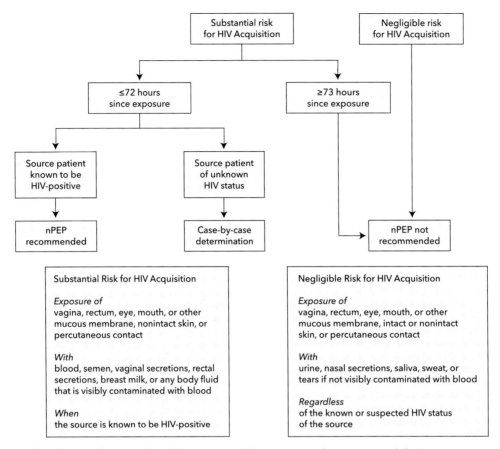

FIGURE 22. Algorithm for evaluation and treatment of possible HIV exposure. nPEP = nonoccupational postexposure prophylaxis.

Centers for Disease Control and Prevention. Updated guidelines for antiretroviral postexposure prophylaxis after sexual, injection drug use, or other nonoccupational exposure to HIV—United States, 2016. Available at https://stacks.cdc.gov/view/cdc/38856. Accessed January 29, 2018.

KEY POINTS *(continued)*

- Pre-exposure prophylaxis with two antiretroviral medications (tenofovir disoproxil fumarate and emtricitabine) is recommended in select persons at high risk for exposure to HIV to reduce the risk of infection.

Pathophysiology and Natural History

Acute Retroviral Syndrome

Most persons with acute HIV infection are symptomatic; however, because symptoms are nonspecific and self-limited, most acute infections are not diagnosed accurately. The frequency of signs and symptoms at presentation is shown in **Table 63**. The differential diagnosis includes Epstein-Barr virus infection, cytomegalovirus infection, and secondary syphilis. During symptomatic acute infection, HIV antibody may not yet be detectable, and diagnosis depends on demonstration of p24 antigen or HIV RNA. Currently recommended HIV testing includes p24 antigen testing as part of the initial evaluation (see Screening and Diagnosis). Persons with acute HIV infection should be immediately linked to care for prompt initiation of treatment.

TABLE 63. Signs and Symptoms of Acute HIV Infection (Acute Retroviral Syndrome)

Sign/Symptom	Frequency (%)
Fever	75
Fatigue	68
Myalgia	49
Rash	48
Headache	45
Pharyngitis	40
Lymphadenopathy	39
Arthralgia	30
Night sweats	28
Diarrhea	27

KEY POINT

- Most persons with acute HIV infection are symptomatic; however, because symptoms are nonspecific and self-limited, most acute infections are not diagnosed accurately.

Chronic HIV Infection and AIDS

Patients with chronic HIV infection may present with opportunistic infections, especially when CD4 counts are less than 200/μL, meeting the definition for AIDS (see Opportunistic Infections). Even before progression to AIDS, patients with HIV infection may present with recurrent or severe episodes of infections that do not qualify as opportunistic, such as bacterial pneumonia, herpes zoster, herpes simplex virus, or vaginal candidiasis. Other symptoms can result from chronic HIV infection itself, including lymphadenopathy, fever, night sweats, fatigue, weight loss, chronic diarrhea, and various oral and skin conditions (see MKSAP 18 Dermatology). HIV should also be considered in patients with unexplained cytopenias or nephropathy.

KEY POINTS

- Before progression to AIDS, patients with chronic HIV infection may present with recurrent or severe episodes of infections that do not qualify as opportunistic, such as bacterial pneumonia, herpes zoster, herpes simplex virus, or vaginal candidiasis.
- Symptoms that can result from chronic HIV infection itself include lymphadenopathy, fever, night sweats, fatigue, weight loss, chronic diarrhea, and various oral and skin conditions.

Screening and Diagnosis

Although any of the presenting symptoms described previously should prompt HIV testing, testing only symptomatic persons neglects numerous persons who are infected. Thus, the CDC, American College of Physicians, Infectious Diseases Society of America, and U.S. Preventive Services Task Force (USPSTF) recommend universal screening for HIV in all adults at least once. The USPSTF suggests those at higher risk (injection drug users and their sexual partners, people who exchange sex for money or drugs, sexual partners of HIV-infected persons, and those with more than one sexual partner since their most recent HIV test) should undergo repeat HIV testing at least annually. In 2017, the CDC reaffirmed its support for this recommendation but noted that clinicians can consider the potential benefits of more frequent HIV screening (for example, every 3 or 6 months) for some asymptomatic sexually active men who have sex with men based on their individual risk factors, local HIV epidemiology, and local policies.

Current (fourth generation) HIV testing uses a combination assay for HIV antibody and HIV p24 antigen, which detects acute infection at least 1 week earlier than older assays. A positive result on the combination assay leads to testing with an HIV-1/HIV-2 antibody differentiation immunoassay, which, if positive, confirms infection. Specimens that test positive on the initial combination assay but negative for HIV antibody are tested for HIV RNA by nucleic acid amplification testing; if positive, acute HIV infection is confirmed (**Figure 23**). Although the initial combination assay has a 99.6% specificity, testing in low prevalence populations (such as general screening) can still result in false positives, so waiting for the results of the confirmatory antibody differentiation immunoassay and nucleic acid amplification testing is important for a definitive diagnosis.

KEY POINTS

- It is recommended that all adults be tested for HIV infection at least once.
- A combination assay for HIV antibody and HIV p24 antigen now detects acute infection at least 1 week earlier than older assays; a positive HIV-1/HIV-2 antibody immunoassay result confirms infection, or a positive HIV RNA nucleic acid amplification test result confirms acute HIV infection.

Initiation of Care

Initial Evaluation and Laboratory Testing

All persons who test positive for HIV should be immediately referred to a health care provider with HIV infection management expertise. Initial evaluation should include complete history (including social and sexual) and examination for signs and symptoms of opportunistic infection or other complications. Patient education and counseling should include information on transmission and prevention. Initial laboratory tests include baseline organ function and evaluation for other infections with higher prevalence in persons with HIV (**Table 64**). A baseline CD4 cell count guides opportunistic infection prophylaxis, and a baseline viral load supports monitoring antiretroviral therapy effectiveness (see Management of HIV Infection).

Immunizations and Prophylaxis for Opportunistic Infections

Numerous immunizations are recommended for all persons with HIV, starting with the 13-valent pneumococcal conjugate and 23-valent pneumococcal polysaccharide vaccines, respectively, at least 8 weeks apart; a 23-valent polysaccharide vaccine booster is also recommended after 5 years. Patients who are not already immune or infected with HBV should receive the hepatitis B vaccine series. Influenza, tetanus-diphtheria-pertussis, hepatitis A, and human papillomavirus vaccinations are indicated as for the general population. Measles-mumps-rubella and varicella vaccines can be given as long as the CD4 cell count is greater than 200/μL. Although the recombinant zoster vaccine is considered safe in immunocompromised persons because it does not contain live virus, safety and efficacy data in patients with HIV are not yet available to inform recommendations. The Advisory Committee on Immunization Practices recommends that all persons with HIV infection be vaccinated for meningococcal disease with the quadrivalent meningococcal vaccine, including boosters every 5 years.

Prophylaxis for opportunistic infections depends on the patient's CD4 cell count (**Table 65**). Before beginning

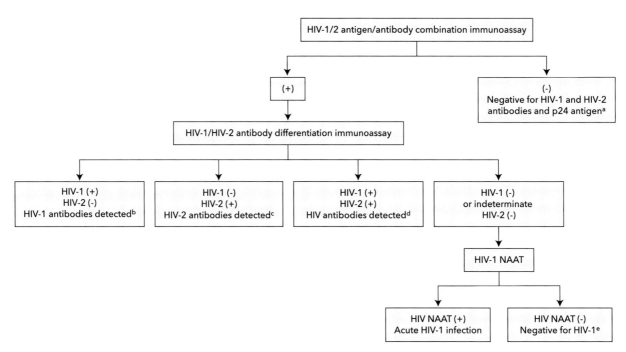

FIGURE 23. CDC-recommended algorithm for laboratory HIV testing. NAAT = nucleic acid amplification test. (+) indicates reactive test result. (−) indicates nonreactive test result.

[a]No evidence of HIV infection.

[b]HIV-1 infection.

[c]HIV-2 infection.

[d]HIV-1 and HIV-2 infection.

[e]HIV-1/2 antigen/antibody combination immunoassay result was a false positive.

Centers for Disease Control and Prevention; Association of Public Health Laboratories. Laboratory testing for the diagnosis of HIV infection: updated recommendations. January 2018. Available at https://stacks.cdc.gov/view/cdc/50872.

TABLE 64. Laboratory Testing as Part of the Evaluation of HIV Infection
Repeat HIV antibody testing if no documentation
Viral resistance testing at baseline and for treatment failure
Quantitative HIV RNA assay (viral load)
T-cell subsets (CD4 cell count)
Complete blood count with differential
Chemistries, including kidney function studies and fasting plasma glucose level
Liver chemistry studies/liver enzyme levels
Fasting serum lipid profile
Urinalysis or quantitative measure of proteinuria
Tuberculin skin test or interferon-γ release assay
Serologic testing for hepatitis A, B, and C virus infection
Serologic testing for syphilis; testing for other sexually transmitted infections
Serologic testing for toxoplasmosis
Cervical Pap test

TABLE 65. Prophylaxis against Opportunistic Infections in HIV/AIDS

Opportunistic Infection	Indication	Preferred Drug
Pneumocystis jirovecii	CD4 cell count <200/μL[a]	TMP-SMX, double-strength or single-strength tablet once daily
Toxoplasmosis	CD4 cell count <100/μL and positive serologic results[a]	TMP-SMX, double-strength tablet once daily
Mycobacterium avium complex	CD4 cell count <50/μL	Azithromycin, 1200 mg once weekly or 600 mg twice weekly; clarithromycin, 500 mg twice daily
Latent tuberculosis	TST >5 mm or positive IGRA results	Isoniazid, 300 mg once daily for 9 months or 900 mg twice weekly, both with pyridoxine, 25 mg once daily

IGRA = interferon-γ release assay; TMP-SMX = trimethoprim-sulfamethoxazole; TST = tuberculin skin test.

[a]Prophylaxis may be discontinued in patients with suppressed viral load and CD4 cell count ≥200/μL for ≥3 months.

prophylaxis, active infection should be ruled out clinically and with any indicated testing to avoid undertreatment and selection for resistance, especially for tuberculosis and disseminated *Mycobacterium avium* complex.

- All persons with HIV should receive the 13-valent pneumococcal conjugate and 23-valent polysaccharide vaccines, hepatitis B vaccine series (in those not already infected or immune), and meningococcal vaccine; influenza, tetanus-diphtheria-pertussis, hepatitis A, and human papillomavirus vaccines are indicated as for the general population.
- Active infection should be ruled out before initiation of prophylaxis for opportunistic infections.

Complications of HIV Infection in the Antiretroviral Therapy Era

Metabolic, Kidney, and Liver Disorders

As HIV has become a treatable illness and persons with HIV age, metabolic disorders and specific organ diseases have become increasingly significant. HIV infection itself may be associated with manifestations of accelerated aging, and neurocognitive impairment can be exacerbated by HIV. Age-associated comorbidities and declines in kidney and liver function can also complicate management through drug interactions and increased toxicity.

HIV infection itself and some antiretrovirals affect lipids and can worsen hyperlipidemia; this is especially true for boosted protease inhibitor–based regimens, which can also worsen insulin resistance. Fasting glucose or hemoglobin A_{1c} and lipid levels should be checked at baseline and 3 months after initiating or changing antiretrovirals.

Chronic kidney disease is increasingly common in HIV infection, although, with effective antiretroviral therapy, it is less often attributed to HIV nephropathy. It is recommended that kidney function be assessed at least every 6 months in patients with HIV. Tenofovir, a very commonly used nucleoside analogue, is associated with risk for tubular nephrotoxicity, which usually manifests as proteinuria. Patients using a regimen containing tenofovir should undergo urinalysis or quantitative measurement of urine protein twice per year.

Bone mineral density is reduced in HIV, and tenofovir is also associated with possible worsening of bone density. Dual-energy x-ray absorptiometry scanning is recommended in men older than 50 years, postmenopausal women, patients with a history of fragility fracture, those with chronic glucocorticoid use, and those at high risk for falls. A newer prodrug of tenofovir, tenofovir alafenamide (TAF), achieves high intracellular levels of active drug with much lower dosing and lower systemic levels compared with the older formulation, tenofovir disoproxil fumarate (TDF). Compared with TDF, TAF has equal antiviral efficacy with reduced kidney and bone toxicity and should be used preferentially over TDF in patients with or at risk for bone or kidney disease.

Liver disease is also increased in HIV infection, often because of coinfection with hepatitis B or C virus. All patients with HIV should be screened for hepatitis B and C viruses. Patients should be immunized if they are HBV negative. If coinfected with HIV and HBV, patients should receive treatment with a tenofovir (either TDF or TAF) plus emtricitabine or lamivudine-based regimen, which treats both viruses. Patients coinfected with hepatitis C virus should be given a course of curative direct-acting antiviral treatment, although attention must be paid to drug interactions between the antiviral regimens (see MKSAP 18 Gastroenterology and Hepatology).

- Fasting glucose or hemoglobin A_{1c} and lipid levels should be checked at baseline and 3 months after initiating or changing antiretroviral therapy.
- Tenofovir disoproxil fumarate (TDF), a very commonly used nucleoside analogue in HIV therapy, is associated with increased risks of tubular nephrotoxicity and worsening of bone mineral density; tenofovir alafenamide should be used preferentially over TDF in patients with or at risk for bone or kidney disease.

Cardiovascular Disease

Rates of cardiovascular disease, including myocardial infarction and stroke, are higher in persons with HIV infection; this association remains after correction for increased risk factors such as smoking. Some of the increase may result from hyperlipidemia, but evidence indicates that the increase partially results from HIV infection being a chronic inflammatory state. It is clear that patients with untreated HIV infection have a higher risk of cardiovascular events compared with patients taking effective antiretroviral therapy, regardless of any worsening of lipid levels from the antiretroviral therapy. Attention to traditional risk factors such as smoking, lipid levels, and hypertension is crucial in patients with HIV, as is use of statin therapy (with attention to drug interactions between some statins and some antiretrovirals) based on current risk calculations. An international multicenter trial is addressing whether patients with HIV should be treated with statins even with a 10-year risk less than 7.5%.

- Rates of cardiovascular disease, including myocardial infarction and stroke, are higher in persons with HIV infection; control of cardiovascular risk factors (smoking, lipid levels, and hypertension) is essential, including statin therapy based on clinical risk calculations.

Immune Reconstitution Inflammatory Syndrome

Immune reconstitution inflammatory syndrome (IRIS) is a disorder associated either with worsening of a pre-existing infectious process (paradoxical IRIS) or with revelation of a previously unrecognized pre-existing infection (unmasking IRIS). It has also been reported with noninfectious complications, such as lymphoma. IRIS usually occurs within a few months of initiating effective antiretroviral therapy in patients with low pretreatment CD4 cell counts (<100/µL). Management of IRIS includes continuing antiretroviral therapy while treating the opportunistic infection. In select patients, NSAIDs or glucocorticoids may be useful in mitigating inflammatory symptoms.

KEY POINT

- Immune reconstitution inflammatory syndrome is caused by an inflammatory response to a pre-existing infectious process; it usually occurs within a few months of initiating effective antiretroviral therapy and presents with a wide variety of infections and noninfectious complications.

Opportunistic Infections

Mucocutaneous *Candida* infections can occur in HIV-infected patients at relatively preserved CD4 cell counts. HIV-infected patients do not usually develop invasive *Candida* infection unless they have other risk factors, such as neutropenia. Oral candidiasis usually presents as thrush, with mucosal whitish plaques, and can be treated topically (for example, with clotrimazole troches) or with a short course of oral fluconazole. Swallowing symptoms suggest esophageal disease, which requires systemic treatment, such as fluconazole, for a longer course; a lack of treatment response is an indication for endoscopy.

Reactivation of latent tuberculosis is also significantly increased in HIV infection, even without a decreased CD4 cell count. Tuberculosis is also more likely to present in extrapulmonary sites or with an atypical chest radiograph. Tuberculosis treatment in HIV must consider interactions of rifamycins with many antiretrovirals.

Infections with other opportunistic organisms usually occur at CD4 cell counts less than 200/µL. *Pneumocystis jirovecii* pneumonia usually presents as a subacute illness with fever, dyspnea, and dry cough in a patient with a CD4 cell count less than 200/µL who is not receiving prophylaxis. Chest radiographs most often show bilateral interstitial infiltrates; cavitation or pleural effusion is unusual and suggests another diagnosis. A normal chest radiograph does not exclude the diagnosis, and chest CT is more sensitive, demonstrating patchy "ground-glass" opacities. Normal lactate dehydrogenase levels and stable exercise oxygen saturation have a high negative predictive value, but elevated lactate dehydrogenase levels and oxygen desaturation with exercise are nonspecific. Diagnosis depends on demonstration of causative organisms and often requires bronchoscopy. The treatment of choice is high-dose trimethoprim-sulfamethoxazole; patients who are hypoxic at presentation should be given adjunctive glucocorticoids to prevent the worsening that may accompany initiation of treatment.

Cryptococcus infection usually presents as subacute meningitis with headache, mental status changes, and fever. Because it often involves the basilar area, cranial nerve deficits may also be seen. The diagnosis can be made most swiftly by antigen testing of cerebrospinal fluid and blood. Management includes antifungal therapy and attention to increased intracranial pressure, which is usually responsible for the morbidity and mortality associated with cryptococcal meningitis (see Fungal Infections).

Toxoplasma gondii infection in AIDS usually presents in patients with CD4 cell counts less than 100/µL. Because it is a reactivation disease, patients are usually serology positive. Clinical presentation includes headache, fever, and focal neurologic deficits. Imaging by CT or MRI (which is more sensitive) reveals multiple ring-enhancing lesions. The differential diagnosis includes primary central nervous system lymphoma, which most often appears as a single lesion on imaging, and progressive multifocal leukoencephalopathy, which is usually nonenhancing. Diagnosis of central nervous system toxoplasmosis is usually presumptive based on presentation, imaging, and response to empiric treatment.

Mycobacterium avium complex infection usually presents as disseminated disease in patients with CD4 cell counts less than 50/µL; symptoms and signs include fever, sweats, weight loss, hepatosplenomegaly, lymphadenopathy, and cytopenias. Blood cultures for acid-fast bacilli will usually grow *Mycobacterium avium* complex, but it may also be found on lymph node or liver biopsy when necessary.

Cytomegalovirus most commonly presents with CD4 cell counts less than 50/µL. Cytomegalovirus retinitis, presenting with vision changes or floaters, is much more likely in AIDS than in other immunocompromised conditions, such as after transplantation. Gastrointestinal cytomegalovirus disease is also common, most often as esophagitis or colitis.

Patients with AIDS are also more likely to develop certain malignancies, especially those related to viruses. Non-Hodgkin lymphoma, especially primary central nervous system lymphoma related to Epstein-Barr virus, is significantly increased compared with age-matched controls. Kaposi sarcoma is caused by human herpes virus type 8 and presents as dark red, brown, or violaceous lesions of the skin or mucous membranes (**Figure 24**); human herpes virus type 8 can also cause primary effusion lymphoma and Castleman disease (giant lymph node hyperplasia). Human papillomavirus–related malignancies are significantly increased in HIV, including cervical and anal cancers, and regular guideline-based screening is important.

KEY POINTS

- *Pneumocystis jirovecii* pneumonia usually presents as a subacute illness with fever, dyspnea, and dry cough; although chest radiographs most often show bilateral interstitial infiltrates, a normal chest radiograph does not exclude the diagnosis.

(Continued)

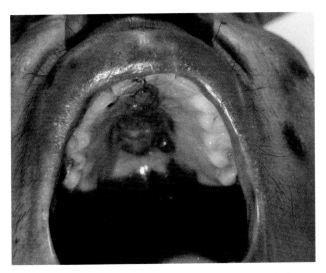

FIGURE 24. Kaposi sarcoma, presenting as firm purple nodules on the face and purple palatal nodules, is seen in a patient with AIDS.

KEY POINTS *(continued)*

- Successful management of *Cryptococcus* infection in patients with HIV includes antifungal therapy and attention to increased intracranial pressure, which is usually responsible for the morbidity and mortality associated with cryptococcal meningitis.

- *Toxoplasma gondii* infection in patients with HIV presents as multifocal central nervous system abscesses; MRI is more sensitive than CT in revealing characteristic ring-enhancing lesions.

- *Mycobacterium avium* complex and cytomegalovirus infections usually present in patients with HIV with CD4 cell counts less than 50/μL.

- Patients with AIDS are more likely to develop certain malignancies, including non-Hodgkin lymphoma, Kaposi sarcoma, and human papillomavirus–related malignancies (cervical and anal cancers).

Management of HIV Infection

When to Initiate Treatment

All persons with HIV infection should begin antiretroviral therapy as soon as they are ready, regardless of CD4 cell count. Previous controversy over whether to start antiretroviral treatment in asymptomatic patients with normal CD4 cell counts has been resolved with demonstration of clear clinical benefit in a large prospective, randomized clinical trial.

Antiretroviral Regimens

Antiretroviral agents used in the United States are shown in **Table 66**. Standards for effective antiretroviral regimens include use of three drugs from two different classes, preferably combining two nucleoside reverse transcriptase inhibitors with an integrase strand transfer inhibitor. Preferred regimens also feature a high barrier to resistance, good tolerability and safety, and combination pills with once-daily dosing to facilitate adherence (**Table 67**).

Patients with or at risk for reduced kidney function or osteopenia should not be given TDF. Patients who are prescribed abacavir must first undergo testing to show they are HLA-B*5701 negative to reduce the risk of hypersensitivity. Many antiretrovirals have interactions with other drugs, and potential drug interactions must always be assessed when beginning HIV therapy or beginning any drug for someone already taking antiretroviral therapy. Such assessment is especially necessary when pharmacokinetic boosters (ritonavir or cobicistat) are used specifically to inhibit drug metabolism and raise levels of antiretrovirals.

Viral load levels and CD4 cell counts are monitored to ensure effectiveness and to assess for immune recovery. With optimal therapy, HIV RNA in blood should become and stay undetectable. CD4 cell counts will increase, although cell counts may take time to improve and may not show full recovery, especially in those who are older or who have other factors affecting lymphocytes. Patients taking antiretroviral therapy who are stable with a CD4 cell count of 500/μL or more for more than 2 years can stop T-cell monitoring as long as viral load remains undetectable.

Resistance Testing

Viral resistance testing should be performed at baseline to ensure selection of a fully active regimen and should be repeated if the viral load increases during antiretroviral treatment. The most common reason for breakthrough viremia is poor medication adherence. In general, plasma levels of HIV RNA must be greater than 500 copies/mL to provide enough virus for resistance testing. Viral resistance testing can be genotypic (looking for mutations associated with drug resistance) or phenotypic (assessing whether virus can replicate in the presence of the drug). Genotypic testing is faster and cheaper, but phenotypic testing may be better in the presence of multiple mutations or for drugs such as protease inhibitors in which the correlation of specific mutations and resistance is less straightforward. Resistance testing results are used to guide selection of a new regimen in the event resistant virus develops, but previous resistance testing results as well as previous regimens and responses must also be considered. Resistance testing may not be reliable if performed while the patient is not taking an antiretroviral regimen because resistance may not be detectable without the selective pressure of the antiretrovirals. Once selected for, previous mutations are generally archived in the viral population and may re-emerge even if resistance testing does not demonstrate the mutation. A regimen may also be switched because of adverse effects or to ease adherence or avoid drug interactions. Laboratory monitoring tests should be repeated 1 month after switching regimens to assess effectiveness and toxicity.

TABLE 66. Antiretroviral Agents Used in the United States to Treat HIV Infection

Class	Agent[a]	Adverse Effects
Nucleoside RTIs	Abacavir	Hypersensitivity[b] (exclude HLA-B*5701 before prescribing)
	Emtricitabine	Minimal toxicity; has activity against HBV, and exacerbations have occurred with discontinuation of therapy
	Lamivudine	Minimal toxicity; has HBV activity, but dosing differs for HIV and HBV treatment
	TDF	Nausea, kidney disease, Fanconi syndrome, decreased bone density; has activity against HBV, and exacerbations have occurred with discontinuation of therapy
	TAF	Nausea; less kidney and bone toxicity than TDF
	Zidovudine	Nausea, headache, anemia[b], leukopenia[b], lactic acidosis[b], lipodystrophy, myopathy[b]
Nonnucleoside RTIs	Efavirenz	Neuropsychiatric symptoms (dizziness, somnolence, sleep disturbance, vivid dreams, mood changes), rash, dyslipidemia
	Etravirine	Nausea, rash
	Nevirapine	Hypersensitivity[b], rash, hepatitis[b]
	Rilpivirine	Rash, headache, insomnia; requires food and gastric acid (no concomitant PPI use) for absorption
Protease inhibitors	Atazanavir	Nausea, hyperbilirubinemia, nephrolithiasis, rash; requires food and gastric acid (no concomitant PPI use) for absorption
	Darunavir	Nausea, diarrhea, rash
	Fosamprenavir	Nausea, diarrhea, rash
	Lopinavir	Nausea, diarrhea, hyperlipidemia, insulin resistance
	Saquinavir	Nausea, diarrhea, hyperlipidemia, QT prolongation
	Tipranavir	Nausea, diarrhea, hyperlipidemia, rash, hepatitis[b], intracranial hemorrhage[b]
CCR5 antagonist	Maraviroc	Hypersensitivity, hepatitis[b]
Integrase inhibitors	Dolutegravir	Elevated creatinine level (decrease in tubular secretion, not GFR), insomnia, headache (generally well tolerated)
	Elvitegravir	Nausea, diarrhea (generally well tolerated)
	Raltegravir	Rash, myopathy (generally well tolerated)
	Bictegravir	Elevated creatinine level (decrease in tubular secretion, not GFR), nausea, diarrhea, headache (generally well tolerated)
Pharmacokinetic boosters	Cobicistat	Elevated creatinine level (decrease in tubular creatinine secretion, not GFR), not recommended if CrCl <70 mL/min
	Ritonavir	Nausea, diarrhea, hyperlipidemia, insulin resistance, lipodystrophy, drug interactions[b]

CrCl = creatinine clearance; GFR = glomerular filtration rate; HBV = hepatitis B virus; PPI = proton pump inhibitor; RTIs = reverse transcriptase inhibitors; TAF = tenofovir alafenamide; TDF = tenofovir disoproxil fumarate.

[a]Many agents are also available as components of combination medications.

[b]Black box warning. Note all nucleoside analogues have a black box warning about possible lactic acidosis, although it is far more likely with stavudine, didanosine, and zidovudine than the other agents.

TABLE 67. Preferred Regimens for Initial Treatment of HIV Infection[a]

Abacavir/lamivudine/dolutegravir

Tenofovir alafenamide/emtricitabine/dolutegravir

Tenofovir alafenamide/emtricitabine/cobicistat/elvitegravir

Tenofovir alafenamide/emtricitabine/raltegravir

Tenofovir alafenamide/emtricitabine/bictegravir

[a]Endorsed by the 2016 International Antiviral Society-USA Panel guidelines and the 2018 Department of Health and Human Services guidelines.

KEY POINTS

- All persons with HIV infection should begin antiretroviral therapy as soon as they are ready, regardless of CD4 cell count.

- Standards for effective antiretroviral regimens include use of three drugs from two different classes; preferred regimens combine two nucleoside reverse transcriptase inhibitors with an integrase strand transfer inhibitor.

- HIV resistance testing may not be reliable if performed while the patient is not taking an antiretroviral regimen because resistance may not be detectable without the selective pressure of the antiretrovirals.

Management of Pregnant Patients with HIV Infection

The management of pregnant women with HIV does not significantly differ from the management of nonpregnant women. Initiating antiretroviral therapy is recommended as soon as possible in pregnant women with HIV who are not already being treated, and it is especially important that women already receiving HIV treatment who become pregnant continue treatment without interruption. Antiretroviral therapy in pregnancy benefits the woman and significantly reduces the risk of perinatal transmission of HIV to her baby. Previous concerns about teratogenicity of some antiretrovirals, including concerns about neural tube defects with efavirenz, have been allayed by data showing no difference in birth defect rates compared with the general population regardless of when therapy was started. Initial treatment regimen selection in pregnant women does not typically differ from nonpregnant women; however, elvitegravir-cobicistat is not recommended because levels are inadequate in the second and third trimesters, and bictegravir and TAF are not recommended until safety and pharmacokinetic data in pregnancy are available. Dolutegravir is not recommended in the first 8 weeks of pregnancy until more data are available regarding possible increased risk of neural tube defects.

KEY POINTS

- Pregnant women should promptly initiate or continue receiving HIV treatment without interruption; previous concerns about teratogenicity of efavirenz and tenofovir disoproxil fumarate have been allayed by data showing no difference in birth defect rates compared with the general population.

- In pregnant women with HIV, bictegravir and tenofovir alafenamide are not recommended until safety and pharmacokinetic data in pregnancy are available; dolutegravir should be avoided in the first 8 weeks of pregnancy until more safety data are available.

Viral Infections

Influenza Viruses

Overview

Three types of influenza viruses primarily infect humans: A, B, and C. Influenza A viruses are divided into subtypes based on two surface proteins, hemagglutinin (H) and neuraminidase (N). Influenza A viruses can infect animals and humans and produce epidemics and pandemics. Influenza B viruses only affect humans and cause yearly epidemics but not pandemics. Influenza C causes mild illness and does not cause epidemics.

Minor changes in the H and N surface envelope glycoproteins (*antigenic drift*) of influenza A and B viruses cause yearly epidemics, and major changes (*antigenic shift*) in influenza A after genetic recombination from animals cause global pandemics. The last influenza pandemic occurred in 2009 and

was caused by H1N1. Emerging subtypes of importance include H7N9, which circulates among poultry in China and can cause severe illness in humans; H5N1, which infects humans through close contact with infected poultry and can spread from person to person; and variants circulating in pigs that can sporadically infect humans.

Clinical Features and Evaluation

During the winter, influenza A causes a self-limiting illness with fever, cough, rhinorrhea, myalgia, and headache in most patients; influenza B causes a milder illness. Older adults (>65 years), young children, pregnant women, and patients with chronic medical conditions (especially chronic lung disease) are at higher risk for severe primary influenza, complications such as superimposed bacterial pneumonia caused by *Streptococcus pneumoniae* or *Staphylococcus aureus*, and death (see Community-Acquired Pneumonia). Less common but severe complications include asthma or chronic obstructive pulmonary disease exacerbations, myocarditis, encephalitis, rhabdomyolysis, myositis, sepsis, and multiorgan failure. Parotitis caused by influenza was reported during the 2015-2016 influenza season.

During the endemic season, patients can be diagnosed within 20 minutes using either rapid antigen tests or polymerase chain reaction (PCR) testing of nasopharyngeal swabs. Both tests are highly specific, but PCR has a sensitivity of nearly 100%; the rapid antigen tests have a sensitivity between 59% and 93%. Starting antiviral therapy following a negative antigen test result is reasonable if clinical suspicion is high. Serologic assays are not used clinically. Testing should be performed in patients at risk for complications (for example, those older than 65 years, patients with chronic medical conditions, immunocompromised patients, pregnant and postpartum women, those with a BMI of 40 or more, and persons with neuromuscular disease) and in health care workers, if the result will influence clinical management (decisions on initiation of antiviral treatment, impact on other diagnostic testing, antibiotic treatment decisions, and infection control practices).

KEY POINTS

- Older adults (>65 years), young children, pregnant women, and patients with chronic medical conditions (especially chronic lung disease) are at higher risk for severe primary influenza, superimposed bacterial pneumonia caused by *Streptococcus pneumoniae* or *Staphylococcus aureus*, and death.

- Rapid antigen and polymerase chain reaction (PCR) tests of nasopharyngeal swabs are highly specific for influenza, but PCR has a higher sensitivity and can identify the virus subtype.

Management

Antiviral therapy should be started within 48 hours of symptom onset in patients with a positive PCR or rapid antigen test result to speed up recovery and decrease hospitalization rates and complications. Antiviral therapy should also be initiated

CONT.

as soon as possible in hospitalized patients because some observational studies have shown decreased adverse outcomes. Treatment initiation should not be delayed while waiting for the results of confirmatory testing.

Neuraminidase inhibitors are active against influenza A and B and can be given orally (oseltamivir), intranasally (zanamivir), or, more recently, intravenously (peramivir). Antiviral therapy is recommended for patients with severe disease, including all hospitalized patients, and those at high risk for complications with confirmed or suspected influenza infection. Antiviral therapy should be given for at least 5 days, but in severely ill or immunosuppressed patients, a longer duration should be considered with repeat follow-up testing to document clearance. Immunosuppressed patients are at risk for neuraminidase inhibitor resistance during or after therapy.

Widespread influenza vaccination is the most important preventive intervention; all persons aged 6 months or older without contraindications and all health care personnel should be vaccinated (see MKSAP 18 General Internal Medicine). Oral oseltamivir and inhaled zanamivir are FDA approved for chemoprophylaxis (zanamivir is not approved in patients with chronic lung diseases) to contain outbreaks in institutional settings (such as long-term care facilities) and hospitals in conjunction with droplet precautions and vaccination. Chemoprophylaxis is given for at least 2 weeks, continuing at least 1 week after the last identified infection. Good hand hygiene and face masks can prevent secondary infections in households.

KEY POINTS

- Widespread influenza vaccination is the most important preventive intervention; all persons aged 6 months or older without contraindications and all health care personnel should be vaccinated.

- Antiviral therapy should be started within 48 hours of symptom onset but can be initiated up to 5 days after symptom onset in hospitalized patients; treatment should not be delayed while awaiting testing.

Novel Coronaviruses

Coronaviruses are RNA viruses that cause respiratory and gastrointestinal diseases. Six known types infect humans, with some infecting animals as well. Two novel coronaviruses, severe acute respiratory syndrome–coronavirus (SARS-CoV) and Middle East respiratory syndrome–coronavirus (MERS-CoV), can infect animals and also cause severe disease and epidemics in humans. In 2002, SARS-CoV emerged in China, causing an acute pneumonia epidemic with a mortality rate of approximately 10%. No infections have been reported since 2004. Treatment is supportive. MERS-CoV emerged in 2012 in Saudi Arabia in humans and camels, with most infections occurring in the Arabian Peninsula. MERS-CoV causes pneumonia,

diarrhea, and kidney failure with a mortality rate of approximately 40%. Because all types of coronaviruses may spread from human to human, contact and airborne precautions should be implemented for hospitalized patients with suspected infection.

KEY POINT

- Middle East respiratory syndrome–coronavirus infection occurs primarily in the Arabian Peninsula and can cause severe pneumonia with diarrhea, kidney failure, and death.

Human Herpesvirus Infections

Human herpesviruses (HHVs) are a group of eight DNA viruses (**Table 68**). In humans, infection with HHV results in lifelong viral latency with the possibility of reactivation and oncogenesis. HHV can be transmitted by physical or sexual contact during active infection or through asymptomatic shedding of the virus (in saliva, semen, or cervical secretions); other routes include blood transfusion, organ transplantation, or maternofetal transmission. Varicella-zoster virus (VZV) is the only HHV that can be transmitted by the airborne route; it is also the only HHV with a vaccine that produces protective humoral immunity. Antivirals are available for some HHVs, and immunoglobulin therapy is available for cytomegalovirus and VZV.

Herpes Simplex Virus Types 1 and 2

Herpes simplex virus (HSV) type 1 infection is transmitted by oral-oral or oral-genital contact. It typically causes oral ulcers and affects 90% of adults (see MKSAP 18 Dermatology). During stress, severe illness, or immunosuppression, patients may experience recurrence of oral stomatitis or esophagitis. The incidence of primary genital infection by HSV-1 is increasing (see Sexually Transmitted Infections). HSV-1 is the most common cause of viral encephalitis (see Central Nervous System Infections).

HSV-2 is sexually transmitted and typically causes genital and rectal ulcers with or without proctitis. HSV-2 affects approximately one sixth of adults in the United States and can also cause recurrent benign lymphocytic meningitis (Mollaret meningitis), myelitis, sacral radiculopathy, and neonatal infection or death (maternofetal transmission in primary genital infection). HSV-1 and HSV-2 can cause herpetic whitlow (on fingers), herpes gladiatorum (a skin infection typically associated with contact sports), keratoconjunctivitis, retinitis, and erythema multiforme.

HSV-1 and HSV-2 infections can be treated and suppressed with oral nucleoside analogues (acyclovir, valacyclovir, and famciclovir). Topical antiviral agents (trifluridine and vidarabine) are used for herpetic keratitis. Intravenous acyclovir is used for severe mucocutaneous disease, disseminated infections in immunosuppressed persons, esophagitis, and suspected HSV encephalitis.

TABLE 68. Human Herpesviruses and Associated Manifestations

Type	Synonym	Subfamily	Manifestations	Latency Site
HHV-1	Herpes simplex virus 1	α	Primary infection: oral and/or genital herpes (predominantly orofacial: gingivostomatitis, pharyngitis, herpes labialis)	Nerve ganglion
			Reactivation: Bell palsy, viral encephalitis; other sites, including skin and eye (recurrent herpes labialis)	
HHV-2	Herpes simplex virus 2	α	Primary infection: oral and/or genital herpes (predominantly genital); meningitis, sacral radiculopathy, and transverse myelitis	Nerve ganglion
HHV-3	Varicella-zoster virus	α	Varicella (chickenpox), herpes zoster (shingles)	Nerve ganglion
HHV-4	Epstein-Barr virus	γ	Infectious mononucleosis, nasopharyngeal carcinoma; in immunocompromised patients: Burkitt lymphoma, central nervous system lymphoma (in patients with AIDS), posttransplant lymphoproliferative disease, hairy leukoplakia	B cell
HHV-5	CMV	β	CMV mononucleosis; in immunocompromised patients: CMV retinitis, leukopenia and thrombocytopenia, pneumonitis, colitis, esophagitis, or hepatitis	Monocyte, lymphocyte, endothelial cell, epithelial cell
HHV-6 (6A and 6B)	Roseolovirus, herpes lymphotropic virus	β	Mononucleosis-like syndrome, roseola (sixth disease, exanthema subitum) in children; may affect various organ systems in transplant patients	T cell
HHV-7	Roseolovirus	β	Usually asymptomatic; may be associated with pityriasis rosea; roseola (sixth disease, exanthema subitum) in children	T cell
HHV-8	Kaposi sarcoma-associated virus	γ	Kaposi sarcoma, PEL, multicentric Castleman disease	B cell, endothelial cell

CMV = cytomegalovirus; HHV = human herpesvirus; PEL = primary effusion lymphoma.

KEY POINTS

- Herpes simplex virus (HSV) type 1 is the most common cause of viral encephalitis, and the incidence of primary genital infection caused by HSV-1 is increasing.
- Intravenous acyclovir is used for severe mucocutaneous herpes, disseminated infections in immunosuppressed persons, esophagitis, and suspected HSV encephalitis.

Varicella-Zoster Virus

Overview

VZV (HHV-3) is transmitted by inhalation and colonization of the respiratory tract, with subsequent viremic dissemination to skin, liver, spleen, and sensory ganglia (varicella, or chickenpox). VZV establishes latency in the ganglia and can later reactivate, causing herpes zoster (shingles), especially in adults older than 60 years or in immunosuppressed patients. Contact and airborne precautions should be used for all hospitalized patients with varicella, for patients with disseminated herpes zoster, and for those with dermatomal zoster who are immunosuppressed.

Clinical Features and Diagnosis

Primary varicella infection (chickenpox) presents with a febrile pruritic vesicular rash affecting the skin and mucocutaneous surfaces (oropharynx, conjunctiva, genitals); the rash commonly begins on the face and trunk, then spreads to the extremities (centrifugal distribution). Lesions may comprise macules, papules, vesicles, and scabs in different stages of development. Skin lesions may become superinfected with *Streptococcus pyogenes* or *Staphylococcus aureus* (impetigo). Most children recover without sequelae, but adults may develop pneumonia, encephalitis, hepatitis, and cerebellar ataxia.

Herpes zoster typically causes a painful vesicular rash that follows a dermatomal distribution that does not cross the midline (see MKSAP 18 Dermatology). Young patients presenting with herpes zoster should be tested for HIV. Immunosuppressed patients can present with multiple dermatomes affected or with disseminated disease. Postherpetic neuralgia, defined as neuropathic pain lasting more than 1 month after resolution of the vesicular rash, is the most significant complication of herpes zoster. Other complications include herpes zoster ophthalmicus with visual loss, Ramsay-Hunt syndrome (vesicular rash in external ear associated with ipsilateral peripheral facial palsy and altered taste), pneumonia, hepatitis, and central nervous system complications such as meningitis, encephalitis, myelitis, and stroke caused by vasculitis (see Central Nervous System Infections).

Varicella or herpes zoster can be diagnosed clinically by the typical vesicular rash and confirmed with VZV PCR testing of the base of a vesicular lesion. VZV is underdiagnosed in the absence of a rash (zoster sine herpete); in such cases, cerebrospinal fluid serologic (VZV IgM and IgG) and PCR testing can be used to diagnose the infections. **H**

Management

Antiviral therapy (acyclovir, valacyclovir, and famciclovir) speeds recovery and decreases the severity and duration of neuropathic pain if begun within 72 hours of VZV rash onset. Intravenous acyclovir should be used for immunosuppressed or hospitalized patients and those with neurologic involvement. **H**

Vaccination is the most important preventive strategy (see MKSAP 18 General Internal Medicine). Postexposure prophylaxis should be provided to susceptible persons (VZV IgG negative); postexposure varicella vaccination is appropriate in immunocompetent persons, and varicella-zoster immune globulin should be used in immunocompromised adults and in pregnant women.

KEY POINTS

- The rash of primary varicella infection (chickenpox) commonly begins on the face and trunk, then spreads to the extremities (centrifugal distribution) and may comprise macules, papules, vesicles, and scabs in various stages of development.

- In immunosuppressed patients, herpes zoster (shingles) can affect multiple dermatomes or present with disseminated disease; young patients presenting with herpes zoster should be tested for HIV.

- Postexposure varicella vaccination is appropriate in immunocompetent persons, and varicella-zoster immune globulin should be used in immunocompromised adults and pregnant women.

- Antiviral therapy speeds recovery and decreases the severity and duration of neuropathic pain if begun within 72 hours of VZV rash onset.

Epstein-Barr Virus

Epstein-Barr virus (EBV) (HHV-4) is highly prevalent; serologic studies show evidence of previous EBV infection in almost all adults. It is most commonly transmitted by saliva and is the main cause of infectious mononucleosis in children and adolescents. Patients present with fever, severe fatigue, exudative pharyngitis, cervical and axillary lymphadenopathy, and splenomegaly. Atypical lymphocytosis and aminotransferase level elevations are clues to the diagnosis, which is established by the presence of heterophile antibodies (Monospot test) or IgM to the EBV viral capsid antigen. The Monospot test result may be negative in the first week of illness. Treatment is supportive, with no role for acyclovir; glucocorticoids may be given to patients with autoimmune hemolytic anemia, central nervous system involvement, or tonsillar enlargement with a compromised airway. EBV is associated with the development of T-cell and B-cell lymphomas, Hodgkin and Burkitt lymphoma, nasopharyngeal carcinoma, and posttransplant lymphoproliferative disease in solid organ transplantation.

KEY POINTS

- Epstein-Barr virus infection, the primary cause of infectious mononucleosis, presents with fever, severe fatigue, exudative pharyngitis, cervical and axillary lymphadenopathy, and splenomegaly.

- The diagnosis of Epstein-Barr virus is established by the presence of heterophile antibodies on the Monospot test, although this test result may be negative during the first week of illness.

Human Cytomegalovirus

Cytomegalovirus (HHV-5) infections are most commonly asymptomatic but may present with a mononucleosis-like syndrome without pharyngitis and with negative heterophile antibody results. Cytomegalovirus may be transmitted through the placenta (congenital cytomegalovirus), breastfeeding, saliva, blood transfusion, or organ transplantation (cytomegalovirus-positive donor to cytomegalovirus-seronegative recipient). Approximately 60% to 90% of adults have latent cytomegalovirus infection with reactivation of disease more common in immunosuppressed persons (those with AIDS, transplant recipients, those receiving glucocorticoid therapy). Cytomegalovirus can cause retinitis, pneumonitis, hepatitis, bone marrow suppression, colitis, esophagitis, and adrenalitis in immunocompromised persons. Immunocompetent patients occasionally also present with colitis.

Because cytomegalovirus can cause a myriad of clinical manifestations, a high index of clinical suspicion is important. Diagnosis is commonly confirmed with molecular tests, such as PCR testing of serum, bronchoalveolar lavage fluid, or cerebrospinal fluid, or by demonstrating typical cytopathic "owl's-eye" intracellular inclusions on biopsy specimens (**Figure 25**). Pathologic diagnosis is confirmed by cytomegalovirus immunostains. Serologic assays have limited diagnostic utility because most adults are seropositive; however, they are performed routinely in pretransplant evaluations to assess the risk of cytomegalovirus reactivation after transplantation and to determine appropriate prophylaxis.

Antiviral therapy with intravenous ganciclovir or oral valganciclovir is used in immunocompromised patients or in immunocompetent patients with severe disease. Oral valganciclovir is also used as prophylaxis or pre-emptive therapy (treat if the PCR serum testing result is positive) in transplant

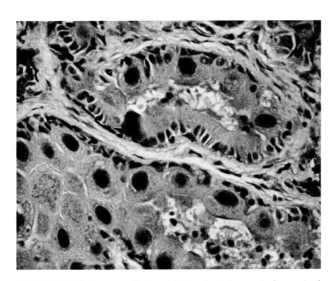

FIGURE 25. Under a magnification of 500X, a photomicrograph of a sample of kidney tissue reveals the presence of what are referred to as cytomegalic inclusion cells. With enlarged, darkly stained nuclei, such cells are also known as owl's-eye inclusion cells and are caused by cytomegalic inclusion disease resulting from cytomegalovirus.

CONT. recipients. Foscarnet and cidofovir can be used in instances of ganciclovir resistance or intolerance.

KEY POINTS

- Serologic assays for cytomegalovirus have limited diagnostic utility because most adults are seropositive; however, they are performed routinely in pretransplant evaluations to assess the risk of cytomegalovirus reactivation following transplantation and to determine appropriate prophylaxis.

- Diagnosis of cytomegalovirus is confirmed with molecular tests of infected fluids, by demonstrating typical cytopathic "owl's-eye" intracellular inclusions on biopsy specimens, or by cytomegalovirus immunostaining of pathologic samples.

Stewardship and Emerging Resistance

Introduction

Emergence of antibiotic resistance is potentiated by all antibiotic use. Careful antibiotic use is essential to preserving the armamentarium. Among outpatient visits, 12.6% are associated with antibiotic prescriptions, and 30% of those prescriptions are considered inappropriate. Most prescriptions are for acute respiratory infections (usually caused by viruses) and asymptomatic bacteriuria not requiring antibiotic treatment. One fifth of emergency department visits for adverse drug events are related to antibiotics. Inpatient antibiotic use accounts for 38.5% of all antibiotic use; half of hospitalized

patients receive antibiotics, and half of these medications are considered unnecessary or inappropriate. The World Health Organization has named carbapenem-resistant *Acinetobacter baumannii* and *Pseudomonas aeruginosa* and carbapenem-resistant and extended-spectrum β-lactamase (ESBL)–producing Enterobacteriaceae as priority-one pathogens, for which new antibiotics are critically needed.

Antimicrobial Stewardship and the Value of Infectious Disease Consultation

Antibiotic stewardship refers to coordinated interventions to improve antibiotic use and clinical outcomes by promoting optimal antibiotic regimens. Goals include minimizing adverse events (5% risk per antibiotic per patient), risk of *Clostridium difficile* infection, and emergence of resistance. A key aspect of stewardship is avoiding antibiotic administration when not indicated. Antibiotic selection, dosing, therapy duration, and route of administration are also considered. Furthermore, antimicrobial stewardship programs include simplifying unnecessary combination therapy, avoiding redundant double anaerobic coverage, converting intravenous to oral agents, streamlining de-escalation, and minimizing duration of therapy.

Combination therapy does not prevent the emergence of resistance. However, it may be considered in specific circumstances, such as empiric therapy regimens, to broaden the spectrum of activity or provide coverage for potential antimicrobial-resistant organisms pending culture and susceptibility results. Antibiotic combination therapy may also provide synergistic activity in limited situations, such as enterococcal endocarditis and bacteremia caused by carbapenem-resistant Enterobacteriaceae (CRE).

Conversion from an intravenous to an oral antimicrobial agent should be considered for ease of administration and to limit intravenous catheter access and use, thereby decreasing the risk of catheter-related bloodstream infection. Factors supporting readiness for conversion include a temperature of 38 °C (100.4 °F) or less, an improving leukocyte count, clinical stability and improvement of signs and symptoms related to infection, a functioning gastrointestinal tract and ability to swallow medications or having a nasogastric tube in place, no diagnostic indication for intravenous therapy (endocarditis, *Staphylococcus aureus* bacteremia), and availability of a suitable oral alternative with good oral bioavailability (fluoroquinolones, oxazolidinones, metronidazole, clindamycin, trimethoprim-sulfamethoxazole, fluconazole, doxycycline, voriconazole).

Antimicrobial stewardship programs use various interventions to optimize antimicrobial use. Interventions that have been shown to be effective in improving outcomes, decreasing resistance, and decreasing costs include preauthorization and prospective audit with feedback to the

TABLE 69.	Newer Antimicrobial Agents						
Agent	**Class**	**Mechanism of Action**	**Route**	**Adverse Effects**	**Issues/Limitations**	**FDA Indications**	**Relative Cost**
Ceftolozane-tazobactam	Antipseudomonal cephalosporin with novel β-lactamase inhibitor	Inhibits cell wall synthesis by binding to PBP; tazobactam irreversibly inhibits activity of many penicillinases and cephalosporinases	IV, every 8 hours	Similar to other cephalosporins	Reduced efficacy in patients with creatinine clearance ≤50 mL/min	Complicated intra-abdominal infections (combined with metronidazole); complicated urinary tract infections, including pyelonephritis Active against many gram-negative organisms, including some ESBL-producing Enterobacteriaceae and multidrug-resistant *Pseudomonas aeruginosa*, including carbapenem-resistant strains	$$$
Ceftaroline	Cephalosporin	Inhibits cell wall synthesis by high affinity binding to PBPs; high affinity for PBP2a that leads to activity against MRSA	IV, every 12 hours	Similar to other cephalosporins	Limited clinical experience for MRSA outside of skin infections	Community-acquired pneumonia (not caused by MRSA, clinical trial data lacking), ABSSSI caused by susceptible organisms (including MRSA)	$$
Ceftazidime-avibactam	Third-generation cephalosporin with novel β-lactamase inhibitor	Inhibits cell wall synthesis by binding to PBP; avibactam inhibits broader range of β-lactamases than other available β-lactamase inhibitors	IV, every 8 hours	Similar to other cephalosporins	Approved on limited clinical safety and efficacy data Reserve use for patients with limited or no alternative treatment options Decreased efficacy in patients with baseline creatinine clearance between 30-50 mL/min Monitor kidney function daily; adjust dose as needed	Complicated intra-abdominal infections (combined with metronidazole); complicated urinary tract infections, including pyelonephritis Active against many multidrug-resistant gram-negative organisms, ESBL, and carbapenemases Not active against metallo-β-lactamases or gram-negative organisms that overexpress efflux pumps or have porin mutations	$$$$$
Dalbavancin	Lipoglycopeptide	Disrupts cell wall membrane synthesis	IV, once weekly	Nausea, headache, diarrhea, elevation of liver enzyme levels	Rapid IV infusion may cause flushing of the upper body, urticaria, pruritus, rash	ABSSSI caused by susceptible strains of gram-positive organisms (*Staphylococcus aureus* including MRSA, *Streptococcus pyogenes*, *Streptococcus agalactiae*, *Streptococcus anginosus* group)	$$$$

Drug	Class	Mechanism	Route/Dosing	Adverse effects	Warnings/Interactions	Indications	Cost
Delafloxacin	Fluoroquinolone	Acts on DNA gyrase and topoisomerase IV inhibiting DNA replication	IV, oral twice daily	Nausea, headache, diarrhea, aminotransferase elevation	Tendinitis, tendon rupture, peripheral neuropathy, central nervous system effects Avoid coadministration of oral formulation with chelating agents, such as antacids	ABSSSI caused by susceptible gram-positive organisms, including MRSA Has activity against gram-negative organisms, including P. aeruginosa Studies ongoing for community-acquired pneumonia and complicated urinary tract infection	$$$
Oritavancin	Lipoglycopeptide	Disrupts cell wall membrane synthesis, disrupts cell membrane integrity	IV, one dose	Headache, nausea, elevation of liver enzyme levels	Interaction with anticoagulation tests to monitor heparin; increases warfarin level by 30%, monitor patients for bleeding	ABSSSI caused by susceptible gram-positive organisms: S. aureus (MRSA and MSSA), S. pyogenes, S. agalactiae, Streptococcus dysgalactiae, S. anginosus group, and vancomycin-susceptible Enterococcus faecalis	$$$
Tedizolid	Oxazolidinone	Disrupts bacterial protein synthesis initiation	IV, oral, once daily for 6 days	Nausea, headache, diarrhea	Patients taking selective serotonin reuptake inhibitors were excluded from clinical trials	ABSSSI caused by susceptible gram-positive organisms (MRSA, MSSA, linezolid-resistant S. aureus, S. pyogenes, S. agalactiae, S. anginosus group, Streptococcus intermedius, Streptococcus constellatus, E. faecalis)	$$
Telavancin	Glycopeptide	Disrupts cell wall synthesis and function	IV, once daily	Nephrotoxicity	Interaction with coagulation tests to monitor heparin; may prolong QTc interval; decreased efficacy in pre-existing chronic kidney disease (eGFR <90 mL/min/1.73 m^2)	Complicated skin and soft tissue infections caused by susceptible organisms and S. aureus (including MRSA) hospital-acquired pneumonia	$$$

ABSSSI = acute bacterial skin and skin-structure infection; eGFR = estimated glomerular filtration rate; ESBL = extended-spectrum β-lactamase; IV = intravenous; MRSA = methicillin-resistant Staphylococcus aureus; MSSA = methicillin-sensitive Staphylococcus aureus; PBP = penicillin-binding protein.

prescriber, targeting antibiotics associated with a high risk of *C. difficile* infection (such as clindamycin, broad-spectrum antibiotics, and fluoroquinolones), using dedicated pharmacokinetic monitoring and adjustment programs, increasing the use of oral antimicrobial agents, and reducing antimicrobial therapy to the shortest effective duration.

KEY POINT

- Important components of antimicrobial stewardship programs include avoiding unnecessary antibiotic use, simplifying unnecessary combination therapy, avoiding double anaerobic coverage, converting intravenous to oral agents, streamlining de-escalation, and minimizing duration of therapy.

Newer Antibacterial Drugs

Two newer cephalosporin antibiotics, ceftazidime-avibactam and ceftolozane-tazobactam, have enhanced activity against β-lactamase–producing organisms, particularly ESBLs, and against some carbapenemase-producing CRE. Three agents are available in the lipoglycopeptide class of antibiotics with activity against aerobic gram-positive organisms, such as *S. aureus* (including methicillin-resistant *S. aureus*), streptococci, and vancomycin-susceptible *Enterococcus faecalis*. Ceftaroline is a fifth-generation cephalosporin with a unique spectrum of activity that covers methicillin-resistant *S. aureus*. Delafloxacin is a new anionic fluoroquinolone with gram-positive (including methicillin-resistant *S. aureus*) and gram-negative activity (**Table 69**).

Antibiotics for Antibiotic-Resistant Organisms

Enterococcus faecium, *S. aureus*, *Klebsiella pneumoniae*, *Acinetobacter* species, *Pseudomonas aeruginosa*, and *Enterobacter* species are particularly problematic antibiotic-resistant organisms. This group includes ESBL and carbapenemase-producing CRE (*Klebsiella pneumoniae* carbapenemases and New Delhi metallo-β-lactamase) that destroy carbapenems. Few effective antibiotics are available to treat infections with these pathogens. However, several older, less commonly used antibiotics retain their activity. Infectious disease consultation should be considered for infections with organisms in this group.

Minocycline

Resurgence in the use of minocycline, available in intravenous and oral forms, is partly because of its activity against multidrug-resistant *Acinetobacter*. In vitro susceptibility to minocycline can be inferred from susceptibility to tetracycline; however, some tetracycline-resistant strains are sensitive to minocycline. Minocycline has been used to treat ventilator-associated pneumonia with an 80% clinical response rate and

is also useful for treating infections caused by *Stenotrophomonas maltophilia*, a problematic ICU pathogen with intrinsic antibiotic resistance. The adverse effects of minocycline are similar to those of tetracycline, including photosensitivity, gastrointestinal disturbance, and skin pigmentation changes with prolonged use.

KEY POINT

- Minocycline has activity against multidrug-resistant *Acinetobacter* and *Stenotrophomonas maltophilia*.

Fosfomycin

Fosfomycin (available in the United States) is a bactericidal oral antibiotic with gram-negative and gram-positive activity (including methicillin-resistant *S. aureus* and vancomycin-resistant Enterobacteriaceae). It achieves high concentrations in the urine and may be used to treat cystitis caused by vancomycin-resistant Enterobacteriaceae and other multidrug-resistant uropathogens such as carbapenemase-producing *K. pneumoniae*.

KEY POINT

- Fosfomycin has gram-negative and gram-positive activity (including methicillin-resistant *S. aureus* and vancomycin-resistant Enterobacteriaceae) and achieves high concentrations in the urine, making it useful for treating cystitis.

Colistin

Colistin (polymyxin E) is a bactericidal agent used to treat multidrug- and pan-resistant aerobic gram-negative infections, including *P. aeruginosa*. *Proteus*, *Providencia*, *Burkholderia*, *Morganella*, and *Serratia* species are resistant to colistin. Colistin resistance has been described in some multidrug-resistant gram-negative infections (mostly carbapenemase-producing *K. pneumoniae*), leading to completely untreatable infections. Colistin can be administered by nebulized aerosol or intravenously. The most common adverse effect is nephrotoxicity (up to 50% of patients), which is usually reversible.

KEY POINT

- Nephrotoxicity occurs in up to 50% of patients treated with colistin, although it is usually reversible.

Outpatient Parenteral Antibiotic Therapy

Outpatient parenteral antibiotic therapy (OPAT) is defined as administration of at least two doses of intravenous antibiotics on different days without intervening hospitalization. Approximately 250,000 patients per year in the United States are treated with OPAT. OPAT allows patients to complete parenteral antibiotic therapy at home or in other outpatient settings when an oral antibiotic is not appropriate or available. Bone and joint infections compose most of the infections treated with OPAT; other candidates include endocarditis, cardiac device infections, abdominal infections, skin and soft tissue infections, and antibiotic-resistant infections for which parenteral antibiotics are the only option (such as urinary tract infection).

Patients should be clinically stable and their infection improving before starting OPAT; OPAT is not appropriate if the patient's care needs would be better met in the hospital. When considering OPAT, it is important to assess the type of infection being treated, the prescribed antibiotic and dosing frequency, the planned therapy duration, the administration site, the intravenous catheter type, and the monitoring process for possible complications. Increasingly, OPAT is being started without initial hospitalization after careful medical assessment by a well-established and organized OPAT program. OPAT requires close monitoring, including antibiotic levels (vancomycin, aminoglycosides), complete blood count, creatinine level, liver chemistry tests, and coagulation tests if relevant for the antibiotic; patients receiving daptomycin therapy in particular should undergo baseline measurement of kidney function and creatine kinase level, followed by weekly monitoring. Antibiotic doses and timing should be adjusted based on monitoring results. Treatment failure may result from relapse or progression of primary infection (60% and 21%, respectively) and therapeutic complications (19%). Successful OPAT requires patient participation; supervised infectious disease OPAT programs have been shown to be safe, efficient, and clinically effective.

KEY POINT

- Bone and joint infections are the primary infections treated with outpatient parenteral antibiotic therapy (OPAT); other candidates for OPAT include serious infections (endocarditis, cardiac device infections, abdominal infections, and skin and soft tissue infections) and antibiotic-resistant infections for which parenteral antibiotics are the only option (such as urinary tract infection).

Bibliography

Central Nervous System Infections

Castelblanco RL, Lee M, Hasbun R. Epidemiology of bacterial meningitis in the USA from 1997 to 2010: a population-based observational study. Lancet Infect Dis. 2014;14:813-9. [PMID: 25104307] doi:10.1016/S1473-3099(14)70805-9

Hasbun R. Central nervous system device infections. Curr Infect Dis Rep. 2016;18:34. [PMID: 27686676] doi:10.1007/s11908-016-0541-x

Hasbun R, Rosenthal N, Balada-Llasat JM, Chung J, Duff S, Bozzette S, et al. Epidemiology of meningitis and encephalitis in the United States, 2011-2014. Clin Infect Dis. 2017;65:359-363. [PMID: 28419350] doi:10.1093/cid/cix319

McGill F, Heyderman RS, Michael BD, Defres S, Beeching NJ, Borrow R, et al. The UK joint specialist societies guideline on the diagnosis and management of acute meningitis and meningococcal sepsis in immunocompetent adults. J Infect. 2016;72:405-38. [PMID: 26845731] doi:10.1016/j.jinf.2016.01.007

Srihawan C, Castelblanco RL, Salazar L, Wootton SH, Aguilera E, Ostrosky-Zeichner L, et al. Clinical characteristics and predictors of adverse outcome in adult and pediatric patients with healthcare-associated ventriculitis and meningitis. Open Forum Infect Dis. 2016;3:ofw077. [PMID: 27419154] doi:10.1093/ofid/ofw077

Tunkel AR, Hasbun R, Bhimraj A, Byers K, Kaplan SL, Michael Scheld W, et al. 2017 Infectious Diseases Society of America's clinical practice guidelines for healthcare-associated ventriculitis and meningitis. Clin Infect Dis. 2017. [PMID: 28203777] doi:10.1093/cid/ciw861

van de Beek D, Brouwer M, Hasbun R, Koedel U, Whitney CG, Wijdicks E. Community-acquired bacterial meningitis. Nat Rev Dis Primers. 2016;2:16074. [PMID: 27808261] doi:10.1038/nrdp.2016.74

van de Beek D, Cabellos C, Dzupova O, Esposito S, Klein M, Kloek AT, et al; ESCMID Study Group for Infections of the Brain (ESGIB). ESCMID guideline: diagnosis and treatment of acute bacterial meningitis. Clin Microbiol Infect. 2016;22 Suppl 3:S37-62. [PMID: 27062097] doi:10.1016/j.cmi.2016.01.007

Venkatesan A, Tunkel AR, Bloch KC, Lauring AS, Sejvar J, Bitnun A, et al; International Encephalitis Consortium. Case definitions, diagnostic algorithms, and priorities in encephalitis: consensus statement of the international encephalitis consortium. Clin Infect Dis. 2013;57:1114-28. [PMID: 23861361] doi:10.1093/cid/cit458

Wang AY, Machicado JD, Khoury NT, Wootton SH, Salazar L, Hasbun R. Community-acquired meningitis in older adults: clinical features, etiology, and prognostic factors. J Am Geriatr Soc. 2014;62:2064-70. [PMID: 25370434] doi:10.1111/jgs.13110

Prion Diseases of the Central Nervous System

Das AS, Zou WQ. Prions: beyond a single protein. Clin Microbiol Rev. 2016;29:633-58. [PMID: 27226089] doi:10.1128/CMR.00046-15

Geschwind MD. Prion diseases. Continuum (Minneap Minn). 2015;21:1612-38. [PMID: 26633779] doi:10.1212/CON.0000000000000251

Haïk S, Brandel JP. Infectious prion diseases in humans: cannibalism, iatrogenicity and zoonoses. Infect Genet Evol. 2014;26:303-12. [PMID: 24956437] doi:10.1016/j.meegid.2014.06.010

Kim MO, Geschwind MD. Clinical update of Jakob-Creutzfeldt disease. Curr Opin Neurol. 2015;28:302-10. [PMID: 25923128] doi:10.1097/WCO.0000000000000197

Knight R. Creutzfeldt-Jakob disease: a rare cause of dementia in elderly persons. Clin Infect Dis. 2006;43:340-6. [PMID: 16804850]

Skin and Soft Tissue Infections

Bystritsky R, Chambers H. Cellulitis and soft tissue infections. Ann Intern Med. 2018;168:ITC17-ITC32. [PMID: 29404597] doi:10.7326/AITC201802060

Case definitions for infectious conditions under public health surveillance. Centers for Disease Control and Prevention. MMWR Recomm Rep. 1997;46:1-55. [PMID: 9148133]

Lipsky BA, Berendt AR, Cornia PB, Pile JC, Peters EJ, Armstrong DG, et al; Infectious Diseases Society of America. 2012 Infectious Diseases Society of America clinical practice guideline for the diagnosis and treatment of diabetic foot infections. Clin Infect Dis. 2012;54:e132-73. [PMID: 22619242] doi:10.1093/cid/cis346

Liu C, Bayer A, Cosgrove SE, Daum RS, Fridkin SK, Gorwitz RJ, et al; Infectious Diseases Society of America. Clinical practice guidelines by the Infectious Diseases Society of America for the treatment of methicillin-resistant *Staphylococcus aureus* infections in adults and children. Clin Infect Dis. 2011;52:e18-55. [PMID: 21208910] doi:10.1093/cid/ciq146

Poulakou G, Giannitsioti E, Tsiodras S. What is new in the management of skin and soft tissue infections in 2016? Curr Opin Infect Dis. 2017;30:158-171. [PMID: 28134678] doi:10.1097/QCO.0000000000000360

Stevens DL, Bisno AL, Chambers HF, Dellinger EP, Goldstein EJ, Gorbach SL, et al; Infectious Diseases Society of America. Practice guidelines for the diagnosis and management of skin and soft tissue infections: 2014 update by the Infectious Diseases Society of America. Clin Infect Dis. 2014;59:e10-52. [PMID: 24973422] doi:10.1093/cid/ciu444

Thomas KS, Crook AM, Nunn AJ, Foster KA, Mason JM, Chalmers JR, et al; U.K. Dermatology Clinical Trials Network's PATCH I Trial Team. Penicillin to prevent recurrent leg cellulitis. N Engl J Med. 2013;368:1695-703. [PMID: 23635049] doi:10.1056/NEJMoa1206300

Weng QY, Raff AB, Cohen JM, Gunasekera N, Okhovat JP, Vedak P, et al. Costs and consequences associated with misdiagnosed lower extremity cellulitis. JAMA Dermatol. 2016. [PMID: 27806170] doi:10.1001/jamadermatol.2016.3816

Wong CH, Khin LW, Heng KS, Tan KC, Low CO. The LRINEC (Laboratory Risk Indicator for Necrotizing Fasciitis) score: a tool for distinguishing necrotizing fasciitis from other soft tissue infections. Crit Care Med. 2004;32:1535-41. [PMID: 15241098]

Community-Acquired Pneumonia

Eliakim-Raz N, Robenshtok E, Shefet D, Gafter-Gvili A, Vidal L, Paul M, et al. Empiric antibiotic coverage of atypical pathogens for community-acquired pneumonia in hospitalized adults. Cochrane Database Syst Rev. 2012:CD004418. [PMID: 22972070] doi:10.1002/14651858.CD004418.pub4

Jain S, Self WH, Wunderink RG; CDC EPIC Study Team. Community-acquired pneumonia requiring hospitalization [Letter]. N Engl J Med. 2015;373:2382. [PMID: 26650159] doi:10.1056/NEJMc1511751

Kolditz M, Tesch F, Mocke L, Höffken G, Ewig S, Schmitt J. Burden and risk factors of ambulatory or hospitalized CAP: a population based cohort study. Respir Med. 2016;121:32-38. [PMID: 27888989] doi:10.1016/j.rmed.2016.10.015

Lee JS, Giesler DL, Gellad WF, Fine MJ. Antibiotic therapy for adults hospitalized with community-acquired pneumonia: a systematic review. JAMA. 2016;315:593-602. [PMID: 26864413] doi:10.1001/jama.2016.0115

Mandell LA, Wunderink RG, Anzueto A, Bartlett JG, Campbell GD, Dean NC, et al; Infectious Diseases Society of America. Infectious Diseases Society of America/American Thoracic Society consensus guidelines on the management of community-acquired pneumonia in adults. Clin Infect Dis. 2007;44 Suppl 2:S27-72. [PMID: 17278083]

Musher DM, Thorner AR. Community-acquired pneumonia. N Engl J Med. 2014;371:1619-28. [PMID: 25337751] doi:10.1056/NEJMra1312885

Postma DF, van Werkhoven CH, van Elden LJ, Thijsen SF, Hoepelman AI, Kluytmans JA, et al; CAP-START Study Group. Antibiotic treatment strategies for community-acquired pneumonia in adults. N Engl J Med. 2015; 372:1312-23. [PMID: 25830421] doi:10.1056/NEJMoa1406330

Restrepo MI, Reyes LF, Anzueto A. Complication of community-acquired pneumonia (including cardiac complications). Semin Respir Crit Care Med. 2016;37:897-904. [PMID: 27960213]

Siemieniuk RA, Meade MO, Alonso-Coello P, Briel M, Evaniew N, Prasad M, et al. Corticosteroid therapy for patients hospitalized with community-acquired pneumonia: a systematic review and meta-analysis. Ann Intern Med. 2015;163:519-28. [PMID: 26258555] doi:10.7326/M15-0715

Tang KL, Eurich DT, Minhas-Sandhu JK, Marrie TJ, Majumdar SR. Incidence, correlates, and chest radiographic yield of new lung cancer diagnosis in 3398 patients with pneumonia. Arch Intern Med. 2011;171:1193-8. [PMID: 21518934] doi:10.1001/archinternmed.2011.15

Tick-Borne Diseases

Biggs HM, Behravesh CB, Bradley KK, Dahlgren FS, Drexler NA, Dumler JS, et al. Diagnosis and management of tickborne rickettsial diseases: Rocky Mountain spotted fever and other spotted fever group rickettsioses, ehrlichioses, and anaplasmosis - United States. MMWR Recomm Rep. 2016;65:1-44. [PMID: 27172113] doi:10.15585/mmwr.rr6502a1

Goddard J. Not all erythema migrans lesions are Lyme disease. Am J Med. 2017;130:231-233. [PMID: 27612442] doi:10.1016/j.amjmed.2016.08.020

Hu LT. Lyme disease. Ann Intern Med. 2016;164:ITC65-ITC80. [PMID: 27136224] doi:10.7326/AITC201605030

Lantos PM. Chronic Lyme disease. Infect Dis Clin North Am. 2015;29:325-40. [PMID: 25999227] doi:10.1016/j.idc.2015.02.006

Moore A, Nelson C, Molins C, Mead P, Schriefer M. Current guidelines, common clinical pitfalls, and future directions for laboratory diagnosis of Lyme disease, United States. Emerg Infect Dis. 2016;22. [PMID: 27314832] doi:10.3201/eid2207.151694

Sanchez E, Vannier E, Wormser GP, Hu LT. Diagnosis, treatment, and prevention of Lyme disease, human granulocytic anaplasmosis, and babesiosis: a review. JAMA. 2016;315:1767-77. [PMID: 27115378] doi:10.1001/jama.2016.2884

Weitzner E, McKenna D, Nowakowski J, Scavarda C, Dornbush R, Bittker S, et al. Long-term assessment of post-treatment symptoms in patients with culture-confirmed early Lyme disease. Clin Infect Dis. 2015;61:1800-6. [PMID: 26385994] doi:10.1093/cid/civ735

Urinary Tract Infections

Geerlings SE, Beerepoot MA, Prins JM. Prevention of recurrent urinary tract infections in women: antimicrobial and nonantimicrobial strategies. Infect Dis Clin North Am. 2014;28:135-47. [PMID: 24484580] doi:10.1016/j.idc.2013.10.001

Hooton TM. Clinical practice. Uncomplicated urinary tract infection. N Engl J Med. 2012;366:1028-37. [PMID: 22417256] doi:10.1056/NEJMcp1104429

Johnson JR, Russo TA. Acute pyelonephritis in adults. N Engl J Med. 2018; 378:48-59. [PMID: 29298155]

Nicolle LE. Asymptomatic bacteriuria. Curr Opin Infect Dis. 2014;27:90-6. [PMID: 24275697] doi:10.1097/QCO.0000000000000019

Schaeffer AJ, Nicolle LE. Clinical practice. Urinary tract infections in older men. N Engl J Med. 2016;374:562-71. [PMID: 26863357] doi:10.1056/NEJMcp1503950

Mycobacterium tuberculosis Infection

Horsburgh CR Jr, Barry CE 3rd, Lange C. Treatment of tuberculosis. N Engl J Med. 2015;373:2149-60. [PMID: 26605929] doi:10.1056/NEJMra1413919

Jamil SM, Oren E, Garrison GW, Srikanth S, Lewinsohn DM, Wilson KC, et al. Diagnosis of tuberculosis in adults and children. Ann Am Thorac Soc. 2017;14:275-278. [PMID: 28146376] doi:10.1513/AnnalsATS.201608-636CME

Lewinsohn DM, Leonard MK, LoBue PA, Cohn DL, Daley CL, Desmond E, et al. Official American Thoracic Society/Infectious Diseases Society of America/Centers for Disease Control and Prevention clinical practice guidelines: diagnosis of tuberculosis in adults and children. Clin Infect Dis. 2017;64:111-115. [PMID: 28052967] doi:10.1093/cid/ciw778

Nahid P, Dorman SE, Alipanah N, Barry PM, Brozek JL, Cattamanchi A, et al. Executive summary: official American Thoracic Society/Centers for Disease Control and Prevention/Infectious Diseases Society of America clinical practice guidelines: treatment of drug-susceptible tuberculosis. Clin Infect Dis. 2016;63:853-67. [PMID: 27621353] doi:10.1093/cid/ciw566

Pai M, Schito M. Tuberculosis diagnostics in 2015: landscape, priorities, needs, and prospects. J Infect Dis. 2015;211 Suppl 2:S21-8. [PMID: 25765103] doi:10.1093/infdis/jiu803

Salinas JL, Mindra G, Haddad MB, Pratt R, Price SF, Langer AJ. Leveling of tuberculosis incidence - United States, 2013-2015. MMWR Morb Mortal Wkly Rep. 2016;65:273-8. [PMID: 27010173] doi:10.15585/mmwr.mm6511a2

Nontuberculous Mycobacterial Infections

Chand M, Lamagni T, Kranzer K, Hedge J, Moore G, Parks S, et al. Insidious risk of severe Mycobacterium chimaera infection in cardiac surgery patients. Clin Infect Dis. 2017;64:335-342. [PMID: 27927870] doi:10.1093/cid/ciw754

Griffith DE, Aksamit T, Brown-Elliott BA, Catanzaro A, Daley C, Gordin F, et al; ATS Mycobacterial Diseases Subcommittee. An official ATS/IDSA statement: diagnosis, treatment, and prevention of nontuberculous mycobacterial diseases. Am J Respir Crit Care Med. 2007;175:367-416. [PMID: 17277290]

Guglielmetti L, Mougari F, Lopes A, Raskine L, Cambau E. Human infections due to nontuberculous mycobacteria: the infectious diseases and clinical microbiology specialists' point of view. Future Microbiol. 2015;10:1467-83. [PMID: 26344005] doi:10.2217/fmb.15.64

Koh WJ, Jeong BH, Kim SY, Jeon K, Park KU, Jhun BW, et al. Mycobacterial characteristics and treatment outcomes in Mycobacterium abscessus lung disease. Clin Infect Dis. 2017;64:309-316. [PMID: 28011608] doi:10.1093/cid/ciw724

Fungal Infections

Azie N, Neofytos D, Pfaller M, Meier-Kriesche HU, Quan SP, Horn D. The PATH (Prospective Antifungal Therapy) Alliance® registry and invasive fungal infections: update 2012. Diagn Microbiol Infect Dis. 2012;73:293-300. [PMID: 22789847] doi:10.1016/j.diagmicrobio.2012.06.012

Castillo CG, Kauffman CA, Miceli MH. Blastomycosis. Infect Dis Clin North Am. 2016;30:247-64. [PMID: 26739607] doi:10.1016/j.idc.2015.10.002

Farmakiotis D, Kontoyiannis DP. Mucormycoses. Infect Dis Clin North Am. 2016;30:143-63. [PMID: 26897065] doi:10.1016/j.idc.2015.10.011

Mahajan VK. Sporotrichosis: an overview and therapeutic options. Dermatol Res Pract. 2014;2014:272376. [PMID: 25614735] doi:10.1155/2014/272376

Maziarz EK, Perfect JR. Cryptococcosis. Infect Dis Clin North Am. 2016;30:179-206. [PMID: 26897067] doi:10.1016/j.idc.2015.10.006

McCarty TP, Pappas PG. Invasive candidiasis. Infect Dis Clin North Am. 2016;30:103-24. [PMID: 26739610] doi:10.1016/j.idc.2015.10.013

Pappas PG, Kauffman CA, Andes DR, Clancy CJ, Marr KA, Ostrosky-Zeichner L, et al. Executive summary: clinical practice guideline for the management of candidiasis: 2016 update by the Infectious Diseases Society of America. Clin Infect Dis. 2016;62:409-17. [PMID: 26810419] doi:10.1093/cid/civ1194

Patterson TF, Thompson GR 3rd, Denning DW, Fishman JA, Hadley S, Herbrecht R, et al. Executive summary: practice guidelines for the diagnosis and management of aspergillosis: 2016 update by the Infectious Diseases Society of America. Clin Infect Dis. 2016;63:433-42. [PMID: 27481947] doi:10.1093/cid/ciw444

Stockamp NW, Thompson GR 3rd. Coccidioidomycosis. Infect Dis Clin North Am. 2016;30:229-46. [PMID: 26739609] doi:10.1016/j.idc.2015.10.008

Wheat LJ, Azar MM, Bahr NC, Spec A, Relich RF, Hage C. Histoplasmosis. Infect Dis Clin North Am. 2016;30:207-27. [PMID: 26897068] doi:10.1016/j.idc.2015.10.009

Sexually Transmitted Infections

Bibbins-Domingo K, Grossman DC, Curry SJ, Davidson KW, Epling JW Jr, García FA, et al; US Preventive Services Task Force (USPSTF). Screening for syphilis infection in nonpregnant adults and adolescents: US Preventive Services Task Force Recommendation Statement. JAMA. 2016;315:2321-7. [PMID: 27272583] doi:10.1001/jama.2016.5824

Brunham RC, Gottlieb SL, Paavonen J. Pelvic inflammatory disease. N Engl J Med. 2015;372:2039-48. [PMID: 25992748] doi:10.1056/NEJMra1411426

Gnann JW Jr, Whitley RJ. Clinical practice. Genital herpes. N Engl J Med. 2016;375:666-74. [PMID: 27532832] doi:10.1056/NEJMcp1603178

Moi H, Blee K, Horner PJ. Management of non-gonococcal urethritis. BMC Infect Dis. 2015;15:294. [PMID: 26220178] doi:10.1186/s12879-015-1043-4

Stoner BP, Cohen SE. Lymphogranuloma venereum 2015: clinical presentation, diagnosis, and treatment. Clin Infect Dis. 2015;61 Suppl 8:S865-73. [PMID: 26602624] doi:10.1093/cid/civ756

Workowski KA, Bolan GA; Centers for Disease Control and Prevention. Sexually transmitted diseases treatment guidelines, 2015. MMWR Recomm Rep. 2015;64:1-137. [PMID: 26042815]

Osteomyelitis

American College of Radiology Appropriateness Criteria. Expert Panel on Musculoskeletal Imaging: suspected osteomyelitis, septic arthritis or soft tissue infection (excluding spine and diabetic foot) https://acsearch.acr.org/list (accessed 2/2/2017)

Berbari EF, Kanj SS, Kowalski TJ, Darouiche RO, Widmer AF, Schmitt SK, et al. 2015 Infectious Diseases Society of America (IDSA) clinical practice guidelines for the diagnosis and treatment of native vertebral osteomyelitis in adults. Clin Infect Dis. 2015;61:e26-46. [PMID: 26229122] doi:10.1093/cid/civ482

Choi SH, Sung H, Kim SH, Lee SO, Lee SH, Kim YS, et al. Usefulness of a direct 16S rRNA gene PCR assay of percutaneous biopsies or aspirates for etiological diagnosis of vertebral osteomyelitis. Diagn Microbiol Infect Dis. 2014;78:75-8. [PMID: 24231384] doi:10.1016/j.diagmicrobio.2013.10.007

Conterno LO, Turchi MD. Antibiotics for treating chronic osteomyelitis in adults. Cochrane Database Syst Rev. 2013:CD004439. [PMID: 24014191] doi:10.1002/14651858.CD004439.pub3

Grigoropoulou P, Eleftheriadou I, Jude EB, Tentolouris N. Diabetic foot infections: an update in diagnosis and management. Curr Diab Rep. 2017;17:3. [PMID: 28101794] doi:10.1007/s11892-017-0831-1

Lipsky BA, Berendt AR, Cornia PB, Pile JC, Peters EJ, Armstrong DG, et al; Infectious Diseases Society of America. 2012 Infectious Diseases Society of America clinical practice guideline for the diagnosis and treatment of diabetic foot infections. Clin Infect Dis. 2012;54:e132-73. [PMID: 22619242] doi:10.1093/cid/cis346

Mears SC, Edwards PK. Bone and joint infections in older adults. Clin Geriatr Med. 2016;32:555-70. [PMID: 27394023] doi:10.1016/j.cger.2016.02.003

Fever of Unknown Origin

Cunha BA, Lortholary O, Cunha CB. Fever of unknown origin: a clinical approach. Am J Med. 2015;128:1138.e1-1138.e15. [PMID: 26093175] doi:10.1016/j.amjmed.2015.06.001

Primary Immunodeficiencies

Abbott JK, Gelfand EW. Common variable immunodeficiency: diagnosis, management, and treatment. Immunol Allergy Clin North Am. 2015;35:637-58. [PMID: 26454311] doi:10.1016/j.iac.2015.07.009

Abolhassani H, Sagvand BT, Shokuhfar T, Mirminachi B, Rezaei N, Aghamohammadi A. A review on guidelines for management and treatment of common variable immunodeficiency. Expert Rev Clin Immunol. 2013;9:561-74; quiz 575. [PMID: 23730886] doi:10.1586/eci.13.30

Audemard-Verger A, Descloux E, Ponard D, Deroux A, Fantin B, Fieschi C, et al. Infections revealing complement deficiency in adults: a French nationwide study enrolling 41 patients. Medicine (Baltimore). 2016;95:e3548. [PMID: 27175654] doi:10.1097/MD.0000000000003548

Azar AE, Ballas ZK. Evaluation of the adult with suspected immunodeficiency. Am J Med. 2007;120:764-8. [PMID: 17765042]

Frazer-Abel A, Sepiashvili L, Mbughuni MM, Willrich MA. Overview of laboratory testing and clinical presentations of complement deficiencies and dysregulation. Adv Clin Chem. 2016;77:1-75. [PMID: 27717414] doi:10.1016/bs.acc.2016.06.001

Bioterrorism

Adalja AA, Toner E, Inglesby TV. Clinical management of potential bioterrorism-related conditions. N Engl J Med. 2015;372:954-62. [PMID: 25738671] doi:10.1056/NEJMra1409755

Breman JG, Henderson DA. Diagnosis and management of smallpox. N Engl J Med. 2002;346:1300-8. [PMID: 11923491]

Hendricks KA, Wright ME, Shadomy SV, Bradley JS, Morrow MG, Pavia AT, et al; Workgroup on Anthrax Clinical Guidelines. Centers for Disease Control and Prevention expert panel meetings on prevention and treatment of anthrax in adults. Emerg Infect Dis. 2014;20. [PMID: 24447897] doi:10.3201/eid2002.130687

McFee RB. Viral hemorrhagic fever viruses. Dis Mon. 2013;59:410-25. [PMID: 24314803] doi:10.1016/j.disamonth.2013.10.003

Prentice MB, Rahalison L. Plague. Lancet. 2007;369:1196-207. [PMID: 17416264]

Thomas LD, Schaffner W. Tularemia pneumonia. Infect Dis Clin North Am. 2010;24:43-55. [PMID: 20171544] doi:10.1016/j.idc.2009.10.012

Zhang JC, Sun L, Nie QH. Botulism, where are we now? Clin Toxicol (Phila). 2010;48:867-79. [PMID: 21171845] doi:10.3109/15563650.2010.535003

Travel Medicine

Delord M, Socolovschi C, Parola P. Rickettsioses and Q fever in travelers (2004-2013). Travel Med Infect Dis. 2014;12:443-58. [PMID: 25262433] doi:10.1016/j.tmaid.2014.08.006

Franco MP, Mulder M, Gilman RH, Smits HL. Human brucellosis. Lancet Infect Dis. 2007;7:775-86. [PMID: 18045560]

Freedman DO, Chen LH, Kozarsky PE. Medical considerations before international travel. N Engl J Med. 2016;375:247-60. [PMID: 27468061] doi:10.1056/NEJMra1508815

Giddings SL, Stevens AM, Leung DT. Traveler's diarrhea. Med Clin North Am. 2016;100:317-30. [PMID: 26900116] doi:10.1016/j.mcna.2015.08.017

Hahn WO, Pottinger PS. Malaria in the traveler: how to manage before departure and evaluate upon return. Med Clin North Am. 2016;100:289-302. [PMID: 26900114] doi:10.1016/j.mcna.2015.09.008

Patterson J, Sammon M, Garg M. Dengue, Zika and chikungunya: emerging arboviruses in the New World. West J Emerg Med. 2016;17:671-679. [PMID: 27833670]

Petersen LR, Jamieson DJ, Powers AM, Honein MA. Zika virus. N Engl J Med. 2016;374:1552-63. [PMID: 27028561] doi:10.1056/NEJMra1602113

Sanford CA, Jong EC. Immunizations. Med Clin North Am. 2016;100:247-59. [PMID: 26900111] doi:10.1016/j.mcna.2015.08.018

Suwanmanee S, Luplertlop N. Dengue and Zika viruses: lessons learned from the similarities between these Aedes mosquito-vectored arboviruses. J Microbiol. 2017;55:81-89. [PMID: 28120186] doi:10.1007/s12275-017-6494-4

Weaver SC, Lecuit M. Chikungunya virus and the global spread of a mosquito-borne disease. N Engl J Med. 2015;372:1231-9. [PMID: 25806915] doi:10.1056/NEJMra1406035

Infectious Gastrointestinal Syndromes

Debast SB, Bauer MP, Kuijper EJ; European Society of Clinical Microbiology and Infectious Diseases. European Society of Clinical Microbiology and Infectious Diseases: update of the treatment guidance document for Clostridium difficile infection. Clin Microbiol Infect. 2014;20 Suppl 2:1-26. [PMID: 24118601] doi:10.1111/1469-0691.12418

DuPont HL. Acute infectious diarrhea in immunocompetent adults. N Engl J Med. 2014;370:1532-40. [PMID: 24738670] doi:10.1056/NEJMra1301069

McDonald LC, Gerding DN, Johnson S, Bakken JS, Carroll KC, Coffin SE, et al. Clinical practice guidelines for Clostridium difficile infection in adults and children: 2017 update by the Infectious Diseases Society of America (IDSA) and Society for Healthcare Epidemiology of America (SHEA). Clin Infect Dis. 2018 Feb 15. [Epub ahead of print] [PMID: 29462280] doi:10.1093/cid/cix1085.

Riddle MS, DuPont HL, Connor BA. ACG clinical guideline: diagnosis, treatment, and prevention of acute diarrheal infections in adults. Am J Gastroenterol. 2016;111:602-22. [PMID: 27068718] doi:10.1038/ajg.2016.126

Shane AL, Mody RK, Crump JA, Tarr PI, Steiner TS, Kotloff K, et al. 2017 Infectious Diseases Society of America clinical practice guidelines for the diagnosis and management of infectious diarrhea. Clin Infect Dis. 2017;65:e45-e80. [PMID: 29053792] doi:10.1093/cid/cix669

Surawicz CM, Brandt LJ, Binion DG, Ananthakrishnan AN, Curry SR, Gilligan PH, et al. Guidelines for diagnosis, treatment, and prevention of Clostridium difficile infections. Am J Gastroenterol. 2013;108:478-98; quiz 499. [PMID: 23439232] doi:10.1038/ajg.2013.4

Infections in Transplant Recipients

Ariza-Heredia EJ, Nesher L, Chemaly RF. Cytomegalovirus diseases after hematopoietic stem cell transplantation: a mini-review. Cancer Lett. 2014;342:1-8. [PMID: 24041869] doi:10.1016/j.canlet.2013.09.004

Fishman JA. From the classic concepts to modern practice. Clin Microbiol Infect. 2014;20 Suppl 7:4-9. [PMID: 24528498] doi:10.1111/1469-0691.12593

Fleming S, Yannakou CK, Haeusler GM, Clark J, Grigg A, Heath CH, et al. Consensus guidelines for antifungal prophylaxis in haematological malignancy and haemopoietic stem cell transplantation, 2014. Intern Med J. 2014;44:1283-97. [PMID: 25482741] doi:10.1111/imj.12595

Lumbreras C, Manuel O, Len O, ten Berge IJ, Sgarabotto D, Hirsch HH. Cytomegalovirus infection in solid organ transplant recipients. Clin Microbiol Infect. 2014;20 Suppl 7:19-26. [PMID: 26451404]

Rubin LG, Levin MJ, Ljungman P, Davies EG, Avery R, Tomblyn M, et al; Infectious Diseases Society of America. 2013 IDSA clinical practice guideline for vaccination of the immunocompromised host. Clin Infect Dis. 2014;58:309-18. [PMID: 24421306] doi:10.1093/cid/cit816

Ullmann AJ, Schmidt-Hieber M, Bertz H, Heinz WJ, Kiehl M, Krüger W, et al; Infectious Diseases Working Party of the German Society for Hematology and Medical Oncology (AGIHO/DGHO) and the DAG-KBT (German Working Group for Blood and Marrow Transplantation). Infectious diseases in allogeneic haematopoietic stem cell transplantation: prevention and prophylaxis strategy guidelines 2016. Ann Hematol. 2016;95:1435-55. [PMID: 27339055] doi:10.1007/s00277-016-2711-1

Health Care–Associated Infections

Allegranzi B, Bischoff P, de Jonge S, Kubilay NZ, Zayed B, Gomes SM, et al; WHO Guidelines Development Group. New WHO recommendations on preoperative measures for surgical site infection prevention: an evidence-based global perspective. Lancet Infect Dis. 2016;16:e276-e287. [PMID: 27816413] doi:10.1016/S1473-3099(16)30398-X

Chenoweth CE, Saint S. Urinary tract infections. Infect Dis Clin North Am. 2016;30:869-885. [PMID: 27816141] doi:10.1016/j.idc.2016.07.007

Holland TL, Arnold C, Fowler VG Jr. Clinical management of Staphylococcus aureus bacteremia: a review. JAMA. 2014;312:1330-41. [PMID: 25268440] doi:10.1001/jama.2014.9743

Kalil AC, Metersky ML, Klompas M, Muscedere J, Sweeney DA, Palmer LB, et al. Management of adults with hospital-acquired and ventilator-associated pneumonia: 2016 clinical practice guidelines by the Infectious Diseases Society of America and the American Thoracic Society. Clin Infect Dis. 2016;63:e61-e111. [PMID: 27418577] doi:10.1093/cid/ciw353

Magill SS, Edwards JR, Bamberg W, Beldavs ZG, Dumyati G, Kainer MA, et al; Emerging Infections Program Healthcare-Associated Infections and Antimicrobial Use Prevalence Survey Team. Multistate point-prevalence survey of health care-associated infections. N Engl J Med. 2014;370:1198-208. [PMID: 24670166] doi:10.1056/NEJMoa1306801

Marston HD, Dixon DM, Knisely JM, Palmore TN, Fauci AS. Antimicrobial resistance. JAMA. 2016;316:1193-1204. [PMID: 27654605] doi:10.1001/jama.2016.11764

Meddings J, Saint S, Fowler KE, Gaies E, Hickner A, Krein SL, et al. The Ann Arbor criteria for appropriate urinary catheter use in hospitalized medical patients: results obtained by using the RAND/UCLA appropriateness method. Ann Intern Med. 2015;162:S1-34. [PMID: 25938928] doi:10.7326/M14-1304

Nuckols TK, Keeler E, Morton SC, Anderson L, Doyle B, Booth M, et al. Economic evaluation of quality improvement interventions for bloodstream infections related to central catheters: a systematic review. JAMA Intern Med. 2016;176:1843-1854. [PMID: 27757564] doi:10.1001/jamainternmed.2016.6610

Weiner LM, Fridkin SK, Aponte-Torres Z, Avery L, Coffin N, Dudeck MA, et al. Vital signs: preventing antibiotic-resistant infections in hospitals - United States, 2014. MMWR Morb Mortal Wkly Rep. 2016;65:235-41. [PMID: 26963489] doi:10.15585/mmwr.mm6509e1

Yokoe DS, Anderson DJ, Berenholtz SM, Calfee DP, Dubberke ER, Ellingson KD, et al. A compendium of strategies to prevent healthcare-associated infections in acute care hospitals: 2014 updates. Infect Control Hosp Epidemiol. 2014;35 Suppl 2:S21-31. [PMID: 25376067]

HIV/AIDS

Brown TT, Hoy J, Borderi M, Guaraldi G, Renjifo B, Vescini F, et al. Recommendations for evaluation and management of bone disease in HIV. Clin Infect Dis. 2015;60:1242-51. [PMID: 25609682] doi:10.1093/cid/civ010

Centers for Disease Control and Prevention. Preexposure prophylaxis for the prevention of HIV infection in the United States—2014. A clinical practice guideline. Available at https://stacks.cdc.gov/view/cdc/23109.

Centers for Disease Control and Prevention. Updated guidelines for antiretroviral postexposure prophylaxis after sexual, injection drug use, or other nonoccupational exposure to HIV—United States, 2016. Available at https://stacks.cdc.gov/view/cdc/38856.

Centers for Disease Control and Prevention and Association of Public Health Laboratories. Laboratory testing for the diagnosis of HIV infection: updated recommendations. Available at http://dx.doi.org/10.15620/cdc.23447. Published June 27, 2014. Available at http://www.cdc.gov/hiv/testing/laboratorytests.html.

Günthard HF, Saag MS, Benson CA, del Rio C, Eron JJ, Gallant JE, et al. Antiretroviral drugs for treatment and prevention of HIV infection in adults:

2016 recommendations of the International Antiviral Society-USA Panel. JAMA. 2016;316:191-210. [PMID: 27404187] doi:10.1001/jama.2016.8900

Kay ES, Batey DS, Mugavero MJ. The HIV treatment cascade and care continuum: updates, goals, and recommendations for the future. AIDS Res Ther. 2016;13:35. [PMID: 27826353]

Lucas GM, Ross MJ, Stock PG, Shlipak MG, Wyatt CM, Gupta SK, et al; HIV Medicine Association of the Infectious Diseases Society of America. Clinical practice guideline for the management of chronic kidney disease in patients infected with HIV: 2014 update by the HIV Medicine Association of the Infectious Diseases Society of America. Clin Infect Dis. 2014;59:e96-138. [PMID: 25234519] doi:10.1093/cid/ciu617

Panel on Antiretroviral Guidelines for Adults and Adolescents. Guidelines for the use of antiretroviral agents in HIV-1-infected adults and adolescents. Department of Health and Human Services. Updated March 27, 2018. Available at https://aidsinfo.nih.gov/guidelines/html/1/adult-and-adolescent-arv/0

Panel on Opportunistic Infections in HIV-Infected Adults and Adolescents. Guidelines for the prevention and treatment of opportunistic infections in HIV-infected adults and adolescents: recommendations from the Centers for Disease Control and Prevention, the National Institutes of Health, and the HIV Medicine Association of the Infectious Diseases Society of America. Updated March 7, 2018. Available at https://aidsinfo.nih.gov/guidelines/html/4/adult-and-adolescent-opportunistic-infection/0

Panel on Treatment of HIV-Infected Pregnant Women and Prevention of Perinatal Transmission. Recommendations for use of antiretroviral drugs in pregnant HIV-1 infected women for maternal health and interventions to reduce perinatal HIV transmission in the United States. Updated March 27, 2018. Available at https://aidsinfo.nih.gov/guidelines/html/3/perinatal/0

Yarchoan R, Uldrick TS. HIV-associated cancers and related diseases. N Engl J Med. 2018;378:1029-1041. [PMID: 29539283] doi:10.1056/NEJMra1615896

Viral Infections

Cohen JI. Clinical practice: Herpes zoster. N Engl J Med. 2013;369:255-63. [PMID: 23863052] doi:10.1056/NEJMcp1302674

Gnann JW Jr, Whitley RJ. Clinical practice. Genital herpes. N Engl J Med. 2016;375:666-74. [PMID: 27532832] doi:10.1056/NEJMcp1603178

Haagmans BL, Al Dhahiry SH, Reusken CB, Raj VS, Galiano M, Myers R, et al. Middle East respiratory syndrome coronavirus in dromedary camels: an outbreak investigation. Lancet Infect Dis. 2014;14:140-5. [PMID: 24355866] doi:10.1016/S1473-3099(13)70690-X

Harper SA, Bradley JS, Englund JA, File TM, Gravenstein S, Hayden FG, et al; Expert Panel of the Infectious Diseases Society of America. Seasonal influenza in adults and children—diagnosis, treatment, chemoprophylaxis, and institutional outbreak management: clinical practice guidelines of the Infectious Diseases Society of America. Clin Infect Dis. 2009;48:1003-32. [PMID: 19281331] doi:10.1086/598513

Paules C, Subbarao K. Influenza. Lancet. 2017. [PMID: 28302313] doi:10.1016/S0140-6736(17)30129-0

Zaki AM, van Boheemen S, Bestebroer TM, Osterhaus AD, Fouchier RA. Isolation of a novel coronavirus from a man with pneumonia in Saudi Arabia. N Engl J Med. 2012;367:1814-20. [PMID: 23075143] doi:10.1056/NEJMoa1211721

Stewardship and Emerging Resistance

Barlam TF, Cosgrove SE, Abbo LM, MacDougall C, Schuetz AN, Septimus EJ, et al. Implementing an antibiotic stewardship program: guidelines by the Infectious Diseases Society of America and the Society for Healthcare Epidemiology of America. Clin Infect Dis. 2016;62:e51-77. [PMID: 27080992] doi:10.1093/cid/ciw118

Deak D, Outterson K, Powers JH, Kesselheim AS. Progress in the fight against multidrug-resistant bacteria? A review of U.S. Food and Drug Administration-approved antibiotics, 2010-2015. Ann Intern Med. 2016;165:363-72. [PMID: 27239977] doi:10.7326/M16-0291

Doi Y, Paterson DL. Carbapenemase-producing Enterobacteriaceae. Semin Respir Crit Care Med. 2015;36:74-84. [PMID: 25643272] doi:10.1055/s-0035-1544208

Petrak RM, Skorodin NC, Fliegelman RM, Hines DW, Chundi VV, Harting BP. Value and clinical impact of an infectious disease-supervised outpatient parenteral antibiotic therapy program. Open Forum Infect Dis. 2016; 3:ofw193. [PMID: 27807591]

Ritchie DJ, Garavaglia-Wilson A. A review of intravenous minocycline for treatment of multidrug-resistant Acinetobacter infections. Clin Infect Dis. 2014;59 Suppl 6:S374-80. [PMID: 25371513] doi:10.1093/cid/ciu613

Schmitt S, McQuillen DP, Nahass R, Martinelli L, Rubin M, Schwebke K, et al. Infectious diseases specialty intervention is associated with decreased mortality and lower healthcare costs. Clin Infect Dis. 2014;58:22-8. [PMID: 24072931] doi:10.1093/cid/cit610

Infectious Disease Self-Assessment Test

This self-assessment test contains one-best-answer multiple-choice questions. Please read these directions carefully before answering the questions. Answers, critiques, and bibliographies immediately follow these multiple-choice questions. The American College of Physicians (ACP) is accredited by the Accreditation Council for Continuing Medical Education (ACCME) to provide continuing medical education for physicians.

The American College of Physicians designates MKSAP 18 Infectious Disease for a maximum of 25 *AMA PRA Category 1 Credits*™. Physicians should claim only the credit commensurate with the extent of their participation in the activity.

Successful completion of the CME activity, which includes participation in the evaluation component, enables the participant to earn up to 25 medical knowledge MOC points in the American Board of Internal Medicine's Maintenance of Certification (MOC) program. It is the CME activity provider's responsibility to submit participant completion information to ACCME for the purpose of granting MOC credit.

Earn Instantaneous CME Credits or MOC Points Online

Print subscribers can enter their answers online to earn instantaneous CME credits or MOC points. You can submit your answers using online answer sheets that are provided at mksap.acponline.org, where a record of your MKSAP 18 credits will be available. To earn CME credits or to apply for MOC points, you need to answer all of the questions in a test and earn a score of at least 50% correct (number of correct answers divided by the total number of questions). Please note that if you are applying for MOC points, you must also enter your birth date and ABIM candidate number.

Take either of the following approaches:

- Use the printed answer sheet at the back of this book to record your answers. Go to mksap.acponline.org, access the appropriate online answer sheet, transcribe your answers, and submit your test for instantaneous CME credits or MOC points. There is no additional fee for this service.

- Go to mksap.acponline.org, access the appropriate online answer sheet, directly enter your answers, and submit your test for instantaneous CME credits or MOC points. There is no additional fee for this service.

Earn CME Credits or MOC Points by Mail or Fax

Pay a $20 processing fee per answer sheet and submit the printed answer sheet at the back of this book by mail or fax, as instructed on the answer sheet. Make sure you calculate your score and enter your birth date and ABIM candidate number, and fax the answer sheet to 215-351-2799 or mail the answer sheet to Member and Customer Service, American College of Physicians, 190 N. Independence Mall West, Philadelphia, PA 19106-1572, using the courtesy envelope provided in your MKSAP 18 slipcase. You will need your 10-digit order number and 8-digit ACP ID number, which are printed on your packing slip. Please allow 4 to 6 weeks for your score report to be emailed back to you. Be sure to include your email address for a response.

If you do not have a 10-digit order number and 8-digit ACP ID number, or if you need help creating a username and password to access the MKSAP 18 online answer sheets, go to mksap.acponline.org or email custserv@acponline.org.

CME credits and MOC points are available from the publication date of December 31, 2018, until December 31, 2021. You may submit your answer sheet or enter your answers online at any time during this period.

Directions

*Each of the numbered items is followed by lettered answers. Select the **ONE** lettered answer that is **BEST** in each case.*

Self-Assessment Test

Item 1

A 68-year-old man is being evaluated for measures to decrease his risk of acquiring a surgical site infection; he is scheduled for coronary artery bypass graft surgery in 5 weeks for limiting chronic angina despite maximal medical therapy. Medical history includes chronic stable angina, hyperlipidemia, hypertension, and diabetes. Medications are low-dose aspirin, propranolol, isosorbide dinitrate, ranolazine, chlorthalidone, lisinopril, and atorvastatin.

On physical examination, blood pressure is 126/72 mm Hg; all other vital signs are normal. On cardiac examination, an S_4 is present. The remainder of the examination is noncontributory.

Which of the following is the most appropriate measure to prevent surgical site infection?

(A) Evaluate for *Staphylococcus aureus* nasal carriage
(B) Provide postoperative vancomycin prophylaxis for 7 days
(C) Provide preoperative vancomycin prophylaxis
(D) Shave patient's chest hair the morning of surgery

Item 2

A 25-year-old man is evaluated in the emergency department for fever, productive cough, dyspnea, and pleuritic chest pain that began several days ago. He reports no other symptoms. Intravenous ceftriaxone and oral azithromycin are initiated, and he is hospitalized. Medical history is significant for a recent diagnosis of HIV infection, for which he began antiretroviral therapy 1 month ago. Other medications are lamivudine, abacavir, and dolutegravir.

On physical examination, temperature is 39.2 °C (102.6 °F), blood pressure is 136/84 mm Hg, pulse rate is 110/min, and respiration rate is 20/min. Oxygen saturation is 90% breathing ambient air. Cardiac examination is normal, and the lungs are clear bilaterally.

Laboratory studies at the time of HIV diagnosis showed a viral load of 95,420 copies/mL and CD4 cell count of 256/μL. The interferon-γ release assay for tuberculosis was indeterminate because of inadequate response to the positive control. One week ago, HIV viral load was 1077 copies/mL and CD4 cell count was 313/μL.

A chest radiograph shows an infiltrate in the right middle lobe and bilateral hilar enlargement.

Sputum acid-fast bacilli smear shows acid-fast bacilli; culture results are pending.

Which of the following is the most appropriate management?

(A) Await culture results
(B) Pause antiretroviral therapy
(C) Start prednisone
(D) Start rifabutin, isoniazid, ethambutol, and pyrazinamide

Item 3

A 27-year-old man is evaluated in the hospital for a 1-month history of fever, drenching night sweats, malaise, fatigue,

chest pain, and a nonproductive cough. He recently completed a 7-day course of levofloxacin with no improvement in symptoms. The patient is in the military, works as a car mechanic on base, and is stationed in Bakersfield, California.

On physical examination, temperature is 37.8 °C (100.0 °F), blood pressure is 128/76 mm Hg, pulse rate is 99/min, respiration rate is 24/min, and oxygen saturation is 92% with the patient breathing room air. The remainder of the physical examination is unremarkable.

Laboratory studies:

Hemoglobin	12.4 g/dL (124 g/L)
Leukocyte count	11,900/μL (11.9 × 10⁹/L), with 30% eosinophils, 60% neutrophils, and 10% lymphocytes
Interferon-γ release assay	Negative

A chest radiograph shows a right lower lobe infiltrate and ipsilateral hilar lymphadenopathy.

Which of the following is the most likely diagnosis?

(A) Coccidioidomycosis
(B) Sarcoidosis
(C) *Streptococcus pneumoniae* pneumonia
(D) Tuberculosis

Item 4

A 44-year-old man is evaluated in the emergency department in January for a 3-day history of dyspnea, cough, and fever. Medical history is otherwise unremarkable, and he takes no medications.

On physical examination, temperature is 38.5 °C (101.3 °F), blood pressure is 118/80 mm Hg, pulse rate is 113/min, and respiration rate is 33/min. Oxygen saturation is 89% breathing 6 L/min oxygen by nasal cannula. The patient appears uncomfortable and is oriented only to person. Breath sounds are decreased bilaterally with scattered crackles. No rash is noted.

Laboratory studies:

Leukocyte count	19,000/μL (19 × 10⁹/L)
Platelet count	274,000/μL (274 × 10⁹/L)
Blood urea nitrogen	36 mg/dL (12.9 mmol/L)
Creatinine	1.45 mg/dL (128 μmol/L)

Sputum Gram stain shows 2+ polymorphonuclear cells and 1+ epithelial cells; no organisms are seen. A respiratory viral panel from a nasopharyngeal swab is positive for rhinovirus.

A chest radiograph is shown on the next page.

The patient will be transferred to the ICU.

Which of the following is the most appropriate treatment?

(A) Azithromycin
(B) Ceftazidime plus azithromycin
(C) Ceftriaxone plus levofloxacin
(D) Piperacillin-tazobactam plus ciprofloxacin

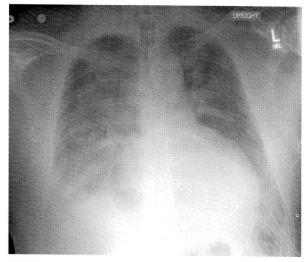

ITEM 4

Item 5

A 43-year-old man is seen in follow-up for fever up to 38.3 °C (101 °F) occurring periodically over the past 3 months. He has no associated symptoms other than fatigue. He reports no recent travel, animal exposures, or tick or insect bites. He does not eat raw meats, raw seafood, or unpasteurized dairy products. He returns for further evaluation after initial testing. Family history is negative for undiagnosed fevers. He takes no medications.

On physical examination, temperature is 37.8 °C (100.1 °F), blood pressure is 114/72 mm Hg, pulse rate is 88/min, and respiration rate is 14/min. A complete physical examination is unremarkable.

Laboratory studies:

Erythrocyte sedimentation rate	10 mm/h
Hematocrit	44%
Leukocyte count	4200/µL (4.2 × 10⁹/L) with a normal differential
Platelet count	320,000/µL (320 × 10⁹/L)
Alkaline phosphatase	Normal
Lactate dehydrogenase	Normal
Kidney and liver chemistry tests	Normal
Urinalysis	Normal

HIV testing is negative. An interferon-γ release assay for tuberculosis is negative. Three sets of blood cultures are negative.

A chest radiograph is normal.

Which of the following is the most appropriate diagnostic test to perform next?

(A) Bone marrow biopsy
(B) CT of the abdomen and pelvis
(C) Liver biopsy
(D) Lumbar puncture

Item 6

A 34-year-old woman is evaluated in the emergency department for a 2-day history of fever, severe headache, malaise,

fatigue, dry cough, and shortness of breath. She underwent deceased-donor kidney transplantation 1 year ago; 2 weeks ago, she developed acute graft rejection and was treated with alemtuzumab. Other medications are tacrolimus, prednisone, and trimethoprim-sulfamethoxazole.

On physical examination, temperature is 37.5 °C (99.5 °F), blood pressure is 80/53 mm Hg, pulse rate is 90/min, and respiration rate is 22/min. Bibasilar crackles are heard on auscultation of the lungs.

Initial laboratory studies show a hemoglobin level of 6.9 mg/dL (69 g/L) and a leukocyte count of 4800/µL (4.8 × 10⁹/L).

A head CT scan shows multiple acute infarcts in the frontal lobe and cerebellum without superimposed hematomas. A lumbar puncture is performed.

Cerebrospinal fluid studies:

Cell count	2 erythrocytes/hpf; 77 leukocytes/hpf, with 90% neutrophils and 10% lymphocytes
Glucose	80 mg/dL (4.4 mmol/L)
Pressure (opening)	140 mm H₂O
Protein	100 mg/dL (1000 mg/L)
Cryptococcal antigen	Negative
Gram stain	No organisms

A chest radiograph shows diffuse bilateral lung nodules.

Which of the following is the most appropriate next diagnostic test?

(A) Brain biopsy
(B) Bronchoscopy with biopsy and bronchoalveolar lavage
(C) Fungal blood culture
(D) Serum galactomannan assay

Item 7

A 19-year-old woman is evaluated in the emergency department for a 2-day history of fever, headaches, and jaundice. She vacationed in Hawaii 1 month ago and reports swimming in lakes and rivers. She was diagnosed with a flu-like illness 2 weeks ago that resolved spontaneously. She reports no history of a rash. She is sexually active with one partner. She takes no medications other than an oral contraceptive.

On physical examination, she is alert and oriented. Temperature is 38.9 °C (102 °F), blood pressure is 92/60 mm Hg, pulse rate is 124/min, and respiration rate is 24/min. Generalized lymphadenopathy, conjunctival suffusion, and scleral icterus are noted. She has photophobia, and passive neck flexion elicits resistance and discomfort. The remainder of the examination is unremarkable.

Laboratory studies:

Bilirubin, total	5.6 mg/dL (95.8 µmol/L)
Creatinine	2.3 mg/dL (203 µmol/L)
Cerebrospinal fluid	
Leukocyte count	152/µL (152 × 10⁶/L)
Glucose	72 mg/dL (4.0 mmol/L)
Protein	78 mg/dL (780 mg/L)

Cerebrospinal fluid Gram stain is negative and culture results are pending.

CONT.

Which of the following is the most likely cause of the patient's findings?

(A) Acute retroviral syndrome

(B) Herpes simplex virus infection

(C) Leptospirosis

(D) Neurosyphilis

Item 8

A 66-year-old woman is evaluated in the emergency department with a 2-day history of fever and nonbloody diarrhea occurring several times a day. She recently completed a 10-day course of cephalexin for cellulitis of the leg.

On physical examination, temperature is 39.0 °C (102.2 °F), blood pressure is 98/60 mm Hg, pulse rate is 110/min, and respiration rate is 23/min. She appears uncomfortable but is not confused. Her abdomen is distended and bowel sounds are decreased. She has tenderness and abdominal guarding to palpation. Cellulitis has resolved.

Laboratory studies:

Leukocyte count	30,000/µL (30×10^9/L) (with 80% neutrophils, 15% band forms, and 5% lymphocytes)
Albumin	2.5 mg/dL (25 g/L)
Creatinine	2.5 mg/dL (221 µmol/L) (baseline 1.0 mg/dL [88.4 µmol/L])
Lactate	2.8 mEq/L (2.8 mmol/L)

Stool polymerase chain reaction assay is positive for *Clostridium difficile* toxin gene. Abdominal imaging reveals evidence of toxic megacolon.

The patient is admitted to the ICU, and a surgical consultation is requested.

Which of the following is the most appropriate medical treatment?

(A) Fecal microbiota transplant

(B) Oral metronidazole

(C) Oral vancomycin

(D) Oral vancomycin and intravenous metronidazole

(E) Oral vancomycin and oral metronidazole

Item 9

A 44-year-old woman is evaluated for persistent fatigue, headache, myalgia, and arthralgia. Early localized Lyme disease was diagnosed 2 months ago after the patient returned from a camping trip in western New Jersey with the symptoms described and a skin eruption of erythema migrans. She was treated with a 14-day course of doxycycline with resolution of the cutaneous lesions but continuation of the other symptoms, which now are adversely affecting her work and personal life. Her only medication is ibuprofen.

On physical examination, vital signs are normal. The patient has full range of motion of the joints. No skin lesions, synovitis, or effusions are noted.

Results of laboratory studies, including a complete blood count, comprehensive metabolic panel, and lactate dehydrogenase measurement, are all within normal limits.

Which of the following is the most likely diagnosis?

(A) Anaplasmosis

(B) Babesiosis

(C) Late-stage Lyme disease

(D) Post–Lyme disease syndrome

(E) Powassan virus infection

Item 10

A 67-year-old man is evaluated for a chronic, nonhealing ulcer on his left foot of 3 months' duration. The patient states he was at a local sauna when he sustained an abrasion to the bottom of his foot after stepping on a sharp object. He subsequently developed an ulcer at the site of the injury and received several courses of antibiotics, including trimethoprim-sulfamethoxazole, doxycycline, and cephalexin, with no improvement. The ulcer continues to expand in size and deepen. Medical history is notable for hypertension and a 40-pack-year smoking history. His only medication is hydrochlorothiazide.

On physical examination, the vital signs are normal except for a temperature of 37.3 °C (99.2 °F). The legs and feet are without edema or discoloration. Pedal and popliteal pulses are symmetrical and intact. Lower extremity sensation is intact. He has a 2- × 2-cm ulcerated lesion on the plantar aspect of the metatarsal region of the great toe, with surrounding erythema, yellowish discharge, and firm edges.

Which of the following is the most likely cause of his ulcer?

(A) *Mycobacterium avium*

(B) *Mycobacterium fortuitum*

(C) *Mycobacterium kansasii*

(D) *Mycobacterium leprae*

Item 11

A 26-year-old woman is evaluated in the emergency department for lower abdominal pain with vaginal discharge. She reports no nausea or vomiting but noted vaginal bleeding after intercourse the previous night. She is sexually active, with two partners in the past 3 months, but she does not use condoms consistently. She has an intrauterine device for contraception and takes no medications.

On physical examination, vital signs are normal. Pelvic examination is shown; uterine and cervical motion tenderness are noted, but she has no adnexal tenderness or masses.

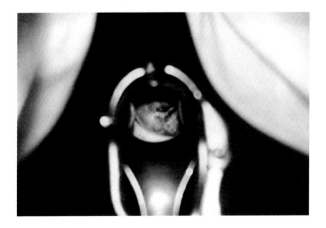

A urine pregnancy test is negative. Samples are obtained for nucleic acid amplification testing for *Neisseria gonorrhoeae* and *Chlamydia trachomatis*.

Which of the following is the most appropriate empiric treatment?

(A) Intramuscular ceftriaxone plus oral doxycycline
(B) Intravenous cefoxitin plus oral doxycycline
(C) Intravenous clindamycin plus intravenous gentamicin
(D) Oral amoxicillin-clavulanate plus oral doxycycline

Item 12

A 72-year-old man undergoes preprocedural evaluation. He is scheduled to undergo cystoscopy and possible biopsy in follow-up for a previously diagnosed non–muscle invasive bladder cancer followed by an elective right total hip arthroplasty for chronic hip pain. He is otherwise asymptomatic. Medical history is significant for diabetes mellitus, hypertension, kidney transplantation, and osteoarthritis. Medications are metformin, amlodipine, pravastatin, prednisone, and tacrolimus.

On physical examination, vital signs are normal. External rotation of the right hip elicits pain. The examination is otherwise normal.

On microscopic urinalysis, leukocyte count is 20 to 40/hpf, erythrocyte count is 0 to 1/hpf, 2+ bacteria are present, and no squamous epithelial cells are seen. Urine culture grew 10,000 to 50,000 colony-forming units of *Proteus mirabilis*.

Kidney ultrasonography is unremarkable.

Which of the following is the primary indication for antimicrobial therapy in this patient?

(A) Cystoscopy and biopsy
(B) Diabetes mellitus
(C) Kidney transplant
(D) Total hip arthroplasty

Item 13

A 33-year-old woman is evaluated after sustaining a needle-stick puncture in an infusion clinic, where she works as a nurse. The needle was being placed for intravenous therapy and had blood on it; it is from a patient at the clinic who is known to have HIV infection and is taking antiretrovirals, but the recent viral load is unknown. The nurse has already cleaned her wound. Medical history is unremarkable, and she takes no medications.

On physical examination, vital signs are normal, and other examination findings are noncontributory.

Which of the following is the most appropriate immediate management?

(A) Begin tenofovir and emtricitabine
(B) Begin tenofovir, emtricitabine, and dolutegravir
(C) Begin tenofovir, emtricitabine, and ritonavir-boosted darunavir
(D) Determine source patient's viral load

Item 14

A 38-year-old woman undergoes follow-up evaluation in the office. She was evaluated in the emergency department 3 nights ago with fever and flank pain following 2 days of dysuria. A urine culture and two sets of blood cultures were collected. She was given intravenous ceftriaxone and discharged with a 7-day course of ciprofloxacin. She is now asymptomatic. Medications are ciprofloxacin and an oral contraceptive.

On physical examination, vital signs and other findings are normal.

Escherichia coli susceptible to ciprofloxacin was isolated from her urine culture and one blood culture.

Which of the following is the most appropriate management?

(A) Completion of oral ciprofloxacin course
(B) Completion of oral ciprofloxacin course with follow-up blood cultures
(C) Extended oral ciprofloxacin therapy for 2 weeks
(D) Intravenous ceftriaxone
(E) Kidney ultrasonography

Item 15

A 25-year-old woman is evaluated for chronic intermittent nonbloody diarrhea with associated abdominal cramping, burping, and bloating. Symptoms began several months ago. She has a history of selective IgA deficiency with recurrent sinopulmonary infections. She has not taken antibiotics in the past 6 months.

On physical examination, temperature is 37.3 °C (99.1 °F); the vital signs are otherwise normal. On abdominal examination, bowel sounds are present with minimal diffuse tenderness to palpation.

Stool testing for occult blood is negative.

Which of the following is the most likely cause of this patient's diarrheal illness?

(A) *Clostridium difficile*
(B) Enterohemorrhagic *Escherichia coli*
(C) *Giardia lamblia*
(D) *Listeria monocytogenes*
(E) Nontyphoidal *Salmonella*

Item 16

A 28-year-old woman arrives to discuss possible recent exposure to Zika virus. She is pregnant, at 8 weeks' gestation, and feels well. Her husband returned home from Brazil 4 weeks ago; while away, he experienced a 5-day febrile illness, which was accompanied by a faint rash, headache, and myalgias, all of which resolved before he arrived home. After his return, they engaged in unprotected sexual intercourse. Her only medication is a prenatal vitamin.

On physical examination, vital signs are normal, and other examination findings are unremarkable.

Which of the following is the most appropriate test to perform next?

(A) Dengue virus IgM and IgG antibodies test
(B) Uterine ultrasonography every 3 weeks

(C) Zika virus IgM antibody test

(D) Zika virus RNA nucleic acid amplification test

Item 17

A 72-year-old woman is evaluated for a 2-day history of left facial droop and severe burning and stinging pain on the left ear helix and into the ear canal, with muffled hearing and tinnitus. She received the live-attenuated zoster vaccine at age 60 years. She takes no medications.

On physical examination, vital signs are normal. She has a left-sided peripheral facial droop. The tympanic membrane appears normal. No rash is present. Hearing is diminished to a whisper in the left ear. The remainder of the examination is unremarkable.

Which of the following is the most likely cause of this patient's findings?

(A) *Borrelia burgdorferi*

(B) Herpes simplex virus type 1

(C) Herpes simplex virus type 2

(D) Varicella-zoster virus

Item 18

A 45-year-old man is evaluated for a 3-day history of fever, myalgia, headache, and nonproductive cough. He works as a large-animal veterinarian. Medical history is unremarkable, and he takes no medications.

On physical examination, vital signs are normal except for a temperature of 38.2 °C (100.8 °F). Oxygen saturation is 94% breathing ambient air. The examination is otherwise unremarkable.

A chest radiograph shows a patchy right lower lobe interstitial infiltrate.

Which of the following is the most likely cause of his illness?

(A) *Bacillus anthracis*

(B) *Coxiella burnetii*

(C) *Chlamydia psittaci*

(D) *Francisella tularensis*

(E) *Yersinia pestis*

Item 19

A 46-year-old woman is evaluated for new-onset fever and discomfort at the site of a peripherally inserted central catheter (PICC). She was hospitalized for acute pancreatitis and required the PICC for intravenous access and hydration.

On physical examination, temperature is 37.8 °C (100.1 °F), and the remaining vital signs are normal. Right brachial PICC line site is tender, without erythema. Cardiac examination is without murmurs.

Two sets of peripheral blood cultures are obtained, showing gram-positive cocci and clusters. Both sets of blood cultures are growing coagulase-negative *Staphylococcus* resistant to methicillin. Vancomycin is initiated.

Which of the following is the most appropriate additional management?

(A) Maintain PICC line and continue vancomycin for 4 weeks

(B) Maintain PICC line and perform transesophageal echocardiography

(C) Remove PICC line

(D) Remove PICC line and repeat blood cultures

Item 20

A 39-year-old man is evaluated in the hospital after a motorcycle accident that necessitated an open reduction and internal fixation of a femur fracture. During the emergency department evaluation, an indwelling urinary catheter was placed. Medical history is noncontributory, and he takes no medications.

On physical examination, he is alert and oriented. Vital signs are normal. The left leg is tender, with a sterile dressing over the incision.

Which of the following is the most appropriate urinary catheter management?

(A) Change catheter to an antimicrobial or antiseptic-coated catheter

(B) Initiate prophylactic antibiotics

(C) Maintain catheter placement until patient is ambulatory

(D) Remove catheter and observe for spontaneous voiding

Item 21

A 50-year-old woman is evaluated in the emergency department for fever and tenderness at the site of a cat bite sustained on the dorsum of her right hand 2 days ago. She indicates that she works at an animal shelter. Medical history is significant for a methicillin-resistant *Staphylococcus aureus* skin infection 6 months ago; she is up to date on all vaccinations, including rabies and tetanus. She takes no medications.

On physical examination, temperature is 38.5 °C (101.3 °F), blood pressure is 98/66 mm Hg, pulse rate is 110/min, and respiration rate is 22/min. A tender puncture wound is noted on the dorsum of the right hand; it is warm and surrounded by significant erythema. Some purulent discharge is noted from the wound.

Blood cultures are obtained.

A plain radiograph of the right hand shows no evidence of gas, foreign body, or bony involvement.

In addition to surgical consultation, which of the following antibiotic regimens is the most appropriate treatment at this time?

(A) Ampicillin-sulbactam plus vancomycin

(B) Ceftriaxone plus metronidazole

(C) Ciprofloxacin plus aztreonam

(D) Imipenem

(E) Vancomycin and clindamycin

Item 22

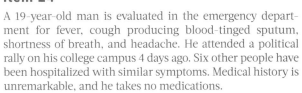

A 42-year-old man is evaluated for headache and progressive weakness. He was hospitalized yesterday with a 9-day history of fever, headache, and myalgia. He is a trail runner, and 10 days ago participated in a 10-kilometer race in North Carolina. He is not aware of any tick bite.

On physical examination, the patient appears ill. Temperature is 39.4 °C (102.9 °F), blood pressure is 102/78 mm Hg, pulse rate is 102/min, and respiration rate is 24/min. No tonsillar enlargement, cervical lymphadenopathy, hepatosplenomegaly, or skin lesion is noted.

Laboratory studies:

Leukocyte count	1500/µL (1.5×10^9/L), with 70% neutrophils and no atypical lymphocytes
Platelet count	34,000/µL (34×10^9/L)
Alanine aminotransferase	667 U/L
Aspartate aminotransferase	995 U/L

Empiric doxycycline therapy is initiated for a possible tick-borne infection. Within 24 hours, he defervesces, and within 48 hours, the leukocyte and platelet counts normalize. Serologic tests for *Rickettsia rickettsii* and *Ehrlichia chaffeensis* obtained on admission have negative results.

Which of the following is the most likely diagnosis?

(A) Heartland virus infection
(B) Human monocytic ehrlichiosis
(C) Infectious mononucleosis
(D) Rocky Mountain spotted fever

Item 23

A 32-year-old man is evaluated in the hospital for a 4-day history of fever and leukocytosis that began 1 week after cranial surgery and a 1-day history of worsening mental status. He experienced traumatic intracranial hemorrhage requiring a craniotomy for drainage and placement of an external ventricular drain. He remains intubated with mechanical ventilation. Medications are empiric vancomycin and cefepime, initiated 4 days ago.

On physical examination, temperature is 39.2 °C (102.5 °F), blood pressure is 108/62 mm Hg, pulse rate is 102/min, and respiration rate is 20/min. He was previously awake and able to follow simple commands, but now he is obtunded. Nuchal rigidity is noted. Other examination findings are unremarkable.

Cerebrospinal fluid (CSF) evaluation shows a leukocyte count of 134/µL (134×10^6/L) with 50% neutrophils, erythrocyte count of 10,000/µL ($10,000 \times 10^6$/L), glucose level of 35 mg/dL (1.9 mmol/L), protein level of 112 mg/dL (1120 mg/L), and elevated lactate level of 5.4 mg/dL.

Blood cultures taken at onset of fever are negative, as are CSF cultures.

A chest radiograph shows no infiltrates.

Which of the following is the most appropriate management?

(A) Continue current care
(B) Discontinue vancomycin and cefepime and begin linezolid

(C) Remove the external ventricular drain
(D) Switch to intraventricular administration of antibiotics

Item 24

A 19-year-old man is evaluated in the emergency department for fever, cough producing blood-tinged sputum, shortness of breath, and headache. He attended a political rally on his college campus 4 days ago. Six other people have been hospitalized with similar symptoms. Medical history is unremarkable, and he takes no medications.

On physical examination, the patient is alert and oriented. Temperature is 39.1 °C (102.4 °F), blood pressure is 98/58 mm Hg, pulse rate is 110/min, and respiration rate is 24/min. Oxygen saturation is 92% breathing oxygen 2 L/min by nasal cannula. Neurologic examination is nonfocal, and no meningeal signs are present. Dyspnea, bilateral pulmonary rhonchi, and tubular breath sounds are noted on pulmonary examination. No rash is present, and the abdomen is nontender.

Sputum Gram stain reveals many polymorphonuclear cells and abundant gram-negative coccobacilli demonstrating bipolar staining.

A chest radiograph shows bilateral patchy infiltrates.

Which of the following is the most appropriate treatment?

(A) Ceftriaxone and azithromycin
(B) Ciprofloxacin
(C) Gentamicin
(D) Piperacillin-tazobactam and levofloxacin

Item 25

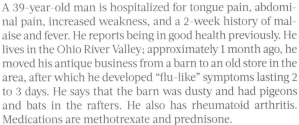

A 39-year-old man is hospitalized for tongue pain, abdominal pain, increased weakness, and a 2-week history of malaise and fever. He reports being in good health previously. He lives in the Ohio River Valley; approximately 1 month ago, he moved his antique business from a barn to an old store in the area, after which he developed "flu-like" symptoms lasting 2 to 3 days. He says that the barn was dusty and had pigeons and bats in the rafters. He also has rheumatoid arthritis. Medications are methotrexate and prednisone.

On physical examination, the patient is lethargic. Temperature is 39.7 °C (103.5 °F), blood pressure is 90/50 mm Hg, pulse rate is 128/min, and respiration rate is 24/min. A shallow ulceration is visible on the right buccal mucosa and left lateral tongue. His neck is supple. Lungs are clear to percussion and auscultation. There is moderate hepatosplenomegaly.

Results of laboratory studies show a hemoglobin level of 9 g/dL (90 g/L), a leukocyte count of 10,500/µL (10.5×10^9/L), and a platelet count of 90,000/µL (90×10^9/L).

Posteroanterior and lateral chest radiographs are unremarkable.

Which of the following is the most appropriate treatment?

(A) Ceftriaxone and azithromycin
(B) Colchicine
(C) Itraconazole
(D) Liposomal amphotericin B

Item 26

A 45-year-old man is evaluated in the ICU for continued daily fevers. He was hospitalized 6 days ago after 4 days of left-sided pleuritic chest pain, fever, and cough productive of yellow sputum with occasional blood streaks. He has a history of injection drug use and last injected heroin 7 days ago. Chest radiograph obtained at admission revealed a left lower lobe infiltrate. A sputum Gram stain showed gram-positive cocci in clusters. Empiric antibiotic therapy including vancomycin was begun. Sputum and two sets of blood cultures taken at admission grew methicillin-resistant *Staphylococcus aureus*, and antibiotic therapy was de-escalated to vancomycin monotherapy on hospital day 3. His only medication is vancomycin.

On physical examination, temperature is 38.5 °C (101.3 °F), blood pressure is 94/68 mm Hg, pulse rate is 118/min, and respiration rate is 28/min. Oxygen saturation is 92% breathing 6 L/min oxygen by nasal cannula. Decreased breath sounds are heard at the left lung base.

A vancomycin trough measurement is therapeutic at 15 µg/mL. Repeat blood cultures from hospital day 3 were negative at 72 hours. Repeat sputum Gram stain shows 3+ leukocytes and 1+ gram-positive cocci.

A transthoracic echocardiogram was negative for valvular vegetations. A repeat chest radiograph is shown.

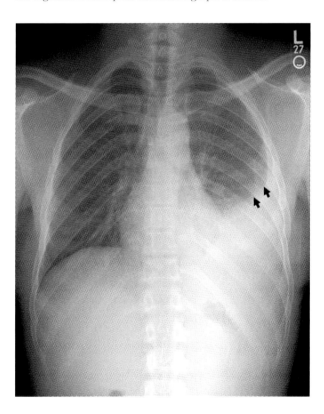

Which of the following is the most appropriate management at this time?

(A) Add methylprednisolone
(B) Add piperacillin-tazobactam
(C) Perform thoracentesis
(D) Procalcitonin measurement
(E) Switch to daptomycin

Item 27

A 27-year-old woman is hospitalized with a 5-day history of intermittent fever, headache, muscle pains, and abdominal cramps. She returned 8 days ago from a 1-week trip to Kenya and Tanzania. She spent time outdoors in the evening and went hiking in a wooded park. She is pregnant at 20 weeks' gestation. She declined pretravel immunizations as well as antimalarial chemoprophylaxis. Her only medication is a prenatal vitamin.

On physical examination, temperature is 39.1 °C (102.3 °F), blood pressure is 98/64 mm Hg, pulse rate is 112/min, and respiration rate is 16/min. Her conjunctivae are icteric. Cardiopulmonary examination reveals regular tachycardia. The remainder of the examination is unremarkable.

A peripheral blood smear is shown.

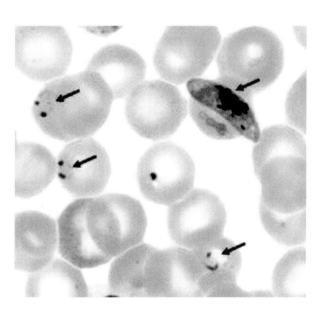

Which of the following is the most likely causative agent?

(A) *Plasmodium falciparum*
(B) *Plasmodium knowlesi*
(C) *Plasmodium malariae*
(D) *Plasmodium ovale*
(E) *Plasmodium vivax*

Item 28

A 64-year-old man is evaluated in the emergency department for acute onset of severe lower back pain that radiates down his legs, with associated numbness and fever. Medical history is significant for end-stage kidney disease, for which he receives hemodialysis. Medications are erythropoietin, iron, lisinopril, nifedipine, and sevelamer.

On physical examination, temperature is 38.6 °C (101.5 °F), blood pressure is 110/62 mm Hg, pulse rate is 114/min, and respiration rate is 20/min. The lower extremities have decreased sensation to touch, diminished reflexes, and mild weakness.

Laboratory studies show a leukocyte count of 15,450/µL (15.5×10^9/L). Blood cultures are pending.

CONT.

MRI of the lumbar spine shows discitis in L2 to L3 with epidural abscess.

Which of the following is the most appropriate management?

(A) Await blood cultures before starting antimicrobial therapy
(B) Empiric antibiotic therapy alone
(C) Empiric antibiotic therapy and surgical drainage
(D) Surgical drainage alone

Item 29

A 19-year-old man is hospitalized with a 6-day history of lightheadedness and nightly fevers. He also reports sore throat, headache, joint and muscle aches, and a dry cough. He recalls a blotchy rash on his trunk and arms, which has resolved. He returned home 12 days ago from a trip to Vietnam, for which he did not receive specific immunizations or other prophylaxis. During the second week of his trip, he experienced 2 days of diarrhea; he has had none since, but abdominal discomfort and anorexia persist.

On physical examination, the patient is lethargic. Temperature is 39.9 °C (103.9 °F), blood pressure is 98/58 mm Hg, pulse rate is 68/min, and respiration rate is 16/min. No skin rash or evidence of jaundice is present. The abdomen is distended, with diminished bowel sounds, but nontender. Neurologic examination is nonfocal.

Which of the following is the most likely diagnosis?

(A) Brucellosis
(B) Leptospirosis
(C) Melioidosis
(D) Typhoid (enteric) fever

Item 30

A 31-year-old man arrives to establish care for newly diagnosed HIV infection. He is asymptomatic. Medical history is otherwise noncontributory, and he takes no medications.

On physical examination, vital signs are normal, and the remainder of the examination is unremarkable.

A review of his previous laboratory studies shows a normal complete blood count, and chemistries, including glucose, creatinine, and liver enzyme levels, are within normal limits. The HIV-1/2 antigen/antibody combination immunoassay is reactive. The HIV-1/2 antibody differentiation assay is positive for HIV-1 antibody, and HIV-1 RNA is quantified at 27,313 copies/mL. CD4 cell count is 455/µL.

Which of the following is the most appropriate next step in management?

(A) Genotypic viral resistance testing
(B) Glycohemoglobin level
(C) Phenotypic viral resistance testing
(D) Repeat HIV viral load and CD4 cell count in 1 month

 ## Item 31

A 33-year-old woman is evaluated in the emergency department in January with a 3-day history of fever, headache, stiff neck, and photophobia. She was previously well, and medical history is negative for recent travel; she takes no medications.

On physical examination, temperature is 38.5 °C (101.3 °F), blood pressure is 136/86 mm Hg, pulse rate is 100/min, and respiration rate is 18/min. The general medical examination is unremarkable. On neurologic examination, she shows photophobia, and a nondilated funduscopic examination shows no papilledema. The remainder of the examination is nonfocal.

Cerebrospinal fluid evaluation shows a leukocyte count of 324/µL (324 × 10⁶/L) with 60% neutrophils, glucose level of 58 mg/dL (3.2 mmol/L), and protein level of 125 mg/dL (1250 mg/L). Gram stain of the cerebrospinal fluid is negative, and culture is pending.

Which of the following is the most likely cause of this patient's symptoms?

(A) Enterovirus
(B) Herpes simplex virus type 2
(C) Mumps virus
(D) West Nile virus

Item 32

A 22-year-old man returns for follow-up evaluation; he was recently diagnosed with HIV infection, and he began antiretroviral therapy 2 weeks ago. He also received influenza vaccination and the 13-valent pneumococcal conjugate vaccine at that time. He reports that he has sex with men. Medical history is notable for previous chlamydia infection and genital warts. Medications are tenofovir, emtricitabine, and dolutegravir.

On physical examination, vital signs are normal. A few small lesions consistent with warts are noted on the penis. The examination is otherwise unremarkable.

Laboratory studies:

CD4 cell count	527/µL
Hepatitis A IgG	Positive
Hepatitis A IgM	Negative
Hepatitis B surface antibody	Negative
Hepatitis B surface antigen	Positive

Which of the following is the most appropriate immunization to be given today?

(A) 23-Valent pneumococcal polysaccharide vaccine
(B) Hepatitis A vaccine
(C) Hepatitis B vaccine
(D) Human papillomavirus vaccine

Item 33

A 22-year-old man is evaluated in the emergency department 1 hour after awakening with right-sided facial weakness. He reports a 2-day history of headache but has had no fever. He lives in Minnesota and has removed two embedded ticks from himself and three from his dog over the past 3 weeks. The patient is otherwise healthy and takes no medication.

On physical examination, vital signs are normal. Nuchal rigidity and right facial nerve (cranial nerve VII) palsy are noted. Mental status is intact. Skin examination findings are shown on the next page.

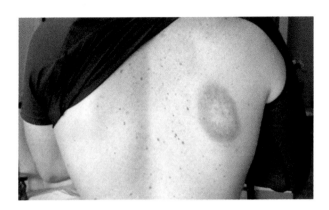

All other physical examination findings are unremarkable. Results of laboratory studies show a leukocyte count of 11,500/µL (11.5 × 10⁹/L).

CONT.

Which of the following is the most appropriate initial management?

(A) *Borrelia burgdorferi* antibody testing

(B) Ceftriaxone administration

(C) Doxycycline administration

(D) Head CT

(E) Lumbar puncture

Item 34

A 34-year-old woman is seeking medical advice. She is pregnant at 24 weeks' gestation. Her husband returned home 1 week ago from a medical mission in the Middle East. Spores of anthrax were discovered in the hospital where he was working. Her husband, who is asymptomatic, has begun taking ciprofloxacin and will receive a vaccination series. The patient questions if she is at risk for infection. Her only medication is a prenatal vitamin.

On physical examination, vital signs are normal. The examination is unremarkable.

Which of the following is the most appropriate management?

(A) Doxycycline and vaccination

(B) Nasopharyngeal swab and anthrax blood test

(C) Raxibacumab injection

(D) No treatment

Item 35

A 27-year-old man is evaluated during a routine health maintenance visit with his internist. He asks about reducing his risk for HIV infection because he has sex with men, has multiple partners, and reports using condoms "sometimes." Medical history is unremarkable, and he takes no medications.

The physical examination is normal.

Laboratory studies show a normal serum creatinine level. A serum rapid plasma reagin test is negative. Nucleic acid amplification testing for gonorrhea and chlamydia from urine, pharynx, and rectum are all negative. An HIV test is negative.

Which of the following is the most appropriate preventive measure?

(A) Reinforce consistent condom use and avoid antiretroviral therapy

(B) Tenofovir and emtricitabine single dose before each sexual encounter

(C) Tenofovir and emtricitabine single dose after each sexual encounter

(D) Tenofovir disoproxil fumarate and emtricitabine daily

Item 36

A 67-year-old woman is hospitalized for an ulcer on the bottom of her right foot; it has expanded over the past 2 months. The patient has type 2 diabetes mellitus, hypertension, stage 3 chronic kidney disease, and peripheral neuropathy. Medications are insulin glargine, insulin lispro, lisinopril, and gabapentin.

On physical examination, temperature is 37.3 °C (99.1 °F); the remaining vital signs are normal. A deep 3- × 4-cm ulcer is located on the distal medial compartment of the plantar surface of the right foot. The base of the ulcer is necrotic and malodorous; a probe-to-bone test is negative. No surrounding erythema or increased warmth is noted. Both feet are warm with palpable pulses.

Erythrocyte sedimentation rate and C-reactive protein level are elevated. Results of a complete blood count are normal.

A plain radiograph reveals soft tissue swelling and ulceration; an MRI reveals findings consistent with osteomyelitis of the distal head of the first metatarsal.

Which of the following is the most appropriate management?

(A) Bone biopsy and culture

(B) Forefoot amputation

(C) Swabbing and culture of wound base

(D) Vancomycin and piperacillin-tazobactam

Item 37

A 32-year-old woman arrives to establish primary care. She is sexually active with a new male partner and reports consistent condom use. Medical history is significant for chlamydia cervicitis 5 years ago and treatment for syphilis 6 years ago. Her only medication is an oral contraceptive.

On physical examination, vital signs and the remainder of the examination are unremarkable.

A syphilis enzyme immunoassay is positive; rapid plasma reagin testing is negative. A fluorescent treponemal antibody test is positive. Nucleic acid amplification testing is negative for *Neisseria gonorrhoeae* and *Chlamydia trachomatis*. HIV antigen/antibody combination testing is negative.

Which of the following is the most appropriate management?

(A) Intramuscular benzathine penicillin, single dose

(B) Intramuscular benzathine penicillin, weekly for 3 weeks

(C) Repeat serology with *Treponema pallidum* particle agglutination assay

(D) No further testing or treatment

Item 38

A 25-year-old woman returns for counseling regarding results of HIV testing completed during a recent routine health maintenance visit. She reports no known exposure or risk factors for HIV infection. Medical history is unremarkable, and she takes no medications.

Laboratory studies show a reactive HIV-1/2 antigen/antibody combination immunoassay, a negative HIV-1/2 antibody differentiation immunoassay, and no RNA detected on HIV-1 RNA nucleic acid amplification testing.

Which of the following is the most appropriate management?

(A) Initiate combination antiretroviral therapy after counseling
(B) Order T-cell subset testing to check CD4 cell count
(C) Perform HIV genotypic resistance testing
(D) Perform Western blot HIV antibody testing
(E) Tell the patient she does not have HIV infection

Item 39

An 18-year-old man is evaluated for a 4-day history of frequent, large-volume diarrhea, with associated abdominal cramping, emesis, fever, and nausea. He is a lifeguard at a freshwater municipal pool, and several other swimmers who use the pool have recently developed similar symptoms.

On physical examination, temperature is 37.5 °C (99.5 °F); the vital signs are otherwise normal. On abdominal examination, bowel sounds are present, palpation elicits minimal tenderness, and no guarding or rebound is noted.

Modified acid-fast staining of the stool reveals oocysts that are about 5 microns in diameter.

Which of the following is the most likely cause of this patient's diarrhea?

(A) *Cryptosporidium*
(B) Enterohemorrhagic *Escherichia coli*
(C) Norovirus
(D) *Nocardia*
(E) *Vibrio parahaemolyticus*

Item 40

A 31-year-old woman undergoes consultation regarding preventive strategies for travelers' diarrhea. She is planning a 7-day vacation to Mexico. Her itinerary includes 3 days in Mexico City followed by 4 days in the Yucatan Peninsula. Medical history is significant for Crohn colitis, which is currently in remission with maintenance therapy. Medications are adalimumab and as-needed loperamide; she is allergic to aspirin.

On physical examination, vital signs are normal, and other findings are unremarkable.

Which of the following is the most appropriate preventive measure for this patient?

(A) Azithromycin
(B) Bismuth subsalicylate
(C) Ciprofloxacin
(D) Probiotics
(E) No prophylaxis

Item 41

An 82-year-old woman is hospitalized with hypotension and volume depletion resulting from gastroenteritis. Medical history is noncontributory, and she takes no medications.

On physical examination, temperature is 36.8 °C (98.3 °F), blood pressure is 92/66 mm Hg, pulse rate is 110/min, and respiration rate is 16/min. The remainder of the examination is unremarkable.

Because of difficulty in inserting a peripheral venous access line, an internal jugular central venous catheter will be placed for volume resuscitation.

Which of the following is the most appropriate measure to prevent catheter-related bloodstream infection in this patient?

(A) Assess catheter daily for necessity and potential removal
(B) Give one dose of vancomycin after catheter insertion
(C) Replace catheter every 7 days
(D) Use a small sterile drape when inserting the catheter

Item 42

A 36-year-old man is evaluated for a 10-day history of abdominal cramping, diarrhea, malaise, and nausea. Diarrhea is watery without mucus or blood. He returned 2 weeks ago from a 7-day trip to Lima, Peru.

On physical examination, temperature is 37.7 °C (99.9 °F); the remaining vital signs are normal. On abdominal examination, bowel sounds are present with diffuse tenderness to palpation. The abdomen is not distended; no guarding or rebound is noted.

Stool polymerase chain reaction assay is positive for *Cyclospora*.

Which of the following is the most appropriate treatment?

(A) Atovaquone
(B) Metronidazole
(C) Pyrimethamine
(D) Quinacrine
(E) Trimethoprim-sulfamethoxazole

Item 43

A 25-year-old woman is seen for counseling. She is newly pregnant at 7 weeks' gestation and has HIV infection diagnosed 6 years ago. HIV has been well controlled with an antiretroviral regimen, which she tolerates well. Medications are tenofovir disoproxil fumarate (TDF), emtricitabine, and efavirenz.

On physical examination, vital signs and other findings are normal.

Laboratory studies show HIV viral load is undetectable and the CD4 cell count is normal.

Which of the following is the most appropriate management?

(A) Continue TDF, emtricitabine, and efavirenz
(B) Pause antiretroviral therapy until after the first trimester
(C) Perform resistance testing
(D) Switch to zidovudine, lamivudine, and ritonavir-boosted lopinavir

Item 44

A 31-year-old man undergoes pretravel consultation. He plans to leave in 8 days for a safari trip to Kenya. He received yellow fever and typhoid vaccinations 18 months ago, and he is undergoing a work-related three-dose hepatitis B vaccination series. He also has a prescription for prophylactic antimalarial medication. No serum IgG antibodies to hepatitis A were detected in a recent blood test. He smokes cigarettes and occasionally drinks an alcoholic beverage.

On physical examination, vital signs are normal, and other findings are unremarkable.

Which of the following is the most appropriate pretravel management for this patient?

(A) First dose of hepatitis A vaccine with a second dose in 7 days
(B) Immune globulin
(C) Single dose of hepatitis A vaccine
(D) Single dose of hepatitis A vaccine plus immune globulin
(E) No intervention

Item 45

A 92-year-old man is hospitalized with a complicated urinary tract infection (UTI). He resides in a nursing home and has a chronic indwelling urinary catheter. In the nursing home, a urinalysis and urine culture were performed for possible UTI, and empiric ciprofloxacin therapy was initiated 1 day before transfer to the hospital. In the emergency department, ciprofloxacin was changed to piperacillin-tazobactam, and blood cultures were obtained. Medical history is notable for dementia, benign prostatic hyperplasia, chronic kidney disease, and recurrent UTIs. Medications are donepezil, memantine, and piperacillin-tazobactam.

On physical examination, temperature is 38.5 °C (101.3 °F), blood pressure is 108/70 mm Hg, pulse rate is 100/min, and respiration rate is 16/min. Suprapubic tenderness is noted, and the urinary catheter is draining cloudy urine. Other examination findings are noncontributory.

Laboratory studies show a leukocyte count of 15,200/µL (15.2×10^9/L) and a serum creatinine level of 1.9 mg/dL (168 µmol/L). Urinalysis reveals leukocytes too numerous to count but no erythrocytes.

Urine culture obtained from the nursing home shows more than 10^5 colony-forming units of *Escherichia coli* sensitive to piperacillin-tazobactam, gentamicin, cefepime, and meropenem (resistant to ceftriaxone, ceftazidime, cefotaxime, and ciprofloxacin); it is confirmed to be an extended-spectrum β-lactamase–producing organism. Blood cultures are pending.

No infiltrates are seen on the chest radiograph.

Which of the following is the most appropriate treatment?

(A) Add gentamicin
(B) Continue piperacillin-tazobactam
(C) Switch piperacillin-tazobactam to cefepime
(D) Switch piperacillin-tazobactam to meropenem

Item 46

A 58-year-old man is assessed for discharge from the hospital. He was admitted 3 days ago with fever and chills. He has non-Hodgkin lymphoma and a tunneled subclavian venous catheter used for chemotherapy infusion. Blood cultures at admission grew vancomycin-resistant *Enterococcus faecium*. The patient's catheter was removed, a peripherally inserted central catheter (PICC) was placed for intravenous access, and daptomycin therapy was initiated. Blood cultures are now negative, and the patient is afebrile.

The patient is ready to be discharged to complete intravenous daptomycin therapy as an outpatient. At the time of discharge, his complete blood count and comprehensive chemistry profile are normal.

Which of the following is the most appropriate weekly monitoring of his daptomycin therapy?

(A) Electrocardiography and blood glucose
(B) Hemoglobin and platelet count
(C) Serum amylase and triglycerides
(D) Serum creatinine and creatine kinase

Item 47

A 32-year-old man is evaluated for a 2-month history of painless, violaceous skin nodules with surrounding edema on the chest, back, and lower extremities. He reports that he has sex with men. Medical history is significant for AIDS, with a CD4 cell count of 54/µL. He is not following an antiretroviral therapy regimen.

On physical examination, temperature is 38.1 °C (100.5 °F), blood pressure is 135/62 mm Hg, pulse rate is 68/min, and respiration rate is 20/min. Several nodules are seen in the mouth during oral examination (shown).

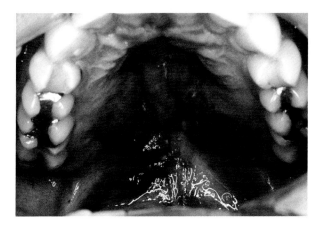

Which of the following is the most likely cause of these findings?

(A) Cytomegalovirus
(B) Epstein-Barr virus
(C) Human herpes virus type 6
(D) Human herpes virus type 8

Item 48

A 42-year-old man is evaluated in the hospital for increased pain and drainage from a previously healed surgical wound over the left fibula. He underwent open reduction and internal fixation of a fracture 4 weeks ago. The patient has undergone incision and surgical debridement of the wound. A bone culture revealed methicillin-sensitive *Staphylococcus aureus*. Medical history is otherwise noncontributory, and his only medication is ibuprofen for pain.

On physical examination, vital signs are normal. A surgical wound over the left lateral leg is well approximated with no erythema or drainage.

A plain radiograph before debridement shows nonunion of the fracture with screws and K-wires in place.

Which of the following is the most appropriate treatment?

(A) Cefazolin
(B) Cefazolin and rifampin
(C) Ceftaroline
(D) Vancomycin and rifampin

Item 49

A 34-year-old man is evaluated immediately after a dog bite to his thigh. Medical history is notable for splenectomy 5 years ago. The patient and dog are up to date on all immunizations. He takes no medications.

On physical examination, vital signs are normal. A tiny puncture wound is located on the right mid-thigh with minimal surrounding erythema.

Which of the following is the most appropriate management?

(A) Amoxicillin-clavulanate
(B) Ciprofloxacin
(C) Metronidazole
(D) Observation

Item 50

A 76-year-old woman is evaluated in the hospital for recurrent diverticulitis. She has had multiple episodes of diverticulitis treated with ciprofloxacin and metronidazole over the past 18 months. During this hospitalization, an abscess was noted on a CT scan of the abdomen and pelvis, and a percutaneous drain was placed and the fluid sent for culture. Piperacillin-tazobactam is started empirically.

On physical examination, temperature is 39.2 °C (102.6 °F), blood pressure is 126/82 mm Hg, pulse rate is 100/min, and respiration rate is 15/min. She has diffuse abdominal tenderness to palpation.

Laboratory studies show a leukocyte count of 22,000/µL (22 × 10⁹/L) and a serum creatinine level of 1.3 mg/dL (115 µmol/L).

Gram stain of the abscess fluid reveals 4+ gram-negative rods; fluid culture grows *Pseudomonas aeruginosa* resistant to ceftazidime, piperacillin-tazobactam, ciprofloxacin, meropenem, and doripenem. Blood cultures are negative.

The *Pseudomonas* isolate should be tested for susceptibility to which of the following antibiotics?

(A) Ceftolozane-tazobactam and colistin
(B) Ertapenem and tobramycin
(C) Fosfomycin
(D) Minocycline

Item 51

A 25-year-old woman is hospitalized with a 4-day history of fever and cough productive of brown sputum. She is at 14 weeks' gestation with her first pregnancy. Medical history is significant for mild persistent asthma. Medications are an albuterol inhaler, beclomethasone inhaler, and a prenatal vitamin.

On physical examination, temperature is 38.2 °C (100.8 °F), blood pressure is normal, pulse rate is 122/min, and respiration rate is 24/min. Oxygen saturation is 94% breathing ambient air. Crackles are heard at the left lung base on pulmonary auscultation.

Chest radiograph shows a left lower lobe infiltrate.

Which of the following is the most likely cause of pneumonia in this patient?

(A) *Escherichia coli*
(B) *Klebsiella pneumoniae*
(C) *Listeria monocytogenes*
(D) *Staphylococcus aureus*
(E) *Streptococcus pneumoniae*

Item 52

A 67-year-old woman is evaluated in December for a 2-day history of runny nose, fever, headache, myalgia, cough, and sore throat. Medical history is notable for heart failure. She lives at home with her husband and is able to eat, drink, and take her oral medications. Her medications are carvedilol and enalapril. She received a standard-dose influenza immunization in October.

On physical examination, temperature is 38.6 °C (101.5 °F), blood pressure is 145/62 mm Hg, pulse rate is 98/min, and respiration rate is 20/min. The patient has rhinorrhea, and the pharynx is erythematous. Lungs are clear to auscultation.

A chest radiograph shows no infiltrates.

A nasopharyngeal swab is positive for influenza B.

Which of the following is the most appropriate treatment?

(A) Amantadine
(B) Oseltamivir
(C) Peramivir
(D) Rimantadine

Item 53

A 74-year-old man is evaluated in the emergency department for new onset of confusion and 2 days of fever and rigors. Medical history is significant for diabetes mellitus, hypertension, and benign prostatic hyperplasia. Medications are lisinopril, hydrochlorothiazide, metformin, tamsulosin, and aspirin.

On physical examination, the patient is confused. Temperature is 39.1 °C (102.4 °F), blood pressure is 102/56 mm Hg, pulse rate is 88/min, and respiration rate is 22/min. Oxygen saturation is 93% breathing ambient air. Neurologic examination is nonfocal and without meningeal signs. On abdominal examination, the abdomen is soft and the urinary bladder is distended. Other examination findings are noncontributory.

Laboratory studies:

Hemoglobin	15.2 g/dL (152 g/L)
Leukocyte count	17,480/µL (17.5 × 10^9/L)
Blood urea nitrogen	72 mg/dL (25.7 mmol/L)
Creatinine	2.1 mg/dL (186 µmol/L)
Urinalysis (catheterized sample)	Volume 780 mL (780 µL); cloudy; 1.244 specific gravity; >100 leukocytes/hpf; 0-5 erythrocytes/hpf; 4+ bacteria

Urine culture and two sets of blood cultures are obtained.

A portable chest radiograph shows no signs of acute cardiopulmonary disease.

In addition to supportive care, which of the following is the most appropriate management?

(A) Intravenous cefepime and kidney ultrasonography

(B) Intravenous ciprofloxacin

(C) Intravenous levofloxacin and digital prostate massage

(D) Intravenous piperacillin-tazobactam and contrast-enhanced abdominal and pelvic CT

 Item 54

A 26-year-old woman is evaluated in the emergency department for fever and low back pain that has progressed for the past 3 weeks. She injects heroin daily. Medical history is unremarkable, and she takes no medications.

On physical examination, temperature is 38.1 °C (100.6 °F), blood pressure is 90/60 mm Hg, pulse rate is 110/min, and respiration rate is 28/min. The lower lumbar spine is tender to palpation. Neurologic examination and other physical examination findings are normal.

Aggressive fluid resuscitation is initiated. Complete blood count, metabolic profile, erythrocyte sedimentation rate, and blood culture and urinalysis are obtained.

MRI is shown (top of next column).

Which of the following is the most appropriate antibiotic management?

(A) Cefazolin and gentamicin

(B) Vancomycin

(C) Vancomycin and cefepime

(D) Withhold antibiotics while awaiting bone biopsy

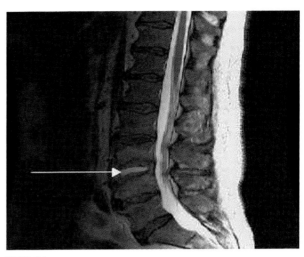

ITEM 54

Item 55

A 21-year-old man is evaluated for cold symptoms beginning last week, including malaise, fatigue, swollen lymph nodes in the neck, and sore throat, which resolved before his appointment today. He has no other symptoms. He reports occasionally having sex with men, usually using condoms, but has had no known HIV exposure. Medical history is unremarkable, and he takes no medications.

On physical examination, vital signs are normal. A few shotty cervical lymph nodes are palpable, but no other lymphadenopathy is noted. No rash is present. Other examination findings are normal.

Laboratory studies show a reactive HIV-1/2 antigen/antibody combination immunoassay. The HIV-1/HIV-2 antibody differentiation immunoassay is negative. HIV-1 RNA nucleic acid amplification testing is positive, with quantification of 11,540 copies/mL.

Which of the following is the most likely diagnosis?

(A) Acute HIV infection

(B) Chronic HIV infection

(C) False-positive HIV test

(D) HIV-2 infection

Item 56

A 19-year-old man is evaluated at an urgent care clinic for a 3-day history of dysuria, with purulent discharge at the urethral meatus this morning. He reports no urgency, frequency, or fever. He returned last week from a spring break trip, during which he had oral sex with a new female partner. Medical history is otherwise noncontributory, he takes no medications, and he has no medication allergies.

On physical examination, vital signs are normal. Purulent discharge is noted at the urethral meatus. The examination is otherwise unremarkable.

Nucleic acid amplification testing for *Neisseria gonorrhoeae* and *Chlamydia trachomatis* is performed on a first-catch urine sample.

Which of the following is the most appropriate empiric treatment?

(A) Ceftriaxone plus azithromycin

(B) Doxycycline

(C) Trimethoprim-sulfamethoxazole

(D) Valacyclovir

Item 57

A 30-year-old woman undergoes predischarge evaluation 1 month after allogeneic hematopoietic stem cell transplantation for acute myeloid leukemia. The posttransplant course was complicated by prolonged neutropenia and *Escherichia coli* bacteremia. The infection and neutropenia have resolved with broad-spectrum antibiotic therapy. She received all indicated pretransplant immunizations. Medications are trimethoprim-sulfamethoxazole for pneumocystis pneumonia prophylaxis and tacrolimus.

On physical examination, vital signs are normal. The indwelling central line site appears normal without erythema, swelling, or tenderness. Lungs are clear throughout. No skin lesions are present.

Laboratory studies show a leukocyte count of 2700/µL (2.7×10^9/L) (differential of 57% polymorphonuclear cells, 30% lymphocytes, 10% monocytes, and 3% eosinophils) and a serum creatinine level of 0.7 mg/dL (61.9 µmol/L).

Pretransplant serologies were positive for cytomegalovirus, Epstein-Barr virus, varicella-zoster virus, and *Toxoplasma*.

In addition to continuing the trimethoprim-sulfamethoxazole, which of the following is the most appropriate outpatient prophylaxis for this patient?

(A) Acyclovir

(B) Ciprofloxacin

(C) Posaconazole

(D) Valganciclovir

Item 58

A 34-year-old man is hospitalized with a 4-week history of fever, headaches, and stiff neck. He recently emigrated from Mexico, but his medical history is otherwise noncontributory, and he takes no medications.

On physical examination, the patient is alert. Temperature is 38.9 °C (102 °F), blood pressure is 92/60 mm Hg, pulse rate is 124/min, and respiration rate is 24/min. Neurologic examination is normal. Passive neck flexion elicits painful resistance.

Cerebrospinal fluid (CSF) analysis reveals a leukocyte count of 424/µL (424×10^6/L) with 92% lymphocytes, glucose level of 22 mg/dL (1.2 mmol/L), and protein level of 278 mg/dL (2780 mg/L).

Rapid point-of-care antibody screening for HIV infection is negative. CSF Gram stain and cryptococcal antigen test results are negative. Results from cultures of the CSF and blood and from the interferon-γ release assay are pending.

The chest radiograph is normal.

Which of the following is the most appropriate management?

(A) Amphotericin B and 5-fluorocytosine

(B) Rifampin, isoniazid, pyrazinamide, and ethambutol

(C) Rifampin, isoniazid, pyrazinamide, ethambutol, and dexamethasone

(D) Vancomycin, ceftriaxone, and dexamethasone

Item 59

A 25-year-old man undergoes follow-up consultation regarding a positive interferon-γ release assay. He reports working for the past year in Vietnam and having a negative tuberculin skin test before departing. He is asymptomatic. He has had no known exposure to anyone with a history of tuberculosis. He has otherwise been well and takes no medications.

On physical examination, vital signs and examination are normal.

HIV testing is negative.

Posteroanterior and lateral chest radiograph is normal.

Which of the following is the most appropriate treatment?

(A) Isoniazid and rifapentine once weekly for 24 weeks

(B) Isoniazid daily for 9 months

(C) Isoniazid, rifampin, pyrazinamide, and ethambutol for 8 weeks followed by isoniazid and rifampin for 4 months

(D) No treatment or testing

Item 60

A 37-year-old man is hospitalized with abdominal pain, fever, and increasing diarrhea of 3 days' duration. He underwent kidney transplantation 3 weeks ago. The postoperative course has been complicated by pneumonia and wound infection, which resolved with antibiotic treatment. The patient was seronegative for cytomegalovirus before transplantation, but the transplant donor was seropositive. Medications are prednisone, tacrolimus, mycophenolate mofetil, valganciclovir, and trimethoprim-sulfamethoxazole.

On physical examination, temperature is 38.4 °C (101.2 °F), blood pressure is 122/85 mm Hg, pulse rate is 110/min, and respiration rate is 18/min. Abdominal palpation elicits tenderness, especially in the left lower quadrant, without rebound or guarding.

Which of the following is the most likely diagnosis?

(A) *Clostridium difficile* colitis

(B) Cytomegalovirus colitis

(C) Mycophenolate adverse effect

(D) Polyoma BK virus

Item 61

A 22-year-old woman arrives for her annual gynecologic examination, including a Pap smear and refill of her oral contraceptive prescription. She indicates she recently became sexually active with a new partner. Medical history is otherwise unremarkable. Her only medication is her oral contraceptive.

On physical examination, vital signs are normal. Pelvic examination is normal. The remainder of the examination is noncontributory.

A urine pregnancy test is negative. The Pap smear is normal. Nucleic acid amplification testing is positive for *Neisseria gonorrhoeae* and negative for *Chlamydia trachomatis*. The HIV antigen/antibody combination immunoassay is negative.

Which of the following is the most appropriate treatment?

(A) Cefixime

(B) Ceftriaxone

(C) Ceftriaxone plus azithromycin

(D) Ciprofloxacin

Item 62

A 51-year-old man is evaluated in the emergency department for a 12-hour history of fever, chills, headache, and weakness. He works on his farm in Maine and spends a considerable part of most days outside, but he is not aware of any tick or mosquito bites. He has had no diarrhea, cough, or rash. The patient had his spleen surgically removed 20 years ago after being involved in a motor vehicle collision. He has had no recent travel outside of the United States, and he is up to date on all immunizations.

On physical examination, temperature is 39.6 °C (103.3 °F), blood pressure is 88/42 mm Hg, pulse rate is 135/min, respiration rate is 28/min, and oxygen saturation is 90% with the patient receiving 4 L/min of oxygen via a nasal cannula. Lethargy, scleral icterus, jaundiced skin, hepatomegaly, and lower extremity petechiae are noted.

Laboratory studies:

Haptoglobin	<8 mg/dL (80 mg/L)
Hematocrit	25%
Leukocyte count	4500/µL (4.5 × 10⁹/L)
Platelet count	109,000/µL (109 × 10⁹/L)
Bilirubin, total	3.9 mg/dL (66.7 µmol/L)
Creatinine	1.0 mg/dL (88.4 µmol/L)
Lactate dehydrogenase	909 U/L

A blood smear from this patient is most likely to show which of the following abnormalities?

(A) Cytoplasmic morulae in leukocytes

(B) Intraerythrocytic banana-shaped gametocytes

(C) Intraerythrocytic tetrad forms

(D) Intraneutrophilic gram-positive diplococci

(E) Schistocytes

Item 63

A 55-year-old man is evaluated in the hospital for antibiotic management of a diabetic foot ulcer. He was hospitalized 3 days ago for debridement of a draining great toe ulcer. A radiograph of the left foot showed osteomyelitis of the great toe. Empiric piperacillin-tazobactam was started after debridement of the ulcer, and a bone biopsy was obtained

intraoperatively. Medical history is significant for diabetes mellitus with nephropathy. Medications are metformin, insulin glargine, and piperacillin-tazobactam. Today the patient is clinically improved.

On physical examination, vital signs are normal. A large, deep plantar ulcer penetrates to the bone of the left great toe with minimal surrounding erythema and no evidence of necrotic tissue.

The bone culture grows *Pseudomonas aeruginosa* (sensitive to piperacillin-tazobactam, ceftazidime, ciprofloxacin, aztreonam, and tobramycin) and *Bacteroides fragilis*.

Which of the following is the most appropriate management?

(A) Add tobramycin to piperacillin-tazobactam

(B) Switch piperacillin-tazobactam to aztreonam

(C) Switch piperacillin-tazobactam to ceftazidime

(D) Switch piperacillin-tazobactam to oral ciprofloxacin and metronidazole

Item 64

A 55-year-old man is hospitalized for acute diverticulitis. Seventy-two hours after initiating treatment with piperacillin-tazobactam through a percutaneously inserted central venous catheter, he becomes hypotensive and tachycardic and is transferred to the ICU. He has a 5-year history of type 2 diabetes mellitus. His only medication is metformin.

On physical examination, temperature is 40 °C (104.0 °F), blood pressure is 89/46 mm Hg, pulse rate is 136/min, respiration rate is 32/min, and oxygen saturation is 92% with the patient breathing ambient air. The patient is somnolent. The funduscopic examination is unremarkable. Abdominal examination reveals a soft, slightly tender left lower quadrant. Other examination findings are unremarkable.

A blood culture is positive for yeast.

The intravenous catheter is removed, and a replacement catheter is inserted at a different site.

Which of the following is the most appropriate management?

(A) Begin empiric therapy with an echinocandin

(B) Begin empiric therapy with fluconazole

(C) Confirm candidemia with a second positive blood culture

(D) Perform antifungal susceptibility testing before initiating therapy

(E) No additional therapy is required

Item 65

A 58-year-old man is evaluated in follow-up after being hospitalized with uncomplicated L3 vertebral osteomyelitis that presumably resulted from bacteremia during hemodialysis for end-stage kidney disease. In the hospital, a CT-guided bone biopsy identified a methicillin-susceptible *Staphylococcus aureus* infection. The patient completed 2 weeks of cefazolin antibiotic therapy and has responded with resolution of fever and improvement in pain. Other medications are sevelamer and amlodipine.

On physical examination, vital signs are normal. The lower lumbar spine is minimally tender to palpation. The remainder of the physical examination is noncontributory.

Which of the following is the most appropriate treatment?

(A) Continue cefazolin to complete 6 weeks of antibiotic therapy

(B) Continue cefazolin to complete 12 weeks of antibiotic therapy

(C) Discontinue cefazolin now

(D) Discontinue cefazolin when follow-up MRI demonstrates improvement

Item 66

A 40-year-old man is hospitalized for a 2-day history of diarrhea. He has five liquid bowel movements per day. One week ago, he completed a course of levofloxacin for treatment of community-acquired pneumonia.

On physical examination, temperature is 38.1 °C (100.5 °F), blood pressure is 116/70 mm Hg, pulse rate is 98/min, and respiration rate is 19/min. The abdomen is nondistended with normal bowel sounds. Moderate abdominal tenderness is present, without guarding or rebound. Mental status is normal.

Laboratory studies:

Leukocyte count	18,000/μL (18.0 × 10 ^{9}/L) (differential: 78% neutrophils, 3% band forms, 19% lymphocytes)
Albumin	2.8 g/dL (28 g/L)
Creatinine	1.6 mg/dL (141.4 μmol/L) (baseline, 1.0 mg/dL [88.4 μmol/L])
Lactate	Normal

Stool polymerase chain reaction assay is positive for *Clostridium difficile* toxin gene.

Which of the following is the most appropriate treatment?

(A) Fecal microbiota transplant

(B) Intravenous vancomycin

(C) Oral metronidazole

(D) Oral vancomycin

(E) Oral vancomycin and intravenous metronidazole

Item 67

An 18-year-old man is evaluated in the emergency department for new-onset seizures. The previous afternoon, he was evaluated in the university health service for acute onset of fever, severe myalgia, headache, and nausea; he was diagnosed with influenza and sent home with oseltamivir and ibuprofen. He received the quadrivalent meningococcal vaccine 7 months ago. Medical history is otherwise noncontributory. Other than oseltamivir and ibuprofen, he takes no medications.

On physical examination, temperature is 38.9 °C (102.0 °F), blood pressure is 90/55 mm Hg, pulse rate is 130/min, and respiration rate is 28/min. The patient is confused and lethargic. Photophobia, meningismus, and a diffuse petechial rash are present.

CT scan of the head is unremarkable.

Microscopic examination of the cerebrospinal fluid demonstrates gram-negative diplococci. Blood and cerebrospinal fluid cultures are pending.

Which of the following is the most likely bacterial agent causing this patient's meningitis?

(A) *Haemophilus influenzae*

(B) *Listeria monocytogenes*

(C) *Neisseria meningitides* group B

(D) *Streptococcus pneumoniae*

Item 68

A 28-year-old man is evaluated for anal discharge accompanied by tenesmus of 3 days' duration. He reports no abdominal pain, diarrhea, or hematochezia. He is sexually active with men and women, practices anal receptive intercourse, and uses condoms inconsistently. Medical history is unremarkable, and he takes no medications.

On physical examination, vital signs are normal. Erythema and discharge are noted in the perianal region, but no ulcers are visible. Anoscopy is not available.

Nucleic acid amplification testing for *Neisseria gonorrhoeae* and *Chlamydia trachomatis* is performed on an anal swab sample. Testing for herpes, syphilis, and HIV infections is also initiated.

Which of the following is the most appropriate treatment?

(A) Azithromycin

(B) Budesonide foam

(C) Ceftriaxone and doxycycline

(D) Ciprofloxacin

Item 69

A 42-year-old woman is hospitalized with dyspnea, dry cough, and fever that has been increasing over the past few days. She underwent allogeneic hematopoietic stem cell transplantation (HSCT) 7 months ago, with a recent occurrence of graft-versus-host disease of the skin and gastrointestinal tract. Donor and recipient were both cytomegalovirus seropositive before transplantation, the patient received monitoring for cytomegalovirus reactivation for 6 months after transplantation, and the cytomegalovirus nucleic acid amplification test was negative 1 month ago. Medications are prednisone, tacrolimus, trimethoprim-sulfamethoxazole, and acyclovir.

On physical examination, temperature is 38.1 °C (100.6 °F), blood pressure is 125/78 mm Hg, pulse rate is 104/min, and respiration rate is 24/min. Oxygen saturation is 88% breathing ambient air. Crackles are audible bilaterally on pulmonary examination. No lymphadenopathy is noted. The remainder of the examination is noncontributory.

Laboratory studies show a leukocyte count of 3500/μL (3.5 × 10⁹/L), with 85% polymorphonuclear cells, 8% lymphocytes, 5% monocytes, and 2% eosinophils.

A chest radiograph shows bilateral diffuse infiltrates. Chest CT scan shows bilateral diffuse ground-glass opacities without pleural effusions.

In addition to starting broad-spectrum antibacterial therapy, which of the following is the most appropriate initial treatment?

(A) Atovaquone

(B) Ganciclovir

(C) Liposomal amphotericin

(D) No additional therapy

Item 70

A 47-year-old man is hospitalized with a 1-month history of increasingly severe low back pain and a 3-day history of fever and chills. He reports injection drug use (last injected 1 week ago). Medical history is otherwise unremarkable, and he takes no medications.

On physical examination, temperature is 38 °C (100.4 °F), blood pressure is 110/76 mm Hg, pulse rate is 88/min, and respiration rate is 16/min. Neurologic examination reveals no deficits, and no murmur is heard on cardiac auscultation. Palpation of the spine elicits point tenderness over L2-L4.

Laboratory studies show an erythrocyte sedimentation rate of 98 mm/h and a leukocyte count of 18,300/µL (18.3 × 10^9/L).

MRI is positive for spondylodiskitis at L3-L4.

Blood samples were obtained, and empiric vancomycin was initiated.

Two sets of blood cultures are positive for methicillin-resistant *Staphylococcus aureus*, with a vancomycin minimum inhibitory concentration of 1.5 µg/mL; repeat blood cultures are pending. The vancomycin trough level is 19 µg/mL.

Transesophageal echocardiography shows no valvular vegetations.

Which of the following is the most appropriate treatment?

(A) Add gentamicin to vancomycin

(B) Add rifampin to vancomycin

(C) Change vancomycin to daptomycin

(D) Continue vancomycin

Item 71

A 28-year-old woman undergoes follow-up evaluation after a recent hospitalization for meningococcal bacteremia. Lumbar puncture results during hospitalization were negative for meningitis. She completed a course of ceftriaxone 1 week ago and reports feeling well since stopping antibiotics. Medical history is notable for gonococcal arthritis of her knee 2 years ago. She has a sister with a history of meningococcal meningitis. She takes no medications.

On physical examination, vital signs are normal. The remainder of the examination is unremarkable.

Which of the following is the most appropriate preventive measure?

(A) Intravenous immune globulin

(B) Plasma infusion

(C) Prophylactic ciprofloxacin

(D) Quadrivalent meningococcal conjugate vaccine

Item 72

A 33-year-old woman is evaluated for redness over her right calf at the site of a scratch that occurred 2 days ago. She has been well otherwise and takes no medications.

On physical examination, vital signs are normal. Tender erythema measuring 4 × 3 cm is noted over the right lower leg. No purulence, induration, or fluctuance is present.

Which of the following is the most appropriate treatment?

(A) Clindamycin

(B) Doxycycline

(C) Trimethoprim-sulfamethoxazole

(D) Vancomycin

Item 73

An 82-year-old man is admitted to the ICU with a 7-day history of fever and cough productive of green sputum. He is unable to climb the stairs to his bedroom without becoming short of breath. Medical history is remarkable for bronchiectasis and polymyalgia rheumatica. His only medication is prednisone, 10 mg/d.

On physical examination, temperature is 38.8 °C (101.8 °F), blood pressure is normal, pulse rate is 115/min, and respiration rate is 25/min. Oxygen saturation is 88% breathing ambient air. Crackles are heard in the right lung base.

A sputum Gram stain shows 3+ polymorphonuclear cells and 2+ gram-negative organisms.

A chest radiograph is shown.

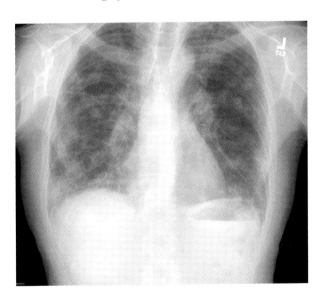

Which of the following is the most appropriate treatment?

(A) Ampicillin-sulbactam and levofloxacin

(B) Aztreonam and ciprofloxacin

(C) Cefepime and ciprofloxacin

(D) Ceftriaxone and azithromycin

(E) Ceftriaxone and levofloxacin

Item 74

A 21-year-old man is hospitalized with a 3-day history of fever and cough productive of green sputum. He was in the hospital 2 months ago for giardiasis and a year ago for pneumonia. Medical history is also notable for frequent episodes of sinusitis, bronchitis, and otitis media dating back to childhood.

On physical examination, temperature is 38.2 °C (100.8 °F), blood pressure is 118/80 mm Hg, pulse rate is 108/min, and respiration rate is 24/min. Pulmonary examination reveals crackles at the right lung base.

Chest radiograph is significant for a right lower lobe consolidation, and empiric antibiotic therapy is initiated.

A sputum culture grows *Streptococcus pneumoniae*.

Which of the following is the most likely underlying diagnosis?

(A) AIDS
(B) Chronic granulomatous disease
(C) Common variable immunodeficiency
(D) Myeloperoxidase deficiency

Item 75

A 28-year-old man undergoes follow-up evaluation of an injury to his right fourth finger sustained 10 weeks ago; he is a sport fisherman and obtained the injury from a tropical fish fin. He received separate 10-day courses of cephalexin and clindamycin without response. He takes no medications.

On physical examination, vital signs are normal. Swelling is present along the dorsum of the finger, with one 2- × 3-cm erythematous, papulonodular, fluctuant lesion located between the proximal and metacarpophalangeal joints. Pain is noted along the flexor tendon.

A plain radiograph of the finger shows no evidence of bony involvement or presence of a foreign body. Surgical exploration is performed, and intraoperative tissue specimens reveal noncaseating granulomas and inflammatory granulation tissue; Gram stain is negative.

Which of the following is the most likely cause of this patient's infection?

(A) *Clostridium perfringens*
(B) Herpes simplex virus type 1
(C) *Mycobacterium marinum*
(D) *Streptococcus pyogenes*

Item 76

A 32-year-old woman is evaluated following a generalized erythematous rash that developed 1 week ago. The rash has now resolved, and she reports no additional symptoms. She was diagnosed with HIV infection and AIDS 6 months ago when she was treated for *Pneumocystis jirovecii* pneumonia. She began antiretroviral therapy and daily trimethoprim-sulfamethoxazole for secondary pneumonia prophylaxis. She stopped taking trimethoprim-sulfamethoxazole last week when the rash developed. Current therapy consists of lamivudine, abacavir, and dolutegravir.

On physical examination, vital signs are normal. No rash is noted. No lesions are present on the eyes or in the mouth. No lymphadenopathy is noted. The lungs are clear bilaterally, and the abdomen is soft and nontender.

Complete blood count with differential and liver enzyme levels are normal. CD4 cell count is 291/μL (130/μL 6 months ago). HIV quantitative RNA is undetectable (31,840 copies/mL 6 months ago); 3 months ago, the CD4 cell count was 209/μL, and viral load was undetectable.

Which of the following is the most appropriate management?

(A) Begin atovaquone
(B) Begin primaquine and clindamycin
(C) Continue current therapy
(D) Restart trimethoprim-sulfamethoxazole
(E) Switch to tenofovir, emtricitabine, and dolutegravir

Item 77

A 67-year-old woman is evaluated after a diagnosis of ventilator-associated pneumonia. She was transferred to the ICU 3 days ago for respiratory failure secondary to Guillain-Barré syndrome and was intubated. Yesterday, the ventilator-associated pneumonia diagnosis was made and empiric antibiotics were started. Today her antibiotic therapy was de-escalated to oxacillin after her sputum culture grew methicillin-sensitive *Staphylococcus aureus*. Blood cultures were negative. Her medications are oxacillin and low-molecular-weight heparin; she is also undergoing plasmapheresis.

On physical examination, temperature is 37.6 °C (99.6 °F), blood pressure and pulse rate are normal, and respiration rate is 15/min. Oxygen saturation is 97% breathing 40% FiO_2. Pulmonary examination reveals scattered rhonchi.

A chest radiograph shows right middle and lower lobe infiltrates without effusions.

Which of the following is the most appropriate antibiotic management?

(A) Continue antibiotic therapy for a total of 7 days
(B) Continue antibiotic therapy for a total of 14 days
(C) Continue antibiotics until extubation
(D) Obtain sputum for Gram stain and culture before stopping antibiotics

Item 78

A 29-year-old woman is evaluated in the emergency department in January for a 5-day history of fever, severe headaches, delusions, and paranoid behavior. Medical history is noncontributory, and she takes no medications.

On physical examination, she is confused and combative. Temperature is 37.9 °C (100.2 °F), blood pressure is 107/48 mm Hg, pulse rate is 102/min, and respiration rate is 20/min. The neck is supple. Occasionally, choreoathetoid movements of the bilateral upper extremities are observed. She has no paralysis. After the examination, she has a generalized seizure in the emergency department.

CONT. Lumbar puncture is performed, and results show a cerebrospinal fluid leukocyte count of 310/μL (310 × 10⁶/L) with 94% lymphocytes, glucose level of 60 mg/dL (3.3 mmol/L), and protein level of 55 mg/dL (550 mg/L).

Cerebrospinal fluid bacterial and fungal cultures are negative. Polymerase chain reaction for herpes simplex virus is negative.

An MRI scan of the brain is normal.

Which of the following is the most likely diagnosis?

(A) Anti-N-methyl-D-aspartate receptor encephalitis

(B) Lyme meningitis

(C) Tuberculous meningitis

(D) West Nile virus encephalitis

Item 79

A 45-year-old man is evaluated for extreme fatigue accompanied by a 9.1-kg (20 lb) weight loss over the past 2 months. He also has had an occasional productive cough for 1 month. He is unemployed and has been sleeping in homeless shelters for approximately 6 months. He drinks alcohol daily, consuming a fifth of vodka approximately every 2 to 3 days; he does not smoke or use illicit drugs.

On physical examination, temperature is 38.3 °C (100.9 °F), blood pressure is 110/60 mm Hg, pulse rate is 90/min, and respiration rate is 18/min. Bilateral crackles are present throughout inspiration over the upper posterior thorax. The remainder of the examination is unremarkable.

Interferon-γ release assay is positive. HIV antibody testing is negative.

The chest radiograph is shown.

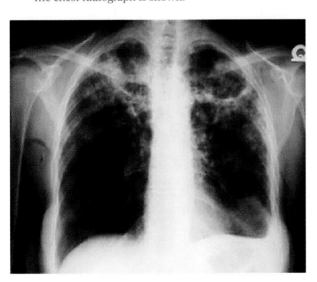

Which of the following is the most appropriate management?

(A) Initiate isoniazid plus pyridoxine

(B) Initiate isoniazid, rifampin, pyrazinamide, and ethambutol

(C) Initiate piperacillin-tazobactam

(D) Obtain sputum specimen for acid-fast bacilli stain and culture

Item 80

A 19-year-old man is evaluated for multiple episodes of nonbloody diarrhea, fever, occasional vomiting, malaise, and crampy abdominal pain that began yesterday. He is a college student who adopted a pet corn snake 2 months ago; the snake is healthy.

On physical examination, temperature is 38.3 °C (100.9 °F), blood pressure is 110/60 mm Hg, pulse rate is 100/min, and respiration rate is 19/min. He appears to be in mild distress. On abdominal examination, bowel sounds are present, as is tenderness to palpation. No rebound or guarding is noted.

Stool testing for occult blood is positive.

Which of the following is the most likely cause of this patient's diarrheal illness?

(A) *Chlamydia psittaci*

(B) *Erysipelothrix rhusiopathiae*

(C) *Mycobacterium marinum*

(D) Nontyphoidal *Salmonella* species

Item 81

A 72-year-old woman undergoes follow-up evaluation for persistent bacteremia. She was hospitalized 12 days ago with fever and chills, which started abruptly 1 week after a cardiac catheterization procedure. Blood cultures were positive for methicillin-sensitive *Staphylococcus aureus*, and cefazolin therapy was initiated. Medical history is otherwise noncontributory, and she takes no other medications.

On physical examination, temperature is 39.4 °C (100.8 °F), blood pressure is 116/76 mm Hg, pulse rate is 92/min, and respiration rate is 16/min. A systolic murmur is present and is unchanged from previous examinations. Abdominal examination reveals right upper quadrant tenderness. The remainder of the examination is noncontributory.

Laboratory studies show an alanine aminotransferase level of 53 U/L, aspartate aminotransferase level of 58 U/L, and alkaline phosphatase level of 104 U/L.

Repeated blood cultures are positive for *S. aureus*.

A transthoracic echocardiogram shows a small aortic valve vegetation. An electrocardiogram is normal.

Which of the following is the most appropriate management?

(A) Perform abdominal CT

(B) Perform head CT

(C) Switch cefazolin to daptomycin

(D) Switch cefazolin to vancomycin

Item 82

A 48-year-old man is evaluated in the emergency department for skin trauma sustained in a freshwater lake 2 days ago, with abrasions and tiny lacerations over the right forearm; he developed a fever and pain at the site of trauma 1 day ago. Medical history is remarkable for cirrhosis secondary to alcohol use. He takes no medications.

On physical examination, temperature is 39.1 °C (102.4 °F), blood pressure is 100/70 mm Hg, pulse rate is 120/min, and

CONT.

respiration rate is 25/min. The right forearm is tender and warm, with several hemorrhagic bullae noted. The remainder of the examination is unremarkable.

A plain radiograph of the right forearm shows no evidence of gas or a foreign body. Surgical exploration and debridement is performed, confirming a diagnosis of necrotizing fasciitis. Gram stain of intraoperative tissue specimens reveals gram-negative bacilli. Empiric antibiotic treatment with vancomycin plus piperacillin-tazobactam is initiated. Twenty-four hours later, the tissue culture grows *Aeromonas hydrophila*.

Which of the following is the most appropriate treatment?

(A) Ciprofloxacin plus doxycycline
(B) Linezolid plus metronidazole
(C) Nafcillin plus rifampin
(D) Vancomycin plus clindamycin

Item 83

A 33-year-old woman is evaluated 4 days after removing an embedded tick from her left arm. She reports that the tick was attached for less than 12 hours. She noticed itching at the site of tick attachment 2 days ago but otherwise has been asymptomatic. She preserved the tick in a bottle, and it is confirmed visually to be an adult black-legged deer tick (*Ixodes scapularis*).

On physical examination, vital signs are normal. A small area of induration is noted on the left arm, with no erythema, tenderness, or warmth. All other physical examination findings are unremarkable.

Which of the following is the most appropriate initial management?

(A) *Borrelia burgdorferi* polymerase chain reaction testing of the tick
(B) *Borrelia burgdorferi* serologies
(C) Doxycycline
(D) Reassurance that the risk of Lyme disease is low

Item 84

A 34-year-old man is evaluated for smallpox (variola) exposure. He feels wells. He is an Air Force surgeon and returned 2 days ago from a mission to the Middle East. Two others who accompanied him on his mission are being evaluated for a febrile illness characterized by headache, sore throat, and a vesicular rash on their faces, arms, and legs. The other men have been placed in airborne precautions because their clinical presentation is consistent with probable active variola infection. Medical history is notable for Crohn disease; he is up to date on all recommended immunizations. His only medication is infliximab.

On physical examination, vital signs are normal, and other physical examination findings are unremarkable.

A complete blood count and comprehensive metabolic profile are normal.

Which of the following is the most appropriate treatment?

(A) Airborne precautions
(B) Tecovirimat
(C) Vaccinia immune globulin
(D) Vaccinia immunization

Item 85

A 22-year-old man is evaluated in the emergency department for a 2-day history of painful rash on the left side of his posterior chest. Medical history is unremarkable, and he takes no medications.

On physical examination, temperature is 37.5 °C (99.5 °F), blood pressure is 115/62 mm Hg, pulse rate is 78/min, and respiration rate is 20/min. A vesicular rash is shown.

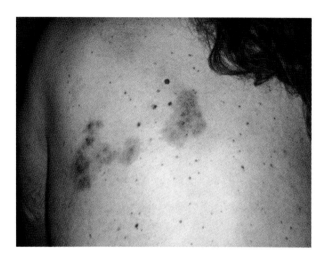

Which of the following is the most appropriate test to perform next?

(A) CH_{50} activity
(B) Fourth generation HIV-1/2 antigen/antibody combination immunoassay
(C) IgA measurement
(D) Quantitative immunoglobulin measurement

Item 86

A 57-year-old woman is hospitalized with a 1-month history of diminished concentration, memory, and judgment, with recent mental status fluctuations and gait disorder. Medical history is remarkable for hypertension. Medications are enalapril and hydrochlorothiazide.

On physical examination, vital signs are normal. She is somnolent but responds to verbal commands. The neck is supple. Deep-tendon reflexes are increased in the upper extremities and decreased in the lower extremities. Movement of the extremities is associated with myoclonus. The remainder of the examination is normal.

Complete blood count, comprehensive metabolic profile, thyroid studies, and vitamin B_{12} measurements are normal.

Lumbar puncture:

Opening pressure	70 mm H$_2$O
Leukocyte count	4/µL (4 × 10⁶/L)
Erythrocyte count	5/µL (5 × 10⁶/L)
Glucose	108 mg/dL (6 mmol/L)
Protein	57 mg/dL (570 mg/L)

Gram stain of cerebrospinal fluid is negative. Polymerase chain reaction of cerebrospinal fluid for herpes simplex virus is negative.

Brain MRI shows abnormally increased T2 and FLAIR signal intensity in the putamen and head of the caudate.

Which of the following is the most likely diagnosis?

(A) Cryptococcal meningoencephalitis
(B) Sporadic Creutzfeldt-Jakob disease
(C) Tuberculous meningitis
(D) Vascular neurocognitive disorder

Item 87

A 74-year-old homeless woman is evaluated for hospital discharge. She was admitted 6 days ago with a diagnosis of community-acquired pneumonia, and empiric ceftriaxone and azithromycin were begun. Her fever resolved within 48 hours of admission; however, hospital discharge was delayed because of difficulty arranging posthospitalization placement. Medical history is otherwise noncontributory. She takes no other medications.

On physical examination, vital signs are normal. Oxygen saturation is 96% breathing ambient air. The remainder of the examination is unremarkable.

Sputum culture obtained at admission is growing *Streptococcus pneumoniae* sensitive to penicillin, ceftriaxone, levofloxacin, and vancomycin and resistant to erythromycin. Blood cultures obtained at admission show no growth.

The patient has been accepted into a group home and is ready for hospital discharge.

Which of the following is the most appropriate management at discharge?

(A) Continue only azithromycin
(B) Continue only ceftriaxone
(C) Stop all antibiotics
(D) Stop ceftriaxone and azithromycin and switch to amoxicillin
(E) Stop ceftriaxone and azithromycin and switch to levofloxacin

Item 88

A 46-year-old man is evaluated for pain and swelling of the left index finger that began 2 weeks ago. Ten weeks ago, the patient sustained a deep laceration to the finger while doing construction work. A plain radiograph at that time showed no evidence of fracture. The laceration was sutured, and the wound completely healed. History is significant for poorly controlled type 2 diabetes mellitus. Medications are metformin and glipizide.

On physical examination, vital signs are normal. A 4-cm wound along the medial aspect of the left index finger is completely healed. The finger is edematous and tender when palpated but without erythema.

Laboratory studies reveal an erythrocyte sedimentation rate of 120 mm/h, a leukocyte count of 7800/μL (7.8 × 10⁹/L), and a serum creatinine level of 0.6 mg/dL (53.0 μmol/L).

Which of the following is the most appropriate diagnostic test to perform next?

(A) CT with contrast
(B) MRI with gadolinium
(C) Plain radiography
(D) Three-phase nuclear bone scan
(E) Ultrasonography

Item 89

A 42-year-old man is admitted to the ICU for nonresponsive pneumonia with a 7-day history of shortness of breath and cough. He was diagnosed with pneumonia and prescribed levofloxacin 3 days ago and has been adherent to his medication; however, his shortness of breath has worsened to the point he is unable to climb one flight of stairs. Medical history is remarkable for hospitalization 5 years ago for alcohol withdrawal and delirium tremens. He drinks a six-pack of beer every weekday and a case of beer on the weekends. His only medication is levofloxacin.

On physical examination, he is in mild respiratory distress but alert and oriented. Temperature is 38.7 °C (101.7 °F), blood pressure is normal, pulse rate is 122/min, and respiration rate is 24/min. Oxygen saturation is 89% breathing ambient air. Pulmonary auscultation reveals decreased breath sounds at the right lung base.

Laboratory studies show a leukocyte count of 18,700/μL (18.7 × 10⁹/L) and a serum creatinine level of 2.3 mg/dL (203 μmol/L).

A chest radiograph shows a right lower lobe infiltrate. Levofloxacin is discontinued.

In addition to initiating azithromycin, which of the following is the most appropriate antibiotic treatment?

(A) Ceftriaxone
(B) Clindamycin
(C) Metronidazole
(D) Piperacillin-tazobactam

Item 90

A 27-year-old man is evaluated in the emergency department for a 2-day history of bloody diarrhea with abdominal cramping. He reports attending a picnic 5 days before symptom onset where he ate a rare (undercooked) hamburger. Medical history is otherwise unremarkable, and he takes no medications.

On physical examination, temperature is 37.1 °C (98.8 °F), blood pressure is 120/76 mm Hg, pulse rate is 100/min, and respiration rate is 16/min. On abdominal examination, bowel sounds are present with diffuse tenderness to palpation but no guarding or rebound.

Laboratory studies:

Hematocrit	39%
Leukocyte count	18,000/μL (18.0 × 10⁹/L) (differential: 80% neutrophils, 20% lymphocytes)
Platelet count	190,000/μL (190 × 10⁹/L)
Creatinine	1.3 mg/dL (114.9 μmol/L)

Stool assay is positive for presence of Shiga-like toxin.

Which of the following is the most appropriate management?

(A) Ceftriaxone
(B) Ciprofloxacin
(C) Loperamide
(D) Trimethoprim-sulfamethoxazole
(E) Supportive care

Item 91

A 45-year-old man is hospitalized with a 5-day history of fever, bloody diarrhea, and abdominal pain. Medical history is significant for end-stage kidney disease, for which he underwent kidney transplantation 1 year ago. Medications are prednisone, mycophenolate, and tacrolimus.

On physical examination, vital signs are normal. Conjunctival pallor is present. Abdominal palpation elicits diffuse abdominal pain. The remainder of the examination is unremarkable.

Laboratory studies:

Hemoglobin	9.5 mg/dL (95 g/L)
Leukocyte count	3400/µL (3.4 × 10⁹/L)
Platelet count	98,000/µL (98 × 10⁹/L)
Alanine aminotransferase	99 U/L
Aspartate aminotransferase	88 U/L
Creatinine	1.5 mg/dL (133 µmol/L)

Which of the following is the most likely diagnosis?

(A) Cytomegalovirus infection
(B) *Entamoeba histolytica* infection
(C) *Salmonella enteritidis* infection
(D) *Strongyloides stercoralis* infection

Item 92

A 23-year-old man is evaluated for a 2-day history of erythema and drainage from a surgical incision site. He reports no fever or chills. He underwent a left inguinal hernia repair 10 days ago. Medical history is otherwise noncontributory, and he takes no medications.

On physical examination, vital signs are normal. The left inguinal incision is erythematous around the edges, is tender, and exudes a small amount of serosanguineous, cloudy drainage from a small area of incision breakdown. No induration is noted around the incision area.

Laboratory studies show a leukocyte count of 8700/µL (8.7 × 10⁹/L).

Which of the following is the most appropriate diagnostic test to perform next?

(A) Blood culture
(B) CT of upper thigh and pelvis
(C) Gram stain and culture of incision site drainage
(D) Gram stain and culture of incision site swabbing

Item 93

A 55-year-old man is evaluated in the emergency department for a 1-week history of chills and altered mental status and a 2-week history of fever and severe headache. He has end-stage liver disease secondary to alcohol abuse. Medications are propranolol, furosemide, spironolactone, and lactulose.

On physical examination, temperature is 38.6 °C (101.5 °F), blood pressure is 110/85 mm Hg, pulse rate is 111/min, and respiration rate is 22/min. The patient is somnolent, cachectic, and jaundiced. Funduscopic examination shows no papilledema. Bibasilar crackles are heard on auscultation of the lungs. The abdomen is distended and tense. No focal neurologic findings are present.

A CT scan of the head with contrast shows cerebral atrophy. A lumbar puncture is performed.

Cerebrospinal fluid studies:

Cell count	2 erythrocytes/hpf; 98 leukocytes/hpf, with 70% neutrophils and 30% lymphocytes
Glucose	20 mg/dL (1.1 mmol/L)
Pressure, opening	180 mm H₂O
Protein	170 mg/dL (1700 mg/L)
Cryptococcal antigen titer	1:2048
Gram stain	Negative

Which of the following is the most appropriate treatment?

(A) Fluconazole
(B) Itraconazole
(C) Liposomal amphotericin B and flucytosine
(D) Micafungin

Item 94

A 64-year-old woman is evaluated for a 6-week history of right knee swelling and pain. She has had no recent injury, fevers, or chills. She retired as a horticulturist and moved from Massachusetts to Florida 3 months ago. She takes NSAIDs, which provide partial pain relief, but the swelling persists.

On physical examination, vital signs are normal. The right knee has a moderately sized effusion but no erythema or warmth. Slight pain is present on passive movement of the knee.

Results of laboratory studies show an equivocal *Borrelia burgdorferi* enzyme immunoassay of 1.07; leukocyte count and rheumatoid factor titer are within normal limits.

Which of the following is the most appropriate next diagnostic test?

(A) *Borrelia burgdorferi* IgG Western blot
(B) C6 enzyme immunoassay antibody test
(C) Polymerase chain reaction of joint fluid
(D) No further testing

Item 95

A 63-year-old man undergoes discharge evaluation. He was hospitalized 24 hours ago after a diagnosis of acute bacterial prostatitis, for which ciprofloxacin was initiated. His fever has resolved. Medical history is otherwise unremarkable, and he takes no other medications.

He is being discharged home to complete 6 weeks of oral ciprofloxacin therapy.

CONT. Which of the following is the most appropriate monitoring for this patient?

(A) Serum lipase level

(B) Serum sodium level

(C) Stool for *Clostridium difficile* toxin

(D) Symptoms of tendon or joint pain

Item 96

A 30-year-old man is evaluated for a 1-week history of sore throat and odynophagia. He reports no fever, nausea, vomiting, diarrhea, or other symptoms. He was recently diagnosed with HIV infection and began antiretroviral therapy 2 weeks ago. Medications are tenofovir alafenamide, emtricitabine, dolutegravir, and trimethoprim-sulfamethoxazole.

On physical examination, vital signs are normal. Oral examination findings (shown) include whitish plaques on the posterior pharynx. Lymph nodes are palpable in the anterior and posterior cervical regions bilaterally. The remainder of the examination is normal.

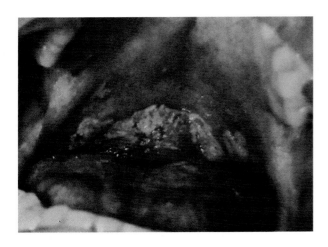

Laboratory studies at the time of HIV diagnosis showed a CD4 cell count of 55/μL and HIV viral load of 138,855 copies/mL.

Which of the following is the most appropriate management?

(A) Intravenous caspofungin

(B) Oral fluconazole

(C) Nystatin swish-and-swallow

(D) Upper endoscopy

(E) Valganciclovir

Item 97

A 47-year-old woman is evaluated in the hospital for pyelonephritis not responding to antibiotic therapy. Five days ago she was evaluated in an urgent care center for abdominal and back pain, nausea, fever, and dysuria. She was started on oral ciprofloxacin for a urinary tract infection (UTI). Symptoms did not respond to this treatment, and two days ago, she was hospitalized. Acute pyelonephritis was diagnosed, and she was treated with intravenous fluids, vancomycin, and cefepime. Since hospitalization, her clinical condition has deteriorated, with continued fever and worsening flank pain. She also has stage 2 chronic kidney disease, recurrent UTIs, and a 6-year history of poorly controlled type 2 diabetes mellitus. Medications are amoxicillin, metformin, and insulin glargine.

On physical examination, temperature is 38.2 °C (100.8 °F), blood pressure is 130/60 mm Hg, pulse rate is 106/min, and respiration rate is 22/min. Abdominal examination reveals diminished bowel sounds, bilateral costovertebral angle tenderness, and suprapubic pain. Other examination findings are unremarkable.

Laboratory studies:

Hemoglobin	11 g/dL (110 g/L)
Leukocyte count	21,000/μL (21 × 10⁹/L) with 91% neutrophils and 9% lymphocytes
Platelet count	167,000/μL (167 × 10⁹/L)
Creatinine	1.8 mg/mL (159 μmol/L)
Urinalysis	10 erythrocytes/hpf, leukocytes too numerous to count, many yeast forms, trace protein, and 4+ glucose

Urine culture results show 10,000 colony-forming units of *Candida glabrata*. Blood culture results are negative.

A CT scan of the abdomen with contrast shows bilateral perinephric stranding, no masses, and no renal abscesses.

Which of the following is the most likely diagnosis?

(A) Acute diverticulitis

(B) Antibiotic-resistant bacterial pyelonephritis

(C) *Candida* pyelonephritis

(D) Renal infarction

Item 98

A 25-year-old man is evaluated for a 3-day history of painful lesions on his penis accompanied by generalized myalgia and malaise. He has been sexually active with one female partner for the past 6 months; he does not use condoms. Medical history is unremarkable for previous genital ulcers and is otherwise noncontributory. He takes no medications but indicates he develops a rash with penicillin use.

On physical examination, vital signs are normal except for a temperature of 38.2 °C (100.8 °F). Bilateral, tender inguinal lymphadenopathy is noted. Lesions on the penile shaft are shown on the next page.

Which of the following is the most appropriate diagnostic test to perform next?

(A) Darkfield examination

(B) Direct fluorescence assay

(C) Nucleic acid amplification testing

(D) Type-specific antibody testing

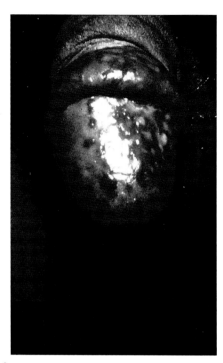

ITEM 98

Item 99

A 25-year-old man is evaluated in the emergency department for left hand pain at the site of injection drug use. All of his immunizations are up to date. He takes no medications.

On physical examination, temperature is 39.3 °C (102.7 °F), blood pressure is 88/50 mm Hg, pulse rate is 110/min, and respiration rate is 26/min. A violaceous, swollen, indurated area is noted on the dorsum of the left hand at the site of recent injection drug use; it is warm to the touch and tender.

Laboratory studies:

Hematocrit	36%
Leukocyte count	25,000/µL (25 × 10⁹/L)
Platelet count	100,000/µL (100 × 10⁹/L)
Alanine aminotransferase	65 U/L
Aspartate aminotransferase	105 U/L
Creatinine	2.5 mg/dL (221 µmol/L)

Empiric treatment with vancomycin and piperacillin-tazobactam is initiated and he undergoes surgical debridement. Intraoperative findings confirm necrotizing fasciitis, and tissue and blood cultures grow group A *Streptococcus*.

Which of the following is the most appropriate antibiotic treatment?

(A) Continue vancomycin and piperacillin-tazobactam
(B) Change to doxycycline and ceftazidime
(C) Change to linezolid and imipenem
(D) Change to penicillin and clindamycin

Item 100

A 78-year-old woman undergoes routine evaluation. She has been feeling relatively well but experiences occasional urinary incontinence when she coughs, sneezes, or laughs. Medical history is significant for hypertension. Medications are chlorthalidone and lisinopril.

On physical examination, vital signs and other physical examination findings are normal.

On dipstick urinalysis, urine is yellow and clear, specific gravity is 1.010, pH is 7.0, and moderate leukocyte esterase and nitrites are present; the urinalysis is negative for blood or glucose but 2+ for bacteria.

Which of the following is the most appropriate management?

(A) Ciprofloxacin
(B) Cystoscopy
(C) Microscopic urinalysis
(D) Urine culture and sensitivity
(E) No further investigation or treatment

Item 101

A 52-year-old woman is evaluated in the emergency department for fever, headache, muscular pain, and a diffuse, nonpruritic rash that began on the arms. She returned 5 days ago from a 3-week trip in southern Spain. She recalls a dark, raised, scab-like lesion on her ankle that she attributed to an insect bite. Her medical history is otherwise unremarkable.

On physical examination, the patient is lethargic. Temperature is 38.7 °C (101.6 °F), blood pressure is 118/70 mm Hg, pulse rate is 82/min, and respiration rate is 16/min. Neurologic examination is nonfocal and without meningismus. A right inguinal lymph node is enlarged. A maculopapular pink rash is present on the trunk, arms, legs, palms, and soles. A black eschar is present on the right ankle that measures 1.5 × 1.5 cm. Other examination findings are normal.

Which of the following is the most likely diagnosis?

(A) Human granulocytic anaplasmosis
(B) Lyme disease
(C) Mediterranean spotted fever
(D) Rocky Mountain spotted fever

Item 102

A 24-year-old man is evaluated in the emergency department in October for a 10-day history of headaches, fever, and stiff neck. He reports camping and hiking in the woods on Nantucket Island 2 months ago. Medical history is unremarkable, and he takes no medications.

On physical examination, he is alert and oriented. Temperature is 38.3 °C (101.0 °F), blood pressure is 134/85 mm Hg, pulse rate is 104/min, and respiration rate is 20/min. Right-sided facial palsy is noted, and neck flexion elicits resistance and discomfort, but the neurologic examination is otherwise normal. No rash is present.

A lumbar puncture is performed, and cerebrospinal fluid evaluation shows a leukocyte count of 235/µL (235 × 10⁶/L) with 84% lymphocytes. Gram stain is negative and cultures are pending.

CONT.

Which of the following is the most likely cause of the patient's findings?

(A) *Borrelia burgdorferi*
(B) Enterovirus
(C) Herpes simplex virus type 2
(D) Varicella-zoster virus
(E) West Nile virus

Item 103

A 26-year-old man is hospitalized for a 3-month history of fever, night sweats, and weakness. Medical history is notable for kidney transplantation 5 years ago. Medications are prednisone and mycophenolate.

On physical examination, temperature is 38.1 °C (100.5 °F), blood pressure is 135/62 mm Hg, pulse rate is 68/min, and respiration rate is 20/min. The sclerae are pale. Cervical, supraclavicular, and axillary lymphadenopathy are noted. Abdominal examination reveals hepatosplenomegaly.

Laboratory studies:

Hemoglobin	8.4 mg/dL (84 g/L)
Leukocyte count	2300/µL (2.3×10^9/L)
Platelet count	98,000/µL (98×10^9/L)
Creatinine (stable)	1.1 mg/dL (97.2 µmol/L)

Which of the following is the most likely cause of his symptoms?

(A) Cytomegalovirus
(B) Epstein-Barr virus
(C) Herpes simplex virus type 1
(D) Polyoma BK virus

Item 104

A 23-year-old man is evaluated for a furuncle on the left forearm that appeared 1 day ago. Medical history is notable only for anaphylaxis with administration of trimethoprim-sulfamethoxazole. He is otherwise well and takes no medications.

On physical examination, temperature is 38.3 °C (100.9 °F), blood pressure is 124/75 mm Hg, pulse rate is 95/min, and respiration rate is 15/min. A 2- × 2-cm fluctuant lesion is present on the right forearm with 1 cm of surrounding erythema. The remainder of the examination is unremarkable.

After incision and drainage of the abscess, a culture is obtained.

Which of the following is the most appropriate additional treatment?

(A) Oral cephalexin
(B) Oral clindamycin
(C) Oral doxycycline
(D) Oral penicillin
(E) Clinical follow-up

Item 105

A 55-year-old woman undergoes annual tuberculin skin testing. An 8-mm induration is recorded after 48 hours. She

reports no symptoms or exposures. She works as a clerk in an internal medicine outpatient clinic at a metropolitan hospital in New York City. Medical history is unremarkable, and she takes no medications.

On physical examination, vital signs and examination are normal.

Which of the following is the most appropriate management?

(A) Chest radiography
(B) Induce sputum for culture
(C) Initiate isoniazid for treatment of latent tuberculosis
(D) Move patient to nonpatient care areas
(E) No further testing or treatment

Item 106

A 35-year-old man is evaluated during a follow-up consultation. He was diagnosed with HIV 6 months ago; at that time, his CD4 cell count was 30/µL. He immediately began antiretroviral therapy and has been adherent to his regimen. His initial screening tests included a nonreactive tuberculin skin test (TST). He states that he has been unemployed for more than 2 years and has lived in a variety of different homeless shelters. Medications are tenofovir-emtricitabine and raltegravir.

On physical examination, vital signs and other findings are unremarkable.

Today, a repeat CD4 cell count is 100/µL and a repeat TST results in 5 mm of induration.

A posteroanterior and lateral chest radiograph is unremarkable.

Which of the following is the most appropriate management?

(A) Initiate isoniazid plus pyridoxine
(B) Initiate isoniazid, rifampin, pyrazinamide, and ethambutol
(C) Obtain an interferon-γ release assay
(D) Repeat TST in 2 weeks

Item 107

A 24-year-old woman is evaluated for cystitis symptoms of 4 days' duration. She reports no fever, chills, flank pain, or vaginal discharge. She has had similar symptoms three times within the past 10 months. She has been treated each time with trimethoprim-sulfamethoxazole at an urgent care center. The last episode was 5 weeks ago. She has sexual intercourse infrequently. Her only medication is an oral contraceptive.

On physical examination, vital signs and other findings are unremarkable.

On microscopic urinalysis, leukocytes are too numerous to count, erythrocyte count is 10/hpf, 4+ bacteria are present, and rare squamous epithelial cells are seen.

Which of the following is the most appropriate management?

(A) Nitrofurantoin
(B) Trimethoprim-sulfamethoxazole
(C) Urine culture plus ampicillin
(D) Urine culture plus cefpodoxime
(E) Urine culture plus ciprofloxacin

Item 108

A 41-year-old woman is evaluated in the emergency department for total loss of vision in the left eye. She also reports a 3-day history of left-sided tunnel vision and a 2-week history of sinus pain and rhinorrhea. The patient has a 20-year history of type 1 diabetes mellitus, which has been poorly controlled for the past 18 months. Medications are insulin glargine and insulin aspart.

On physical examination, temperature is 37.2 °C (99.0 °F), blood pressure is 140/66 mm Hg, pulse rate is 110/min, and respiration rate is 18/min. Left eye proptosis and chemosis are noted; the left pupil is nonreactive. The left nasal mucosa has gray-black exudate and an eschar. A 2- × 3-cm black eschar is seen on the hard palate. Neurologic examination shows occulomotor, trochlear, trigeminal, and abducens nerve (cranial nerves III, IV, V, and VI) palsy on the left.

A CT scan of the head without contrast shows a mass in the maxillary sinus with extension into the left frontal lobe and surrounding edema.

Which of the following is the most likely diagnosis?

(A) Anthrax

(B) Aspergillosis

(C) Lemierre syndrome

(D) Mucormycosis

Answers and Critiques

Item 1   Answer: A

Educational Objective: Prevent *Staphylococcus aureus* surgical site infection by evaluating for *S. aureus* nasal carriage.

The most appropriate measure to prevent surgical site infection is to evaluate for *Staphylococcus aureus* nasal carriage 2 weeks before surgery and decolonize if positive. *S. aureus* is the most common pathogen (23%) associated with surgical site infections (SSIs). SSIs after coronary artery bypass graft surgery can be serious and devastating, with mediastinitis related to *S. aureus* of particular concern. The 2016 World Health Organization guidelines recommend that patients known to be nasal carriers of *S. aureus* who are scheduled to undergo cardiothoracic or orthopedic surgery should have preoperative decolonization (mupirocin ointment for 5 days with or without chlorhexidine gluconate body wash) to decrease the risk of developing *S. aureus*–related SSI.

Data do not support extending antibiotic prophylaxis beyond 24 hours after cardiac surgery even while drains remain in place. For most other surgeries, no additional doses of antibiotic should be given postoperatively, even in cases of intraoperative spillage of gastrointestinal contents. Postoperative antibiotics are only indicated when treating an active infection.

Preoperative antibiotic prophylaxis reduces the risk of SSI by decreasing the concentration of pathogens at or around the incision site. The agent used and the timing of administration are key. For cardiac surgery, cefazolin is recommended unless a patient is known to have methicillin-resistant *S. aureus* colonization or has a severe (anaphylactic) β-lactam allergy, in which case vancomycin is used. For optimal benefit, the antibiotic should be administered 1 to 2 hours before incision. For procedures lasting more than several hours, the antibiotic should be redosed during surgery (for example, redose at 3-4 hours for cefazolin).

Preoperative shaving in the area of the planned incision increases the risk of SSI. Shaving causes microscopic abrasions of the skin, which promotes bacterial proliferation. Recommendations indicate only removing hair from the surgical site if it will interfere with the procedure, in which case clipping is preferred.

KEY POINT

- Patients undergoing cardiothoracic or orthopedic surgery should be screened for nasal carriage of *Staphylococcus aureus* and, if positive, should have preoperative decolonization.

Bibliography

Schweizer ML, Chiang HY, Septimus E, Moody J, Braun B, Hafner J, et al. Association of a bundled intervention with surgical site infections among patients undergoing cardiac, hip, or knee surgery. JAMA. 2015;313:2162-71. [PMID: 26034956] doi:10.1001/jama.2015.5387

Item 2   Answer: D   H

Educational Objective: Treat tuberculosis and immune reconstitution inflammatory syndrome in a patient with HIV.

The most appropriate management for this patient is to start rifabutin, isoniazid, ethambutol, and pyrazinamide therapy for tuberculosis. He began antiretroviral therapy 1 month ago and has responded well, with a significant decrease in viral load and increased CD4 cell count. The timing of his presentation is consistent with the immune reconstitution inflammatory syndrome (IRIS) (median 48 days), the return of a robust immune response resulting from treatment of the HIV that "unmasks" a pre-existing infection that appears like a new acute infection. This presentation is common with tuberculosis, which may present as a much more acute pulmonary illness resembling bacterial pneumonia. He had an indeterminate result on interferon-γ release assay (IGRA) because of an inadequate response to the positive control, which was the result of immunocompromise at the time of presentation; additionally, the results of IGRA testing are a poor indicator of active tuberculosis infection. He should begin four-drug antituberculous therapy while results of culture and susceptibility testing are pending. Nucleic acid amplification testing of the specimen may give information on the identification of the organisms and even the possibility of rifamycin resistance. Initial empiric treatment for tuberculosis should include a rifamycin as one of the four drugs, but rifabutin is often preferred over rifampin in patients with HIV because of fewer drug-drug interactions between rifabutin and antiretrovirals, including dolutegravir.

If this patient does have active tuberculosis, treatment is needed urgently; culture results may take weeks, so waiting would be inappropriate.

Antiretrovirals should not be stopped when IRIS occurs. Therapy should be continued while providing treatment for the newly diagnosed infection.

Prednisone can be added if IRIS is life threatening or involves the pericardium or central nervous system. None of these is the case in this patient; giving glucocorticoids without a known diagnosis increases the risk of worsening an infection that is not being directly treated.

KEY POINT

- Immune reconstitution inflammatory syndrome is the return of a robust immune response resulting from treatment of HIV that may "unmask" a pre-existing infection; when this occurs, the underlying infection should be treated while antiretroviral therapy is continued.

Bibliography

Panel on Opportunistic Infections in HIV-Infected Adults and Adolescents. Guidelines for the prevention and treatment of opportunistic infections in HIV-infected adults and adolescents: recommendations from the Centers for Disease Control and Prevention, the National Institutes of Health, and the HIV Medicine Association of the Infectious Diseases Society of America. Available at https://aidsinfo.nih.gov/guidelines/html/4/adult-and-adolescent-opportunistic-infection/0. Accessed April 12, 2018.

Item 3   Answer: A

Educational Objective: Diagnose pulmonary coccidioidomycosis.

This patient has disseminated coccidioidomycosis manifesting as a pulmonary infection. The fungus *Coccidioides* is inhaled and causes an initial pulmonary infection. In endemic areas, as many as one third of cases of community-acquired pneumonia (CAP) are caused by *Coccidioides* species. Healthy persons generally contain the initial infection owing to intact cell-mediated immunity; however, immunocompromised persons are at risk for dissemination. This endemic dimorphic fungal infection is known to mimic other diseases, including tuberculosis, histoplasmosis, sarcoidosis, and cancer. The patient is stationed in Bakersfield, California, an epicenter for this infection. In addition, his assignment as a car mechanic, with much of his work likely conducted outside, increases the risk of infection. Another clue is his peripheral eosinophilia. A definitive diagnosis generally is made on the basis of serology and histopathologic analysis of tissue. When coccidioidomycosis is diagnosed, first-line therapy is fluconazole to prevent progressive or disseminated disease.

Sarcoidosis is a systemic disease of unknown cause. It is slightly more frequent in black persons in their 20s and 30s, especially women. It frequently presents in the respiratory tract as bilateral hilar lymphadenopathy, with or without diffuse parenchymal lung changes. Unilateral hilar lymphadenopathy is distinctly unusual, as is eosinophilia. In addition, sarcoidosis tends to be a much more indolent process, presenting over several months to years with progressive cough and dyspnea. This patient developed symptoms acutely, over a 1-month period.

The most commonly identified organism causing CAP is *Streptococcus pneumoniae*. Suggestive clinical symptoms include fever, cough, sputum production, and dyspnea. Radiographic findings can be characterized as interstitial infiltrates, lobar consolidation, or cavitary lesions; unilateral hilar lymphadenopathy would be distinctly unusual. Finally, symptoms lasting for a month and peripheral eosinophilia are not characteristic of a bacterial lung infection.

Primary pulmonary tuberculosis may present with mid- to lower-zone unilateral infiltrates, unilateral hilar lymphadenopathy, and pleural effusions. Early in the course of the disease, laboratory findings are often normal; eosinophilia is not present. Finally, pulmonary tuberculosis is excluded by the negative interferon-γ release assay.

KEY POINT

- In endemic areas, as many as one third of cases of community-acquired pneumonia are caused by *Coccidioides* species.

Bibliography

Stockamp NW, Thompson GR 3rd. Coccidioidomycosis. Infect Dis Clin North Am. 2016;30:229-46. [PMID: 26739609] doi:10.1016/j.idc.2015.10.008

Item 4   Answer: C

Educational Objective: Treat community-acquired pneumonia in a hospitalized patient requiring ICU support.

The most appropriate treatment is ceftriaxone plus levofloxacin. This otherwise healthy patient presents with severe community-acquired pneumonia (CAP). The initial evaluation reveals respiratory failure (tachypnea and hypoxia), uremia, altered mentation, and multilobar infiltrates, all of which are minor criteria for severe disease based on Infectious Diseases Society of America/American Thoracic Society (IDSA/ATS) criteria. Patients with at least three minor criteria for severe disease have increased risk of mortality and are best managed in the ICU. Guideline-based recommendations for empiric therapy of CAP requiring ICU care include a third-generation cephalosporin or ampicillin-sulbactam to treat *Streptococcus pneumoniae*, gram-negative bacilli, or *Haemophilus influenzae* plus an agent active against *Legionella*, such as a macrolide or quinolone. The initial evaluation of this patient was positive for rhinovirus on a respiratory viral panel (RVP). Respiratory viruses are increasingly recognized among hospitalized patients with CAP; however, the significance of this finding is uncertain. Respiratory viruses may predispose patients to a secondary bacterial pneumonia or be present as a copathogen. Considering the severity of this patient's illness, antibiotics should be initiated and continued despite the positive RVP until a bacterial cause is excluded.

Azithromycin monotherapy is an appropriate choice for treatment of CAP in a previously healthy outpatient. Patients with more severe CAP are at risk for infections with numerous organisms, as well as with drug-resistant pathogens. For this reason, patients with CAP admitted to the ICU should receive combination therapy with an antipneumococcal β-lactam and either a macrolide or a fluoroquinolone.

Ceftazidime is a third-generation cephalosporin that is effective against *Pseudomonas* but has minimal activity against gram-positive organisms, including *S. pneumoniae*, and therefore would not be an appropriate choice, even as combination therapy with a macrolide, to treat CAP.

Piperacillin-tazobactam plus ciprofloxacin would be indicated when concern for *Pseudomonas* pneumonia is present; however, in a previously healthy patient with minimal health care interactions or previous antibiotic use, *Pseudomonas* would be an unlikely pathogen.

KEY POINT

- Guideline-based recommendations for empiric therapy of community-acquired pneumonia requiring ICU admission include a third-generation cephalosporin or ampicillin-sulbactam to treat *Streptococcus pneumoniae*, gram-negative bacilli, or *Haemophilus influenzae* plus an agent active against *Legionella*, such as a macrolide or quinolone.

Bibliography

Mandell LA, Wunderink RG, Anzueto A, Bartlett JG, Campbell GD, Dean NC, et al; Infectious Diseases Society of America. Infectious Diseases Society of America/American Thoracic Society consensus guidelines on the management of community-acquired pneumonia in adults. Clin Infect Dis. 2007;44 Suppl 2:S27-72. [PMID: 17278083]

Item 5   Answer: B

Educational Objective: Evaluate fever of unknown origin.

The most appropriate diagnostic test in this patient is CT of the abdomen and pelvis. He meets the criteria for classic fever of unknown origin, which is defined by fever of 38.3 °C (100.9 °F) or greater for 3 or more weeks that remains undiagnosed after two visits in the ambulatory setting. Taking a careful, detailed history is the starting point in evaluating a patient with fever of unknown cause. The history may need to be repeated on subsequent visits because subtle clues may be revealed only later. All symptoms should be considered relevant. A history of comorbid conditions and a surgical, obstetric or gynecologic (in women), medication, travel, and social history should be elicited followed by a careful physical examination that includes full neurologic, musculoskeletal, ear-nose-throat, eye or funduscopic, skin, lymphatic, and urogenital examinations. The results of basic laboratory and imaging studies along with the history and physical examination findings are used to guide further evaluation. In this patient, the initial evaluation for infectious causes (tuberculosis, endocarditis, urinary tract infection), neoplasms (lymphoma, leukemia), and connective tissue disease is unrevealing. Therefore, the patient should undergo CT of the abdomen and pelvis (with and without contrast) to evaluate for abscess, neoplasm (hepatoma, renal cell carcinoma), splenomegaly, and lymphadenopathy. The prognosis is good for adults who remain undiagnosed after extensive evaluation.

Bone marrow biopsy is generally considered when the complete blood count is abnormal and a process involving the bone marrow (such as tuberculosis, histoplasmosis, or malignancy) is evident.

Liver biopsy is considered in the setting of abnormal liver chemistry tests and a suggested abnormality on imaging. It would not be appropriate at this time.

If signs or symptoms referable to the central nervous system are evident, imaging of the head and lumbar puncture should be considered. However, this patient has no central nervous system findings.

KEY POINT

- Initial studies for fever of unknown origin in most patients typically include a complete blood count with differential, complete metabolic profile with kidney and liver studies, at least three blood culture sets and cultures of other bodily fluids (such as urine or from other sources based on clinical suspicion), an erythrocyte sedimentation rate, tuberculosis testing, and serology for HIV; it is reasonable to perform chest imaging (radiography or CT) as initial diagnostic imaging.

Bibliography

Mulders-Manders C, Simon A, Bleeker-Rovers C. Fever of unknown origin. Clin Med (Lond). 2015;15:280-4. [PMID: 26031980] doi:10.7861/clinmedicine.15-3-280

Item 6   Answer: B

Educational Objective: Diagnose invasive aspergillosis.

This patient most likely has disseminated aspergillosis with lung and brain involvement. Aspergillus invades blood vessels and causes distal infarction of infected tissue. Patients with invasive pulmonary aspergillosis may have fever, cough, chest pain, and hemoptysis at presentation. Pulmonary infiltrates, nodules, or wedge-shaped densities resembling infarcts may also be seen on chest radiographs; CT scans may show a target lesion with a necrotic center surrounded by a ring of hemorrhage (halo sign). Central nervous system involvement may manifest as a brain abscess or infarction. Other sites of involvement include blood vessels in the heart, gastrointestinal tract, or skin. Risk factors for invasive or disseminated aspergillosis include profound and prolonged neutropenia and hematopoietic stem cell transplantation. The second most common risk group for invasive aspergillosis is solid organ (heart, lung, liver, kidney) transplant recipients. The infection has also increasingly been reported in patients who are critically ill and in ICUs, especially those with exposure to glucocorticoids. The most efficient way to establish a definitive diagnosis (and then initiate antifungal therapy) is with bronchoalveolar lavage (BAL) and biopsy. In patients with disseminated aspergillosis, the serum galactomannan assay has a sensitivity of less than 30% and is not very useful; in contrast, the BAL galactomannan assay has a much higher sensitivity and specificity. Therefore, BAL fluid samples should be collected for analysis, and tissue biopsy should be performed.

A brain biopsy is sometimes useful to establish a definitive diagnosis but carries a much greater risk of causing adverse effects than bronchoscopy and BAL. If the lung biopsy is negative, then a brain biopsy should be considered.

Fungal blood cultures have a low sensitivity in all invasive mold infections but especially in invasive aspergillosis, in which less than 1% of patients with infection have a positive culture.

KEY POINT

- Risk factors for invasive or disseminated aspergillosis include profound and prolonged neutropenia and stem cell and solid organ transplantation; patients have fever, cough, chest pain, and hemoptysis at presentation, and pulmonary infiltrates, nodules, or wedge-shaped densities may be seen on chest radiographs.

Bibliography

Cadena J, Thompson GR 3rd, Patterson TF. Invasive aspergillosis: current strategies for diagnosis and management. Infect Dis Clin North Am. 2016;30:125-42. [PMID: 26897064] doi:10.1016/j.idc.2015.10.015

Item 7   Answer: C

Educational Objective: Diagnose leptospiral meningitis.

The most likely diagnosis is leptospirosis. She presents with a biphasic illness after freshwater exposure in an area highly endemic for leptospirosis. Infection occurs by direct exposure to urine or tissues of infected animals or indirectly through contaminated water or soil. Rodents and other small mammals are the most significant sources of human disease. Leptospiral meningitis usually develops weeks after exposure, in the second phase of the illness, but may merge with the first phase in severe disease and can present with uveitis, rash, conjunctival suffusion (conjunctival redness without exudate), sepsis, lymphadenopathy, kidney injury, and hepatosplenomegaly. Subconjunctival suffusion may be subtle but is a finding that rarely occurs in other infections. The cerebrospinal fluid (CSF) findings resemble enteroviral meningitis, but empiric treatment with doxycycline should be started pending confirmation.

Most persons who develop HIV infection experience an acute symptomatic illness, referred to as acute retroviral syndrome, within a few weeks of acquiring the infection. Symptoms are most often consistent with an infectious mononucleosis with fever, malaise, lymphadenopathy, rash, and pharyngitis. Some of these patients will develop meningitis or meningoencephalitis. Meningitis caused by acute HIV infection is typically self-limited and may be clinically indistinguishable from other viral meningitis syndromes, but jaundice, kidney injury, and subconjunctival suffusion are not seen with acute HIV infection.

Patients with herpes simplex meningitis have typical meningitis symptoms, such as fever, nuchal rigidity, headache, and photophobia. Jaundice, kidney injury, and subconjunctival suffusion are not characteristic of herpes simplex meningitis.

Treponema pallidum meningitis can occur in the secondary or tertiary phase of syphilis. Headache and meningismus are common; decreased visual acuity secondary to uveitis, vitreitis, retinitis, or optic neuropathy can be seen, as well as other cranial neuropathies. The CSF usually shows a lymphocytic pleocytosis with an elevated protein level. This patient's clinical course is not compatible with syphilitic meningitis.

KEY POINT

- Leptospiral meningitis usually develops weeks after exposure, during the second phase of illness, and can present with uveitis, rash, conjunctival suffusion, sepsis, lymphadenopathy, kidney injury, and hepatosplenomegaly.

Bibliography

Londeree WA. Leptospirosis: the microscopic danger in paradise. Hawaii J Med Public Health. 2014;73:21-3. [PMID: 25478298]

Item 8   Answer: D

Educational Objective: Treat fulminant *Clostridium difficile* infection.

The most appropriate treatment is oral vancomycin plus intravenous metronidazole. Treatment of *Clostridium dif-*

ficile infection (CDI) should be stratified according to its severity. The Society for Healthcare Epidemiology of America and the Infectious Diseases Society of America define severe CDI by a leukocyte count ≥15,000/µL (15×10^9/L) or a serum creatinine level >1.5 mg/dL (133 µmol/L). The American College of Gastroenterology defines severe CDI by the presence of hypoalbuminemia (<3 g/dL [30 g/L]) plus leukocytosis (≥15,000/µL [15×10^9/L]) or abdominal tenderness. Fulminant CDI is defined as severe infection complicated by ileus, hypotension, shock, or toxic megacolon.

Medical therapy for fulminant CDI includes oral vancomycin plus intravenous metronidazole; vancomycin enemas may also be added if ileus is present. Complications are treated on an individual basis, although the presence of toxic megacolon requires surgical consultation to determine if emergent colectomy is indicated.

Fecal microbiota transplant is effective for treatment of recurrent episodes of CDI, but it is not recommended for an initial episode of CDI, regardless of severity.

Oral metronidazole alone for 10 days can be used for patients who present with an initial episode of nonsevere CDI when oral vancomycin or fidaxomicin is not available.

Oral vancomycin alone for 10 days is recommended for treatment of an initial episode of nonsevere and severe CDI. Oral fidaxomicin can also be used.

Oral metronidazole does not add benefit when used in addition to oral vancomycin.

KEY POINT

- Fulminant *Clostridium difficile* infections require oral vancomycin plus intravenous metronidazole; vancomycin enemas may also be added if ileus is present.

Bibliography

McDonald LC, Gerding DN, Johnson S, Bakken JS, Carroll KC, Coffin SE, et al. Clinical practice guidelines for *Clostridium difficile* infection in adults and children: 2017 update by the Infectious Diseases Society of America (IDSA) and Society for Healthcare Epidemiology of America (SHEA). Clin Infect Dis. 2018;66:987-994. [PMID: 29562266] doi:10.1093/cid/ciy149

Item 9   Answer: D

Educational Objective: Diagnose post–Lyme disease syndrome.

This patient most likely now has post–Lyme disease syndrome (PLDS). In a patient who lives in or has visited an area endemic for Lyme disease, a skin lesion consistent with erythema migrans is sufficient to make a clinical diagnosis of early localized Lyme disease. Early localized Lyme disease is treated with doxycycline for 10 to 21 days. Despite appropriate therapy, this patient continues to experience nonspecific but debilitating symptoms that have persisted for several months. She most likely has PLDS, a poorly understood sequela of Lyme disease that sometimes is misclassified as "chronic Lyme disease" despite a lack of microbiologic evidence of a persistent viable organism. PLDS is thought to be due to a disordered immunologic response to the preceding infection. Most patients slowly improve over a period of

6 months, and treatment is directed toward symptom amelioration. Randomized controlled trials have shown that patients with PLDS do not respond to prolonged courses of antibiotic therapy, and such treatment is not warranted in this population.

Anaplasma phagocytophilum, *Babesia microti*, and Powassan virus are all transmitted by the same tick vector as *Borrelia burgdorferi*, the causative spirochete of Lyme disease, and coinfections may occur. Anaplasmosis is treated with doxycycline, and the patient's previous course of treatment should have eradicated any incubating disease.

In contrast, doxycycline is not effective therapy for babesiosis. Mild babesiosis may present as a nonspecific flu-like illness, although fever typically is present. The hallmark of babesiosis is hemolytic anemia, and normal laboratory studies in this patient essentially exclude this diagnosis.

In the United States, late-stage Lyme disease most commonly presents as an inflammatory arthritis involving larger joints. The patient has no physical findings consistent with this diagnosis and had appropriate treatment to prevent progression to late-stage Lyme disease.

Powassan virus causes meningoencephalitis rather than the nonspecific symptoms manifested by this patient.

KEY POINT

- Post–Lyme disease syndrome is a poorly understood sequela of Lyme disease thought to be due to a disordered immunologic response to the preceding infection; most patients slowly improve over a 6-month course, and treatment is directed toward symptom amelioration.

Bibliography

Aucott JN. Posttreatment Lyme disease syndrome. Infect Dis Clin North Am. 2015;29:309-23. [PMID: 25999226] doi:10.1016/j.idc.2015.02.012

Item 10   Answer: B

Educational Objective: Diagnose *Mycobacterium fortuitum* infection.

This patient most likely has an infection with *Mycobacterium fortuitum*. *M. fortuitum* is one of the rapidly growing, nontuberculous mycobacteria (NTM) capable of producing chronic, nonhealing wounds anywhere the bacteria has been introduced, including skin, soft tissue, surgical sites, and occasionally on prosthetic devices. Although *M. fortuitum* is not part of the differential diagnosis of acute wound infections, NTM should always be considered in chronic wounds, especially when conventional antimicrobial therapy has been ineffective. To diagnose an NTM infection, a deep biopsy of chronic wound tissue should be performed. The biopsy specimen should be sent for histopathology to stain for bacteria, mycobacteria, and fungi, and a portion should be sent to the microbiology laboratory for similar stains and cultures.

Pulmonary disease is the most common manifestation of NTM infection, and *Mycobacterium avium* complex

(MAC) infection is the most common causative species. MAC is also responsible for most cases of NTM lymphadenitis. Disseminated MAC infection develops in patients with HIV who have CD4 cell counts less than 50/μL and are not receiving MAC prophylaxis. The clinical presentation often includes fever, night sweats, weight loss, and gastrointestinal symptoms. MAC would not be responsible for a solitary, nonhealing cutaneous ulcer.

Mycobacterium kansasii most commonly causes a lung infection that mimics tuberculosis, with cough, fever, weight loss, and cavitary lung disease. Risk factors for infection include COPD, cancer, HIV, alcohol abuse, and drug-associated immunosuppression. *M. kansasii* does not cause isolated chronic skin or soft tissue infections.

Leprosy is caused by the acid-fast bacillus *Mycobacterium leprae*, a slow-growing organism. Leprosy should be considered in the setting of chronic skin lesions that fail to respond to treatment of common skin conditions or when sensory loss is observed within lesions or in extremities. This patient's rapid development of a nonhealing ulcer after an initial injury 1 month ago is not compatible with infection caused by *M. leprae*.

KEY POINT

- Rapidly growing, nontuberculous mycobacteria, such as *Mycobacterium fortuitum*, can produce chronic, nonhealing wounds that do not respond to conventional antimicrobial therapy.

Bibliography

Guglielmetti L, Mougari F, Lopes A, Raskine L, Cambau E. Human infections due to nontuberculous mycobacteria: the infectious diseases and clinical microbiology specialists' point of view. Future Microbiol. 2015;10:1467-83. [PMID: 26344005] doi:10.2217/fmb.15.64

Item 11   Answer: A

Educational Objective: Treat pelvic inflammatory disease in an outpatient.

The most appropriate treatment for this patient is a single dose of intramuscular ceftriaxone (250 mg) plus oral doxycycline (100 mg twice daily) for 14 days. The patient has risk factors for sexually transmitted infections (multiple partners and inconsistent condom use) and presents with symptoms suggesting pelvic inflammatory disease (PID). Uterine and cervical motion tenderness are sensitive findings for the diagnosis of PID; the likelihood of PID is further increased by the presence of mucopurulent cervical discharge. Antibiotic therapy should begin before diagnostic testing results are received. Although PID is a polymicrobial infection, testing only for the common sexually transmitted pathogens, *Neisseria gonorrhoeae* and *Chlamydia trachomatis*, is recommended. Although a positive result for either pathogen significantly increases the probability of PID, even if the result is negative, a treatment course for PID should be completed based on clinical findings. Women with an intrauterine device can be treated successfully with the device in place in most cases. In addition to the diagnostic testing obtained from the cervical discharge, this patient should be screened for HIV and syphilis.

This patient has no signs of systemic toxicity or findings to suggest a potential surgical emergency, so hospitalization is not indicated. She is not pregnant and has no history suggesting she would be unable to tolerate oral therapy, so ambulatory treatment is appropriate. Intravenous cefoxitin plus doxycycline and intravenous clindamycin plus gentamicin are regimens for inpatient management of PID. Intravenous ampicillin-sulbactam plus doxycycline is an alternate regimen for hospitalized patients; however, oral amoxicillin-clavulanate is not recommended for the treatment of PID.

KEY POINT

- In patients with a high likelihood of pelvic inflammatory disease without indications for hospitalization, empiric therapy with intramuscular ceftriaxone and oral doxycycline is appropriate without waiting for microbiologic testing results.

Bibliography

Brunham RC, Gottlieb SL, Paavonen J. Pelvic inflammatory disease. N Engl J Med. 2015;372:2039-48. [PMID: 25992748] doi:10.1056/NEJMra1411426

 Item 12 **Answer: A**

Educational Objective: Manage asymptomatic bacteriuria in a patient undergoing an invasive urologic procedure.

The indication for antimicrobial therapy in this patient is an invasive urologic procedure. Because urine is a sterile body fluid, the presence of significant bacteriuria is considered to be an infection. In men, either 10^5 cfu/mL of bacteria from voided urine or at least 10^2 cfu/mL of a single bacterial species from a clean intermittent catheterized sample is required to distinguish true bacteriuria from contamination. Asymptomatic bacteriuria (ASB) is diagnosed when no signs or symptoms of active infection referable to the urinary tract are present. Depending on variables such as age and genitourinary abnormalities, older adult men have an ASB prevalence of approximately 5% to 20% in the community, rising to 15% to 40% in long-term care facilities. It is important to recognize that screening for and possibly treating asymptomatic bacteriuria is supported by only two indications: pregnancy and risk mitigation before an invasive urologic procedure. The use of prophylactic antibiotics before minor noninvasive urologic interventions without mucosal bleeding does not provide any benefit and is not recommended.

Likewise, screening for and treating ASB in patients about to undergo orthopedic surgery, including total joint arthroplasty, is without proven merit because it is not a cause of postoperative surgical site infection.

Data are insufficient to advocate the routine treatment of ASB in kidney transplant recipients or patients with diabetes.

KEY POINT

- Screening for and possibly treating asymptomatic bacteriuria is supported by only two indications: pregnancy and medical clearance before an invasive urologic procedure.

Bibliography

Nicolle LE. Asymptomatic bacteriuria. Curr Opin Infect Dis. 2014;27:90-6. [PMID: 24275697] doi:10.1097/QCO.0000000000000019

Item 13 **Answer: B**

Educational Objective: Prevent HIV infection after exposure.

This patient has sustained a possible exposure to HIV and should begin postexposure prophylaxis as soon as possible with a three-drug regimen of tenofovir, emtricitabine, and dolutegravir. Significant risk factors for the exposure include that it was a hollow-bore needle with visible blood. If the source patient was known to have an undetectable viral load in blood, the risk would be reduced but not eliminated; however, the source patient's viral load is unknown at this time. Drug selection may be modified depending on the source patient's history of viral resistance, but the preferred empiric postexposure prophylaxis regimens include tenofovir disoproxil fumarate, emtricitabine, and either dolutegravir or raltegravir, and should be given for 4 weeks. The same recommendations are appropriate whether the exposure was occupational or nonoccupational. The exposed patient should be tested for HIV immediately, 4 to 6 weeks later, and 3 months after the exposure. Exposed persons should also be counseled on transmission, symptoms of acute infection, and toxicity of the medications being prescribed.

A two-drug regimen for postexposure prophylaxis (compared with pre-exposure prophylaxis) is no longer recommended.

Protease inhibitors such as darunavir, whether boosted or not, are not recommended for prophylaxis because of their higher rates of adverse effects.

Because postexposure prophylaxis must begin promptly to be most effective, it would not be appropriate to wait for results of the source patient's viral load before determining therapy. The source patient should also be tested for other blood-borne pathogens, such as hepatitis B and C.

KEY POINT

- Preferred HIV postexposure prophylaxis regimens include tenofovir disoproxil fumarate, emtricitabine, and either dolutegravir or raltegravir and are appropriate whether the exposure was occupational or nonoccupational.

Bibliography

Centers for Disease Control and Prevention. Updated guidelines for antiretroviral postexposure prophylaxis after sexual, injection drug use, or other nonoccupational exposure to HIV–United States, 2016. Available at https://stacks.cdc.gov/view/cdc/38856. Accessed November 2, 2017.

Item 14   Answer: A

Educational Objective: Manage acute pyelonephritis with bacteremia in a woman.

This patient should complete her prescribed 7-day course of oral ciprofloxacin. She has acute uncomplicated pyelonephritis, which can usually be managed with outpatient oral antimicrobial therapy. Ciprofloxacin for 1 week or levofloxacin for 5 days are the recommended first-line treatment regimens. An initial dose of a long-acting parenteral antibiotic (such as ceftriaxone or aminoglycoside) is suggested when local fluoroquinolone resistance (>10%) is a concern. When a fluoroquinolone antibiotic cannot be used or the bacterial isolate proves resistant, an alternative second-line oral antibiotic should be substituted. Available options include trimethoprim-sulfamethoxazole or the less well-studied oral β-lactam agents.

With the exception of pregnancy, follow-up microbiologic cultures and urinalysis are not required or indicated after resolution of infection.

Extending the duration of ciprofloxacin therapy beyond 7 days would be warranted for complicated pyelonephritis but should not be influenced by the discovery of the single bloodstream isolate in this otherwise healthy woman.

Transient bacteremia does not necessitate hospitalization for parenteral antimicrobial therapy except when the pathogen is found to be multidrug resistant or when complicating features are present (severe illness, obstruction, pregnancy).

In adult women with acute kidney infections, urinary tract imaging by ultrasonography or CT is not routinely performed. However, urologic imaging may be useful and is recommended in evaluating patients who do not clinically improve after 72 hours of adequate antimicrobial therapy or when complications such as obstruction or perinephric and renal abscesses are suspected. Such studies should also be considered when evaluating women who experience an excessive number of recurrent urinary tract infections.

KEY POINT

- Acute, uncomplicated pyelonephritis can usually be managed with oral outpatient antimicrobial therapy, with the fluoroquinolones ciprofloxacin and levofloxacin being the preferred, first-line agents.

Bibliography
Kumar S, Dave A, Wolf B, Lerma EV. Urinary tract infections. Dis Mon. 2015;61:45-59. [PMID: 25732782] doi:10.1016/j.disamonth.2014.12.002

Item 15   Answer: C

Educational Objective: Diagnose *Giardia lamblia* infection.

This patient with selective IgA deficiency most likely has chronic diarrhea due to a *Giardia lamblia* infection. Typical symptoms of *Giardia* include watery diarrhea that is fatty and foul smelling, bloating, crampy abdominal pain, flatulence, and nausea; fever is uncommon. In immunocompetent hosts, *Giardia* infection symptoms typically resolve within 2 to 4 weeks, but in patients with humoral immunodeficiency, such as hypogammaglobulinemia or selective IgA deficiency, *Giardia* infection may be prolonged because of impaired protection against *Giardia* adherence to the intestinal epithelium. Patients with selective IgA deficiency have impaired humoral immunity but no impairment in neutrophil, T-cell, or complement function. Infectious complications of selective IgA deficiency typically include recurrent respiratory tract infections and chronic diarrhea caused by *Giardia.*

Although *Clostridium difficile* can cause recurrent disease, this patient does not have a history of recent antibiotic use or any other risk factors for *C. difficile* infection such as advanced age, chemotherapy, gastrointestinal surgery, inflammatory bowel disease, or gastric acid suppression with proton pump inhibitors.

Enterohemorrhagic *Echerichia coli* (EHEC) infection is usually spread by ingestion of undercooked meat or fecally contaminated food. EHEC typically presents with bloody acute diarrhea, crampy abdominal pain, and no fever.

Listeria monocytogenes can cause an acute gastroenteritis syndrome associated with diarrhea, emesis, fever, headache, and nonbloody watery diarrhea associated with pain in muscles and joints. But such an infection typically lasts less than 2 days. Invasive complications of infection, including bacteremia and meningitis, are seen in conditions primarily associated with cell-mediated immune dysfunction such as pregnancy, use of glucocorticoids, and extremes of age (neonates or those older than 65 years).

Nontyphoidal *Salmonella* is the most common cause of foodborne illness. Infection usually results from ingesting fecally contaminated water or food of animal origin. Symptoms are typically self-limited and include crampy abdominal pain, fever, headache, nonbloody diarrhea, nausea, and vomiting. Severe invasive disease may occur in patients with cell-mediated immunodeficiency, but the clinical presentation is not significantly altered in selective IgA deficiency.

KEY POINT

- Patients with selective IgA deficiency are susceptible to *Giardia lamblia* infection, manifesting as abdominal cramping, bloating, and chronic diarrhea.

Bibliography
Einarsson E, Ma'ayeh S, Svärd SG. An up-date on Giardia and giardiasis. Curr Opin Microbiol. 2016;34:47-52. [PMID: 27501461] doi:10.1016/j.mib.2016.07.019

Item 16   Answer: C

Educational Objective: Evaluate a patient with recent Zika virus exposure.

Testing for Zika virus IgM antibodies is the most appropriate management for this pregnant patient, who has had possible exposure to Zika virus through unprotected sexual activity. Asymptomatic pregnant women not living in an area with active Zika virus transmission who may have been exposed more than 2 weeks previously require testing for Zika virus IgM antibodies; a positive result would indicate probable recent infection. Men who have had symptomatic or asymptomatic infection have been proven to have detectable Zika virus RNA in their semen for up to several weeks, with subsequent sexual transmission to their female partner. Under such circumstances, condoms should be used with each sexual encounter for at least 3 months. Her husband's recent viral-like illness occurring in an endemic geographic area, although unconfirmed, must be presumed to have been Zika virus infection. Evaluating her for evidence of asymptomatic infection is of paramount importance to provide counseling and investigate the possible risk of congenital Zika syndrome, of which microcephaly is the most frequent manifestation.

Patients with dengue may be asymptomatic or present with acute febrile illness associated with frontal headache, retro-orbital pain, myalgia, and arthralgia, with or without purpura, melena, or conjunctival injection. Gastrointestinal or respiratory symptoms may predominate. Severe lumbosacral pain is characteristic ("breakbone fever"). As the fever abates, a macular or scarlatiniform rash, which spares the palms and soles and evolves into areas of petechiae on extensor surfaces, may develop. The husband's symptoms are not compatible with dengue. Even if he did have dengue, he cannot transmit the infection to his wife, and testing her for dengue infection is not indicated.

Pregnant women with proven or presumptive recent Zika virus infection require serial ultrasonography every 3 to 4 weeks to assess fetal anatomy and growth. Frequent ultrasonographic monitoring may be appropriate if recent Zika infection is confirmed.

RNA nucleic acid amplification testing for the presence of Zika virus in serum and urine has a greatly diminished sensitivity if performed more than 2 weeks after symptomatic or asymptomatic exposure. In this case, Zika virus IgM antibody testing is preferred.

KEY POINT

- In patients with potential Zika virus exposure more than 2 weeks previously, testing for Zika virus IgM antibodies is necessary.

Bibliography

Petersen LR, Jamieson DJ, Powers AM, Honein MA. Zika virus. N Engl J Med. 2016;374:1552-63. [PMID: 27028561] doi:10.1056/NEJMra1602113

Item 17   Answer: D

Educational Objective: Diagnose Ramsay Hunt syndrome caused by varicella-zoster virus infection.

Varicella-zoster virus (VZV) is the most likely cause of this patient's findings. VZV reactivation presents with pain or paresthesias in a specific dermatome; the characteristic rash develops several days later. In order of frequency, the thoracic, trigeminal, lumbar, and cervical cutaneous dermatomes are most often involved. More than 50% of cases occur in persons older than 60 years; immunocompromised

patients are also at risk. Involvement of the geniculate ganglion may cause herpes zoster oticus, also known as the Ramsay Hunt syndrome, characterized by pain and vesicles in the external ear canal, ipsilateral peripheral facial palsy, and altered or absent taste. Patients may also experience hearing loss, tinnitus, and altered lacrimation. Most experts consider Ramsay Hunt syndrome to be a polycranial neuropathy, with frequent involvement of cranial nerves V, IX, and X. A vesicular rash may be absent in patients with VZV (zoster sine herpete) and should not deter physicians from ordering polymerase chain reaction testing for VZV. Acyclovir is typically prescribed for this syndrome. The live attenuated zoster vaccine has 64% efficacy that decreases to 36% after 6 years. A novel recombinant zoster vaccine, approved in 2017, has 97% efficacy and should be given to this patient.

The most common neurologic manifestation of early disseminated Lyme disease is facial nerve palsy, which may be unilateral or bilateral. Treatment of early localized disease prevents progression of infection. Untreated patients may progress to early disseminated infection. This stage typically presents as a febrile illness associated with erythema migrans at multiple sites distant from the initial tick attachment. Constitutional symptoms are common and include fever, myalgia, arthralgia, and headache. Neurologic Lyme disease without a history of tick bite, erythema migrans rash, or systemic symptoms is highly unlikely.

Bell palsy is defined as an isolated paralysis of the facial nerve that leads to complete unilateral facial paralysis. Herpes simplex virus (HSV) type 1 reactivation is the likely cause of Bell palsy in most cases. However, most cases of Bell palsy are diagnosed as "idiopathic" because it is difficult in clinical practice to prove that reactivation of HSV-1 is the cause of this peripheral neuropathy.

HSV type 2 is more commonly associated with genital ulcers, recurrent aseptic meningitis, or myelitis than with Bell palsy. Neither Lyme disease nor HSV reactivation can explain the burning and stinging ear pain, tinnitus, hearing loss, and facial palsy experienced by this patient as well as VZV reactivation can.

KEY POINT

- Varicella-zoster virus is a cause of Ramsay Hunt syndrome, which usually presents with ear pain, a vesicular rash in the external ear (although the rash may be absent), and ipsilateral peripheral facial palsy.

Bibliography

Cohen JI. Clinical practice: Herpes zoster. N Engl J Med. 2013;369:255-63. [PMID: 23863052] doi:10.1056/NEJMcp1302674

Item 18   Answer: B

Educational Objective: Diagnose Q fever pneumonia.

The most likely cause of this patient's illness is *Coxiella burnetii*. He presents with community-acquired pneumonia not requiring hospitalization, which is most frequently caused by atypical bacteria, *Streptococcus pneumoniae*, or a viral pathogen. His occupation puts him at risk for zoonotic causes of pneumonia as well. Many zoonotic organisms can potentially cause pulmonary infection, but they can usually be differentiated based on illness severity and animal reservoir. In this patient, the relatively mild infection coupled with exposure to livestock makes *C. burnetii* the most likely culprit. *C. burnetii*, which causes Q fever pneumonia, is most frequently associated with exposure to farm animals, parturient animals in particular. High rates of seropositivity have been reported in farmers, veterinarians, and abattoir workers. Infection can occur without direct animal exposure; increased rates of Q fever pneumonia have been found among persons residing in proximity to livestock farms. Infection occurs after inhalation of aerosolized bodily fluids from infected animals. Acute pulmonary infection ranges from subclinical to severe, but it is rarely fatal. Treatment with doxycycline is indicated to decrease symptom duration and to prevent progression to chronic Q fever.

Bacillus anthracis is the causative agent of anthrax. Cutaneous anthrax is the most common naturally occurring form of the disease. In the United States, inhalation anthrax is almost exclusively of concern as an agent of bioterrorism. In endemic areas, pulmonary infection may occur after inhalation of spores from the fur or hide of infected livestock, particularly goats and cattle. Inhalation anthrax is a fulminant, often fatal infection.

Chlamydia psittaci is the causative agent of psittacosis, which typically presents as pneumonia associated with abrupt onset of fever, severe headache, and dry cough. This organism is associated with inhalation of dried bird droppings, so bird owners or breeders and poultry farmers are at particularly high risk for this infection.

Pneumonic tularemia occurs either after direct inhalation or through secondary spread of *Francisella tularensis* into the lungs. Pneumonic tularemia is characterized by a nonproductive cough, dyspnea, and substernal or pleuritic chest pain. Chest radiographs show infiltrates, hilar lymphadenopathy, and pleural effusion. In the United States, most infections are transmitted through animal exposure. Hunters are at particularly high risk for primary tularemia pneumonia through skinning and dressing of infected rabbits or other wild game.

Yersinia pestis infection of the lung causes pneumonic plague. Rodents serve as the primary reservoir for plague. Pulmonary infection occurs through droplet transmission from an infected host or secondary spread from an extrapulmonary source. Patients present with sudden high fever, pleuritic chest pain, a productive cough, and hemoptysis. Pneumonic plague is almost uniformly fatal unless recognized and treated promptly.

KEY POINT

- Many zoonotic organisms have the potential to cause pulmonary infection, but they can be differentiated based on the severity of illness and animal reservoir; relatively mild infection coupled with exposure to livestock indicates likely *Coxiella burnetii* infection.

Bibliography

Freidl GS, Spruijt IT, Borlée F, Smit LA, van Gageldonk-Lafeber AB, Heederik DJ, et al. Livestock-associated risk factors for pneumonia in an area of intensive animal farming in the Netherlands. PLoS One. 2017;12:e0174796. [PMID: 28362816] doi:10.1371/journal.pone.0174796

Item 19   Answer: D

Educational Objective: Treat coagulase-negative *Staphylococcus* central line–associated bloodstream infection.

The most appropriate management is to remove the peripherally inserted central catheter (PICC) and repeat blood cultures. Central line–associated bloodstream infections (CLABSIs) can occur with any type of catheter, including short-term peripheral intravenous catheters and PICCs. They are most commonly caused by coagulase-negative *Staphylococcus* followed by *S. aureus*. Coagulase-negative *Staphylococcus* is less virulent than *S. aureus* and is less likely to cause metastatic infection or endocarditis in patients without prosthetic devices or endovascular hardware (such as prosthetic heart valves) in place. Coagulase-negative *Staphylococcus* CLABSIs often resolve with removal of the catheter. Blood cultures should be repeated after catheter removal to document clearance of the organism. Alternatively, patients with coagulase-negative *Staphylococcus* CLABSIs can be treated with antibiotics for 5 to 7 days if the catheter is removed and for 10 to 14 days in combination with antibiotic lock therapy if the catheter is not removed.

Most uncomplicated CLABSIs are treated for 7 to 14 days; *S. aureus* CLABSIs may require treatment for 4 to 6 weeks after catheter removal. Shorter therapy durations (14 days) may be considered in select patients with *S. aureus* CLABSI whose catheters have been removed and who do not have diabetes mellitus, are not immunosuppressed, have no implanted prosthetic devices, have no evidence of endocarditis by echocardiography (preferably transesophageal), and have no evidence of infected thrombophlebitis; whose fever and bacteremia resolve within 72 hours of starting appropriate therapy; and whose physical examination and diagnostic tests do not suggest the presence of metastatic infection.

In patients with persistent bacteremia or endovascular hardware, transesophageal echocardiography may be pursued to evaluate for endocarditis. In patients with endovascular hardware, longer durations of antibiotics are generally required. Catheters should always be removed when endocarditis, metastatic infection, hemodynamic instability, suppurative thrombophlebitis, or persistent bacteremia is evident.

KEY POINT

- Coagulase-negative *Staphylococcus* is less virulent than *S. aureus* and is less likely to cause metastatic infection or endocarditis in patients without prosthetic devices or endovascular hardware in place (such as prosthetic heart valves) and may be treated with simple removal of the intravenous catheter.

Bibliography

Mermel LA, Allon M, Bouza E, Craven DE, Flynn P, O'Grady NP, et al. Clinical practice guidelines for the diagnosis and management of intravascular catheter-related infection: 2009 update by the Infectious Diseases Society of America. Clin Infect Dis. 2009;49:1–45. [PMID: 19489710] doi:10.1086/599376

Item 20   Answer: D

Educational Objective: Prevent catheter-associated urinary tract infection by removing the catheter.

The proper management of the patient's urinary catheter is to remove it and observe the patient for spontaneous voiding. Catheters should be used for appropriate indications only, which include urinary retention and bladder outlet obstruction, measurement of urinary output in critically ill patients, perioperative use for selected surgical procedures, assistance with healing of perineal or sacral wounds in patients with incontinence, use in patients requiring prolonged immobilization, and contribution to comfort at the end of life. An indwelling urinary catheter is sometimes inserted in the emergency department during trauma evaluation; however, the need for continuing the catheter should be assessed when the initial evaluation has been completed. If this patient required prolonged immobilization (for example, multiple traumatic injuries such as pelvic fractures), continuing the indwelling urinary catheter may be appropriate. Patients should be monitored closely for their ability to void spontaneously when a catheter is removed. Bladder ultrasonography can be used to determine residual postvoid volume; if more than 200 mL remain, consider intermittent catheterization for a short amount of time rather than placing a new indwelling urinary catheter. Early removal of urinary catheters should be considered when possible and can be encouraged by reminder systems. Additionally, nurse-initiated removal protocols have been shown to be effective in limiting duration of catheterization. Catheter-associated urinary tract infection (CAUTI) prevention strategies are summarized by the acronym ABCDE: Adhere to general infection control principles, perform Bladder ultrasonography to potentially avoid catheterization, use Condom catheters or intermittent catheterization when appropriate, Do not use an indwelling catheter if criteria for use are not met, and remove catheters Early when they are no longer indicated using computerized reminders or nurse-driven removal protocols.

Antimicrobial-impregnated or antiseptic-coated catheters have not been shown to decrease CAUTIs with short-term (<14 days) catheterization. Information is scarce on their benefits with long-term urinary catheters. Early removal of the catheter is a better care strategy.

Administering antibiotics with the goal of preventing infection is not effective and promotes antibiotic-resistant bacteria and fungal CAUTIs and is not indicated in this case.

KEY POINT

- Early removal of urinary catheters should be considered when possible, and patients should be monitored for their ability to void spontaneously after catheter removal.

Bibliography

Chenoweth CE, Saint S. Urinary tract infections. Infect Dis Clin North Am. 2016;30:869–885. [PMID: 27816141] doi:10.1016/j.idc.2016.07.007

Item 21   Answer: A

Educational Objective: Treat an infected cat bite in a patient with risk factors for methicillin-resistant *Staphylococcus aureus*.

This patient should receive antibiotic treatment with ampicillin-sulbactam plus vancomycin in addition to undergoing surgical consultation. She has a cat bite–associated wound infection with accompanying low blood pressure and tachypnea and requires hospitalization. Cat bites are more likely than dog bites to cause infection because of cats' sharp, narrow teeth; infections are caused by organisms from the animal's mouth flora and the host's skin flora. This flora comprises a mix of anaerobic and aerobic organisms, including streptococci, staphylococci, and *Bacteroides*, *Fusobacterium*, *Porphyromonas*, and *Pasteurella* species. *Pasteurella* is a facultative anaerobic gram-negative rod that is the most common bacteria in a cat's mouth. Intravenous piperacillin-tazobactam, ampicillin-sulbactam, imipenem, or meropenem would address these organisms but not potential methicillin-resistant *Staphylococcus aureus* (MRSA). If pus is present, the patient has MRSA risk factors such as a previous MRSA infection or colonization within the last year, or local MRSA prevalence is high, then coverage should also include agents that target MRSA, such as vancomycin or daptomycin. Consequently, the combination of ampicillin-sulbactam and vancomycin would be the best choice for empiric antibiotic coverage because this regimen is effective against serious infections caused by MRSA and the microbiota of a cat's mouth.

Ceftriaxone and metronidazole would be effective against many of the organisms encountered in a cat bite–associated skin infection, but it would not cover the possibility of MRSA infection in this patient.

Ciprofloxacin and aztreonam also lack coverage for MRSA and some anaerobes likely to be associated with a bite wound.

Imipenem is a broad-spectrum antibiotic effective against many of the organisms associated with cat bite wounds, but it does not provide MRSA coverage.

Neither vancomycin nor clindamycin provides adequate coverage against *Pasteurella* species, so this regimen would not be effective for a cat bite–associated infection.

KEY POINT

- Cat bite–associated wound infections comprise a mix of anaerobic and aerobic organisms, including *Pasteurella* species, which require treatment with antibiotic agents such as piperacillin-tazobactam, ampicillin-sulbactam, imipenem, and meropenem; coverage for methicillin-resistant *Staphylococcus aureus* must be included in select patients who have risk factors for this infection.

Bibliography

Bystritsky R, Chambers H. Cellulitis and soft tissue infections. Ann Intern Med. 2018;168:ITC17-ITC32. [PMID: 29404597] doi:10.7326/AITC201802060

Item 22   Answer: B

Educational Objective: Diagnose human monocytic ehrlichiosis.

This patient most likely has human monocytic ehrlichiosis (HME), a tick-borne illness primarily caused by *Ehrlichia chaffeensis*. His symptoms include a nonfocal febrile illness associated with leukopenia, thrombocytopenia, and elevated hepatic enzyme levels, all of which are characteristic of HME. His participation in outdoor activities in wooded areas places him at risk for exposure to ticks. HME is endemic in the mid-Atlantic, southern, and southeastern United States; his clinical presentation is highly suggestive of this illness. The prompt response to doxycycline is classic for a tick-borne rickettsial illness, such as HME; a lack of response within 48 hours of therapy would suggest an alternative diagnosis or a coinfection. The negative serologic results for *E. chaffeensis* do not disprove the diagnosis and should not prompt early discontinuation of doxycycline. The sensitivity of antibody testing is low in the first week of illness; seroconversion typically occurs within 2 to 4 weeks of symptom onset, and acute and convalescent titers are useful for retrospective confirmation of infection. During the acute illness, buffy-coat staining (to reveal the presence of morulae, which are basophilic inclusion bodies in the cytoplasm of monocytes representing clusters of bacteria [shown]) or polymerase chain reaction of whole blood specimens may allow an early diagnosis.

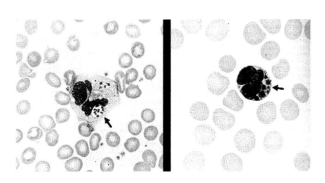

Although many infections present identically to HME, the salient feature in this patient was the rapid response to doxycycline therapy, which essentially excludes a viral process. Heartland virus, a newly described Bunyavirus transmitted by the same vector as *E. chaffeensis*, is clinically indistinguishable from HME and should be suspected when no improvement is seen within 48 hours of starting doxycycline therapy.

Infectious mononucleosis can present with fever, cytopenia, and elevated aminotransferase levels. However, other components of the infectious mononucleosis triad (fever, pharyngitis, and cervical lymphadenopathy) were absent in this patient.

The rapid response to doxycycline treatment is consistent with Rocky Mountain spotted fever (RMSF) infection. However, the pronounced leukopenia and absence of a rash more than 1 week into the illness argue against this diagnosis.

> **KEY POINT**
>
> - Human monocytic ehrlichiosis infection is characterized by a nonfocal febrile illness associated with leukopenia, thrombocytopenia, elevated hepatic enzyme levels, and a rapid response to tetracycline.

Bibliography

Biggs HM, Behravesh CB, Bradley KK, Dahlgren FS, Drexler NA, Dumler JS, et al. Diagnosis and management of tickborne rickettsial diseases: Rocky Mountain spotted fever and other spotted fever group rickettsioses, ehrlichioses, and anaplasmosis – United States. MMWR Recomm Rep. 2016;65:1-44. [PMID: 27172113] doi:10.15585/mmwr.rr6502a1

Item 23   Answer: C

Educational Objective: Treat health care–associated ventriculitis and meningitis.

The most appropriate management in this patient is removal of his ventricular drain. After drain removal, clinical monitoring for intracranial hypertension will be important. Health care–associated ventriculitis or meningitis (HCAVM) or nosocomial meningitis may present a diagnostic and treatment challenge to clinicians. It typically occurs after head trauma or a neurosurgical procedure (craniotomy, lumbar puncture) or secondary to device infection (for example, cerebrospinal fluid [CSF] shunts or drains, intrathecal pumps, deep brain stimulator). *Staphylococcus* species and enteric gram-negative bacteria are the most common causes, but up to 50% of patients can have negative cultures because more than 50% receive antibiotic therapy before CSF studies are performed, as occurred in this patient. Worsening mental status, new fever, or stiff neck in a patient who recently underwent surgery should raise the possibility of HCAVM. An elevated CSF lactate level greater than 4 mg/dL, an elevated CSF procalcitonin level, or a combination of both, may be useful in the diagnosis of health care–associated bacterial ventriculitis and meningitis in culture-negative cases. Empiric therapy should include vancomycin and a β-lactam with antipseudomonal activity (such as cefepime or meropenem) and device removal, if present.

For patients with health care–associated ventriculitis and meningitis caused by staphylococci in whom β-lactam agents or vancomycin cannot be used, treatment with linezolid, daptomycin, or trimethoprim-sulfamethoxazole is recommended with selection based on in vitro susceptibility testing. However, the priority in this patient is removing the ventricular drain, not changing the antibiotic regimen.

Intraventricular or intrathecal antimicrobial therapy should be considered for patients with health care–associated ventriculitis and meningitis in whom the

CONT. infection responds poorly to systemic antimicrobial therapy alone. This strategy is not appropriate in a patient with a potentially infected ventricular drain.

KEY POINT

- In patients with health care–associated ventriculitis or meningitis, device removal, if present, should accompany empiric antimicrobial therapy.

Bibliography

Tunkel AR, Hasbun R, Bhimraj A, Byers K, Kaplan SL, Michael Scheld W, et al. 2017 Infectious Diseases Society of America's clinical practice guidelines for healthcare-associated ventriculitis and meningitis. Clin Infect Dis. 2017. [PMID: 28203777] doi:10.1093/cid/ciw861

Item 24   Answer: C

Educational Objective: Treat pneumonic plague.

The most appropriate treatment is gentamicin. This patient most likely has pneumonic plague caused by the bacteria *Yersinia pestis*, one of the biologic agents classified as an A-list bioterrorism pathogen because of its high potential lethality and ease of dissemination. Sputum Gram stain (and possibly blood smear) may identify gram-negative coccobacilli demonstrating the classic bipolar staining or "safety pin" shape shown. Although most pulmonary involvement occurs through secondary hematogenous spread to the lungs from a bubo or other source, primary pneumonic plague can occur after close contact with another person with plague pneumonia, after animal exposure, or as a result of intentional aerosol release for the purpose of terrorism, as in this case. Recommended first-line treatment is either streptomycin or gentamicin.

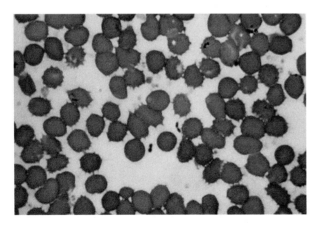

Anthrax is caused by *Bacillus anthracis*, a gram-positive, aerobic organism. It appears as a sporulating gram-positive rod on microscopic examination. Patients with inhalational anthrax present with low-grade fever, malaise, myalgia, and headache accompanied by cough, dyspnea, and chest pain. A chest radiograph showing mediastinal widening from hemorrhagic lymphadenitis is characteristic. Ciprofloxacin, levofloxacin, moxifloxacin, or doxycycline should be provided as soon as possible after any actual or suspected case of anthrax that raises concern for a bioterrorism attack.

Ambulatory empiric therapy for community-acquired pneumonia (CAP) is directed against *Streptococcus pneumoniae*, *Haemophilus influenzae*, and atypical bacteria, even though a significant proportion of patients with CAP infected with viral pathogens do not benefit from antibiotic therapy. The combination of ceftriaxone and azithromycin would be an appropriate choice for the treatment of CAP but would be inadequate for treating plague, which requires either streptomycin or gentamicin.

When clinical concern for *Pseudomonas* is present, dual therapy with two active agents is indicated. Options include an antipseudomonal β-lactam (piperacillin-tazobactam, cefepime, or meropenem) in conjunction with either a quinolone (levofloxacin or ciprofloxacin) or an aminoglycoside. *Pseudomonas* infection should be considered in immunocompromised patients and patients with underlying structural lung disease (bronchiectasis or cystic fibrosis) or medical conditions requiring repeated courses of antibiotics. The combination of piperacillin-tazobactam and levofloxacin would be ideal for a seriously ill patient with CAP and concern for *Pseudomonas* infection but not for this patient most likely infected with *Yersinia pestis*.

KEY POINT

- First-line treatment for primary pneumonic plague is either streptomycin or gentamicin.

Bibliography

Adalja AA, Toner E, Inglesby TV. Clinical management of potential bioterrorism-related conditions. N Engl J Med. 2015;372:954-62. [PMID: 25738671] doi:10.1056/NEJMra1409755

Item 25   Answer: D

Educational Objective: Treat disseminated histoplasmosis.

The most appropriate treatment for this patient is liposomal amphotericin B. He has disseminated histoplasmosis, for which he has numerous risk factors. He lives in an area endemic for histoplasmosis (Ohio River Valley), and because he takes prednisone and methotrexate for his rheumatoid arthritis, he is immunosuppressed. He has had significant exposure working in an old barn with bats. He also is hypotensive and diaphoretic and has oral ulcerations and hepatosplenomegaly, which are typical of disseminated infection, as is pancytopenia. Approximately 10% of patients with histoplasmosis develop disseminated infection; if not diagnosed early, the mortality rate is greater than 90%. The treatment of choice for disseminated histoplasmosis is liposomal amphotericin B initially, with de-escalation to itraconazole for several months. A definitive diagnosis can be established by detection of the urinary antigen for histoplasmosis (95% specificity), blood cultures, or a biopsy of the oral lesions.

Ceftriaxone and azithromycin are the recommended drugs of choice for community-acquired pneumonia. The

CONT.

patient's physical examination and chest radiograph are unremarkable, which effectively rules out pneumonia and the need for these antibiotics.

Behçet syndrome is a form of vasculitis associated with recurrent painful oral and genital ulcerations; patients also may demonstrate additional distinctive features, including hypopyon and pathergy. Central nervous system involvement can manifest as headaches, stroke, and behavioral changes. Gastrointestinal involvement may be hard to distinguish from inflammatory bowel disease. Low-dose prednisone or colchicine is used for oral or genital ulcers, and high-dose prednisone and immunomodulating agents are used for more severe disease. Behçet syndrome does not explain the patient's fever, hemodynamic instability, pancytopenia, or hepatomegaly, and colchicine therapy is not warranted.

Itraconazole is an azole triazole used to treat many endemic fungal infections, including histoplasmosis. However, it is not as effective as liposomal amphotericin B in disseminated infection. It may be used for subacute or chronic histoplasmosis, such as pulmonary histoplasmosis.

KEY POINT

- Liposomal amphotericin B is the treatment of choice for disseminated histoplasmosis.

Bibliography

Hage CA, Azar MM, Bahr N, Loyd J, Wheat LJ. Histoplasmosis: up-to-date evidence-based approach to diagnosis and management. Semin Respir Crit Care Med. 2015 Oct;36(5):729-45. doi: 10.1055/s-0035-1562899. Review. PMID: 26398539.

 Item 26   Answer: C

Educational Objective: Evaluate a patient for complications of pneumonia (empyema).

The most appropriate management at this time is to perform thoracentesis. This patient has nonresponsive pneumonia demonstrated by persistent fever of more than 72 hours despite directed therapy (vancomycin) against the causative organism (methicillin-resistant *Staphylococcus aureus* [MRSA]). Lack of response to therapy is a poor prognostic factor and is associated with excess mortality. Antibiotic therapy failure may indicate a noninfectious cause mimicking pneumonia, antibiotic-resistant bacterial infection, infection with a nonbacterial organism, or loculated infection such as an empyema. This patient's chest radiograph shows opacification of the left heart border and hemidiaphragm, raising concern for pleural fluid adjacent to a pulmonary infiltrate. Parapneumonic pleural effusions are present in up to 40% of patients hospitalized with CAP. Determining the need for chest tube drainage requires analysis of the pleural fluid. A finding of purulent or foul-smelling material or a positive Gram stain is diagnostic of an empyema, and a pleural fluid pH less than 7.2 or a pleural fluid glucose level less than 60 mg/dL (3.33 mmol/L) is highly suggestive. Chest tube placement in addition to antibiotics is necessary to treat infection localized to the pleural space. Delayed drainage

may result in ongoing fever, sepsis, or fibrosis ultimately requiring surgical intervention.

The role of glucocorticoids in CAP remains controversial. Evidence is accumulating that early administration of glucocorticoids may reduce the host inflammatory response, particularly in patients with acute respiratory distress syndrome; however, the routine use of glucocorticoids for CAP has not been established.

The addition of piperacillin-tazobactam would be indicated if a secondary hospital-acquired pulmonary infection were a concern, but the persistent fever and Gram stain showing only gram-positive cocci makes superinfection less likely.

Procalcitonin is produced by cells as a response to bacterial toxins, which result in elevated serum procalcitonin levels in bacterial infections. In viral infections, procalcitonin levels are reduced. Procalcitonin measurement is only one of several factors in determining a bacterial versus a viral cause and should be considered as adjunctive to other diagnostic tools. In this patient, there is little doubt concerning the microbiologic diagnosis, and determining the procalcitonin level will not be helpful.

Daptomycin is contraindicated for use in pulmonary infections because it binds to surfactant and does not achieve adequate levels in the alveoli.

KEY POINT

- In patients with pneumonia unresponsive to appropriate antibiotic therapy, a noninfectious cause mimicking pneumonia, antibiotic-resistant bacterial infection, infection with a nonbacterial organism, or loculated infection such as an empyema may be the cause.

Bibliography

McCauley L, Dean N. Pneumonia and empyema: causal, casual or unknown. J Thorac Dis. 2015;7:992-8. [PMID: 26150912] doi:10.3978/j.issn.2072-1439.2015.04.36

Item 27   Answer: A

Educational Objective: Diagnose *Plasmodium falciparum* malaria.

This pregnant woman has contracted *Plasmodium falciparum* malaria after visiting a part of the world where malaria is endemic. Her clinical presentation and peripheral blood smear showing many parasitized erythrocytes demonstrating signet ring forms, together with the absence of trophozoites and schizonts, are typical for infection with *P. falciparum*. Of returning travelers with acute and potentially life-threatening febrile diseases, *P. falciparum* malaria accounts for most infections. Furthermore, pregnant women are at increased risk of severe disease and a heightened mortality rate, which is likely related to a reduced immune response. Additionally, effects on the microvasculature and sequestering of organisms in the placenta during pregnancy are known to significantly increase the risk of miscarriage,

CONT.

premature delivery, low-birth-weight neonates, congenital infection, and fetal demise.

Accurate identification of *P. falciparum* and *Plasmodium knowlesi* is critical because of the risk for severe and potentially lethal infection. *P. falciparum* should be suspected if the patient traveled to Africa, symptoms begin soon after return from an endemic area, and the peripheral blood smear shows a high level of parasitemia. *P. knowlesi* is a more recently recognized human pathogen; infection may be severe because of high levels of parasitemia. Examination of the peripheral blood smear reveals all stages of the parasite. The epidemiologic history is helpful because *P. knowlesi* is not encountered in Africa but rather South and Southeast Asia.

Plasmodium malariae, Plasmodium ovale, and *Plasmodium vivax* are all associated with a low or very low degree of parasitemia, typically less than 2%, and although the risk of recurrence is high, with the exception of *P. vivax,* the risk for severe disease is low.

KEY POINT

- *Plasmodium falciparum* infection should be suspected if the patient traveled to Africa, symptoms begin soon after return from an endemic area, and the peripheral blood smear shows a high level of parasitemia.

Bibliography

Hahn WO, Pottinger PS. Malaria in the traveler: how to manage before departure and evaluate upon return. Med Clin North Am. 2016;100:289-302. [PMID: 26900114] doi:10.1016/j.mcna.2015.09.008

 ### Item 28   Answer: C

Educational Objective: Treat spinal epidural abscess.

The most appropriate treatment of this patient is empiric antibiotic therapy and surgical drainage of the abscess. Spinal epidural abscesses (SEAs) usually result from contiguous spread from infected vertebrae or intervertebral body disc spaces or from hematogenous dissemination from a distant site. SEA can be challenging to diagnose because symptoms can be mild or nonspecific and fever may not always be present. A high index of suspicion, particularly in patients with atypical or persistent back pain, will facilitate more prompt diagnosis. Symptoms may progress from back pain to accompanying neurologic symptoms, such as bowel or bladder dysfunction, lower extremity weakness, paresthesias, and, in the last stages, paralysis. MRI of the spine with contrast is the preferred imaging modality for diagnosis. Blood cultures should be performed before starting antibiotic therapy to identify the cause, and, in certain cases, cultures may avoid the need for aspiration of the spinal abscess. Medical therapy alone is often successful if no neurologic deficits are present at the time of diagnosis or if substantial complications from surgery are likely because of comorbid conditions. However, surgical drainage is recommended in patients who present with neurologic symptoms or evidence

of progression or recurrence despite proper antimicrobial therapy. Serial clinical evaluations and follow-up MRI of the spine (at approximately 4-6 weeks into therapy or with any sign of clinical deterioration) are necessary adjuncts to management without surgery. Empiric parenteral antimicrobial therapy should include coverage for *Staphylococcus aureus* (accounts for approximately 50% of infections), *Streptococcus* species, and gram-negative bacilli and may be narrowed based on culture results, if available. Therapy typically lasts between 6 and 8 weeks (or until resolution of abscess on follow-up MRI) but may require modification depending on clinical and radiographic recovery.

Patients with sepsis or neurologic compromise, as in this patient, should start empiric broad-spectrum antimicrobial therapy pending blood and abscess cultures. Otherwise, empiric antimicrobial therapy may be withheld until a cause is confirmed. This patient has an indication for immediate empiric antibiotic therapy and surgical drainage.

KEY POINT

- Patients with spinal epidural abscess who also have neurologic compromise should immediately begin broad-spectrum antimicrobial therapy and undergo surgical drainage.

Bibliography

Berbari EF, Kanj SS, Kowalski TJ, Darouiche RO, Widmer AF, Schmitt SK, et al. 2015 Infectious Diseases Society of America (IDSA) clinical practice guidelines for the diagnosis and treatment of native vertebral osteomyelitis in adults. Clin Infect Dis. 2015;61:e26-46. [PMID: 26229122] doi:10.1093/cid/civ482

Item 29   Answer: D

Educational Objective: Diagnose typhoid (enteric) fever.

This patient most likely has typhoid fever, also known as enteric fever, caused by either of the typhoidal *Salmonella* strains, *S. typhi* or *S. paratyphi.* Infection is transmitted by ingestion of food or water contaminated by feces. In resource-poor areas, organisms may be spread in community food or, more frequently, by water. In developed countries, transmission is chiefly by food that has been contaminated during preparation by healthy carriers. Symptoms of enteric fever are generally nonspecific. Fever is the major manifestation, typically rising over 2 to 3 nights and persisting for several days. A pulse-temperature dissociation (relative bradycardia) is often present. A brief period of diarrhea followed by constipation, abdominal discomfort, nonproductive cough, mild confusion, and transient small blanching skin lesions (rose spots) are other clinical features. Ceftriaxone is the preferred empiric antibiotic agent, with ciprofloxacin and azithromycin as additional options if resistance is not encountered.

Human brucellosis can develop after exposure to one of four *Brucella* species through contact with viable organisms in secretions or excretions of infected animals, ingestion of undercooked meat or milk products, or, less often, inhalation. Patients experience numerous nonspecific symptoms as well as recurring or "undulating" waves of fever, but rash, gastrointestinal symptoms, and relative bradycardia are not typical.

Humans acquire leptospirosis after contact with infected urine spread by carrier animals. Classically, illness is biphasic, beginning with a septicemic phase followed by an immune phase, which correlates with the appearance of antibodies in serum. Clinically apparent leptospirosis presents with the abrupt onset of fever, rigors, myalgias, and headache. Conjunctival suffusion in a patient with a nonspecific febrile illness should raise suspicion for the diagnosis of leptospirosis. A more severe form, known as Weil syndrome (icteric leptospirosis), consisting of jaundice, azotemia, and anemia, may also occur. Gastrointestinal symptoms are infrequent.

The gram-negative bacillus *Burkholderia pseudomallei*, found in soil and water in endemic areas such as Southeast Asia, is the causative agent of melioidosis. After acquisition through direct skin contact, ingestion, or inhalation, an acute pulmonary, septicemic, or localized suppurative infection may occur. The patient's findings are not compatible with melioidosis.

KEY POINT

- Fever is the major manifestation of typhoid fever and is often associated with a relative bradycardia; additional symptoms may include a brief period of diarrhea followed by constipation, abdominal discomfort, nonproductive cough, mild confusion, and transient small blanching skin lesions (rose spots).

Bibliography

Thwaites GE, Day NP. Approach to fever in the returning traveler. N Engl J Med. 2017;376:548-560. [PMID: 28177860] doi:10.1056/NEJMra1508435

Item 30   Answer: A

Educational Objective: Manage newly diagnosed HIV infection.

This patient needs baseline genotypic HIV resistance testing. Because of the possibility of transmitted virus having resistance mutations, it is recommended to obtain baseline resistance testing before starting an antiretroviral regimen. If the patient is ready, antiretrovirals can be started the same day, while waiting for resistance testing results, with regimen modification if necessary based on results. Virologic failure of a regimen (rebound of a suppressed viral load or failure to achieve undetectable viral load with therapy) is also an indication for resistance testing to guide the change in regimen. Genotypic testing looks for mutations in the viral genome associated with antiviral drug resistance. Phenotypic testing actually tests the virus's ability to grow in the presence of differing concentrations of the drug and is therefore more useful in the presence of multiple interacting mutations or unclear correlations of mutation and resistance, such as occurs with resistance to protease inhibitors. Genotypic testing is faster and less

expensive because all that is necessary is sequencing of the respective genes for the patient's viral isolate. When significant resistance is not expected and information is needed more quickly, genotypic testing would be preferred over phenotypic testing.

Some antiretroviral agents have been associated with increased insulin resistance and risk for hyperglycemia, and assessing for this at baseline and during therapy is recommended. This patient, however, already has a normal glucose level at baseline testing, so measuring the glycohemoglobin is not necessary at this time.

All patients with HIV should begin antiretroviral therapy as soon as they are ready. Prompt initiation of therapy benefits the patient and reduces the risk of transmission to others, so waiting for repeat viral load and CD4 cell count is inappropriate and unnecessary.

KEY POINT

- Genotypic viral resistance testing is recommended immediately after a diagnosis of HIV infection to guide the selection of active agents for the antiretroviral regimen or after virologic failure of a regimen to guide adjustment of antiretroviral therapy.

Bibliography

Panel on Antiretroviral Guidelines for Adults and Adolescents. Guidelines for the use of antiretroviral agents in adults and adolescents living with HIV. Department of Health and Human Services. Available at https://aidsinfo.nih.gov/guidelines/html/1/adult-and-adolescent-arv/0. Accessed April 12, 2018.

Item 31   Answer: B

Educational Objective: Diagnose meningitis caused by herpes simplex virus type 2.

The most likely diagnosis in this patient is meningitis caused by herpes simplex virus (HSV) type 2. Viral meningitis is the most common cause of "aseptic" meningitis, in which cerebrospinal fluid (CSF) Gram stain and cultures are negative. Most patients have typical meningitis symptoms, such as fever, nuchal rigidity, headache, and photophobia. HSV meningitis syndromes can be related to primary infections, with central nervous system involvement as a secondary consequence, or reactivation of latent infection presenting as aseptic meningitis. HSV-2 is more commonly associated with meningitis and is the most common cause of recurrent meningitis (recurrent benign lymphocytic meningitis). HSV-1 is associated with encephalitis. HSV can cause meningitis year round. CSF findings resemble enteroviral meningitis, with lymphocytic pleocytosis, a normal glucose level, and a mildly elevated protein level as in this patient. CSF polymerase chain reaction studies may be used for diagnosing HSV and enterovirus meningitis.

Enteroviruses are the most common cause of viral meningitis, but they usually present between May and November in the Western Hemisphere, with symptoms including headache, fever, nuchal rigidity, photophobia, nausea, vomiting, myalgias, pharyngitis, maculopapular rash, and cough. This

CONT.

patient's presentation in the winter makes this an unlikely cause of her illness.

Mumps virus can cause meningitis, with typical symptoms of fever, headache, and neck stiffness. Since the advent of universal childhood vaccination for measles, mumps, and rubella, the incidence of mumps-related meningitis has dramatically decreased. Meningitis from mumps virus can occur at any point during the course of clinical mumps infection. Parotitis or orchitis may be present. The patient's clinical presentation is not consistent with mumps meningitis.

Focal motor weakness is a common finding in West Nile neuroinvasive disease (WNND), either combined with meningoencephalitis or as an isolated myelitis. In its most severe form, infection of the anterior horn cells can cause a symmetric or asymmetric flaccid paralysis, analogous to that seen with polio in the prevaccination era. The diagnosis of WNND can be confirmed through identification of the IgM antibody in CSF. West Nile virus is a mosquito-borne illness most commonly seen between June and October, making this an unlikely cause of this patient's illness.

KEY POINT

- Herpes simplex virus type 2 can cause acute aseptic meningitis year round and is the most common cause of recurrent viral meningitis.

Bibliography

Nigrovic LE. Aseptic meningitis. Handb Clin Neurol. 2013;112:1153-6. [PMID: 23622323] doi:10.1016/B978-0-444-52910-7.00035-0

Item 32   Answer: D

Educational Objective: Provide appropriate immunizations for a patient with HIV infection.

Human papillomavirus (HPV) is the most appropriate immunization for this patient at this time. He was recently diagnosed with HIV infection and has begun antiretroviral therapy. At baseline, his CD4 cell count is normal. He is in an age group for which HPV immunization is recommended, and that recommendation is the same regardless of HIV status. The presence of genital warts does not change the indication for HPV vaccination. He should begin the HPV vaccine series with the first injection today. Indications for influenza, tetanus-diphtheria-pertussis, and hepatitis A virus (HAV) vaccines are also the same for patients with HIV infection as for the general population.

Pneumococcal vaccination is important for all persons with HIV infection, regardless of CD4 cell count. As with other immunocompromised persons, patients with HIV should receive the 13-valent conjugate and 23-valent polysaccharide vaccines, in that order. This patient has already received the pneumococcal conjugate vaccine and needs the polysaccharide vaccine, but at least 8 weeks must elapse between these two vaccines to allow for better immune response in this prime-boost strategy. Therefore, giving him

the pneumococcal polysaccharide vaccine at this visit would be premature.

Serum IgM antibodies to HAV are detectable at the time of symptom onset and remain detectable for approximately 3 to 6 months. Serum IgG antibodies appear in convalescence and remain detectable for decades. The presence of anti-HAV IgG in the absence of anti-HAV IgM indicates past infection or vaccination. This patient does not need vaccination against HAV.

Hepatitis B virus (HBV) surface antibody testing is negative, indicating a lack of immunity to HBV; he also has risk factors for HBV that would warrant HBV vaccination. However, the patient tested positive for hepatitis B surface antigen, indicating he already has HBV infection and would not benefit from immunization with the HBV vaccine.

KEY POINT

- Indications for influenza, tetanus-diphtheria-pertussis, hepatitis A virus, and human papillomavirus vaccines are the same for patients with HIV infection as for the general population.

Bibliography

Panel on Opportunistic Infections in HIV-Infected Adults and Adolescents. Guidelines for the prevention and treatment of opportunistic infections in HIV-infected adults and adolescents: recommendations from the Centers for Disease Control and Prevention, the National Institutes of Health, and the HIV Medicine Association of the Infectious Diseases Society of America. Available at https://aidsinfo.nih.gov/guidelines/html/4/adult-and-adolescent-opportunistic-infection/0. Accessed April 12, 2018.

Item 33   Answer: E

Educational Objective: Diagnose neuroborreliosis.

This patient should undergo lumbar puncture. He has unilateral facial nerve palsy, headache, neck stiffness, and a circular rash with central clearing that is clinically consistent with erythema migrans. The presence of erythema migrans in a patient with risk factors for Lyme disease is diagnostic of infection. Neuroborreliosis occurs in 10% to 15% of patients with Lyme disease, and cranial nerve palsy, particularly of the facial nerve (cranial nerve VII), is the most common presentation. When unilateral or bilateral facial nerve palsy is present in isolation, oral doxycycline treatment for 14 to 28 days is sufficient for Lyme disease. However, when the central nervous system is involved, parenteral therapy with ceftriaxone, cefotaxime, or penicillin is recommended. In this patient, the presence of headache and nuchal rigidity raise concern for concomitant meningitis. Because confirmation of meningeal involvement would change therapy, a lumbar puncture is first necessary to determine appropriate therapy. Cerebrospinal fluid (CSF) findings in Lyme meningitis are indistinguishable from other forms of aseptic meningitis.

Testing for antibodies to *Borrelia burgdorferi* adds little to the diagnosis because the presence of erythema migrans with cranial neuropathy is sufficient for diagnosis of neuroborreliosis. Serum antibody testing for *B. burgdorferi*

CONT.

infection would be important in the absence of a compatible skin lesion or with inconsistent exposure history.

In neuroborreliosis, a delay in starting antimicrobial treatment is not associated with adverse outcomes as it is in bacterial meningitis, and empiric therapy can be deferred until CSF cell counts are available.

Performing a head CT is unnecessary because Lyme neuroborreliosis is rarely associated with intraparenchymal lesions, and thus the risk of lumbar puncture in this previously healthy, cognitively intact patient is low.

KEY POINT

- In a patient with Lyme disease and possible central nervous system involvement, positive findings on lumbar puncture can support the diagnosis of neuroborreliosis, which necessitates parenteral therapy with ceftriaxone, cefotaxime, or penicillin.

Bibliography

Halperin JJ. Neuroborreliosis. J Neurol. 2017;264:1292-1297. [PMID: 27885483] doi:10.1007/s00415-016-8346-2

Item 34   Answer: D

Educational Objective: Manage potential bioterrorism-related anthrax exposure.

Because this patient has no known direct exposure to anthrax, no treatment is necessary. In cases of proven or suspected anthrax in a family member, no specific treatment or isolation procedures are required for others in the household because spread in health care or household settings has never been demonstrated. In patients with confirmed or suspected bioterrorism-related anthrax exposure, postexposure prophylactic antibiotics, taken for 60 days, should be started as soon as possible. Ciprofloxacin, levofloxacin, and doxycycline are the approved drugs for postexposure prophylaxis in adult patients. In pregnant women, ciprofloxacin is the drug of choice, and although tetracyclines are not recommended during pregnancy, doxycycline can be used with caution when ciprofloxacin is contraindicated. Therapy can be completed with amoxicillin if the isolate is found to be penicillin susceptible. Because of the possibility that residual dormant spores may become active after antibiotics are completed, three subcutaneous injections of anthrax vaccine should be given at 2-week intervals as part of postexposure prophylaxis.

No test is available for the detection of anthrax infection in an asymptomatic person, so taking a swab or performing a blood test would provide no useful information.

The human monoclonal antibodies against anthrax toxin, raxibacumab (available only from the Centers for Disease Control and Prevention) and obiltoxaximab (FDA approved) can be combined with antibiotics for treatment of inhalation anthrax or for postexposure prophylaxis when alternative preventive therapies are not available or appropriate. In this scenario, they are not indicated for the patient or her husband who has received adequate prophylaxis for anthrax and does not have systemic disease.

KEY POINT

- Patients with no known direct exposure to anthrax do not require treatment or separation from those who may be infected.

Bibliography

Hendricks KA, Wright ME, Shadomy SV, Bradley JS, Morrow MG, Pavia AT, et al; Workgroup on Anthrax Clinical Guidelines. Centers for Disease Control and Prevention expert panel meetings on prevention and treatment of anthrax in adults. Emerg Infect Dis. 2014;20. [PMID: 24447897] doi:10.3201/eid2002.130687

Item 35   Answer: D

Educational Objective: Prevent HIV infection in persons at risk with pre-exposure prophylaxis.

The most appropriate preventive measure for this patient is daily tenofovir disoproxil fumarate and emtricitabine (TDF-FTC). He has multiple risk factors for acquiring HIV infection, including having sex with multiple partners without consistent condom use. Data support the use of pre-exposure prophylaxis (PrEP) in specific populations with ongoing high risk for infection, such as sexual partners of infected persons, men who have sex with men, and injection drug users. PrEP is recommended for persons in such groups who can adhere to the daily regimen. Efficacy has varied depending on adherence to the regimen; rates of reduction in new infections ranged from 42% to 75% and up to 92% in patients whose adherence was documented by monitoring drug blood levels. This patient is in a group shown in clinical trials to benefit from PrEP for HIV. Combination tenofovir alafenamide and emtricitabine is being studied for PrEP, but until results of these studies are known, only TDF should be used. Risk of kidney dysfunction from TDF is low, but kidney function should be checked every 6 months during PrEP. Patients taking PrEP should be counseled to continue using barrier precautions and should undergo testing for HIV, other sexually transmitted infections (STIs), and pregnancy in women, every 3 months.

TDF-FTC given as a single dose before or after each sexual exposure has not been proven effective, and because of concerns for lower effectiveness and possible selection for resistance, these methods should not be used for prevention.

Patients should be counseled regarding the need for continued barrier precautions during sex because the effectiveness of PrEP is less than 100% and to reduce transmission of other STIs. However, counseling the patient about consistent condom use without PrEP places the patient at unnecessary risk for HIV infection. PrEP and barrier protection is now the standard of prevention for men who have sex with men at risk for HIV infection.

KEY POINT

- The combination of tenofovir disoproxil fumarate plus emtricitabine taken once daily is more than 90% effective, if taken consistently, in preventing HIV acquisition.

Bibliography

Riddell J 4th, Amico KR, Mayer KH. HIV preexposure prophylaxis: A review. JAMA. 2018;319:1261-1268. [PMID: 29584848] doi:10.1001/jama.2018.1917

Item 36   Answer: A

Educational Objective: Evaluate osteomyelitis in a diabetic foot infection.

A bone biopsy and culture is the next step in the management of osteomyelitis for this patient. Biopsies can be accomplished by open surgical procedure or percutaneously. Confirming a microbiologic diagnosis is needed before antibiotics can be administered.

Indications for amputation include persistent sepsis, inability to tolerate antibiotic therapy, progressive bone destruction despite therapy, and bone destruction that compromises the mechanical integrity of the foot. None of these indications are present in this patient. Surgical debridement of the ulcer may be needed to remove the necrotic tissue, but this can be done at the time of bone biopsy.

With the exception of *Staphylococcus aureus*, microorganisms isolated from culture samples obtained from superficial wounds or sinus tracts correlate poorly with deep cultures from bone; therefore, this practice is of limited value. Bone biopsy with histopathologic assessment and full microbiologic studies is important for diagnosing osteomyelitis, excluding other entities (such as neoplasm), and isolating the causative pathogen(s).

Because the patient has no signs of skin or soft tissue infection or of sepsis, antibiotics are not immediately needed; furthermore, the provision of empiric antibiotics would also decrease the yield of a subsequent bone biopsy. Vancomycin and piperacillin-tazobactam might be indicated in the future, pending the results of the bone biopsy. However, a histologic and microbiologic diagnosis confirmation is needed before antibiotics can be administered.

KEY POINT

- Osteomyelitis in a patient with a diabetic foot infection and no evidence of skin or soft tissue infection or sepsis requires a bone biopsy before antibiotics are administered.

Bibliography

Lipsky BA, Berendt AR, Cornia PB, Pile JC, Peters EJ, Armstrong DG, et al; Infectious Diseases Society of America. 2012 Infectious Diseases Society of America clinical practice guideline for the diagnosis and treatment of diabetic foot infections. Clin Infect Dis. 2012;54:e132-73. [PMID: 22619242] doi:10.1093/cid/cis346

Item 37   Answer: D

Educational Objective: Manage a patient based on syphilis serology results.

This woman's serologic results are consistent with successfully treated syphilis, and no additional testing or treatment is indicated. Many laboratories use a "reverse" screening strategy, whereby a treponemal test, such as an enzyme immunoassay (EIA), is performed first and, if positive, is followed by a nontreponemal test (rapid plasma regain [RPR] or Venereal Disease Research Laboratory [VDRL] test). If the EIA is positive and the RPR or VDRL is negative, the positive result should be confirmed by a second treponemal test (such as the fluorescent treponemal antibody test performed in this patient). A positive EIA (confirmed by a second test) with a negative RPR is the expected serologic result in a patient who has been treated for syphilis. The treponemal test (EIA) remains positive indefinitely, but the nontreponemal test (RPR or VDRL) should remain negative.

If the nontreponemal test became positive again, it would indicate a new infection, and treatment, based on disease stage, would be indicated. If this patient had reported no history of treatment for syphilis, she should be treated for syphilis of unknown duration, which consists of 3 weekly doses of intramuscular benzathine penicillin. Single-dose benzathine penicillin is indicated for the treatment of primary, secondary, and early latent syphilis.

Because the positive EIA result was already confirmed by a second treponemal test, the fluorescent treponemal antibody, additional testing with another treponemal test, such as the *Treponema pallidum* particle agglutination assay, is not necessary.

KEY POINT

- In patients with previously treated syphilis, treponemal serology results will remain positive, but nontreponemal tests will be negative; these patients require no further testing or treatment.

Bibliography

Workowski KA, Bolan GA; Centers for Disease Control and Prevention. Sexually transmitted diseases treatment guidelines, 2015. MMWR Recomm Rep. 2015;64:1-137. [PMID: 26042815]

Item 38   Answer: E

Educational Objective: Interpret the results of HIV testing.

This woman had a false-positive result for HIV and should be reassured she does not have HIV infection. She has no symptoms to suggest acute infection. The initial HIV combination immunoassay tests for HIV-1 or HIV-2 antibody and p24 antigen. If reactive, an HIV-1/2 antibody differentiation immunoassay is performed, which differentiates between HIV-1 and HIV-2 antibodies. If the antibody differentiation assay is reactive for HIV-1 antibody, then HIV-1 infection is confirmed. If the antibody differentiation assay is negative, then testing for HIV RNA by nucleic acid amplification is performed. A negative antibody differentiation assay with a positive HIV RNA test would indicate acute HIV infection (in the "window" period after infection but before antibody development). But if the HIV RNA assay is also negative (no HIV RNA detected), then no evidence for HIV infection exists, and the initial test was a false positive. Although false-positive findings are rare, in a population with low pre-test probability (such as in screening), false-positive results on the initial antigen/antibody combination immunoas-say may be seen with higher frequency than true-positive results; waiting for the confirmatory testing results is crucial to avoid misdiagnosis and unnecessary additional testing and treatment.

Because the patient does not have HIV infection, it would be inappropriate to begin antiretroviral therapy. Like-wise, baseline HIV resistance testing is not indicated, nor would it be possible because the patient has no detectable HIV RNA to be genotyped.

It is important to assess the CD4 cell count for all per-sons newly diagnosed with HIV infection so the level of immunocompromise and consequent risk for opportunis-tic infections can be determined and prophylaxis can be started, if indicated. But this patient does not have HIV infec-tion. Testing CD4 cell count as a surrogate for HIV infection is inappropriate because the CD4 level is neither sensitive nor specific for HIV infection.

Western blot testing for HIV is no longer performed as part of the laboratory protocol for diagnosing HIV infection because of problems with sensitivity in acute infection and with interpretation of indeterminate results.

KEY POINT

- A screening HIV test result that is positive on the ini-tial antigen/antibody combination immunoassay but negative on the antibody differentiation immunoassay and nucleic acid amplification testing for HIV RNA represents a false-positive result.

Bibliography
Centers for Disease Control and Prevention and Association of Public Health Laboratories. Laboratory testing for the diagnosis of HIV infection: updated recommendations. Available at http://dx.doi.org/10.15620/cdc.23447. Published June 27, 2014. Accessed November 2, 2017.

Item 39   Answer: A

Educational Objective: Diagnose *Cryptosporidium* infection.

This patient has watery diarrhea associated with swimming pool exposure, and the oocysts observed microscopically represent *Cryptosporidium*. This parasitic protozoan is tol-erant to chlorine and can persist for days in a chlorinated pool. *Cryptosporidium* has become the leading cause of swimming pool–related outbreaks of diarrheal illness. Swal-lowing infected water can result in infection. The incuba-tion period is about 1 week, and the clinical presentation typically includes watery diarrhea, crampy abdominal pain, dehydration, fever, malaise, nausea, vomiting, and weight loss. The infection typically resolves in immunocompetent persons, but infection can be more serious and prolonged in those with immunocompromise, particularly in persons with AIDS who are not receiving combination antiretrovi-ral therapy. Diagnosis can be established microscopically

by visualization of oocysts with modified acid-fast stain-ing. Because oocysts are shed intermittently, diagnosis may require stool antigen testing using polymerase chain reac-tion, enzyme immunoassay, or direct fluorescent antibody testing.

Although enterohemorrhagic *Escherichia coli* (EHEC) infection can be acquired by aspiration of contaminated swimming pool water, it typically produces bloody diarrhea. EHEC is a gram-negative rod that does not exhibit modified acid-fast staining.

Norovirus is the most common cause of gastroenteritis and is characterized by explosive vomiting and diarrhea. It is spread person to person through the fecal-oral route, lead-ing to community outbreaks. But the virus is not visualized with modified acid-fast staining. A diagnostic assay for viral gastroenteritis with polymerase chain reaction testing is reserved for public health investigation.

Modified acid-fast staining can detect *Nocardia* species, but the organisms are filamentous branching rods. Infection usually involves the lungs, central nervous system, and skin, but not the gastrointestinal tract.

Vibrio parahaemolyticus lives in salt water and causes diarrhea, usually after consumption of undercooked shellfish, especially oysters. This gram-negative rod is not detected with a modified acid-fast stain and requires special culture media with high salt content for growth.

KEY POINT

- The protozoan *Cryptosporidium* is the most common cause of swimming pool–related outbreaks of diar-rhea; diagnosis is made by microscopic examination of the stool or by stool antigen testing.

Bibliography
Wright SG. Protozoan infections of the gastrointestinal tract. Infect Dis Clin North Am. 2012;26:323-39. [PMID: 22632642] doi:10.1016/j.idc.2012.03.009

Item 40   Answer: C

Educational Objective: Prevent travelers' diarrhea in a patient with inflammatory bowel disease.

Ciprofloxacin is the most appropriate preventive measure for this patient. Travelers' diarrhea, defined as three or more loose or watery bowel movements per day associated with other signs or symptoms such as fever, abdominal pain, cramps, or blood in the stool, is the most common travel-associated infection; it has an incidence of 10% to 40% for trips lasting more than 1 week. Enterotoxigenic *Escherichia coli* is the causative agent in most cases. The risk of infection is related to certain geographic travel destinations (South and Southeast Asia, Central and South America, the Middle East and sub-Saharan Africa) as well as individual characteristics. Persons with chronic inflammatory bowel disease (Crohn and ulcerative colitis) or who are immunocompromised (HIV, organ transplantation, those taking immunosuppressant medications) are particularly susceptible. Although most diarrheal episodes are self-limited and resolve within a few days, they can sometimes be protracted and severe, causing significant volume depletion and electrolyte imbalance. In some persons, chronic diarrhea or irritable bowel syndrome may persist for many months after the initial travel diarrhea episode has subsided. Prevention strategies generally focus on advice for avoiding potentially contaminated water and food, but studies have not conclusively proven these measures to be significantly effective. Prophylactic administration of systemic antibiotics has been determined to be highly effective in preventing infection, but it should only be offered to those at greatest risk for complications should infection occur. Nevertheless, in these higher risk persons, the duration of antibiotic administration should not extend beyond 2 to 3 weeks in an effort to decrease the chances of medication-related adverse effects or the development of drug resistance. The fluoroquinolone antibiotics (ciprofloxacin or norfloxacin) are the preferred drugs.

The macrolide antibiotic azithromycin is a highly effective agent for the treatment of various bacterial pathogens causing enterocolitis, but it has not been adequately evaluated as a prophylactic medication.

More than two thirds of persons who took bismuth subsalicylate to prevent diarrhea while traveling found it effective. However, it requires multiple daily doses, has potential adverse effects, and would be contraindicated in this woman with an aspirin allergy.

Probiotics have been proposed for the prevention and treatment of numerous medical disorders, but proven benefit has been limited to only a handful of disorders; travelers' diarrhea is not one of them.

Even though the risk of infection is less than 50%, this woman has Crohn colitis, so not recommending chemoprophylaxis may place her at undue risk.

KEY POINT

• Persons with chronic inflammatory bowel disease or who are immunocompromised are most susceptible to severe travelers' diarrhea or complications, and prophylaxis (fluoroquinolones preferred) should be provided to these patients.

Bibliography

Steffen R, Hill DR, DuPont HL. Traveler's diarrhea: a clinical review. JAMA. 2015;313:71-80. [PMID: 25562268] doi:10.1001/jama.2014.17006

Item 41   Answer: A

Educational Objective: Prevent central line–associated bloodstream infection.

This patient's central venous catheter (CVC) should be assessed daily for continued necessity and potential removal. Approximately 250,000 central line–associated bloodstream infections (CLABSIs) occur in the United States every year, with 80,000 occurring in the ICU. CLABSIs increase length of hospital stay up to 24 days and have an attributable mortality rate of 35%. Approximately 55% of patients in the ICU

and 24% of those in other units have a central line. Antimicrobial resistance is a problem for most CLABSI pathogens. The risk of CLABSI can be reduced by routinely incorporating the CVC bundle as part of patient care. The CVC insertion bundle includes hand hygiene; use of full barrier precautions (including a large full-body sterile drape to cover the patient during catheter insertion) and personal protective equipment (mask, cap, sterile gown, and gloves); chlorhexidine skin antisepsis; selection of optimal catheter type (such as selecting the minimum number of ports or lumens needed) and site; sterile dressing; and daily review of line necessity with prompt removal of unnecessary catheters. The daily review of line necessity and documentation can be achieved with multidisciplinary rounds, daily reminders, and automated alerts. These practices are important for decreasing the risk of developing CLABSIs. Just as with the insertion bundle, a maintenance bundle helps decrease the risk of introducing organisms during use of the catheter. Components of the maintenance bundle include daily review of line necessity with prompt removal of unnecessary catheters, hand hygiene before manipulation of the intravenous system, care of injection ports, and proper monitoring of catheter site dressing and dressing changes.

Guidelines recommend against routinely replacing CVCs (or arterial catheters) and administering antimicrobial prophylaxis for short-term or tunneled catheter insertion. Neither practice has been shown to decrease central line–associated infections. In fact, routinely changing central catheters may increase the risk of infection by introducing bacteria from the skin at the time of insertion.

KEY POINT

• Central venous catheters should be assessed daily for continued necessity and removed promptly when they are no longer needed.

Bibliography

Marschall J, Mermel LA, Fakih M, Hadaway L, Kallen A, O'Grady NP, et al; Society for Healthcare Epidemiology of America. Strategies to prevent central line-associated bloodstream infections in acute care hospitals: 2014 update. Infect Control Hosp Epidemiol. 2014;35:753-71. [PMID: 24915204] doi:10.1086/676533

Item 42   Answer: E

Educational Objective: Treat *Cyclospora* parasitic infection.

This patient has travel-associated *Cyclospora* infection and should be treated with trimethoprim-sulfamethoxazole. *Cyclospora* protozoan infections are typically acquired after consumption of fecal-contaminated food or water, particularly in countries where the parasite is endemic, such as Peru, Guatemala, Haiti, and Nepal. *Cyclospora* infections may also be acquired through consumption of fresh produce imported from tropical areas. The incubation period is approximately 1 week (range, 2 days to ≥2 weeks). The clinical presentation usually consists of crampy abdominal pain, anorexia, bloating, decreased appetite, fatigue, flatulence, low-grade fever, malaise, nausea, watery diarrhea, and weight loss. Persons with HIV infection may have more severe symptoms associated with wasting.

Diagnosis can be established microscopically by visualization of oocysts with modified acid-fast staining; fluorescence microscopy can be used as well. Several stool specimens may be required because *Cyclospora* oocysts may be shed intermittently and at low levels, even in persons with profuse diarrhea. Polymerase chain reaction assays appear to have the greatest sensitivity for the diagnosis of a *Cyclospora* infection.

The recommended treatment is one double-strength tablet of trimethoprim-sulfamethoxazole taken orally twice daily for 7 to 10 days. The Centers for Disease Control and Prevention states no effective alternative treatments have been identified for persons who are allergic to or cannot tolerate trimethoprim-sulfamethoxazole; observation and symptomatic care is recommended for those patients.

Atovaquone has activity against protozoans such as *Pneumocystis jirovecii*, *Toxoplasma*, *Plasmodium*, and *Babesia*, but not *Cyclospora*.

Metronidazole has activity against some protozoans, including *Giardia*, *Entamoeba*, and *Trichomonas*, but not *Cyclospora*.

Pyrimethamine has activity against protozoans such as *Toxoplasma*, *Pneumocystis jirovecii*, and *Isospora belli*, but not *Cyclospora*.

Quinacrine can be used to treat *Giardia* but is not effective against *Cyclospora*.

KEY POINT

- *Cyclospora* infection is treated with oral trimethoprim-sulfamethoxazole.

Bibliography

Wright SG. Protozoan infections of the gastrointestinal tract. Infect Dis Clin North Am. 2012;26:323-39. [PMID: 22632642] doi:10.1016/j.idc.2012.03.009

Item 43   Answer: A

Educational Objective: Prevent perinatal transmission of HIV.

This pregnant woman with well-controlled HIV infection should continue the same antiretroviral regimen. Antiretroviral therapy during pregnancy is crucial and significantly decreases the risk of perinatal transmission of HIV to the baby. Although most transmission in untreated women occurs at the time of delivery, in utero transmission also occurs, and maintaining therapy throughout pregnancy or starting therapy immediately is important to significantly reduce the risk. Although concerns have been raised regarding the safety of efavirenz and tenofovir disoproxil fumarate in pregnancy, more recent data demonstrate the safety of these agents, including in the first trimester. A woman whose HIV is well controlled and is found to be pregnant should continue the same regimen unless another reason exists to change it.

Pausing antiretroviral therapy would result in rebound of viral replication and viremia, which would significantly increase the risk of in utero transmission of HIV to the developing fetus.

Testing for HIV drug resistance can be genotypic (looking for specific mutations associated with resistance to specific drugs) or phenotypic (assessing whether HIV can replicate in the presence of achievable levels of specific drugs). Resistance testing should always be done before an initial drug regimen is chosen and when treatment failure occurs, as indicated by failure to suppress viral load or an increase in viral load that was previously suppressed. Resistance testing is unnecessary at this time because no virologic failure is evident that would necessitate changing therapy. Moreover, it would not be possible to perform resistance testing in a patient with an undetectable viral load because not enough virus is present to test. A viral load level greater than 500 copies/mL is usually necessary to successfully perform resistance testing.

Zidovudine, lamivudine, and ritonavir-boosted lopinavir is a valid alternative for treating HIV; it was previously a preferred regimen in pregnancy. However, changing this patient's therapy, which is well tolerated and controls her HIV infection well, is unnecessary and would only risk new adverse effects, poor adherence (because of more pills or more frequent dosing), or treatment failure.

KEY POINT

- Antiretroviral therapy during pregnancy is crucial and significantly decreases the risk of perinatal transmission of HIV to the baby.

Bibliography

Panel on Treatment of Pregnant Women with HIV Infection and Prevention of Perinatal Transmission. Recommendations for the use of antiretroviral drugs in pregnant women with HIV infection and interventions to reduce perinatal HIV transmission in the United States. Available at https://aidsinfo.nih.gov/guidelines/html/3/perinatal/0. Accessed April 12, 2018.

Item 44   Answer: C

Educational Objective: Prevent acute hepatitis A infection.

This patient should be given a single dose of hepatitis A vaccine. Worldwide, hepatitis A is the most common cause of acute viral hepatitis. Infection with this human-only RNA picornavirus is spread primarily through the fecal-oral route. Rates of endemicity are highest in developing nations, where hygiene and sanitary measures are less than optimal. Since the availability of effective hepatitis A vaccines in the mid-1990s, this enteric virus has been designated the leading cause of infection and death among vaccine-preventable diseases. Infected adolescents and adults usually present with fever, malaise, nausea, and anorexia, with more than 70% exhibiting jaundice. Most infection is benign and resolves uneventfully. Rarely, patients may experience fulminant hepatitis and acute liver failure. However, hepatitis A does not become a chronic disease. Either of the two inactivated cell culture–produced vaccines that have become part of the recommended routine childhood vaccine schedule can be used. In addition to avoiding potentially contaminated food and water, vaccination is also strongly advised for those planning to travel to areas that pose significant risk of infection. Ideally, vaccination should occur at least 2 to 4 weeks before departure. Nevertheless, a single dose of vaccine given any time before travel provides adequate protection in otherwise healthy persons. Depending on the particular vaccine product used, a second dose is administered between 6 to 18 months later.

Another dose of vaccine administered 7 days after the first would have no immunologic boosting effect.

Passive immunization with intramuscular immune globulin adds no benefit when administered alone or in combination with vaccination for most healthy patients when time before travel is short. However, to optimally guard against infection, immune globulin is recommended with vaccination in persons with chronic liver disease or other chronic medical conditions, immunocompromised states, and older adults if travel is scheduled in less than 2 weeks. Immune globulin alone would also be warranted in persons who are allergic to or decline vaccination and in children younger than 12 months for whom the vaccine is not approved.

Providing no intervention would place this traveler at undue risk of acquiring hepatitis A infection.

KEY POINT

- Hepatitis A vaccination should ideally occur 2 to 4 weeks before travel to an endemic region; however, a single dose of the vaccine given any time before travel provides adequate protection to otherwise healthy persons.

Bibliography

Fiore AE, Wasley A, Bell BP; Advisory Committee on Immunization Practices (ACIP). Prevention of hepatitis A through active or passive immunization: recommendations of the Advisory Committee on Immunization Practices (ACIP). MMWR Recomm Rep. 2006;55:1-23. [PMID: 16708058]

Item 45　　Answer:　D

Educational Objective: Treat multidrug-resistant urinary tract infection.

Antibiotic therapy should be switched from piperacillin-tazobactam to meropenem. This patient has a complicated urinary tract infection (UTI), defined by the presence of a chronic indwelling urinary catheter. The pattern of antibiotic susceptibility of *Escherichia coli* from the urine culture suggests an extended-spectrum β-lactamase (ESBL)–producing organism. ESBL-producing gram-negative organisms are capable of hydrolyzing higher generation cephalosporins that have an oxyimino side chain, including cefotaxime, ceftazidime, ceftriaxone, and cefepime. Laboratory identification of ESBLs is difficult because they are a heteroge-

neous group of enzymes. The carbapenem class of antibiotics (imipenem, meropenem, doripenem, ertapenem) is the preferred class of agents for treating infections with ESBL-producing organisms.

Adding gentamicin would provide no benefit. Additionally, this patient has kidney disease; thus, aminoglycosides should be avoided if at all possible.

On laboratory testing, ESBL-producing gram-negative organisms may appear susceptible to piperacillin-tazobactam; however, susceptibility breakpoints do not always reflect clinical success. Thus, piperacillin-tazobactam may be insufficient to treat infections with ESBL-producing organisms. An exception is uncomplicated UTI, in which piperacillin-tazobactam may be effective because high concentrations of the antibiotic are achievable in urine.

The oxyimino cephalosporins (such as cefepime) should not be used, even if an ESBL-producing organism appears to be susceptible on laboratory testing. Treatment failures are common, even with higher doses, so carbapenems are the preferred antibiotic.

KEY POINT

- The carbapenem class of antibiotics (imipenem, meropenem, doripenem, ertapenem) is the preferred class of agents for treating infections with extended-spectrum β-lactamase–producing organisms.

Bibliography

Kaye KS, Pogue JM. Infections caused by resistant gram-negative bacteria: epidemiology and management. Pharmacotherapy. 2015;35:949-62. [PMID: 26497481] doi:10.1002/phar.1636

Item 46　　Answer:　D

Educational Objective: Monitor for adverse effects of daptomycin therapy in an outpatient.

Patients receiving outpatient daptomycin therapy should undergo baseline measurement of kidney function and creatine kinase (CK) followed by weekly monitoring. Patients should also be screened for symptoms of myopathy. Daptomycin is commonly used for outpatient parenteral antibiotic therapy (OPAT) because of its safety profile, ease of administration (once daily), and good activity against gram-positive bacteria, including vancomycin-resistant enterococci and methicillin-resistant *Staphylococcus aureus*. However, daptomycin is known to cause elevated levels of CK and can contribute to the development of myopathy during therapy. Daptomycin should be discontinued in asymptomatic patients if CK levels increase to greater than 10 times the upper limit of normal or the CK level is greater than 5 times the upper limit of normal with symptoms of myopathy. Concomitant treatment with statins (particularly simvastatin and atorvastatin) may increase the chance of developing an elevated CK level; it is suggested that statins be discontinued if possible during daptomycin treatment. If statins cannot be discontinued, or if kidney dysfunction is evident, the CK level should be monitored more frequently than once weekly. Likewise, the creatinine level should also be monitored because daptomycin dosing may require adjustment (lower dose or dosing interval of every other day), and CK may require more frequent monitoring if the creatinine level increases.

Daptomycin use does not require electrocardiographic monitoring, and it has no effect on the bone marrow (for example, erythrocyte or platelet suppression), pancreas, lipid levels, or blood glucose level; so weekly amylase, triglyceride, glucose, and hemoglobin measurements and platelet count monitoring are unnecessary (although periodic leukocyte counts may be necessary in some patients for monitoring of the primary infection). It is important for patients undergoing OPAT to have close follow-up to monitor for any adverse effects from antibiotic therapy (including development of vascular access infections) as well as resolution of the infection being treated.

KEY POINT

- Patients receiving daptomycin therapy should undergo baseline measurement of kidney function and creatine kinase level followed by weekly monitoring.

Bibliography

Cervera C, Sanroma P, González-Ramallo V, García de la María C, Sanclemente G, Sopena N, et al; DAPTODOM Investigators. Safety and efficacy of daptomycin in outpatient parenteral antimicrobial therapy: a prospective and multicenter cohort study (DAPTODOM trial). Infect Dis (Lond). 2017;49:200-207. [PMID: 27820968] doi:10.1080/23744235.2016.1247292

Item 47   Answer: D

Educational Objective: Identify the cause of Kaposi sarcoma.

This patient has Kaposi sarcoma caused by human herpes virus (HHV) type 8. It is found primarily in men who have sex with other men and who have AIDS. This patient's clinical presentation is typical for Kaposi sarcoma, with painless violaceous skin nodules with oral involvement. The treatment for Kaposi sarcoma includes antiretroviral therapy, local therapies (radiation therapy, intralesional chemotherapy, cryotherapy, or topical retinoids), and systemic therapies such as interferon or chemotherapy.

Cytomegalovirus (HHV-5) infections are most commonly asymptomatic, but they can also present with a mononucleosis-like syndrome and may reactivate in patients with cellular immunodeficiency such as AIDS or in those who have had a solid organ or bone marrow transplantation. Cytomegalovirus does not cause skin nodules but can present with retinitis (in AIDS), pneumonia, hepatitis, adrenalitis, pancytopenia, gastritis, or colitis.

Epstein-Barr virus (EBV) (HHV-4) is the main cause of infectious mononucleosis presenting with fever, exudative pharyngitis, cervical lymphadenopathy, and splenomegaly. EBV reactivation is associated with the development of T-cell and B-cell lymphomas, Hodgkin and Burkitt lymphoma, nasopharyngeal carcinoma, and posttransplant lymphoproliferative disease in solid organ transplantation.

Human herpes virus type 6 causes roseola infantum, febrile seizures in children, and cytomegalovirus-seronegative and EBV-seronegative mononucleosis. It does not cause skin nodules. Recipients of bone marrow transplantation may also develop encephalitis, hepatitis, pneumonia, rash, graft-versus-host disease, and delayed engraftment.

KEY POINT

- Kaposi sarcoma can develop in patients with AIDS infected with human herpes virus type 8, presenting with painless violaceous skin nodules with oral involvement.

Bibliography

De Paoli P, Carbone A. Kaposi's sarcoma herpesvirus: twenty years after its discovery. Eur Rev Med Pharmacol Sci. 2016;20:1288-94. [PMID: 27097948]

Item 48   Answer: B

Educational Objective: Treat osteomyelitis associated with orthopedic hardware.

Cefazolin and rifampin are appropriate therapy for treatment of methicillin-sensitive *Staphylococcus aureus* (MSSA) osteomyelitis associated with orthopedic hardware. Identification of the causative pathogen, administration of adequate antimicrobials for a prolonged duration, surgical debridement (if warranted), and removal of orthopedic prosthetic devices (if feasible) influence the success of osteomyelitis treatment. Optimal management of this patient's infection includes hardware removal; however, this is not possible because the fracture has not yet healed. Hardware-associated infections caused by *S. aureus* are difficult to eradicate because of the biofilm that forms on the hardware. First-line treatment of MSSA osteomyelitis consists of a β-lactam agent such as cefazolin; a randomized controlled trial and systematic review of the literature have demonstrated that if infected hardware cannot be removed, the addition of rifampin increases the chances of therapeutic success compared with an antistaphylococcal agent alone.

Although cefazolin has activity against MSSA as well as good bone penetration, it would not be an appropriate therapeutic option for the treatment of hardware-associated osteomyelitis without the addition of rifampin.

Ceftaroline has coverage for MSSA, methicillin-resistant *S. aureus*, and Enterobacteriaceae, but it is unnecessarily broad coverage for the treatment of this patient's MSSA infection.

Vancomycin, a bacteriostatic agent, is less effective than β-lactam agents for the treatment of MSSA and is typically restricted to patients with drug intolerance or allergy.

KEY POINT

- Rifampin should be used in combination with another antistaphylococcal agent when managing *Staphylococcus aureus* osteomyelitis in the setting of orthopedic hardware if the hardware cannot be removed.

Bibliography

Kim BN, Kim ES, Oh MD. Oral antibiotic treatment of staphylococcal bone and joint infections in adults. J Antimicrob Chemother. 2014;69:309-22. [PMID: 24072167] doi:10.1093/jac/dkt374

Item 49   Answer: A

Educational Objective: **Treat an immunocompromised patient after a dog bite.**

The most appropriate management for this patient would be administration of amoxicillin-clavulanate. Because of asplenia, he is immunodeficient and should receive prophylactic antibiotic therapy after the dog bite, even without evidence of infection. Infections typically result from the host's skin flora and the animal's mouth flora. This flora is a mix of aerobic and anaerobic organisms, including staphylococci, streptococci, *Bacteroides* species, *Porphyromonas* species, *Fusobacterium* species, *Capnocytophaga canimorsus*, and *Pasteurella* species. *C. canimorsus* is a gram-negative bacillus that can cause overwhelming sepsis in patients with functional or anatomic asplenia who have experienced a dog bite or scratch. Because of its activity against pathogens associated with animal bite wounds, a 3- to 5-day course of amoxicillin-clavulanate is recommended for patients who are immunosuppressed (including patients with cirrhosis and asplenia); have wounds with associated edema, lymphatic or venous insufficiency, or crush injury; have wounds involving a joint or bone; have deep puncture wounds; or have moderate to severe injuries, especially when involving the face, genitalia, or hand. If a patient is allergic to penicillin, a combination of trimethoprim-sulfamethoxazole or a fluoroquinolone or doxycycline plus clindamycin or metronidazole can be used.

Because these infections are typically polymicrobial, consisting of aerobic and anaerobic bacteria, neither ciprofloxacin nor metronidazole alone would be adequate. Ciprofloxacin lacks anaerobic bacterial coverage, and metronidazole lacks aerobic activity.

Because of this the patient's immunodeficiency, observation alone would not be recommended by the Infectious Diseases Society of America guidelines.

KEY POINT

- Amoxicillin-clavulanate is recommended for patients with animal bites who are immunosuppressed (including patients with cirrhosis and asplenia); have wounds with associated edema, lymphatic or venous insufficiency, or crush injury; have wounds involving a joint or bone; have deep puncture wounds; or have moderate to severe injuries, especially when involving the face, genitalia, or hand.

Bibliography

Stevens DL, Bisno AL, Chambers HF, Dellinger EP, Goldstein EJ, Gorbach SL, et al. Practice guidelines for the diagnosis and management of skin and soft tissue infections: 2014 update by the infectious diseases society of America. Clin Infect Dis. 2014;59:147-59. [PMID: 24947530] doi:10.1093/cid/ciu296

Item 50   Answer: A

Educational Objective: **Treat multidrug-resistant intra-abdominal infection.**

The *Pseudomonas* isolate should be tested for susceptibility to ceftolozane-tazobactam and colistin. This patient has an intra-abdominal infection caused by carbapenem-resistant (meropenem and doripenem) *Pseudomonas aeruginosa.* The antimicrobial options for treating carbapenem-resistant organisms are limited. Ceftolozane-tazobactam consists of a newer antipseudomonal cephalosporin combined with a β-lactamase inhibitor. It has activity against some extended-spectrum β-lactamase (ESBL)–producing gram-negative organisms as well as carbapenem-resistant strains of *Pseudomonas*. Its efficacy is reduced in patients whose creatinine clearance rate is 50 mL/min or less. Ceftolozane-tazobactam is approved to treat complicated urinary tract infections and complicated intra-abdominal infections. For complicated intra-abdominal infections, ceftolozane-tazobactam must be paired with metronidazole because it lacks antianaerobic activity. This patient's penicillin allergy is not an anaphylactic reaction, so it is reasonable to consider a cephalosporin in her treatment.

Colistin is an older antimicrobial agent that has made a resurgence because of its bactericidal activity against pan-resistant gram-negative organisms (including carbapenem-resistant, gram-negative organisms). Half of patients who are administered colistin develop nephrotoxicity, which limits the drug's usefulness in many cases. Kidney function should be closely monitored during administration, and colistin should be dose adjusted for patients with kidney disease. Paresthesias are a commonly reported neurotoxicity. Unfortunately, colistin resistance has been reported and appears to be increasing.

Ertapenem is a non-antipseudomonal carbapenem, so it would not be an option for this patient. Likewise, tobramycin is an aminoglycoside, which has poor activity and penetration into abscesses and would not be a consideration for this patient.

Fosfomycin is used to treat urinary tract infections caused by several multidrug-resistant organisms (such as vancomycin-resistant enterococci, methicillin-resistant *Staphylococcus aureus*, and resistant *Klebsiella pneumoniae*). Fosfomycin has poor tissue penetration and is not indicated for infections other than uncomplicated urinary tract infections.

Minocycline is another older antimicrobial agent that has been used recently to treat multidrug-resistant *Acinetobacter* as well as *Stenotrophomonas maltophilia* infections, but it does not have activity against *Pseudomonas*.

KEY POINT

- Ceftolozane-tazobactam is a newer antipseudomonal cephalosporin combined with a β-lactamase inhibitor that can be used in the treatment of multidrug-resistant intra-abdominal infection.

Bibliography

Morrill HJ, Pogue JM, Kaye KS, LaPlante KL. Treatment options for carbapenem-resistant Enterobacteriaceae infections. Open Forum Infect Dis. 2015;2:ofv050. [PMID: 26125030] doi:10.1093/ofid/ofv050

Item 51   Answer: E

Educational Objective: Evaluate community-acquired pneumonia in a pregnant patient.

Streptococcus pneumoniae is the most likely cause of this patient's community-acquired pneumonia (CAP). Pneumonia is the most common cause of fatal nonobstetric infection in pregnancy. The microbiology of CAP in pregnancy is similar to that seen in the general population. Among patients requiring hospitalization, the most common pathogens are *S. pneumoniae*, *Haemophilus influenzae*, and atypical organisms, including *Legionella* species, *Chlamydia pneumoniae*, and *Mycoplasma pneumoniae*. Empiric treatment of pregnant patients is similar to that in nonpregnant adults, although quinolones and tetracyclines are relatively contraindicated because of the potential for teratogenic effects. In addition to these common bacterial causes of CAP, pregnant women are at increased risk for serious viral pneumonia from influenza virus and varicella-zoster virus, so it is recommended that pregnant women receive seasonal influenza vaccination.

Gram-negative bacteria, including *Klebsiella pneumoniae*, *Pseudomonas aeruginosa*, *Acinetobacter* species, *Escherichia coli*, and *Enterobacter* species, are rarely implicated in CAP, including among pregnant women hospitalized for pneumonia. Most patients with CAP caused by gram-negative bacteria have a predisposing risk factor, such as bronchiectasis, cystic fibrosis, or COPD, and develop severe pneumonia necessitating admission and care in the ICU.

Pregnancy causes a decrease in T-cell function, and pregnant women are at increased risk for severe *Listeria* infections, including meningitis and sepsis. However, *Listeria* rarely causes pulmonary infection and would be an unlikely cause of infection in this patient.

Staphylococcus aureus is an increasingly recognized cause of CAP, with risk factors including antecedent viral infection or injection drug use. Maternal *S. aureus* infection can occur perinatally, related to delivery, surgery, or indwelling lines, but remains a rare cause of CAP in the prenatal period.

KEY POINT

- The microbiology of community-acquired pneumonia in pregnancy is similar to that seen in the general population; among patients requiring hospitalization, the most common pathogens are *Streptococcus pneumoniae*, *Haemophilus influenzae*, and atypical organisms, including *Legionella* species, *Chlamydia pneumoniae*, and *Mycoplasma pneumoniae*.

Bibliography

Mehta N, Chen K, Hardy E, Powrie R. Respiratory disease in pregnancy. Best Pract Res Clin Obstet Gynaecol. 2015;29:598-611. [PMID: 25997564] doi:10.1016/j.bpobgyn.2015.04.005

Item 52   Answer: B

Educational Objective: Treat influenza virus infection with a neuraminidase inhibitor.

The most appropriate treatment for this patient is the neuraminidase inhibitor oseltamivir. During a confirmed local influenza outbreak, infection can be reliably diagnosed on the basis of clinical criteria alone. When confirmation is needed, rapid antigen tests of respiratory samples from nasopharyngeal swabs detect influenza A and B. Positive test results are highly specific. However, sensitivity ranges from 40% to 80%. Detection of viral nucleic acid by polymerase chain reaction (PCR) is rapid, has high sensitivity and specificity, and can determine the type and subtype of influenza virus. Annual influenza vaccination is the most effective intervention for preventing influenza and is recommended for all persons 6 months or older. Only a few randomized trials have assessed the efficacy of influenza vaccines in older individuals. These trials suggest that the vaccines are approximately 60% effective against influenza in adults 65 years and older. Nevertheless, immunization is likely to prevent hospitalization in older adults. Neuraminidase inhibitors have activity against influenza A and B. They can be given orally (oseltamivir), intranasally (zanamivir), or intravenously (peramivir). Antiviral therapy is recommended for severe disease, including all hospitalized patients or those with confirmed or suspected influenza infection at high risk for complications. Older adult patients (older than ≥65 years), young children, pregnant women, and patients with chronic medical conditions (especially chronic lung disease and heart disease) are at higher risk for severe primary influenza complications such as superimposed bacterial pneumonia caused by *Streptococcus pneumoniae* or *Staphylococcus aureus* and death.

M2 inhibitors, such as amantadine and rimantadine, were the first agents introduced for influenza treatment, but they are only active against influenza A. Therefore, these agents would be ineffective against this patient's infection with influenza B.

Antiviral therapy should be started within 48 hours of symptom onset in patients with a positive rapid influenza test because it decreases recovery time, hospitalization rates, and complications. Because this patient can be treated as an outpatient, either oseltamivir or zanamivir would be appropriate choices. Intravenous peramivir is typically reserved for patients who cannot tolerate or are otherwise incapable of taking inhaled or enteral agents.

KEY POINT

- Neuraminidase inhibitors (oseltamivir, zanamivir, peramivir) are indicated for the treatment of influenza A and B and can be administered through various routes (oral, intranasal, intravenous).

Bibliography

Uyeki TM. Influenza. Ann Intern Med. 2017;167:ITC33-ITC48. [PMID: 28869984] doi:10.7326/AITC201709050

Item 53   Answer: A

Educational Objective: Manage urinary tract infections in men.

This patient should be given intravenous cefepime and fluids and should undergo kidney ultrasonography. According to the 2016 Critical Care Congress Third International Consensus Definition of Sepsis and Septic Shock (Sepsis-3), this man is septic. The probable source of his severe infection is the urinary tract (UTI), likely acute prostatitis, which is the most significant cause of bacteremia in older adult men. The prompt administration of adequate antimicrobial therapy is the most important factor in decreasing morbidity, mortality, and length of hospital stay in patients with sepsis. Cefepime is an appropriate choice because it possesses dependable bactericidal activity against common urinary pathogens as well as potentially drug-resistant organisms, including *Pseudomonas*. In addition to antimicrobial therapy and supportive medical care, men with febrile UTIs require anatomic assessment of the upper and lower urinary tract by either kidney ultrasonography or CT with contrast (more sensitive, but contraindicated with kidney disease) to determine the need for source control. When acute prostatitis is the presumed diagnosis, imaging generally is unnecessary, but assurance that this patient with sepsis does not have a prostatic abscess may prove beneficial if his fever persists beyond 72 hours.

The empiric use of ciprofloxacin or other fluoroquinolone antibiotics in a hospitalized patient with a complicated UTI is no longer recommended because several strains of *Escherichia coli* and other Enterobacteriaceae have become resistant to these agents.

Detection of a boggy and tender prostate gland on gentle digital rectal examination would suggest a prostate focus of infection, but vigorous prostate massage is not indicated in acute prostatitis because of a lack of diagnostic or therapeutic benefit and possibility of facilitating bacteremia.

The β-lactam and β-lactamase inhibitor, piperacillin-tazobactam, would be an adequate initial antibiotic selection but should be avoided in a patient with an undocumented penicillin allergy, even if he has tolerated cephalosporin medications.

KEY POINT

- Men with febrile urinary tract infections require prompt antimicrobial therapy and anatomic assessment of the upper and lower urinary tract.

Bibliography

Schaeffer AJ, Nicolle LE. Clinical practice. Urinary tract infections in older men. N Engl J Med. 2016;374:562-71. [PMID: 26863357] doi:10.1056/NEJMcp1503950

Item 54   Answer: C

Educational Objective: Treat vertebral osteomyelitis in a patient with signs of sepsis.

The patient has vertebral osteomyelitis and clinical findings suggestive of sepsis; empiric antibiotic therapy to cover the most likely pathogens should be initiated. A diagnosis of vertebral osteomyelitis should be considered in patients reporting worsening back or neck pain without an alternate explanation. Local tenderness over the site of spinal infection is frequently detected. Radicular pain, motor weakness, and sensory changes may be present. Common sources of hematogenous osteomyelitis are distant foci of infection (for example, skin and soft tissue, genitourinary, gastrointestinal), intravascular catheters, and infective endocarditis. Hematogenous osteomyelitis is typically monomicrobial, and *Staphylococcus aureus* is the most commonly isolated pathogen; however, aerobic, gram-negative bacilli cause disease in many patients. Certain patient-specific conditions are associated with less common bacterial organisms, including *Salmonella* osteomyelitis in persons with sickle cell disease and *Pseudomonas aeruginosa* bone infection in injection drug users. Lengthy parenteral antimicrobial therapy is the mainstay of treatment. An antistaphylococcal agent with methicillin-resistant *S. aureus* (MRSA) coverage (vancomycin) and a β-lactam with antipseudomonal coverage (cefepime) is an appropriate empiric regimen for suspected osteomyelitis in this patient who uses injection drugs.

Cefazolin does not provide coverage for MRSA, and aminoglycosides, such as gentamicin, have poor penetration into bone.

Vancomycin alone would not provide coverage for gram-negative organisms, which should be included in the empiric therapy for this patient.

Although microbiologic confirmation of the bacterial cause should always be sought, withholding antibiotics in a patient likely to have sepsis (fever, hypotension, tachycardia) is not appropriate. If the patient has positive blood cultures, a presumptive microbiologic diagnosis of vertebral osteomyelitis can usually be made. However, because injection drug users have frequent bacteremia and the patient's bloodstream infection may be unrelated to the vertebral osteomyelitis, some experts would recommend pursuing bone biopsy, even in patients with positive blood cultures.

KEY POINT

- When sepsis is suspected among patients with osteomyelitis, empiric antibiotic therapy should begin, even when the microbial cause of the infection has not yet been determined.

Bibliography

Berbari EF, Kanj SS, Kowalski TJ, Darouiche RO, Widmer AF, Schmitt SK, et al. 2015 Infectious Diseases Society of America (IDSA) clinical practice guidelines for the diagnosis and treatment of native vertebral osteomyelitis in adults. Clin Infect Dis. 2015;61:e26-46. [PMID: 26229122] doi:10.1093/cid/civ482

Item 55   Answer: A

Educational Objective: Diagnose acute HIV infection.

This patient has acute HIV infection. His recent nonspecific viral symptoms are consistent with the acute retroviral syndrome, although they are not diagnostic. Regardless of the presence or absence of symptoms, his HIV testing results support a diagnosis of acute HIV infection. His initial HIV-1/2 antigen/antibody combination immunoassay is reactive, indicating further testing is needed. The HIV-1/HIV-2 antibody differentiation assay is negative, indicating the absence of antibody to HIV; however, the RNA assay is positive for HIV-1 RNA. This finding indicates the patient does not have antibodies to HIV but does demonstrate the presence of virus by nucleic acid amplification testing. The initial combination immunoassay was reactive because of the presence of HIV p24 antigen rather than antibody, which indicates acute infection with HIV before antibody development. The ability to detect acute infection is a key advantage of and improvement in current HIV testing, allowing for earlier detection of infection, faster initiation of treatment, and, consequently, reduced risk of transmission.

In chronic HIV infection, the HIV antibody differentiation immunoassay would have demonstrated antibody to HIV, either HIV-1 (usually) or HIV-2 (rarely). Because no antibody was detected but HIV RNA is present, infection is still in the acute phase before antibody development.

Because the HIV-1 RNA assay was positive at a significant level, the initial HIV antigen/antibody immunoassay result was not a false positive. Although false-positive HIV RNA testing can occur, it is usually at a very low, barely detectable level. This patient's level is substantial, and he has known risk factors and consistent symptoms for acute HIV infection, increasing his pretest probability and making a positive result much more likely a true positive.

HIV-2 infection is rare in the United States. It is ruled out in this patient by the negative HIV-2 antibody result on the HIV-1/HIV-2 antibody differentiation assay.

KEY POINT

- On testing for HIV infection, a positive result on HIV-1/2 antigen/antibody combination immunoassay is followed by testing with the HIV-1/HIV-2 antibody differentiation immunoassay; a negative antibody differentiation immunoassay but a positive follow-up HIV-1 nucleic acid amplification test is diagnostic of acute HIV infection.

Bibliography

Centers for Disease Control and Prevention and Association of Public Health Laboratories. Laboratory testing for the diagnosis of HIV infection: updated recommendations. Available at http://dx.doi.org/10.15620/cdc.23447. Published June 27, 2014. Accessed November 2, 2017.

Item 56   Answer: A

Educational Objective: Treat urethritis with empiric therapy.

The most appropriate treatment is ceftriaxone plus azithromycin. The patient has dysuria and evidence of mucopurulent urethral discharge, which are consistent with urethritis.

Because he is being evaluated in an urgent care setting and may not return for follow-up, empiric therapy is appropriate. A single intramuscular dose of ceftriaxone (250 mg) plus a single oral dose of azithromycin (1 g) will treat *Neisseria gonorrhoeae* and *Chlamydia trachomatis*, the most common causes of urethritis. Diagnostic testing results are still important in case the patient does not respond to empiric therapy and for disease reporting and contact tracing. This man should also be offered HIV and syphilis testing and undergo counseling regarding the use of condoms for all sexual encounters, including oral sex. Some concern exists that sexually active persons, particularly young persons, may believe that oral sex is "safe" and does not pose a risk of sexually transmitted infection (STI) transmission. Most STIs can be acquired through oral sex; the risk of acquiring HIV infection may be lower, but precise data on the relative risk of STI acquisition from specific types of sexual activity are not available.

Doxycycline for 7 days is an alternate therapy for *C. trachomatis*; however, it should be used only when a macrolide allergy precludes the use of azithromycin. It also will not reliably treat *N. gonorrhoeae*.

Trimethoprim-sulfamethoxazole is not an effective treatment for urethritis. Trimethoprim-sulfamethoxazole can potentially be used for empiric therapy for cystitis; however, men with cystitis should not have purulent urethral discharge. Additionally, symptoms of bladder irritation, including increased frequency and urgency, are generally present.

Herpes simplex virus can present as urethritis, and penile ulcers may not be present on physical examination; however, this clinical presentation is less common and should only be considered if the infection fails to respond to treatment for the more common causes of urethritis. Therefore, valacyclovir is not the most appropriate initial empiric therapy for this patient.

KEY POINT

- In a patient with clinical signs and symptoms of urethritis, treatment with ceftriaxone and azithromycin provides appropriate empiric therapy without waiting for microbiologic testing results.

Bibliography

Workowski KA, Bolan GA; Centers for Disease Control and Prevention. Sexually transmitted diseases treatment guidelines, 2015. MMWR Recomm Rep. 2015;64:1-137. [PMID: 26042815]

Item 57   Answer: C

Educational Objective: Prevent opportunistic fungal infections after hematopoietic stem cell transplantation.

Posaconazole is the most appropriate prophylactic therapy for this patient after hospital discharge. Patients who undergo allogeneic hematopoietic stem cell transplantation (HSCT) usually experience a period of prolonged neutropenia after the pretransplant myeloablative conditioning regimen. This prolonged, severe neutropenia is a significant risk factor for invasive bacterial and fungal infections, and prophylaxis for both is indicated. The risk of invasive fungal infection remains elevated, however, even after recovery of neutrophils for the first few months after allogeneic HSCT and even later in the setting of graft-versus-host disease. Therefore, although this patient is doing well and her neutrophil count has recovered, antifungal prophylaxis should be provided in addition to continuing trimethoprim-sulfamethoxazole therapy. Posaconazole provides activity against *Candida* and *Aspergillus* and other moulds that are the cause of an increasing proportion of invasive fungal infections after HSCT.

Acyclovir is used to reduce reactivation of herpes simplex virus during periods of neutropenia, but its administration is no longer needed. Additionally, this patient is seropositive for varicella-zoster virus because of immunization, so varicella-zoster prophylaxis is unnecessary. Finally, acyclovir has no role in preventing reactivation of Epstein-Barr virus or cytomegalovirus, two other infections for which this patient is at risk.

Ciprofloxacin is a preferred agent for antibacterial prophylaxis during neutropenia because it has activity against most of the gram-negative bacteria of greatest concern. But with resolution of neutropenia and completion of therapy for known infection, continued antibacterial therapy should be avoided to lessen toxicities and complications such as *Clostridium difficile* colitis.

Valganciclovir is used to prevent or treat cytomegalovirus infection. This patient is at risk for reactivation cytomegalovirus because of her positive serology. However, because of the leukopenia that is a common toxicity of valganciclovir, a strategy of monitoring for cytomegalovirus and starting pre-emptive therapy only when indicated is preferred over prophylaxis after HSCT.

KEY POINT

- In patients who have undergone hematopoietic stem cell transplantation, the risk of invasive fungal infection remains elevated for the first few months, even after recovery of neutrophil counts, so antifungal prophylaxis should be continued during this time.

Bibliography

Ullmann AJ, Schmidt-Hieber M, Bertz H, Heinz WJ, Kiehl M, Krüger W, et al; Infectious Diseases Working Party of the German Society for Hematology and Medical Oncology (AGIHO/DGHO) and the DAG-KBT (German Working Group for Blood and Marrow Transplantation). Infectious diseases in allogeneic haematopoietic stem cell transplantation: prevention and prophylaxis strategy guidelines 2016. Ann Hematol. 2016;95:1435-55. [PMID: 27339055] doi:10.1007/s00277-016-2711-1

Item 58   Answer: C

Educational Objective: Treat suspected tuberculous meningitis.

The most appropriate management for this patient is four-drug antituberculous therapy (rifampin, isoniazid, pyrazinamide, and ethambutol) plus dexamethasone. Meningitis can be defined as either acute or chronic. The symptoms of acute meningitis typically progress over hours, sometimes days, whereas chronic meningitis generally progresses over 4 or more weeks. Tuberculosis and fungal infection are the most common causes of chronic meningitis. Tuberculous meningitis should be suspected in patients from highly endemic countries who have basilar lymphocytic meningitis associated with cranial neuropathies (particularly involving cranial nerve VI) and hypoglycorrhachia. A history of tuberculosis exposure, an abnormal chest radiograph, a positive tuberculin skin test, and a positive interferon-γ release assay may be clues to the diagnosis, but these can be absent. Cerebrospinal fluid (CSF) acid-fast bacilli stains and cultures are insensitive and may take up to 6 weeks to grow. Patients with a high suspicion for tuberculosis should be treated empirically with rifampin, isoniazid, pyrazinamide, and ethambutol pending culture results and clinical improvement. Adjunctive dexamethasone decreases mortality, especially in patients with normal mental status and no neurologic deficits; it should be started concomitantly with antituberculous therapy.

The most common fungal meningitis in the United States is cryptococcal meningitis. Cryptococcus is inhaled and causes an initial pulmonary infection. Risk factors for dissemination include AIDS, organ transplantation, glucocorticoid treatment, diabetes mellitus, liver dysfunction, and kidney injury. The central nervous system is the most common site of disseminated cryptococcosis. CSF analysis may resemble that of tuberculous meningitis, although monocytes may predominate and the opening pressure is often greater than 200 mm H_2O. An India ink preparation of the CSF will demonstrate cryptococcal organisms in up to 80% of patients with a high organism burden, such as patients with HIV infection, but is only 50% sensitive in patients without HIV. The CSF assay for cryptococcal antigen is highly sensitive and specific for the diagnosis of meningitis and can be obtained soon after lumbar puncture results are available. Recommended induction therapy for cryptococcal meningitis includes amphotericin B and 5-fluorocytosine but is not indicated in this patient who is at low risk for this infection.

Bacterial meningitis is an acute infection with progression of symptoms over hours to days. This patient has chronic lymphocytic meningitis with an extremely low CSF glucose level and a negative CSF Gram stain, making bacterial meningitis unlikely. Initiating vancomycin, ceftriaxone, and dexamethasone is not the most appropriate management.

KEY POINT

- Tuberculosis and cryptococcus are the most common causes of chronic meningitis; empiric treatment for tuberculous meningitis includes four-drug antituberculous therapy (rifampin, isoniazid, pyrazinamide, and ethambutol) plus dexamethasone.

Bibliography

Prasad K, Singh MB, Ryan H. Corticosteroids for managing tuberculous meningitis. Cochrane Database Syst Rev. 2016;4:CD002244. [PMID: 27121755] doi:10.1002/14651858.CD002244.pub4

Item 59   Answer: B

Educational Objective: Treat a patient with latent tuberculosis infection.

The most appropriate management for this patient is to initiate self-administered treatment with isoniazid. He has traveled to a high-risk area for *Mycobacterium tuberculosis*. Before departing for Vietnam, he had a negative tuberculin skin test; however, he returned with a positive screening result for tuberculosis. Because the chest radiograph is negative, he requires treatment for latent tuberculosis rather than treatment with the four-drug regimen for active tuberculosis. Several treatment options exist, and the regimen chosen should be based on comorbidities, knowledge of the drug-susceptibility data from the source patient, and possible drug interactions. Self-administered isoniazid for 9 months is approved for the treatment of latent tuberculosis by the Centers for Disease Control and Prevention for patients with and without HIV infection. In patients being treated for latent tuberculosis who have normal baseline aminotransferase levels and no risk factors for liver disease, routine testing of aminotransferase levels during treatment is unnecessary.

Once-weekly isoniazid and rifapentine only needs to be administered for 12 weeks, not 24 weeks. This regimen must be administered as directly observed therapy (that is, a health care worker directly observes the ingestion of a medication), as are all intermittent therapies. The 12-week regimen can be used instead of 9 months of isoniazid alone for healthy adult patients, including those with HIV coinfection who are not taking antiretroviral agents. It is not recommended for patients suspected of having rifampin- or isoniazid-resistant tuberculosis strains or for patients who are pregnant or plan to become pregnant while taking these agents.

Treatment of active tuberculosis usually consists of multiple drugs for 6 to 9 months administered in two phases: initial and continuation. The core first-line antituberculous agents are isoniazid, rifampin, pyrazinamide, and ethambutol. These agents are administered for 8 weeks as part of the initiation phase. Isoniazid and rifampin are then continued for 4 or 7 months as part of the continuation phase. This patient does not have active tuberculosis (absent symptoms and a normal chest radiograph) and does not require therapy with four antituberculosis drugs.

This patient has latent tuberculosis infection, as detected by the positive interferon-γ release assay. Providing no treatment would put him at risk of developing active disease or exposing close contacts who may then become ill.

KEY POINT

- Prophylactic treatment with isoniazid is recommended for persons with latent tuberculosis infection, determined by a newly positive tuberculosis screening test but no signs or symptoms of active disease; 9 months of daily isoniazid can be self-administered.

Bibliography

Nahid P, Dorman SE, Alipanah N, Barry PM, Brozek JL, Cattamanchi A, et al. Executive summary: Official American Thoracic Society/Centers for Disease Control and Prevention/Infectious Diseases Society of America clinical practice guidelines: treatment of drug-susceptible tuberculosis. Clin Infect Dis. 2016;63:853-67. [PMID: 27621353] doi:10.1093/cid/ciw566

Item 60   Answer: A

Educational Objective: Diagnose *Clostridium difficile* colitis after transplantation.

The most likely diagnosis is colitis caused by *Clostridium difficile*. *C. difficile* infection is the most common cause of health care–associated colitis, and antibiotic use is the most significant risk factor. The patient presents within the first month after solid organ transplantation; this is a time when the most likely infections are nosocomial and similar to those in patients who have had other surgeries. This patient has recently completed antimicrobial treatment for pneumonia and wound infection, increasing his risk for *C. difficile* colitis, which is common in transplant recipients during this time frame. Testing for *C. difficile* colitis and providing treatment would be appropriate at this time. Polymerase chain reaction assays to detect the genes responsible for production of toxins A and B are very sensitive and are increasingly used in the diagnosis of *C. difficile* colitis.

The other concern of most significance in this patient would be cytomegalovirus infection, most likely manifesting as colitis in this scenario. Being a cytomegalovirus-seronegative recipient of an organ from a cytomegalovirus-seropositive donor puts the patient at significant risk for developing cytomegalovirus disease, most commonly in the gastrointestinal tract or as a nonspecific febrile illness. However, because of this risk, he is already receiving prophylaxis with valganciclovir, which significantly lowers the rate of occurrence. His presentation being so early after transplantation also makes cytomegalovirus less likely, because infection most often occurs in the "middle" period, 1 to 6 months after transplantation.

Mycophenolate toxicities include diarrhea, cytopenias, and infection. Although diarrhea is a common adverse effect of mycophenolate, the additional presence of fever and abdominal pain makes this an unlikely cause. *C. difficile* infection must be considered first and ruled out.

Polyoma BK virus causes a nephropathy after transplantation, not diarrhea, and usually occurs later than the first month after transplantation. Definitive diagnosis requires kidney biopsy. When polyoma BK nephropathy occurs, immunosuppression should be reduced to the minimum level necessary to avoid rejection.

KEY POINT

- The first month after solid organ transplantation is when the most likely infections are nosocomial and similar to those in patients who have had other surgeries; patients who have recently completed antimicrobial treatment are particularly at increased risk for *Clostridium difficile* colitis.

Bibliography

Fishman JA. From the classic concepts to modern practice. Clin Microbiol Infect. 2014;20 Suppl 7:4-9. [PMID: 24528498] doi:10.1111/1469-0691.12593

Item 61   Answer: C

Educational Objective: Treat *Neisseria gonorrhoeae* infection.

The most appropriate treatment is ceftriaxone plus azithromycin. This sexually active young woman presented for an annual Pap smear and renewal of oral contraceptives. She was appropriately screened for *Chlamydia trachomatis* and *Neisseria gonorrhoeae* infection using nucleic acid amplification testing. The U.S. Preventive Services Task Force recommends this screening for all sexually active women younger than 25 years. If the patient were older than 25 years, she should be tested because of her new sexual partner. Her screening results are positive for *N. gonorrhoeae*. Even without symptoms or findings on pelvic examination, she should be treated; a significant number of persons with *N. gonorrhoeae* infection are asymptomatic without evidence of cervicitis. Intramuscular ceftriaxone (250 mg) is the preferred therapy for treatment of *N. gonorrhoeae* infection, along with a single dose of oral azithromycin (1 g). Although this regimen is given empirically when *C. trachomatis* and *N. gonorrhoeae* coinfection is suspected (for example, empiric therapy for cervicitis), because of increasing minimum inhibitory concentrations (MIC) to ceftriaxone among *N. gonorrhoeae* isolates in the United States, azithromycin is used even when *C. trachomatis* infection is not present; this combination will increase the success of treatment of the *N. gonorrhoeae* infection.

Oral cefixime does not achieve adequate levels to exceed the MIC of many *N. gonorrhoeae* isolates, so this option should only be used if ceftriaxone is unavailable. In this circumstance, a single dose of oral azithromycin should be administered with the cefixime.

Ciprofloxacin was previously recommended for the treatment of *N. gonorrhoeae* infections; however, the prevalence of fluoroquinolone resistance among *N. gonorrhoeae* isolates has increased, and this antibiotic is no longer recommended.

KEY POINT

- Because of increasing minimum inhibitory concentrations to ceftriaxone among *Neisseria gonorrhoeae* isolates in the United States, this agent should be combined with a single dose of azithromycin.

Bibliography

Workowski KA, Bolan GA; Centers for Disease Control and Prevention. Sexually transmitted diseases treatment guidelines, 2015. MMWR Recomm Rep. 2015;64:1-137. [PMID: 26042815]

Item 62   Answer: C

Educational Objective: Diagnose babesiosis.

This patient's blood smear is most likely to show intraerythrocytic tetrad forms. He has a life-threatening illness characterized by fever and hemolysis and has no spleen. Given his residence in the northeastern United States and his outdoor vocation, severe babesiosis is likely. *Babesia* species are transmitted by the same tick that causes Lyme disease; infection also can be acquired through transfusion of infected erythrocytes outside of the endemic region. Asplenia is a major risk factor for fulminant *Babesia* infection, as is older age, HIV infection, or other immunocompromising conditions. Clinical manifestations are variable, with most relating to severe hemolytic anemia. Infection can be diagnosed by visualization of intraerythrocytic parasites, which appear as either ring forms or tetrads, with the latter often described as having the Maltese cross appearance shown. Complications, including acute respiratory distress syndrome, disseminated intravascular coagulation, heart failure, kidney failure, and coma, are associated with severe anemia (hematocrit level <30%) and parasitemia (exceeding 10%) and are indications for exchange transfusion.

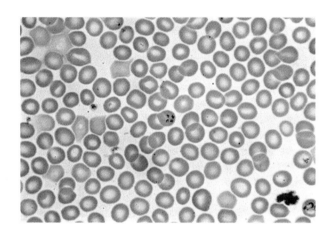

Morulae, basophilic inclusion bodies composed of clusters of bacteria, can be seen in the cytoplasm of monocytes and neutrophils of patients with ehrlichiosis and anaplasmacytosis, respectively. These tick-borne infections cause fever, leukopenia, and thrombocytopenia but are not associated with hemolytic anemia.

Both malaria and babesiosis cause a hemolytic anemia and may present with ring-shaped parasitic inclusions inside erythrocytes. However, banana-shaped gametocytes are seen only with *Plasmodium falciparum* malaria, and the absence of a compatible travel history excludes this diagnosis.

Asplenic patients are at risk for overwhelming pneumococcal sepsis with a high bacterial burden; gram-positive diplococci may be visualized inside neutrophils on buffy-coat stain. Although leukopenia and thrombocytopenia are common with fulminant infection, hemolytic anemia is not a feature of pneumococcal sepsis.

Schistocytes are a manifestation of microangiopathic hemolytic anemia caused by a thrombotic microangiopathy (TMA), such as hemolytic uremic syndrome or thrombotic thrombocytopenic purpura. Although both these syndromes can cause fever, hemolysis, and thrombocytopenia, the absence of acute kidney injury in this patient excludes a TMA.

KEY POINT

- Babesiosis can be diagnosed by visualization of intraerythrocytic parasites in a ring or tetrad form on a blood smear.

Bibliography

Akel T, Mobarakai N. Hematologic manifestations of babesiosis. Ann Clin Microbiol Antimicrob. 2017;16:6. [PMID: 28202022] doi:10.1186/s12941-017-0179-z

Item 63   Answer: D

Educational Objective: Manage conversion of intravenous antimicrobial therapy to oral antimicrobial therapy.

This patient's therapy should be switched from intravenous piperacillin-tazobactam to oral ciprofloxacin and metronidazole. He has a diabetic foot ulcer and osteomyelitis of the left great toe caused by *Pseudomonas aeruginosa* and *Bacteroides fragilis*. Ciprofloxacin and metronidazole have excellent bioavailability and will penetrate bone adequately with oral administration. Continuing intravenous therapy offers no advantage for this patient, and intravenous therapy has risks that include developing a venous catheter–associated bloodstream infection. Intravenous-to-oral antibiotic switching should be considered in patients who have an intact and functioning gastrointestinal tract, whose clinical status is improving, and who are not being treated for an infection for which parenteral therapy is preferred (for example, endocarditis or meningitis). Common infectious scenarios for which a switch from intravenous to oral therapy should be considered include community-acquired pneumonia, bacterial peritonitis, pyelonephritis, septic arthritis, and skin and soft tissue infections. When switching from a parenteral to an oral antibiotic agent, the bioavailability of the oral antibiotics must be considered.

A second antipseudomonal agent is not required for this patient's osteomyelitis. He also has kidney disease, which should discourage use of an aminoglycoside. Therefore, adding tobramycin while continuing intravenous antibiotic therapy would not be the best management for this patient who can de-escalate to oral therapy.

Although aztreonam and ceftazidime have good antipseudomonal activity, neither agent has any anaerobic activity to cover *B. fragilis*.

KEY POINT

- Intravenous-to-oral antibiotic switching should be considered in patients who have an intact and functioning gastrointestinal tract, whose clinical status is improving, and who are not being treated for an infection for which parenteral therapy is preferred.

Bibliography

Cyriac JM, James E. Switch over from intravenous to oral therapy: A concise overview. J Pharmacol Pharmacother. 2014;5:83-7. [PMID: 24799810] doi:10.4103/0976-500X.130042

Item 64   Answer: A

Educational Objective: Manage candidemia with empiric antifungal therapy.

This patient has candidemia. Candidemia occurs most frequently in the presence of an intravascular catheter and may lead to focal organ involvement or disseminated infection as a consequence of hematogenous spread. Risk factors for candidemia and other forms of systemic candidiasis include neutropenia, malignancies, organ transplantation, broad-spectrum antimicrobial agents, immunosuppressive agents, chemotherapeutic agents, intravascular catheters, hemodialysis, parenteral nutrition, and major abdominal surgery. Because systemic candidiasis has a high mortality rate, therapy should be initiated promptly when it is suspected or diagnosed. The finding of yeast in the blood culture is enough to initiate empiric antifungal therapy until the fungal identification is definitive. An echinocandin (anidulafungin, caspofungin, or micafungin) is recommended as empiric therapy for most patients with candidemia. If the *Candida* species is azole susceptible, the patient may be de-escalated to fluconazole to complete the 14-day course of therapy.

Fluconazole is not recommended as initial management for this patient. Several *Candida* species, such as *C. glabrata*, *C. auris*, and *C. krusei*, are known to be intrinsically resistant to azoles.

Systemic candidiasis is usually diagnosed by a positive culture from blood or a normally sterile body site. A positive blood culture should not be treated as a contaminant, and empiric therapy should be instituted immediately, particularly in seriously ill patients such as this one. *Candida* isolated from blood cultures should always prompt a search for the source.

Central venous catheters should be removed as soon as possible in patients with candidemia; however, removal of an implicated catheter is not sufficient treatment for candidemia. All patients must be treated with antifungal drugs.

KEY POINT

- A positive blood culture for *Candida* species should not be treated as a contaminant, and empiric therapy with an echinocandin should be instituted immediately.

Bibliography

Pappas PG, Kauffman CA, Andes DR, Clancy CJ, Marr KA, Ostrosky-Zeichner L, et al. Executive summary: clinical practice guideline for the management of candidiasis: 2016 update by the Infectious Diseases Society of America. Clin Infect Dis. 2016;62:409-17. [PMID: 26810419] doi:10.1093/cid/civ1194

Item 65   Answer: A

Educational Objective: Treat vertebral osteomyelitis.

This patient has a confirmed diagnosis of methicillin-susceptible *Staphylococcus aureus* osteomyelitis and should complete a 6-week course of antibiotics. Although there are no randomized controlled trials regarding the optimal duration of antibiotic therapy for osteomyelitis, a treatment course of 2 weeks is inadequate. For this patient, vertebral osteomyelitis at a single level, not associated with epidural abscess or hardware, has a favorable prognosis; older age, comorbidities, and infection with *S. aureus* are unfavorable factors. However, there is no evidence that antibiotics beyond 6 weeks will enhance therapeutic success. In a recently published clinical trial comparing 6 weeks to 12 weeks of antibiotics for vertebral osteomyelitis, cure rates were not significantly different between the treatment groups. Several retrospective studies have found similar results.

Prolonged courses of antibiotics place the patient at risk for adverse events, including drug-resistant pathogens and *Clostridium difficile*–associated diarrhea.

Cefazolin should not be discontinued now because the patient has only completed 2 weeks of treatment, and 6 weeks is considered the therapeutic minimum.

Monitoring of inflammatory markers during treatment can assist in assessing the success of therapy. Routine follow-up MRI is not recommended in patients who respond clinically. Follow-up MRI may suggest progressive infection and lead to unnecessary additional intervention. Follow-up MRI is indicated with clinical deterioration or if a concomitant epidural or paraspinal abscess was present that was managed medically.

KEY POINT

- The recommended duration of antibacterial therapy for acute vertebral osteomyelitis is 6 weeks.

Bibliography

Berbari EF, Kanj SS, Kowalski TJ, Darouiche RO, Widmer AF, Schmitt SK, et al. 2015 Infectious Diseases Society of America (IDSA) clinical practice guidelines for the diagnosis and treatment of native vertebral osteomyelitis in adults. Clin Infect Dis. 2015;61:e26-46. [PMID: 26229122] doi:10.1093/cid/civ482

Item 66   Answer: D

Educational Objective: Treat severe *Clostridium difficile* infection.

This patient has severe *Clostridium difficile* infection (CDI) and should receive oral vancomycin therapy. All patients with confirmed CDI require antimicrobial treatment, but optimal management depends on whether the episode represents the initial presentation or a recurrence, as well as the severity of the illness. The American College of Gastroenterology defines severe disease by the presence of hypoalbuminemia (<3 g/dL [30 g/L]) plus leukocytosis (leukocyte count ≥15,000/µL [15 × 10^9/L]) or abdominal tenderness. The Society for Healthcare Epidemiology of America and the Infectious Diseases Society of America guidelines define severe disease by a serum creatinine level >1.5 mg/dL (133 µmol/L) or leukocyte count ≥15,000/µL (15 × 10^9/L). Oral vancomycin for 10 days is recommended for the initial episode of a severe CDI infection. Oral fidaxomicin may also be used.

Fecal microbiota transplantation has been advocated as a treatment approach for patients with multiple relapses of CDI. The rationale is that exogenous feces will restore the normal colonic microbiota. Fecal microbiota transplantation is not recommended for an initial episode of CDI.

Intravenous vancomycin is not recommended for treatment of CDI because vancomycin delivered intravenously is not excreted into the large intestine and has no effect on CDI.

Oral metronidazole for 10 days can be used for patients who have an initial episode of nonsevere CDI when neither oral vancomycin nor fidaxomicin is available, but not in this patient with severe disease.

Oral vancomycin plus intravenous metronidazole is recommended for an initial episode of severe infection complicated (that is, fulminant disease) by ileus, hypotension, shock, or toxic megacolon. Fulminant CDI is often associated with ileus-limiting colonic transit of orally dosed medications; therefore, a vancomycin enema through a rectal tube should be considered to maximize colonic luminal concentrations.

KEY POINT

- Oral vancomycin (or fidaxomicin) therapy is recommended for the treatment of an initial episode of severe *Clostridium difficile* infection.

Bibliography

McDonald LC, Gerding DN, Johnson S, Bakken JS, Carroll KC, Coffin SE, et al. Clinical practice guidelines for *Clostridium difficile* infection in adults and children: 2017 update by the Infectious Diseases Society of America (IDSA) and Society for Healthcare Epidemiology of America (SHEA). Clin Infect Dis. 2018;66:987-994. [PMID: 29562266] doi:10.1093/cid/ciy149

Item 67   Answer: C

Educational Objective: Diagnose serogroup B *Neisseria meningitides* in a patient who received the quadrivalent meningococcal vaccine.

Neisseria meningitides serogroup B is the most likely cause of this patient's meningitis. Bacterial meningitis classically presents with fever, nuchal rigidity, and altered mental status. However, all three symptoms may not be present in many patients with confirmed disease. Other clinical manifestations that suggest bacterial meningitis include photophobia and headache. Serogroup B *N. meningitides* accounts for 40% of all bacterial meningitis infections in the United States because the quadrivalent conjugate vaccine (ACYW-135) does not include group B. College students are at higher risk for developing meningococcal meningitis because of risk factors such as living in dormitories, sharing drinks, and kissing multiple partners. Clinical findings that support the diagnosis of meningococcal meningitis include severe myalgia, rapid progression, hemodynamic instability, and early appearance of a petechial or hemorrhagic rash in a previously well person. Finally, the finding of gram-negative diplococci on cerebrospinal fluid (CSF) examination strongly supports the diagnosis.

CONT.

Prevalence of *Haemophilus influenzae* meningitis has decreased in the pediatric age group since the advent of the type B conjugate vaccine, and it is an uncommon cause of meningitis in adults. Adult patients with functional or anatomic asplenia are at greatest risk. Gram stain of the CSF would show small pleomorphic gram-negative coccobacilli, which is not consistent with this patient's findings.

Listeria monocytogenes is responsible for meningitis primarily in immunosuppressed patients with decreased cell-mediated immunity, owing to medications or medical conditions, as well as in the very old or very young. *L. monocytogenes* appears as gram-positive rods and coccobacilli, which are not consistent with this patient's findings. *Streptococcus pneumoniae* is the most common bacterial cause of meningitis in adults of all ages followed by *N. meningitidis*. Since the introduction of the pneumococcal conjugate vaccine in 2000, the rate of pneumococcal meningitis has decreased by about one third, and the greatest reduction is seen in children younger than 5 years. *S. pneumoniae* is a gram-positive diplococcus and is an unlikely cause of this patient's meningitis.

KEY POINT

- The quadrivalent meningococcal vaccine does not include coverage for serogroup B *Neisseria meningitides*, which now accounts for 40% of all meningitis infections in the United States.

Bibliography
van de Beek D, Brouwer M, Hasbun R, Koedel U, Whitney CG, Wijdicks E. Community-acquired bacterial meningitis. Nat Rev Dis Primers. 2016;2:16074. [PMID: 27808261] doi:10.1038/nrdp.2016.74

Item 68   Answer: C

Educational Objective: Treat proctitis in a patient at risk for sexually transmitted infection.

Ceftriaxone and doxycycline should be given empirically to patients with clinical evidence of proctitis who are at risk for sexually transmitted infections (STIs). The differential diagnosis of proctitis in this patient includes *Chlamydia trachomatis* (including the lymphogranuloma venereum serovars), *Neisseria gonorrhoeae*, syphilis, and herpes simplex virus (HSV) infection. In those who also have diarrhea (proctocolitis), *Campylobacter*, *Shigella*, and *Entamoeba histolytica* should be considered as well. In this patient with proctitis, diagnostic evaluation should include nucleic acid amplification testing (NAAT) of a rectal swab specimen for *N. gonorrhoeae*, *C. trachomatis*, and HSV-1 and HSV-2 (even if ulcers are not visible on external examination) as well as serologic testing for syphilis. If anoscopy is not available to further elucidate the most likely diagnosis, initial empiric therapy for *N. gonorrhoeae* and *C. trachomatis* should be prescribed pending diagnostic testing results. If the NAAT is positive for *C. trachomatis*, further testing for lymphogranuloma venereum should be performed, and consultation with an expert in STIs should be sought.

For initial empiric therapy of proctitis, azithromycin would not provide adequate coverage for the possibility of *N. gonorrhoeae* infection.

This patient could have inflammatory bowel disease; however, considering his high risk for STI and the acute nature of his symptoms, an STI is far more likely, and the use of a topical glucocorticoid preparation is not appropriate.

Although it may provide coverage for some of the enteric pathogens implicated in proctocolitis, ciprofloxacin cannot be used as part of empiric therapy for *N. gonorrhoeae* because of high rates of resistance.

KEY POINT

- Ceftriaxone and doxycycline should be given empirically to patients with clinical evidence of proctitis who are at risk for sexually transmitted infections.

Bibliography
Workowski KA, Bolan GA; Centers for Disease Control and Prevention. Sexually transmitted diseases treatment guidelines, 2015. MMWR Recomm Rep. 2015;64:1-137. [PMID: 26042815]

Item 69   Answer: B

Educational Objective: Treat pneumonia after hematopoietic stem cell transplantation.

Ganciclovir for cytomegalovirus is the most appropriate empiric treatment in this patient at this time. The risk of cytomegalovirus reactivation is related to serologic status of the donor and recipient and is unlikely when donor and recipient are both negative. Cytomegalovirus disease after transplantation may manifest as a nonspecific febrile illness; may cause leukopenia and thrombocytopenia; or may cause organ-specific disease, most often pneumonitis, colitis, esophagitis, or hepatitis. This patient is at significant risk for cytomegalovirus infection and has a clinical presentation consistent with cytomegalovirus pneumonia, specifically her presenting symptoms and radiographic findings of diffuse bilateral lung involvement. Although it has been more than 6 months from her hematopoietic stem cell transplantation (HSCT), her recent graft-versus-host disease increases infection risk. She is not receiving cytomegalovirus prophylaxis at this time; her acyclovir therapy is effective prophylaxis for herpes simplex virus and varicella-zoster virus but not for cytomegalovirus. Cytomegalovirus pneumonia after HSCT is associated with poor prognosis and significant mortality. Treatment with ganciclovir should be started while proceeding with the diagnostic evaluation, including nucleic acid amplification testing and bronchoscopy.

Atovaquone is an appropriate treatment for *Pneumocystis jirovecii* pneumonia. Although this patient is at risk for *P. jirovecii* and her presentation is consistent with it, she is taking trimethoprim-sulfamethoxazole, which is effective as prophylaxis, making this infection unlikely.

Liposomal amphotericin would provide broad-spectrum antifungal coverage in this patient who is at risk for fungal infection. However, her presentation and

CONT.

radiographic findings are not consistent with invasive fungal infection, which is more likely to demonstrate nodules on CT. Moreover, the toxicity of amphotericin would preclude its use empirically in this setting.

KEY POINT

- Cytomegalovirus disease after transplantation may manifest as a nonspecific febrile illness; may cause leukopenia and thrombocytopenia; or may cause organ-specific disease, most often pneumonitis, colitis, esophagitis, or hepatitis; ganciclovir therapy should be initiated empirically in patients who present with signs and symptoms of cytomegalovirus infection.

Bibliography

Ariza-Heredia EJ, Nesher L, Chemaly RF. Cytomegalovirus diseases after hematopoietic stem cell transplantation: a mini-review. Cancer Lett. 2014;342:1-8. [PMID: 24041869] doi:10.1016/j.canlet.2013.09.004

Item 70   Answer: D

Educational Objective: Treat methicillin-resistant *Staphylococcus aureus* bacteremia.

The most appropriate management is to continue the vancomycin. Endocarditis and vertebral osteomyelitis are two important complications of *Staphylococcus aureus* bacteremia. Vancomycin is the preferred antimicrobial agent for treatment of bacteremia with methicillin-resistant *S. aureus* (MRSA). An alternative to vancomycin should be considered if the organism is not susceptible or if no clinical or microbiologic (such as persistent bacteremia) response occurs despite adequate source control. Daptomycin is an acceptable alternative if the isolate is susceptible. *S. aureus* with a vancomycin minimum inhibitory concentration (MIC) of 2 µg/mL or less is considered susceptible; intermediate susceptibility is defined as an MIC of 4 to 8 µg/mL. Vancomycin should not be used in the treatment of MRSA bacteremia when the vancomycin MIC is greater than 2 µg/mL because clinical failures have been reported. At MICs close to 2 µg/mL, clinical response (that is, clearance of bacteremia and resolution of fever and leukocytosis) should guide whether to continue vancomycin or change to daptomycin. Source control and appropriate antibiotic therapy are important for improving clinical outcomes. When using vancomycin to treat MRSA bacteremia, a trough level of 15 to 20 µg/mL should be targeted. At trough levels greater than 20 µg/mL, the risk for adverse effects increases without an increase in clinical benefit.

Adding rifampin or gentamicin to vancomycin has not been shown to improve outcomes of MRSA bacteremia and should be avoided. Combination therapy also increases the risk for adverse events (nephrotoxicity with gentamicin, hepatotoxicity and drug interactions with rifampin). Combination therapy is sometimes considered with prosthetic device infections, and an infectious diseases specialist should be consulted for guidance in such cases.

KEY POINT

- When treating methicillin-resistant *Staphylococcus aureus* bacteremia, vancomycin should be used only if the minimum inhibitory concentration is 2 µg/mL or less.

Bibliography

Choo EJ, Chambers HF. Treatment of methicillin-resistant Staphylococcus aureus bacteremia. Infect Chemother. 2016;48:267-273. [PMID: 28032484] doi:10.3947/ic.2016.48.4.267

Item 71   Answer: D

Educational Objective: Prevent infection in patients with terminal complement deficiency.

The most appropriate preventive measure for this patient is immunization with the quadrivalent meningococcal conjugate vaccine. A personal history of recurrent *Neisseria* infection or history of infection in multiple family members suggests a deficiency in one of the terminal complement components that make up the membrane attack complex (MAC). The MAC comprises C5 to C9, and a deficiency in any of these constituents leads to an impaired ability to combat *Neisseria* infections, particularly *N. meningitidis*. Patients are at risk for recurrent meningococcal infection, often caused by unusual serogroups. For unclear reasons, infection in this population is often uncharacteristically mild. Evaluation for terminal complement deficiency is performed by quantitation of total hemolytic complement (CH_{50}). If the CH_{50} is low, more specific testing for individual components of the MAC may be performed. Immunization is the mainstay of infection prevention in patients with defects in terminal complement. The Advisory Committee on Immunization Practices recommends use of a conjugate quadrivalent meningococcal vaccine as well as a vaccine active against serogroup B meningococcal infection, with a booster of the conjugate quadrivalent meningococcal vaccine given every 5 years for adults with terminal complement deficiency. These patients should also receive both pneumococcal (polysaccharide and conjugate) and *Haemophilus influenzae* type B vaccines.

Intravenous immune globulin does not have appreciable levels of complement and would not be useful for infection prevention in a patient with terminal complement deficiency.

Although plasma is rich in complement, plasma infusion is not a feasible long-term approach to repletion of complement levels. Additionally, such treatment would be associated with an increased risk of bloodborne diseases and the potential development of antibody against the missing component.

Prophylactic ciprofloxacin has a role in reducing the risk of meningococcal disease after close exposure to an infected person, but no data support using chronic prophylactic antibiotics in patients with terminal complement deficiencies. Instead, patients should be counseled to be vigilant for development of fever, rash, headache, or other symptoms concerning for *Neisseria* infection.

Bibliography
Stevens DL, Bisno AL, Chambers HF, Dellinger EP, Goldstein EJ, Gorbach SL, et al; Infectious Diseases Society of America. Practice guidelines for the diagnosis and management of skin and soft tissue infections: 2014 update by the Infectious Diseases Society of America. Clin Infect Dis. 2014;59:e10-52. [PMID: 24973422] doi:10.1093/cid/ciu444

KEY POINT

- Immunization with the quadrivalent meningococcal conjugate vaccine is the mainstay of infection prevention in patients with terminal complement deficiency.

Bibliography
Audemard-Verger A, Descloux E, Ponard D, Deroux A, Fantin B, Fieschi C, et al. Infections revealing complement deficiency in adults: a French nationwide study enrolling 41 patients. Medicine (Baltimore). 2016;95:e3548. [PMID: 27175654] doi:10.1097/MD.0000000000003548

Item 72   Answer: A

Educational Objective: Treat a patient with mild nonpurulent cellulitis.

The most appropriate treatment for this patient is clindamycin. Treatment of skin and soft tissue infections is guided by categorizing the infection as purulent or nonpurulent and by grading the severity of the infection as mild, moderate, or severe. This patient has a nonpurulent cellulitis without systemic signs of infection (mild infection). Nonpurulent infections are typically caused by streptococci, and outpatient treatment with an oral agent active against streptococci, including clindamycin, penicillin, cephalexin, or dicloxacillin, is recommended.

After incision and drainage, trimethoprim-sulfamethoxazole or doxycycline would be appropriate empiric therapy for moderate-severity (systemic signs of infection present) purulent skin infections (such as a furuncle or carbuncle) in which the usual cause is *Staphylococcus aureus* (including methicillin-resistant strains [MRSA]).

Because of the increased likelihood of MRSA contributing to infection, intravenous vancomycin would be appropriate to include for empiric treatment of severe purulent skin infections. Severe infections are those that do not improve with incision and drainage plus oral antibiotics or that have specific systemic signs of infection, including temperature greater than 38 °C (100.4 °F), heart rate greater than 90/min, respiration rate greater than 24/min, abnormal leukocyte count (>12,000/μL [12 × 10⁹/L] or <4000/μL [4 × 10⁹/L]), or infection in immunocompromised patients. Intravenous vancomycin is also appropriate for severe nonpurulent necrotizing skin infections (in addition to coverage of gram-negative bacilli and anaerobes). In select patients with cellulitis of moderate severity, vancomycin is recommended for coverage of streptococci and MRSA. These would include cellulitis in patients who are injection drug users, those with nasal MRSA colonization or extracutaneous MRSA infection, or those whose infection is associated with penetrating trauma.

KEY POINT

- Nonpurulent cellulitis without systemic signs of infection is usually caused by streptococci, which can be treated with an oral agent such as clindamycin, penicillin, cephalexin, or dicloxacillin.

Item 73   Answer: C

Educational Objective: Treat community-acquired pneumonia caused by *Pseudomonas aeruginosa*.

The most appropriate empiric treatment regimen for this patient is cefepime and ciprofloxacin. *Pseudomonas aeruginosa* is an uncommon cause of community-acquired pneumonia (CAP), reported in 1% to 8% of patients in various case series. However, it is important to recognize risk factors predisposing patients to this organism because standard treatment regimens for CAP require modification when *Pseudomonas* is suspected. Risk factors for *Pseudomonas* infection include structural lung disease (such as bronchiectasis, COPD, and cystic fibrosis) and frequent COPD exacerbations requiring repeated courses of antibiotics or glucocorticoids. This patient has bronchiectasis, glucocorticoid use, and the presence of gram-negative bacilli on sputum Gram stain as risk factors for *Pseudomonas* infection. Initial treatment with an appropriate antibiotic regimen has been shown to decrease mortality in patients with CAP caused by *Pseudomonas*. For this reason, the use of two agents with antipseudomonal activity is advocated for empiric therapy, with de-escalation when culture and sensitivity results become available. Even in patients with risk factors for *Pseudomonas* infection, it is important to continue treatment with a combination that is also active against *Streptococcus pneumoniae* and *Legionella* species until culture results are available. Recommended regimens include dual therapy with an antipseudomonal, antipneumococcal β-lactam (such as cefepime or piperacillin-tazobactam) or an antipseudomonal carbapenem (such as imipenem or meropenem) and an antipseudomonal quinolone (ciprofloxacin or levofloxacin). The combination of cefepime and ciprofloxacin meets these requirements.

Neither ceftriaxone nor ampicillin-sulbactam is active against *Pseudomonas* and should not be used when this organism is a concern. Although levofloxacin is effective against quinolone-susceptible *Pseudomonas*, administration of a single antipseudomonal agent is not recommended because of the high rates of antibiotic resistance.

The combination of aztreonam and ciprofloxacin provides double coverage against *Pseudomonas*; however, it is inactive against *S. pneumoniae* and therefore is inappropriate for initial empiric therapy.

KEY POINT

- In patients with community-acquired pneumonia and risk factors for *Pseudomonas aeruginosa* infection, the use of dual therapy with antipseudomonal, antipneumococcal β-lactam, or an antipseudomonal carbapenem, and antipseudomonal quinolone agents is recommended for initial empiric therapy.

Answers and Critiques

Bibliography

Cillóniz C, Gabarrús A, Ferrer M, Puig de la Bellacasa J, Rinaudo M, Mensa J, et al. Community-acquired pneumonia due to multidrug- and non-multidrug-resistant Pseudomonas aeruginosa. Chest. 2016;150:415-25. [PMID: 27060725] doi:10.1016/j.chest.2016.03.042

Item 74   Answer: C

Educational Objective: Diagnose common variable immunodeficiency.

This patient has common variable immunodeficiency (CVID). The history of recurrent sinopulmonary and gastrointestinal infections in a young patient should trigger an investigation for an underlying immunodeficiency. CVID refers to a heterogeneous group of disorders that are linked by the presence of low levels of IgG and IgA and an impaired ability to produce antibody to antigenic stimuli. Clinically, patients with CVID are at increased risk for recurrent respiratory tract infections with encapsulated organisms such as *Streptococcus pneumoniae* and *Haemophilus influenzae* as well as *Mycoplasma pneumoniae*. These patients may also develop chronic diarrhea because of enteroviruses, norovirus, or *Giardia*. Based on this patient's history of previous infection with several of these pathogens, further evaluation with quantitative immunoglobulin levels is warranted. Diagnosis of CVID is important; patients with CVID benefit from replacement therapy with exogenous immune globulin. In addition to recurrent infection, patients with CVID are at increased risk for autoimmune diseases, bronchiectasis, enteropathy, and lymphoma.

Patients with advanced HIV infection or AIDS have low levels of CD4 cells and are at risk for opportunistic infections typically controlled through cellular immunity. Mucocutaneous candidiasis infection is one of the most common manifestations of HIV infection. *Cryptococcus* infection typically manifests as subacute or chronic meningitis. *Pneumocystis jirovecii* pneumonia is a common complication in patients with HIV infection who have not received prophylaxis. *Toxoplasma gondii* can cause encephalitis. Tuberculosis and *Mycobacterium avium* complex infection are the most common mycobacterial infections in patients with AIDS. Cytomegalovirus usually manifests as retinitis, esophagitis or colitis, and polyradiculitis or encephalitis. The nature of this patient's infections and history dating back to childhood make advanced AIDS an unlikely diagnosis.

Chronic granulomatous disease (CGD), which is usually diagnosed in childhood, is caused by a defect in neutrophil oxidation. A history of recurrent or unusually severe infections or infections with *Aspergillus* species, *Staphylococcus aureus*, *Burkholderia cepacia* complex, *Serratia marcescens*, or *Nocardia* species suggests the diagnosis. This patient's frequent episodes of sinusitis, bronchitis, otitis media, and giardiasis are not characteristic of CGD.

Myeloperoxidase is an intraleukocytic enzyme that plays a role in the destruction of fungal organisms. Complete deficiency of myeloperoxidase is rare, and most patients with this syndrome remain asymptomatic. This patient's recurrent episodes of infection since childhood are not compatible with myeloperoxidase deficiency.

KEY POINT

- Patients with common variable immunodeficiency are at increased risk of recurrent respiratory tract infections with encapsulated organisms (*Streptococcus pneumoniae, Haemophilus influenzae*), and they may develop chronic diarrhea because of enteroviruses, norovirus, or *Giardia*.

Bibliography

Abbott JK, Gelfand EW. Common variable immunodeficiency: diagnosis, management, and treatment. Immunol Allergy Clin North Am. 2015;35:637-58. [PMID: 26454311] doi:10.1016/j.iac.2015.07.009

Item 75   Answer: C

Educational Objective: Diagnose *Mycobacterium marinum* skin infection.

The most likely cause of this patient's infection is *Mycobacterium marinum*. *M. marinum* is found worldwide in freshwater and saltwater aquatic environments, including swimming pools. Skin infections have typically been reported after skin trauma and contact with fish tanks ("fish tank granuloma"), fish, or shellfish. Hobbies and occupations predisposing to infection include aquatic sports enthusiasts, fishermen, seafood workers, and owners of fish tanks. The incubation period is usually less than 1 month, and the clinical course is often insidious. Infection usually manifests initially as a violaceous or erythematous papule or nodule that may ulcerate at the site of inoculation. Lesions may be solitary or multiple; occasionally, a sporotrichoid distribution along the lymphatic vessels may develop. The upper extremities, including the hands, fingers, or elbows, are commonly involved. Diagnosis is often delayed and is established by isolation of the organism from culture of a biopsy, aspirate, or drainage specimen. Granulomas may be present and provide evidence of potential mycobacterial infection.

This patient's course of infection is indolent and inconsistent with the more acute presentations of *Streptococcus pyogenes* and *Clostridium perfringens* skin and soft tissue infections. Additionally, Gram stain of the intraoperative specimen would have revealed bacterial organisms, and infections secondary to these organisms would have responded to the antibiotics already administered.

Herpes simplex virus type 1 can cause a painful infection of the finger (herpetic whitlow), manifesting as grouped vesicles on an erythematous base. Infection occurs when the virus is inoculated through breaks in the skin. Even without treatment, these infections usually resolve within several weeks and would not be expected to persist for months in an immunocompetent patient.

Answers and Critiques

KEY POINT

- *Mycobacterium marinum* is found worldwide in freshwater and saltwater aquatic environments, typically causing indolent skin or soft tissue infection and usually appearing as papules on extremities after contact and trauma from fish tanks, fish, or shellfish.

Bibliography

Aubry A, Chosidow O, Caumes E, Robert J, Cambau E. Sixty-three cases of Mycobacterium marinum infection: clinical features, treatment, and antibiotic susceptibility of causative isolates. Arch Intern Med. 2002;162:1746-52. [PMID: 12153378]

Item 76   Answer: C

Educational Objective: Discontinue *Pneumocystis* pneumonia prophylaxis in HIV infection.

This patient should discontinue taking trimethoprim-sulfamethoxazole regardless of whether it caused the reported rash the previous week, but she should continue her current antiretroviral regimen. The patient initially presented 6 months ago with *Pneumocystis jirovecii* pneumonia and was diagnosed with HIV and AIDS. Following successful treatment of the pneumonia and initiation of antiretroviral therapy, appropriate secondary prophylaxis was initiated with daily trimethoprim-sulfamethoxazole. She demonstrated an excellent response to antiretrovirals with achievement of undetectable viral load and rising CD4 cell count. Her CD4 cell count has now been higher than 200/µL for more than 3 months, meeting criteria for safe discontinuation of prophylaxis for *Pneumocystis*. Studies have shown that *Pneumocystis* prophylaxis, whether primary or secondary, can be safely discontinued in patients with this level of immune reconstitution.

Atovaquone would be an acceptable alternative to trimethoprim-sulfamethoxazole for prophylaxis of *Pneumocystis*, but this patient no longer requires *Pneumocystis* prophylaxis with any agent.

Primaquine and clindamycin is an appropriate alternative regimen to trimethoprim-sulfamethoxazole for treatment of *Pneumocystis* pneumonia but not for prophylaxis. However, this patient has no evidence of active pneumonia, so treatment is not indicated.

The patient has continued taking her previously prescribed antiretroviral regimen, and the rash resolved, so the rash was unlikely caused by these agents. With the excellent response to this regimen and no apparent adverse effects, the current regimen should be continued rather than switching regimens.

KEY POINT

- Patients with HIV who are taking antiretroviral therapy and achieve CD4 cell counts greater than 200/µL for more than 3 months may safely discontinue prophylaxis for *Pneumocystis jirovecii* infection.

Bibliography

Panel on Opportunistic Infections in HIV-Infected Adults and Adolescents. Guidelines for the prevention and treatment of opportunistic infections in HIV-infected adults and adolescents: recommendations from the Centers for Disease Control and Prevention, the National Institutes of Health, and the HIV Medicine Association of the Infectious Diseases Society of America. Available at https://aidsinfo.nih.gov/guidelines/html/4/adult-and-adolescent-opportunistic-infection/0. Accessed April 12, 2018.

Item 77   Answer: A   [H]

Educational Objective: Treat ventilator-associated pneumonia for 7 days.

The recommended treatment duration for ventilator-associated pneumonia (VAP) is 7 days. VAP is defined as pneumonia developing 48 hours after endotracheal intubation. The most significant VAP risk factor is intubation and mechanical ventilation. Early onset (<5 days after hospitalization or intubation) generally results from antimicrobial-sensitive organisms (*Streptococcus pneumoniae*, *Haemophilus influenzae*, *Staphylococcus aureus*, and antibiotic-susceptible gram-negative bacteria); late onset (≥5 days after hospitalization or intubation) is more likely with multidrug-resistant organisms (MDROs), including *Pseudomonas aeruginosa*, *Klebsiella pneumoniae*, *Acinetobacter* species, *Stenotrophomonas maltophilia*, *Burkholderia cepacia*, and methicillin-resistant *S. aureus*. The recommended therapy duration for VAP is 7 days. A longer antibiotic duration does not improve outcomes, leads to the emergence of antibiotic-resistant organisms, and can increase the risk for adverse effects from antibiotic exposure.

Sputum Gram stain and culture are unnecessary for influencing the timing to stop antibiotics; the implicated organism may remain (colonizing) after treatment has been completed and the patient has improved clinically. Persistence of the infecting organism is not an indication to continue antibiotic therapy.

Antibiotics should not be continued until extubation. The antibiotic therapy duration is the same for patients who are successfully extubated during treatment and patients who remain intubated after 7 days of antibiotic therapy as long as clinical improvement occurs. If the patient does not improve clinically (resolution of fever, decrease in oxygenation and suction requirements) or initially improves and then worsens during treatment, the patient should be evaluated to identify development of infectious complications (pleural effusion, empyema, superinfection, antibiotic resistance) or noninfectious complications.

KEY POINT

- Ventilator-associated pneumonia should be treated with a 7-day course of antibiotics; longer courses contribute to the emergence of antibiotic resistance, increase the risk for antibiotic-related adverse effects, and do not improve outcomes.

Bibliography

Kalil AC, Metersky ML, Klompas M, Muscedere J, Sweeney DA, Palmer LB, et al. Management of adults with hospital-acquired and ventilator-associated pneumonia: 2016 clinical practice guidelines by the Infectious Diseases Society of America and the American Thoracic Society. Clin Infect Dis. 2016;63:e61-e111. [PMID: 27418577] doi:10.1093/cid/ciw353

Bibliography
Dalmau J, Graus F. Antibody-mediated encephalitis. N Engl J Med. 2018;378:840-851. [PMID: 29490181] doi:10.1056/NEJMra1708712

Item 78   Answer: A

Educational Objective: Diagnose anti-*N*-methyl-D-aspartate receptor encephalitis.

The most likely diagnosis is anti-*N*-methyl-D-aspartate receptor (anti-NMDAR) encephalitis. Anti-NMDAR encephalitis has emerged as an increasingly common cause of encephalitis. Anti-NMDAR encephalitis is associated with ovarian teratomas in more than 50% of patients with the disease because of antibody production to a tumor protein that cross-reacts with neuronal tissue. In patients without evidence of teratoma, an inciting antigenic stimulus is rarely identified. The diagnosis is suggested by the presence of choreoathetosis, psychiatric symptoms, seizures, and autonomic instability; detection of anti-NMDAR antibody in serum confirms it. Anti-NMDAR encephalitis should be suspected in young women presenting with encephalitis associated with changes in mood and behavior when initial evaluation for other causes, including herpes simplex virus infection, is negative. Anti-NMDAR encephalitis treatment can include tumor removal (if present), intravenous glucocorticoids, intravenous immune globulin, plasmapheresis, and rituximab.

The most common central nervous system manifestation of Lyme disease is lymphocytic meningitis that may be indistinguishable from viral meningitis with fever, headache, and meningismus. An inflammatory encephalomyelitis may very rarely be observed. Lyme meningitis usually occurs in the summer and fall; it is often associated with peripheral facial palsy and is not associated with altered mental status, psychiatric symptoms, choreoathetosis, or seizure as seen in this patient.

Tuberculous meningitis is a subacute febrile illness with a predilection for inflammatory changes at the base of the brain. After a 2- to 3-week prodromal period, patients often manifest meningismus and varying degrees of cranial nerve and long-tract signs. Tuberculosis is unlikely in this patient because of the lack of chronicity, normal glucose level in cerebrospinal fluid, absence of cranial nerve and long-track signs, and lack of evidence of basilar meningitis on MRI.

West Nile neuroinvasive disease may present with meningitis, encephalitis, or myelitis, either singly or as overlap syndromes in the endemic months between June and October. Limb weakness, which may be symmetric or involve a single extremity, is characteristic. A nonspecific viral exanthema may be found in less than 50% of patients. MRI may show focal lesions of the thalami, basal ganglia, and spinal cord in some patients.

KEY POINT

- When other causes of encephalitis have been ruled out in a patient presenting with associated changes in mood and behavior, anti-*N*-methyl-D-aspartate receptor encephalitis should be suspected.

Item 79   Answer: D

Educational Objective: Diagnose active tuberculosis infection.

The most appropriate management for this patient is to obtain a sputum specimen and perform acid-fast bacilli (AFB) staining and culture. The patient appears to have active pulmonary tuberculosis, based on an indolent course of cough, fever, fatigue, and weight loss and a posteroanterior chest radiograph showing bilateral upper lobe cavitary infiltrates and a left pleural effusion. Although it is essential to initiate antimicrobial therapy promptly, it is important to verify the microbiologic diagnosis of *Mycobacterium tuberculosis* infection first by submitting three sputum specimens for AFB staining and culture. If the AFB stain is positive, nucleic acid amplification testing (NAAT) can be used to differentiate *M. tuberculosis* from other types of mycobacteria, allowing for early initiation of treatment. It is also important to perform susceptibility testing because the frequency of antimicrobial resistance (for isoniazid and rifampin) is increasing.

The tuberculin skin test (TST) and interferon-γ release assay (IGRA) are the initial diagnostic studies used to evaluate for tuberculosis infection. However, neither test can distinguish between latent and active tuberculosis. Latent tuberculosis infection is diagnosed when an asymptomatic patient has a positive TST or IGRA result without clinical evidence of active tuberculosis infection by history, physical examination, or chest imaging. Because this patient has active tuberculosis, treatment for latent tuberculosis with isoniazid plus pyridoxine would not be appropriate. This regimen should only be used in patients with latent tuberculosis.

For active tuberculosis infection, the Centers for Disease Control and Prevention recommends initiating four-drug therapy with isoniazid, rifampin, pyrazinamide, and ethambutol for 8 weeks. In susceptible isolates, isoniazid and rifampin should then be continued for 18 weeks. This treatment regimen is appropriate only after *M. tuberculosis* infection has been confirmed with positive stain and NAAT.

Piperacillin-tazobactam would be an appropriate antibiotic choice if pneumococcus, *Klebsiella pneumoniae*, or *Pseudomonas aeruginosa* were the likely pathogens. However, the presentation of an indolent infection, a positive IGRA, and evidence of fibrocavitary disease in the upper lobes is highly suspicious for pulmonary tuberculosis, not acute bacterial pneumonia.

KEY POINT

- The microbiologic diagnosis of tuberculosis should be verified by acid-fast bacilli staining of sputum samples and nucleic acid amplification testing before initiating antituberculous therapy.

Bibliography

Lewinsohn DM, Leonard MK, LoBue PA, Cohn DL, Daley CL, Desmond E, et al. Official American Thoracic Society/Infectious Diseases Society of America/Centers for Disease Control and Prevention clinical practice guidelines: diagnosis of tuberculosis in adults and children. Clin Infect Dis. 2017;64:111-115. [PMID: 28052967] doi:10.1093/cid/ciw778

Bibliography

Mermin J, Hutwagner L, Vugia D, Shallow S, Daily P, Bender J, et al; Emerging Infections Program FoodNet Working Group. Reptiles, amphibians, and human Salmonella infection: a population-based, case-control study. Clin Infect Dis. 2004;38 Suppl 3:S253-61. [PMID: 15095197]

Item 80   Answer: D

Educational Objective: Diagnose nontyphoidal *Salmonella* infection.

The most likely diagnosis is nontyphoidal *Salmonella* infection. This patient's fever and nonbloody diarrhea are most likely caused by nontyphoidal *Salmonella*, with infection resulting from contact with a colonized snake. Nontyphoidal *Salmonella* infection usually results from ingesting fecally contaminated water or food of animal origin, including poultry, beef, eggs, and milk. Intestinally colonized reptiles and amphibians are asymptomatic and intermittently shed the organism in their feces, creating the potential for fecal-oral route transmission. Handling infected snakes, turtles, iguanas, frogs, or toads or anything in the enclosures in which they live can result in infection. Surfaces contaminated by feces may also serve as a source of infection. The incubation period is usually less than 3 days, and symptoms typically include crampy abdominal pain, diarrhea (not usually visibly bloody), fever, headache, nausea, and vomiting.

Infection with *Chlamydia psittaci* is typically acquired by inhaling the organism in feces from a pet bird. The incubation period is about 1 week and the clinical presentation usually consists of chills, dry cough, fever, headache, and myalgia. Diarrhea may be present but is much less common. Chest radiograph abnormalities are common.

Erysipelothrix rhusiopathiae is a bacterium that infects animals such as fish, swine, and poultry. Human infection is usually occupationally acquired in butchers, fish handlers, and veterinarians. Localized cutaneous violaceous lesions of the fingers and hands are a classic finding, although more diffuse cutaneous infections, bacteremia, and even infective endocarditis can develop.

Mycobacterium marinum is a nontuberculous mycobacterium found worldwide in freshwater and saltwater aquatic environments. Skin infections result from skin trauma and contact with fish tanks ("fish tank granuloma"), fish, or shellfish. Persons predisposed to infection include aquatic sports enthusiasts, fish tank owners, fishermen, and seafood workers. The clinical course is often insidious, manifesting initially as a violaceous or erythematous papule or nodule at the site of inoculation, which may ulcerate. Lesions may be solitary or multiple; occasionally a sporotrichoid distribution along lymphatic vessels may develop. *M. marinum* does not cause diarrhea.

KEY POINT

- Nontyphoidal *Salmonella* is commonly carried asymptomatically by reptiles and amphibians and transferred from the animals' feces to people; human symptoms include crampy abdominal pain, fever, nonbloody diarrhea, and vomiting.

Item 81   Answer: A

Educational Objective: Evaluate persistent *Staphylococcus aureus* bacteremia.

An abdominal CT is the most appropriate next step in the evaluation and management of this patient. Bacteremia persisting more than 72 hours after the start of appropriate antimicrobial therapy suggests a complicated infection, requiring additional evaluation with a longer treatment course. Endocarditis and vertebral osteomyelitis are two important complications of *Staphylococcus aureus* bacteremia. Patients with abdominal pain or flank pain should undergo abdominal CT to evaluate for the presence of metastatic infection of the liver, spleen, or kidney; psoas abscess; or other intra-abdominal source. This patient has aortic valve endocarditis, persistent *S. aureus* bacteremia and fever, new right upper quadrant pain, and abnormal liver chemistry tests, which are concerning for development of liver abscess. Metastatic infections are not uncommon with *S. aureus* bacteremia and require a careful history and physical examination to identify where to look and what tests to perform next. New right upper quadrant pain with liver chemistry test abnormalities should prompt investigation with imaging studies such as CT, which can also evaluate the spleen, kidney, and pararenal structures that may be seeded during bacteremia. Transesophageal echocardiography (TEE) will also need to be performed because of this patient's fever and persistent bacteremia. Development of a perivalvular abscess is a possibility, especially if conduction abnormalities are present on the electrocardiogram. Compared with transthoracic echocardiography, perivalvular abscesses are better visualized with TEE.

Several neurologic complications can arise from *S. aureus* endocarditis, including brain abscess, stroke, and meningitis. Neurologic symptoms can be the presenting signs in *S. aureus* endocarditis (for example, a patient presenting with stroke who has a heart murmur and unexplained fever should be evaluated for endocarditis). New neurologic symptoms that develop during the course of treatment for endocarditis should always be evaluated (such as with head CT). This patient has no neurologic symptoms, so a head CT is not indicated.

Daptomycin is rarely used to treat methicillin-sensitive *S. aureus* (MSSA) infections except in patients with multiple antibiotic allergies that preclude the use of β-lactams or glycopeptides. Persistent bacteremia is likely a failure of source control and requires careful investigation for possible sources of metastatic infection and drainage if amenable.

Cefazolin is more rapidly bactericidal than vancomycin and is preferred over vancomycin for treatment of MSSA. Therefore, switching would be inappropriate.

- *Staphylococcus aureus* bacteremia persisting more than 72 hours after the start of appropriate antimicrobial therapy suggests a complicated infection requiring additional evaluation; endocarditis, osteomyelitis, and intra-abdominal infections are important sites of metastatic infection.

Bibliography

Tong SY, Davis JS, Eichenberger E, Holland TL, Fowler VG Jr. Staphylococcus aureus infections: epidemiology, pathophysiology, clinical manifestations, and management. Clin Microbiol Rev. 2015;28:603-61. [PMID: 26016486] doi:10.1128/CMR.00134-14

Item 82   Answer: A

Educational Objective: Treat necrotizing skin infection caused by *Aeromonas hydrophila.*

The most appropriate treatment for this patient is ciprofloxacin plus doxycycline. This patient has *Aeromonas hydrophila*-associated skin and soft tissue infection. *Aeromonas* species are found in aquatic environments, including fresh water and brackish water, and grow best during warmer months. Lacerations and puncture wounds sustained in these environments can result in wound infection. *Aeromonas* infections of the skin and soft tissue and of the bloodstream are more likely to occur in patients with underlying immunocompromising conditions, such as cirrhosis and cancer, and are more common in men. Necrotizing fasciitis caused by this gram-negative bacillus requires surgery, supportive care, and antibiotics. Pending culture data, empiric therapy for necrotizing skin infections typically consists of broad-spectrum antibiotics such as vancomycin plus piperacillin-tazobactam. When the diagnosis of *A. hydrophila* infection is established, doxycycline plus ciprofloxacin or ceftriaxone is recommended.

The combination of linezolid and metronidazole, although effective against aerobic gram-positive organisms, such as staphylococci and enterococci as well as many anaerobes, is not active against *Aeromonas.*

Nafcillin and rifampin would be active against methicillin-susceptible *S. aureus*, particularly prosthetic joint infections, but is not active against *A. hydrophila.*

Vancomycin plus clindamycin would be effective in necrotizing fasciitis with associated toxic shock caused by methicillin-resistant *S. aureus* but would not be active against *A. hydrophila.*

- Lacerations and puncture wounds sustained in fresh and brackish water environments can result in necrotizing infection with *Aeromonas hydrophila*; this infection should be treated with surgery, supportive care, and antibiotics with gram-negative coverage, such as doxycycline plus ciprofloxacin.

Bibliography

Stevens DL, Bisno AL, Chambers HF, Dellinger EP, Goldstein EJ, Gorbach SL, et al. Practice guidelines for the diagnosis and management of skin and soft tissue infections: 2014 update by the infectious diseases society of America. Clin Infect Dis. 2014;59:147-59. [PMID: 24947530] doi:10.1093/cid/ciu296

Item 83   Answer: D

Educational Objective: Manage a tick bite.

The most appropriate initial management for this patient is reassurance that the risk of Lyme disease is low. In selected patients at high risk, doxycycline prophylaxis has been shown to decrease the risk of Lyme disease if given within 72 hours of tick removal, assuming that the tick has been attached for greater than 36 hours. Knowledge of the epidemiology of Lyme disease in the area of practice is important for making informed decisions about prophylaxis. Even in endemic regions, such as the northeastern and upper midwestern United States, few vector ticks are infected with *Borrelia burgdorferi.* Most patients in highly endemic areas do not develop symptomatic infection after a tick bite because bacterial transmission rarely occurs unless the vector tick has fed for at least 36 hours. In the subset of patients from highly endemic areas seen within 72 hours of tick removal in whom attachment with an *Ixodes* species tick for greater than 36 hours can be substantiated, a single dose of doxycycline (200 mg) has been shown to decrease the risk of developing infection. This patient was exposed to the tick that transmits Lyme disease. However, given the short duration of attachment, her risk for infection is negligible. Furthermore, she is beyond the 72-hour window during which prophylaxis has been shown to be beneficial. The most appropriate management is reassurance, with the caveat that she return for evaluation if she develops a rash, fever, or other suggestive symptoms within a month of the exposure.

Diagnostic testing with polymerase chain reaction to confirm tick infection is not routinely available and not informative because of the low risk of transmission, even if *B. burgdorferi* is identified in the vector.

Checking *B. burgdorferi* titers similarly has low yield because antibodies may not be present during the early stages of infection, and paired serologic testing with a subsequent convalescent specimen in the absence of symptoms is not cost effective.

- In patients at high risk, doxycycline prophylaxis has been shown to decrease the risk of Lyme disease if started within 72 hours of tick removal, assuming that the tick has been attached for at least 36 hours.

Bibliography

Ogden NH, Lindsay LR, Schofield SW. Methods to prevent tick bites and Lyme disease. Clin Lab Med. 2015;35:883-99. [PMID: 26593263] doi:10.1016/j.cll.2015.07.003

Item 84   Answer: D

Educational Objective: Evaluate a patient with potential smallpox exposure.

This man has potentially been exposed to variola and requires active vaccinia immunization to prevent the development of smallpox. Ideally, vaccinia vaccination should be administered no more than 7 days (but preferably within 3) after the presumed exposure. In 1980, the World Health Organization declared that smallpox had been eradicated worldwide. However, because of its ease of deliberate airborne spread, highly contagious nature, and expected significant morbidity and mortality, smallpox has been identified as a member of the A list of potential agents of bioterrorism. Because routine childhood vaccinia immunization is no longer required or recommended in the United States, most of the population is not immune. Smallpox vaccines are available in the event of exposure. Although none of these vaccines contains the actual variola virus, when properly administered the vaccines elicit a significant protective immune response. Although serious adverse events are a greater risk after administration of any live virus vaccine, including those containing vaccinia, persons at high risk for complications from replication-component vaccines are also at higher risk for severe smallpox. Unless the patient is severely immunodeficient (within 4 months of bone marrow transplantation, HIV infection with CD4 cell counts <50/µL, or severe combined immunodeficiency), the vaccine should be given. This patient's use of infliximab would not exclude him from vaccination.

The core protein cysteine protease inhibitor tecovirimat, which has proven activity against members of the orthopox genus, has been approved for the treatment of smallpox in the event of a potential outbreak.

Airborne precautions after potential exposure would only be indicated if fever or other signs of active infection occurred.

Vaccinia immune globulin, available from the Centers for Disease Control and Prevention, consists of pooled human antibodies and is indicated for the treatment of severe vaccinia virus vaccine complications or when vaccination is contraindicated.

KEY POINT

- Vaccinia immunization is appropriate in the event of possible exposure to smallpox (variola).

Bibliography
Petersen BW, Damon IK, Pertowski CA, Meaney-Delman D, Guarnizo JT, Beigi RH, et al. Clinical guidance for smallpox vaccine use in a postevent vaccination program. MMWR Recomm Rep. 2015;64:1-26. [PMID: 25695372]

Item 85   Answer: B

Educational Objective: Evaluate a young patient with herpes zoster for HIV infection.

The most appropriate test to perform next is a fourth generation HIV-1/2 antigen/antibody combination immunoassay.

This test combines an immunoassay for HIV antibody with a test for HIV p24 antigen. This improves the ability of the test to detect early HIV infection because p24 antigen becomes detectable a week before antibody in acute infection. Detection of antigen may help diagnose patients as early as 2 weeks after infection. This patient's painful vesicular rash distributed over a thoracic dermatome is classic for infection with varicella-zoster virus. Older adults and immunocompromised patients, including patients with HIV infection, are at increased risk. Severe or recurrent varicella-zoster virus infections or infection at a young age should prompt an evaluation for HIV infection.

Patients with terminal complement component deficiencies usually present with recurrent, invasive infections with encapsulated bacteria such as *Neisseria meningitides*, *Haemophilus influenzae*, and *Streptococcus pneumoniae*. These patients should be screened for complement deficiency by assaying for CH_{50} activity. If CH_{50} activity is normal, alternate pathway function should be assessed with an alternative complement pathway (AH_{50}) assay. If results of either assay are abnormal, specific component concentrations should be determined.

Selective IgA deficiency is one of the most common B-cell immunodeficiencies. Inheritance may be autosomal dominant or recessive; most cases are sporadic. Patients with selective IgA deficiency may be asymptomatic or present with recurrent sinopulmonary infections (otitis media, sinusitis, pneumonia) or gastrointestinal infections (giardiasis). Other common manifestations include inflammatory bowel disease; celiac disease; an increased frequency of autoimmune disorders, including rheumatoid arthritis, systemic lupus erythematosus, and chronic active hepatitis; and allergic disorders, including asthma, allergic rhinitis, and food allergies.

Common variable immunodeficiency involves B- and T-cell abnormalities and results in clinically significant immune dysregulation. The primary manifestation is hypogammaglobulinemia, and recurrent respiratory infections are a common presentation in adults. The gastrointestinal tract is frequently involved and causes malabsorption or chronic diarrhea. Infection with *Giardia*, *Campylobacter*, or *Yersinia* species may occur, as may opportunistic infections. Concurrent autoimmune disorders occur in up to 25% of patients. The risk for malignancy is increased, including gastrointestinal cancers and non-Hodgkin lymphoma. Patients also have a poor or an absent response to protein and polysaccharide vaccines. Serum immunoglobulin levels are usually low, circulating B cells may be normal or low, and T-cell function varies. The diagnosis is made by confirming low levels of total IgG and IgA or IgM, as well as by a poor antibody response to vaccines.

KEY POINT

- Infection with varicella-zoster virus in a young patient should prompt testing for HIV infection.

Answers and Critiques

Bibliography

Cohen JI. Clinical practice: Herpes zoster. N Engl J Med. 2013;369:255-63. [PMID: 23863052] doi:10.1056/NEJMcp1302674

Bibliography

Kim MO, Geschwind MD. Clinical update of Jakob-Creutzfeldt disease. Curr Opin Neurol. 2015;28:302-10. [PMID: 25923128] doi:10.1097/WCO.0000000000000197

Item 86   Answer: B

Educational Objective: Diagnose sporadic Creutzfeldt-Jakob disease.

This patient most likely has sporadic Creutzfeldt-Jakob disease (sCJD). This is the most common form of prion disease and has no evidence of environmental risk factors. Involvement of several neurologic systems and a rapid onset of apparent dementia are classic manifestations of prion disease. On physical examination, ataxia, myoclonus, and a rapidly progressive dementia are present. MRI abnormalities are not specific for sCJD and vary with the clinical syndrome. Patients with increased T2 signal in the caudate and putamen are more likely to have early dementia and shorter survival. No simple, noninvasive assay is available to diagnose sCJD; however, the presence of T-tau or 14-3-3 protein in cerebrospinal fluid (CSF) can be suggestive. The definitive diagnostic test is a brain biopsy demonstrating widespread spongiform changes with gliosis. No definitive treatment exists for any prion disease, and most are rapidly fatal.

Cryptococcal meningitis may present initially with altered mentation. Cryptococcal meningitis can be seen in apparently immunocompetent persons; however, it is likely that most patients who develop this infection have some underlying immune deficiency. Lumbar puncture may show a high opening pressure, and the CSF typically shows a lymphocytic pleocytosis. The patient's findings are not compatible with this diagnosis.

Tuberculous meningitis may present with waxing and waning mental status changes. However, the CSF in tuberculous meningitis frequently shows high protein (>500 mg/dL [5000 mg/L]) and low glucose (<40 mg/dL [2.22 mmol/L]) levels. Additionally, MRI may reveal basilar pachymeningitis and occasional tuberculomas, which are not seen in this patient.

Vascular neurocognitive disorder (VND) is the term now used to describe cognitive impairment of any degree resulting from cerebrovascular disease. The diagnosis is made when neuroimaging or clinical history reveals evidence of a stroke or subclinical cerebrovascular disease that is responsible for impairment of at least one cognitive domain. The absence of infarcts on MRI and rapid progression of this patient's symptoms are not compatible with VND.

KEY POINT

- Sporadic Creutzfeldt-Jakob disease is the most common form of prion disease, involving several neurologic systems and rapid progression of apparent dementia.

Item 87   Answer: C

Educational Objective: Choose the appropriate treatment duration for uncomplicated community-acquired pneumonia.

The most appropriate management for this patient at discharge is to discontinue her antibiotics. She had pneumococcal pneumonia requiring hospitalization for treatment and stabilization. Her clinical status rapidly improved with appropriate empiric therapy. The Infectious Diseases Society of America/American Thoracic Society guidelines recommend an antibiotic treatment duration for uncomplicated community-acquired pneumonia of 5 to 7 days. A recent randomized trial found no difference in clinical response between patients treated for 5 days compared with control patients who received a median of 10 days of antibiotic therapy. This study was limited to immunocompetent patients who did not require admission to the ICU and who defervesced at least 48 hours before antibiotic discontinuation; short-course therapy has not been validated in patients with complicated infection, including those at risk for *Staphylococcus aureus* or *Pseudomonas* infection. Short-course therapy offers the advantages of minimizing the risk of adverse effects, lowering cost, and potentially decreasing length of hospital stay. Because this patient completed more than 5 days of therapy during hospitalization, no further antibiotics are indicated at discharge.

Under the same circumstances, azithromycin would be contraindicated because the isolate was resistant to erythromycin, indicating a class effect of macrolide resistance.

Continuing ceftriaxone would necessitate either continued inpatient intravenous treatment or placement of an indwelling intravenous line for outpatient therapy, both unnecessary interventions.

The management of patients who have clinically responded before completing 5 days of inpatient therapy can be challenging, especially if cultures are negative. Antibiotic de-escalation from parenteral to oral formulations is appropriate when patients have clinically improved. If this patient had been ready for discharge before completing 5 days of therapy, transition to oral amoxicillin would have been appropriate for completing the antibiotic course.

Although levofloxacin is active against this patient's infection, it is overly broad therapy for a penicillin-sensitive strain of *Streptococcus pneumoniae*.

KEY POINT

- In patients with uncomplicated community-acquired pneumonia not requiring ICU admission, a short course of antibiotic therapy (5-7 days) is sufficient.

Bibliography

Uranga A, España PP, Bilbao A, Quintana JM, Arriaga I, Intxausti M, et al. Duration of antibiotic treatment in community-acquired pneumonia: a multicenter randomized clinical trial. JAMA Intern Med. 2016;176:1257-65. [PMID: 27455166] doi:10.1001/jamainternmed.2016.3633

Item 88   Answer: C

Educational Objective: Diagnose osteomyelitis using radiography.

Plain radiography is the appropriate initial diagnostic test for a patient with suspected osteomyelitis. This patient presents with pain and swelling in his finger after a traumatic injury that has healed. The clinical examination is not consistent with a skin and soft tissue infection (lack of erythema); however, inflammatory markers are elevated, so osteomyelitis due to a contiguous spread of organisms introduced by the injury should be considered. Cortical bone loss must be greater than 50% for a plain radiograph to show findings diagnostic of osteomyelitis, so plain radiography is not sufficiently sensitive to exclude this diagnosis. However, plain radiography is much less expensive than the other available imaging modalities and can be quite specific for bone infection if findings are positive, so this test should be done first. The utility of plain radiography in this patient may be higher because a film was taken at the time of the injury, and subtle changes may be apparent when compared.

If the plain radiograph is not diagnostic, a gadolinium-enhanced MRI would be the next imaging test to pursue. A contrast-enhanced CT can be performed if MRI is contraindicated (for example, because of the presence of hardware). A three-phase bone scan could be ordered with a labeled leukocyte scan, but it should only be done if an MRI or a CT with contrast cannot be obtained. Ultrasonography has limited utility in the diagnosis of osteomyelitis.

With the exception of ultrasonography, all these imaging modalities are expensive and, depending on the technique, unnecessarily expose the patient to contrast agents and excessive radiation; the clinician should always consult with the radiologist if the best imaging modality to confirm the suspected diagnosis is in question.

KEY POINT

- Plain radiography is the most cost-effective diagnostic test that can confirm a suspected case of osteomyelitis, but it is not sufficiently sensitive to exclude the diagnosis.

Bibliography

Beaman FD, von Herrmann PF, Kransdorf MJ, Adler RS, Amini B, Appel M, et al; Expert Panel on Musculoskeletal Imaging. ACR Appropriateness Criteria® suspected osteomyelitis, septic arthritis, or soft tissue infection (excluding spine and diabetic foot). J Am Coll Radiol. 2017;14:S326-S337. [PMID: 28473089] doi:10.1016/j.jacr.2017.02.008

Item 89   Answer: D

Educational Objective: Treat aspiration pneumonia.

In addition to starting azithromycin for empiric coverage of atypical organisms, piperacillin-tazobactam is the most appropriate antibiotic treatment for this patient. He requires ICU admission for severe, progressive community-acquired pneumonia (CAP) after outpatient therapy with levofloxacin has failed to improve his infection. Levofloxacin was an appropriate empiric treatment choice for CAP in this patient, considering his history of heavy alcohol use, which increases the risk of infection with Enterobacteriaceae, including *Klebsiella* species. Antibiotic treatment failure can result from poor adherence, a noninfectious cause of symptoms (such as pulmonary embolism), a nonbacterial infection (such as histoplasmosis), lack of source control (as with empyema), or infection with a resistant organism. The patient's history of heavy alcohol use suggests the possibility of aspiration pneumonia, whereby normal oropharyngeal organisms gain access to the lower airways and cause infection. Other risk factors for aspiration pneumonia include poor dentition, gastroesophageal reflux, dysphagia, vomiting, and reduced consciousness, as can be seen in patients with alcoholism, illicit drug use, or seizures. The localization to the right lower lobe is also consistent with aspiration because this area is dependent when patients are lying supine. In community-dwelling patients with aspiration pneumonia, the most common organisms are anaerobic bacteria, such as microaerophilic streptococci, *Fusobacterium*, *Peptostreptococcus*, and *Prevotella* species; however, Enterobacteriaceae may also be present. Therefore, an empiric agent active against anaerobic organisms and gram-negative bacteria is indicated; piperacillin-tazobactam meets these criteria.

Ceftriaxone has adequate coverage against Enterobacteriaceae (as well as other more common flora such as *Streptococcus pneumoniae*) but has limited activity against anaerobic organisms. Therefore, this agent would not be ideal when aspiration pneumonia is a concern.

Clindamycin is active against gram-positive anaerobic organisms but not against gram-negative agents, such as *Fusobacterium* or *Prevotella*. It also lacks activity against other aerobic gram-negative bacilli, such as *Haemophilus influenzae*.

Metronidazole has excellent activity against anaerobic gram-negative rods but limited utility against anaerobic gram-positive cocci and streptococcal species, so it would not be appropriate as empiric therapy for aspiration pneumonia.

KEY POINT

- In community-dwelling patients with aspiration pneumonia, the most common organisms are anaerobic bacteria, such as microaerophilic streptococci, *Fusobacterium*, *Peptostreptococcus*, and *Prevotella* species as well as Enterobacteriaceae.

Bibliography

DiBardino DM, Wunderink RG. Aspiration pneumonia: a review of modern trends. J Crit Care. 2015;30:40-8. [PMID: 25129577] doi:10.1016/j.jcrc.2014.07.011

Item 90   Answer: E

Educational Objective: Treat enterohemorrhagic *Escherichia coli* infection with supportive care.

This patient has a diarrheal infection caused by enterohemorrhagic *Escherichia coli* (EHEC) and should receive supportive care and monitoring for the development of complications, such as hemolytic-uremic syndrome (HUS). EHEC strains such as *E. coli* O157:H7 and O104:H4 produce a Shiga-like toxin that can cause hemorrhagic colitis; consequently, EHEC is also referred to as Shiga toxin–producing *E. coli* (STEC). Supportive care typically consists of oral hydrations salts; salty liquids such as chicken soup are also effective. Bismuth subsalicylate compounds can help reduce the number of bowel movements.

E. coli infection is typically foodborne, with outbreaks often associated with consumption of a contaminated food source. Beef is commonly responsible when the intestinal contents from an infected animal contaminate the meat during processing. Consumption of fewer than 100 organisms can result in symptoms.

Although EHEC does not invade the mucosa, inflammation is caused by toxin release. The clinical presentation usually consists of abdominal pain, bloody diarrhea, and leukocytosis; fever is often absent or low grade. HUS complicates less than 10% of EHEC infections, manifesting as microangiopathic hemolytic anemia, thrombocytopenia, and kidney injury. It is more commonly seen in children than adults.

Diagnostic testing depends on laboratory protocol. Some laboratories routinely plate all stool samples on media capable of detecting *E. coli* O157:H7; other laboratories restrict testing to only grossly bloody stools or to clinician request. Considering this variability, the laboratory should be notified when STEC is a concern to ensure appropriate testing is performed.

Antibiotics (such as ceftriaxone, ciprofloxacin, and trimethoprim-sulfamethoxazole) and antimotility agents (such as loperamide) are usually not administered to patients with EHEC because they do not provide clinical benefit and their use is associated with an increased risk for HUS.

KEY POINT

- Primary enterohemorrhagic *Escherichia coli* infections should receive supportive care; administration of antibiotics or antimotility medications is associated with increased risk for hemolytic uremic syndrome.

Bibliography

Freedman SB, Xie J, Neufeld MS, Hamilton WL, Hartling L, Tarr PI, et al; Alberta Provincial Pediatric Enteric Infection Team (APPETITE). Shiga toxin-producing Escherichia coli infection, antibiotics, and risk of developing hemolytic uremic syndrome: a meta-analysis. Clin Infect Dis. 2016;62:1251-1258. [PMID: 26917812] doi:10.1093/cid/ciw099

Item 91   Answer: A

Educational Objective: Diagnose cytomegalovirus infection in a solid organ transplant recipient with colitis.

The most likely diagnosis in this patient is cytomegalovirus infection. Approximately 60% to 90% of adults have latent cytomegalovirus infection, with reactivation of disease common in persons who are immunosuppressed (patients with AIDS, transplant recipients, patients taking glucocorticoids). Cytomegalovirus is an important pathogen in kidney transplant recipients, and the risk of cytomegalovirus infection depends on the serologic status of the kidney donor and recipient at the time of transplantation. The highest risk occurs when a seronegative recipient (one who has never had a cytomegalovirus infection) receives a kidney from a seropositive donor. Cytomegalovirus can cause retinitis (especially in persons with AIDS), pneumonitis, hepatitis, bone marrow suppression, colitis with bloody diarrhea, esophagitis, and adrenalitis. This patient recently received a kidney transplant; he has bone marrow suppression (leukopenia and thrombocytopenia), hepatitis (elevated aminotransferase levels), and bloody diarrhea consistent with cytomegalovirus reactivation. Diagnosis relies on isolation of the virus from bodily fluids, such as urine; detection of cytomegalovirus pp65 antigen in leukocytes; cytopathic demonstration of "owl's eye" intracellular inclusions from tissue biopsy (colon in this case) (shown); polymerase chain reaction; and serologic assays. Antiviral treatment is typically indicated in cases of disease reactivation in immunocompromised patients and occasionally in immunocompetent hosts with severe disease. Valganciclovir is the first-line agent and is also used as prophylaxis or pre-emptive therapy in certain transplant patients.

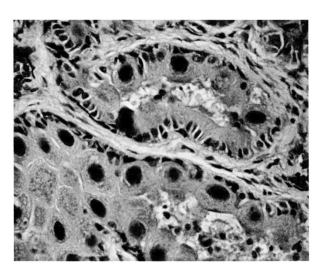

Entamoeba histolytica and *Salmonella enteritidis* can cause bloody diarrhea, but neither presents with pancytopenia. Therefore, they are unlikely possibilities in a solid organ transplant recipient. Furthermore, *E. histolytica* would not cause elevated aminotransferase levels in the absence of a liver abscess.

Strongyloides stercoralis is the only parasite that has an autoinfection route (ability to complete its life cycle entirely within the human host) resulting in an increasing burden of parasites that can survive for decades in patients. Disseminated strongyloidiasis after solid organ transplantation

CONT.

can present with abdominal pain and diarrhea, but it is usually nonbloody. Furthermore, disseminated *Strongyloides* infection may present with sepsis with colonic bacteria, serpiginous rash, meningitis, or eosinophilic pneumonia. All patients scheduled for solid organ transplantation are now screened with a *Strongyloides* antibody and treated with ivermectin to decrease the incidence of this infection.

KEY POINT

- Latent cytomegalovirus infection is present in 60% to 90% of adults, and patients who are immunosuppressed may experience disease reactivation with retinitis, pneumonitis, hepatitis, bone marrow suppression, colitis with bloody diarrhea, esophagitis, or adrenalitis.

Bibliography

Angarone M, Ison MG. Diarrhea in solid organ transplant recipients. Curr Opin Infect Dis. 2015;28:308-16. [PMID: 26098506] doi:10.1097/QCO.0000000000000172

Item 92   Answer: C

Educational Objective: Evaluate surgical site infection.

Gram stain and culture of the drainage from the incision site is the most appropriate test to perform next. Most surgical site infections (SSIs) occur within 30 days of surgery (90 days for surgery involving placement of an implant). The major sources of organisms causing SSIs are from the patient's skin and possibly the alimentary tract or female genital tract, depending on the type of surgery. The organism most often isolated is *Staphylococcus aureus*, followed by coagulase-negative staphylococci, *Escherichia coli*, *Enterococcus faecalis*, and *Pseudomonas aeruginosa*. SSIs are categorized as superficial incisional, deep incisional, and organ/deep organ space infections. A superficial incisional infection involves the underlying soft tissue and presents with inflammatory changes at the incision site (erythema, tenderness), with or without purulent drainage, and few if any systemic signs of infection, such as fever. Such incisions may require reopening to determine the extent of infection, allow complete drainage, and obtain proper specimens for Gram stain and culture to guide antibiotic therapy. Obtaining a culture is important to identify the pathogen involved and obtain antibiotic sensitivity information to determine if antibiotic-resistant organisms are present. Wound drainage fluid, purulent fluid, or infected tissue is the best culture source. Deep tissue or wound cultures are preferable to superficial wound swab cultures, which are more likely to reflect skin or wound colonization and do not necessarily yield the causative pathogen. The most narrow-spectrum oral antibiotic should be used whenever possible.

Deep incisional (involving fascia and/or muscle layers) SSIs usually present with some systemic signs of infection, such as fever and leukocytosis. These infections are managed with debridement and antibiotic therapy guided by results of deep-tissue cultures. Bacteremia may occur with deep or organ space infections, and blood cultures should be considered in such circumstances but are unnecessary in patients with a superficial site infection such as this one.

CT is useful in cases of organ or deep space (tissue deep to the fascia) SSIs to identify abscesses and plan necessary drainage procedures. Imaging, such as ultrasonography or CT, does not provide additional information needed to manage this type of SSI.

A superficial swab of the incision site is likely to pick up skin flora and make interpreting the culture results difficult.

KEY POINT

- A superficial incisional infection involves the underlying soft tissue and presents with inflammatory changes at the incision site (erythema, tenderness), with or without purulent drainage, and few if any systemic signs of infection such as fever; therapy is guided by Gram stain and culture of the wound.

Bibliography

Garner BH, Anderson DJ. Surgical site infections: an update. Infect Dis Clin North Am. 2016;30:909-929. [PMID: 27816143] doi:10.1016/j.idc.2016.07.010

Item 93   Answer: C

Educational Objective: Treat cryptococcal meningitis.

This patient should be treated with liposomal amphotericin B and flucytosine. *Cryptococcus neoformans* is inhaled and causes an initial pulmonary infection. Healthy persons generally contain the initial infection because of intact cell-mediated immunity; however, immunocompromised persons are at risk for dissemination. Risk factors for dissemination include AIDS, organ transplantation, glucocorticoid treatment, diabetes mellitus, liver dysfunction, and kidney injury. The central nervous system is the most common site of disseminated cryptococcosis. The patient most likely has cryptococcal meningitis, as evidenced by the classic triad of headache, fever, and positive cryptococcal antigen titer in the cerebrospinal fluid (CSF). Because the mortality rate may approach 60% in patients without HIV with cryptococcal meningitis, it is imperative that the appropriate antifungal regimen of liposomal amphotericin B and flucytosine be initiated as soon as possible and continued for a minimum of 2 weeks. In addition, although no papilledema or focal neurologic findings are noted, the CSF opening pressure is elevated, and the patient may require serial lumbar punctures.

Fluconazole, an azole antifungal agent, has in vitro and in vivo activity against *C. neoformans*, but it is recommended as de-escalation therapy after the patient has received at least 2 weeks of amphotericin B and flucytosine and is clinically stable. Fluconazole should be continued for at least 2 months after diagnosis, assuming the patient improves and clinical disease manifestations respond to therapy.

Itraconazole, an azole antifungal agent, has some activity in vitro against *C. neoformans*. It is not recommended for primary therapy because of a lack of data. It may be used as an alternative agent and as suppressive therapy or prophylaxis if fluconazole is not available.

Micafungin, an echinocandin antifungal agent, is the drug of choice for candidemia and invasive candidiasis but has no activity against *C. neoformans*.

KEY POINT

- Combination therapy with liposomal amphotericin B and flucytosine is the treatment of choice for cryptococcal meningitis.

Bibliography

Maziarz EK, Perfect JR. Cryptococcosis. Infect Dis Clin North Am. 2016;30:179-206. [PMID: 26897067] doi:10.1016/j.idc.2015.10.006

Item 94   Answer: A

Educational Objective: Diagnose late disseminated Lyme disease.

This patient should have IgG Western blotting to detect antigens to *Borrelia burgdorferi*. She has symptoms of monoarticular arthritis, which has a broad differential diagnosis. Her presentation is most compatible with late disseminated Lyme disease; her previous residence in a Lyme-endemic area and her occupation, with its increased likelihood of tick exposure, increase the probability of this diagnosis. Onset of symptoms of Lyme arthritis typically occurs months, and sometimes years, after the initial infection. Involvement of large joints, particularly the knees, is common. Confirmatory serologic testing using a two-tiered diagnostic approach is required for definitive diagnosis of late disseminated Lyme disease. The initial test is a Lyme enzyme immunoassay antibody titer. This test is very sensitive, and, in a patient suspected of having late disseminated Lyme disease, a negative result essentially excludes the diagnosis. In patients with a positive or equivocal result, as with this patient, a second-tier test is necessary to confirm the diagnosis. Early in the course of infection, both IgM and IgG Western blots are recommended because IgM antibody production predates IgG development. After 4 weeks or more of symptoms, IgG antibody is presumed to be positive, and thus a positive IgM Western blot with a negative IgG likely represents a false-positive result. For this reason, the testing algorithm from the Centers for Disease Control and Prevention specifies that when signs and symptoms are present for more than 30 days, only a confirmatory IgG Western blot should be performed.

The C6 antibody corresponds to a highly conserved protein common to all *Borrelia* strains. Testing using this assay may have a role in diagnosis of infections that occurred outside of the United States. For domestically acquired infections, this test is not currently recommended to replace either component of the conventional two-tier algorithm.

The sensitivity of synovial polymerase chain reaction is low, and this method is not recommended as an initial diagnostic test for Lyme arthritis.

KEY POINT

- Confirmatory serologic testing using a two-tiered diagnostic approach that includes enzyme immunoassay and IgG Western blotting (and, early in the course of disease, IgM Western blotting) is required for definitive diagnosis of late disseminated Lyme disease.

Bibliography

Arvikar SL, Steere AC. Diagnosis and treatment of Lyme arthritis. Infect Dis Clin North Am. 2015;29:269-80. [PMID: 25999223] doi:10.1016/j.idc.2015.02.004

Item 95   Answer: D   ⊞

Educational Objective: Monitor for ciprofloxacin adverse effects.

This patient should be monitored for tendon or joint pain. Fluoroquinolones (such as ciprofloxacin and delafloxacin) are associated with the development of tendinitis and tendon rupture. Most tendinitis occurrences (90%) involve the Achilles tendon and are more common in men and persons older than 60 years. Tendon rupture occurs in 40% of patients and is more common in women. Additional risk factors include concomitant glucocorticoid treatment and solid organ transplantation. Tendinitis can occur anytime during treatment and up to 6 months after discontinuation of the antibiotic. Patients should be counseled to immediately report tendon pain, swelling, or inflammation and stop taking the fluoroquinolone. Other adverse effects involve the nervous system and include headache, dizziness, insomnia, and alteration in mood. Peripheral neuropathy usually occurs early in therapy; symptoms can last years after fluoroquinolone discontinuation and may be irreversible. Another important adverse effect of fluoroquinolones is the potential for QT prolongation and the development of serious arrhythmias. Fluoroquinolones should be avoided in patients with known QT prolongation, risk factors for torsades de pointes, or concomitant administration of other medications that prolong the QT interval. The FDA advises restricting fluoroquinolone use in uncomplicated infections.

The gastrointestinal effects of fluoroquinolones (anorexia, nausea, vomiting, mild abdominal discomfort) do not include pancreatitis, so monitoring the serum lipase level is unnecessary; regardless, the serum lipase level would not be measured unless the patient had symptoms compatible with acute pancreatitis.

Fluoroquinolones are associated with hypoglycemia and hyperglycemia but not with disturbances in sodium level. Therefore, sodium levels do not require monitoring. Hypoglycemia occurs most often in older adult patients with diabetes mellitus but can occur in patients without diabetes. Hyperglycemia has also been associated with the use of fluoroquinolones. Patients should be monitored closely for signs and symptoms of disordered glucose regulation, but monitoring of glucose levels is not recommended in most patients without diabetes.

CONT.

Stool should be tested for *Clostridium difficile* toxin or with polymerase chain reaction assays to detect the genes responsible for production of toxins only if the patient develops diarrhea.

KEY POINT

- Fluoroquinolone antibiotics such as ciprofloxacin are associated with the development of tendinitis and tendon rupture, so patients should be counseled to report tendon or joint pain and swelling.

Bibliography

Lewis T, Cook J. Fluoroquinolones and tendinopathy: a guide for athletes and sports clinicians and a systematic review of the literature. J Athl Train. 2014;49:422-7. [PMID: 24762232] doi:10.4085/1062-6050-49.2.09

Item 96   Answer: B

Educational Objective: Treat *Candida* esophagitis.

Oral fluconazole is the most appropriate management for this patient's likely esophageal candidiasis; he should be treated presumptively and followed for response. The diagnosis of oropharyngeal candidiasis is usually made clinically; although whitish plaques are often prominent, oral candidiasis may also present as diffuse erythema without plaques. The presence of oral candidiasis and painful swallowing symptoms indicates likely esophageal involvement. The preferred treatment is oral fluconazole regardless if the disease is isolated to the oral cavity or extends into the esophagus; however, esophageal involvement warrants a more prolonged course (14-21 days rather than 7-14 days). Clinical response is usually apparent within a few days.

Because this patient is able to swallow pills, oral therapy is appropriate, and intravenous therapy is unnecessary. Additionally, fluconazole has higher rates for complete resolution without relapse of disease than the echinocandins and is preferred therapy unless resistance is documented, which would not be expected in a patient who has not been taking long-term azole therapy.

Topical agents such as nystatin are less effective than systemic fluconazole for oropharyngeal candidiasis and are especially ineffective for esophageal disease.

If presumptive treatment for candida esophagitis is ineffective in improving symptoms, then upper endoscopy is indicated to better define the cause.

Cytomegalovirus esophagitis is seen in immunocompromised patients and rarely occurs in patients with an intact immune system. Although herpes simplex virus (HSV) esophagitis can be seen in immunocompetent and immunocompromised patients, it is much more likely to be found in an immunocompromised person. These viral infections usually manifest as esophageal ulcerative lesions rather than plaques. Biopsies of the ulcer should be performed to confirm cytomegalovirus and HSV. Treatment of cytomegalovirus with valganciclovir (or HSV with acyclovir) would

not be appropriate without first seeing evidence for it on endoscopy.

KEY POINT

- The preferred treatment for oropharyngeal candidiasis, including esophageal disease, is oral fluconazole, although esophageal involvement warrants a more prolonged treatment course.

Bibliography

Panel on Opportunistic Infections in HIV-Infected Adults and Adolescents. Guidelines for the prevention and treatment of opportunistic infections in HIV-infected adults and adolescents: recommendations from the Centers for Disease Control and Prevention, the National Institutes of Health, and the HIV Medicine Association of the Infectious Diseases Society of America. Available at https://aidsinfo.nih.gov/guidelines/html/4/adult-and-adolescent-opportunistic-infection/0. Accessed April 12, 2018.

Item 97   Answer: C

Educational Objective: Diagnose invasive candidiasis.

This patient has *Candida* pyelonephritis, a form of invasive candidiasis. She has several risk factors for candidiasis, such as recently taking broad-spectrum antibiotics, uncontrolled diabetes mellitus, and a history of recurrent urinary tract infections. These risk factors, in combination with the findings of yeast, leukocytes, and erythrocytes in the urine, is classic for this infection. Although the urine culture only grew 10,000 colony-forming units of *Candida glabrata*, the colony count may not correlate with active infection in *Candida* infections of the urinary tract. Thus, antifungal therapy with an echinocandin should be initiated immediately. After identification of the species, the antifungal agent may be de-escalated to an oral azole if the *Candida* species is susceptible to azoles. The total duration should be 10 to 14 days of antifungal therapy.

Acute diverticulitis may present with the same manifestations this patient had. However, the bilateral flank pain and the lack of abdominal pain make diverticulitis less likely. In addition, the urinalysis results showing leukocytes too numerous to count and the classic CT scan finding of perinephric stranding point to a kidney infection.

Antibiotic-resistant bacterial pyelonephritis is a possibility and could explain her progressive symptoms despite appropriate antibiotic therapy for pyelonephritis. However, this diagnosis is excluded by the patient's urine culture, which showed only *Candida* species.

Patients with acute kidney infarction typically present with acute flank pain or generalized abdominal pain, often associated with nausea and vomiting and, less commonly, with fever; hematuria is present in one third of patients. Over half of kidney infarctions are cardioembolic, and atrial fibrillation is commonly found in patients with this diagnosis. A contrast-enhanced CT scan will show a wedge-shaped perfusion defect. This patient's normal abdominal

CONT.

contrast-enhanced CT scan and urinalysis argue against kidney infarction.

KEY POINT

- In patients with invasive candidiasis, antifungal therapy with an echinocandin should be initiated immediately, followed by de-escalation to an oral azole if the identified *Candida* species is susceptible; the total duration of antifungal therapy should be 10 to 14 days.

Bibliography

Pappas PG, Kauffman CA, Andes DR, Clancy CJ, Marr KA, Ostrosky-Zeichner L, et al. Executive summary: clinical practice guideline for the management of candidiasis: 2016 update by the Infectious Diseases Society of America. Clin Infect Dis. 2016;62:409-17. [PMID: 26810419] doi:10.1093/cid/civ1194

Item 98   Answer: C

Educational Objective: Diagnose primary herpes simplex virus genital infection.

The patient's presentation is most consistent with primary genital infection with herpes simplex virus (HSV), and nucleic acid amplification testing (NAAT) for HSV-1 and HSV-2 is the preferred method to confirm the diagnosis. HSV is the most common cause of genital ulcer disease in the United States. The epidemiology of primary genital HSV infections has shifted, and up to half are now caused by HSV-1 rather than HSV-2. However, HSV-1 is less able to establish latency in the genital region, so most recurrent genital infections are caused by HSV-2. NAAT is highly sensitive and specific for HSV. Regardless of type, the initial treatment of primary genital HSV infection is the same (acyclovir, valacyclovir, or famciclovir), but patients with HSV-1 primary genital infection can be counseled that they are less likely to experience recurrent genital ulcers. This patient must also be counseled regarding the natural history of his infection, the need to inform sexual partners of his diagnosis, and the need to avoid sexual contact when ulcers are present. He should be screened for other sexually transmitted infections (STIs), including gonorrhea, chlamydia, syphilis, and HIV, and counseled on the use of condoms to reduce the risk of STI transmission.

Darkfield examination is the appropriate diagnostic test if genital ulcer disease caused by syphilis is suspected. Although syphilitic chancres may appear in multiples and are often accompanied by regional lymphadenopathy, single ulcers are far more common and appear as deeper ulcers with raised regular borders. Syphilitic chancres are generally painless.

Type-specific serologic testing for HSV-1 and HSV-2 should not be used to confirm the diagnosis of genital ulcer disease, especially when ulcers are present. Patients may have evidence of HSV infection on the basis of serologic testing with genital ulcers resulting from another cause.

Direct fluorescence assay testing of the ulcer is not as sensitive as NAAT. Viral culture is a better option if NAAT testing is unavailable.

For all diagnostic tests, sensitivity is improved by obtaining the sample by rotating the swab firmly on the ulcer base after a vesicle is unroofed or from a lesion that has been ulcerated for less than 24 hours.

KEY POINT

- Nucleic acid amplification testing is the most appropriate diagnostic choice for confirming genital ulcer disease caused by herpes simplex virus.

Bibliography

Gnann JW Jr, Whitley RJ. Clinical practice. Genital herpes. N Engl J Med. 2016;375:666-74. [PMID: 27532832] doi:10.1056/NEJMcp1603178

Item 99   Answer: D

Educational Objective: Treat a patient with necrotizing fasciitis and toxic shock syndrome secondary to group A *Streptococcus*.

The antibiotic treatment should be switched from vancomycin and piperacillin-tazobactam to penicillin and clindamycin. This patient has necrotizing fasciitis (NF) secondary to group A *Streptococcus* (GAS) infection (usually *Streptococcus pyogenes*). Additionally, he has toxic shock syndrome, which occurs in approximately 50% of patients with GAS NF. A definitive diagnosis of toxic shock syndrome is established by isolation of the organism from a sterile site (blood and tissue), hypotension, and the presence of multiorgan involvement (in this case, kidney, liver, bone marrow [thrombocytopenia]). Surgical debridement is the primary treatment for GAS NF. The Infectious Diseases Society of America (IDSA) also recommends penicillin plus clindamycin for antibiotic treatment of GAS NF. Although *S. pyogenes* is susceptible to penicillin, clindamycin is added because of its ability to suppress streptococcal toxin production. More studies are needed to establish the exact role of intravenous immune globulin in this setting, and it is not recommended by the IDSA in the latest guidelines.

Doxycycline plus a third-generation cephalosporin, such as ceftazidime, ceftriaxone, or cefotaxime, is recommended by the IDSA for treatment of *Vibrio vulnificus*-associated necrotizing skin and soft tissue infections. This combination would not treat GAS NF adequately because it does not include a protein synthesis inhibitor to suppress toxin production.

Empiric therapy for necrotizing skin and soft tissue infections should address the possibility of mixed aerobic and anaerobic organisms, including methicillin-resistant *Staphylococcus aureus*. Vancomycin or linezolid plus imipenem or meropenem, or piperacillin-tazobactam, or metronidazole plus ceftriaxone, is recommended. When culture results are available, however, antibiotic stewardship principles would advocate discontinuing vancomycin and piperacillin-tazobactam and initiating targeted therapy consisting of penicillin and clindamycin against *S. pyogenes*. The combination of linezolid and imipenem would be too broad in its coverage after the culture results reveal GAS.

- In patients with necrotizing fasciitis caused by group A *Streptococcus*, the combination of penicillin and clindamycin is indicated for antimicrobial therapy after surgical debridement.

Bibliography

Stevens DL, Bisno AL, Chambers HF, Dellinger EP, Goldstein EJ, Gorbach SL, et al. Practice guidelines for the diagnosis and management of skin and soft tissue infections: 2014 update by the infectious diseases society of America. Clin Infect Dis. 2014;59:147-59. [PMID: 24947530] doi:10.1093/cid/ciu296

Item 100   Answer: E

Educational Objective: Manage asymptomatic bacteriuria.

No treatment or further investigation is indicated in this asymptomatic older woman who has bacteriuria discovered on a routine dipstick urinalysis. Although commonly performed, analysis of the urine is not warranted, except when evaluating a patient who presents with clear signs or symptoms of a urinary tract infection (UTI), and may lead to unnecessary administration of antibiotics. Incontinence without urgency or dysuria is not unexpected in many older women. The prevalence of asymptomatic bacteriuria (ASB) is as low as 1% to 5% in healthy premenopausal women (2%-10% in pregnant women) and up to 100% in patients with long-term indwelling urinary catheters. However, most ASB occurs in older adult women and men, with a respective prevalence of 11% to 16% and 4% to 19% in the community, increasing to 25% to 50% and 15% to 40% in long-term care facilities. Except in specific patient groups, well-designed studies have proven that although persons with bacteriuria are at increased risk for symptomatic UTIs, ASB treatment does not decrease the frequency of symptomatic infections or improve other outcomes. ASB is associated with a higher prevalence of potentially dangerous antibiotic-resistant strains in women who progress to an active UTI. Except in pregnant women, who have a known increased prevalence of ASB, which has been demonstrated to lead to serious complications, routine screening for infection in women without symptoms is unwarranted. Screening and treatment are also indicated before invasive urologic procedures. The presence of pyuria accompanying ASB is not an indication for antimicrobial treatment.

This patient does not require treatment for her asymptomatic bacteriuria; additionally, fluoroquinolone antibiotics are no longer recommended for the treatment of symptomatic lower UTIs because of the significant rise in *Escherichia coli* isolates resistant to this class of agents.

Cystoscopy is recommended in the evaluation of microscopic hematuria for all patients older than 35 years or those with risk factors for urologic malignancy. Cystoscopy would possibly be warranted in patients with recurring symptomatic UTIs but is not indicated in this patient.

Culture and sensitivity testing as well as microscopic urinalysis are not necessary in women presenting with classic lower UTI symptoms, including frequency, urgency, and dysuria, without manifestations of systemic or upper tract

disease. Urinalysis and urine culture are not indicated as part of routine health surveillance in asymptomatic patients and should not be performed. They are not necessary in this patient with asymptomatic bacteriuria.

- No treatment is indicated for asymptomatic bacteriuria in otherwise healthy, nonpregnant patients.

Bibliography

Nicolle LE. Urinary tract infections in the older adult. Clin Geriatr Med. 2016;32:523-38. [PMID: 27394021] doi:10.1016/j.cger.2016.03.002

Item 101   Answer: C

Educational Objective: Diagnose Mediterranean spotted fever.

This patient most likely has Mediterranean spotted fever caused by *Rickettsia conorii*. Most rickettsial infections are transmitted by arthropod vectors. Outdoor activities, especially during the spring and summer months, present the greatest opportunity for infection. Mediterranean spotted fever is one of the most severe forms of the spotted fever group of rickettsial diseases likely to be contracted during international travel. Signs and symptoms of illness usually begin following an incubation period of 2 to 14 days after a tick bite, which frequently goes unnoticed. The risk of infection is greatest in northern and southern Europe but also occurs in Africa, India, and the Middle East. Characteristically, fever, myalgia, and headache mark the onset of infection followed shortly by the appearance of a maculopapular and oftentimes petechial rash, generally beginning on the ankles and wrists and typically involving the palms and soles. A distinct eschar (shown) is classically present

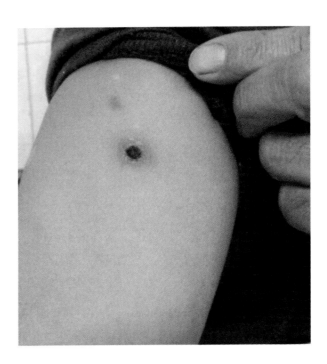

at the site of inoculation along with the development of localized regional lymphadenopathy. Disease is usually mild to moderate; however, vascular dissemination can lead to severe complications, of which neurologic manifestations are the most common. Laboratory findings are nonspecific, but diagnosis may be aided by polymerase chain reaction and serologic assays. A 7- to 10-day course of doxycycline is the treatment of choice.

Anaplasma phagocytophilum, the causative agent of human granulocytic anaplasmosis, can be found worldwide and is transmitted by various *Ixodes* tick species. However, rash is a very uncommon clinical manifestation (<10%).

Lyme disease in Europe mainly results from infection with *Borrelia garinii* or *Borrelia afzelii*, transmitted by *Ixodes ricinus* ticks. In nearly 75% of infected persons, it presents with an erythema migrans rash at the site of inoculation.

Rocky Mountain spotted fever, caused by *R. rickettsii*, is the most common rickettsial infection but is geographically restricted to certain areas of the United States, Central and South America, Mexico, and Canada. Eschar formation at the site of tick attachment is rare.

KEY POINT

- Mediterranean spotted fever characteristically presents with fever, myalgia, and headache followed shortly by the appearance of a maculopapular and oftentimes petechial rash; a distinct black eschar is also classically present at the site of inoculation.

Bibliography

Parola P, Paddock CD, Socolovschi C, Labruna MB, Mediannikov O, Kernif T, et al. Update on tick-borne rickettsioses around the world: a geographic approach. Clin Microbiol Rev. 2013;26:657-702. [PMID: 24092850] doi:10.1128/CMR.00032-13

Item 102   Answer: A

Educational Objective: Diagnose Lyme meningitis.

Lyme disease, caused by infection with *Borrelia burgdorferi*, is the most common vector-borne infection in the United States. The first stage involves localized symptoms occurring 1 to 4 weeks after infection. This early stage is usually characterized by erythema migrans present in 60% to 80% of localized infections. Untreated patients may progress to early disseminated infection, typically presenting as a febrile illness associated with erythema migrans at multiple sites distant from the initial tick attachment. Focal cardiac or neurologic symptoms may also occur in early disseminated disease, typically 2 to 10 weeks after the development of the erythema migrans rash. The most common neurologic manifestation of early disseminated Lyme disease is facial nerve palsy, which may be unilateral or bilateral. Because the cerebrospinal fluid (CSF) findings closely resemble those of other viral infections (enterovirus, herpes simplex virus, varicella-zoster virus, West Nile virus), the "rule of 7s" was derived and validated to accurately classify a patient at low

risk for having Lyme disease (headache duration <7 days, <70% mononuclear cells, and absence of a seventh facial nerve palsy). Nantucket Island is a highly endemic area for Lyme disease; the patient's history of camping 2 months before meningitis onset is consistent with the diagnosis of *Borrelia burgdorferi* infection. The treatment is intravenous ceftriaxone.

Aseptic meningitis caused by herpes simplex virus type 2, West Nile virus, or enterovirus would include a normal neurologic examination. The presence of right-sided facial palsy in this patient makes these unlikely causes.

Varicella-zoster virus can also present with a facial palsy, but this condition usually occurs as part of the Ramsay-Hunt syndrome (with vesicular rash of the external ear). Ramsay-Hunt syndrome is usually seen in young immunosuppressed persons (those with AIDS) or in older adults.

The normal mental status excludes West Nile virus encephalitis as does the presence of facial palsy.

KEY POINT

- For patients presenting with aseptic meningitis and cerebrospinal fluid findings typical for viral infection, the "rule of 7s" can classify a patient at low risk for having Lyme disease (headache duration <7 days, <70% mononuclear cells, and absence of a seventh facial nerve palsy).

Bibliography

Shapiro ED. Clinical practice. Lyme disease. N Engl J Med. 2014;370:1724-31. [PMID: 24785207] doi:10.1056/NEJMcp1314325

Item 103   Answer: B

Educational Objective: Diagnose Epstein-Barr virus infection in a kidney transplant recipient.

This patient's symptoms are most likely caused by infection with Epstein-Barr virus (EBV). He most likely has post-transplant lymphoproliferative disorder (PTLD). His clinical presentation of fever, pancytopenia, generalized lymphadenopathy, and hepatosplenomegaly is consistent with this diagnosis, considering his kidney transplantation and immunosuppressive therapy. PTLD risk is higher in patients with a history of pre-existing EBV infection treated with lymphocyte-depleting agents and in those receiving sirolimus and tacrolimus compared with those receiving mycophenolate and cyclosporine. PTLD can range from a benign monoclonal gammopathy to a malignant lymphoma. PTLD should be considered in any patient presenting with fever and lymphadenopathy or an extranodal mass; treatment includes reduction of immunosuppression and rituximab or other chemotherapy.

Although numerous viral infections can complicate transplantation, cytomegalovirus is the most significant. The risk for reactivation is related to serologic status of the donor and recipient and is most likely in seronegative recipients from a seropositive donor; it is unlikely when donor and recipient are both negative. Like EBV, cytomegalovirus can

CONT.

reactivate and cause pancytopenia, hepatitis, pneumonitis, esophagitis, colitis, or adrenalitis in solid-organ transplant recipients. Cytomegalovirus reactivation is also associated with organ rejection, secondary infection, and an increased risk for graft loss and death. However, cytomegalovirus does not cause generalized lymphadenopathy or hepatosplenomegaly. Cytomegalovirus-seropositive transplant recipients or cytomegalovirus-negative recipients with positive donors should receive prophylactic valganciclovir or undergo routine monitoring for cytomegalovirus viremia.

Herpes simplex virus can also reactivate in the setting of immunosuppressive therapy, but it would be more likely to present with oral or genital ulcers.

Polyoma BK virus reactivation occurs in approximately 5% of kidney transplant recipients and can cause kidney allograft dysfunction or loss. It can present with a gradual, asymptomatic increase in the serum creatinine level with tubulointerstitial nephritis or, less commonly, with ureteral stenosis. Patients may have polyoma BK virus on polymerase chain reaction of the urine or serum or may have polyoma BK virus inclusion-bearing epithelial cells called "decoy cells." The treatment is to reduce immunosuppression. This patient's stable serum creatinine level argues against this diagnosis.

KEY POINT

- Posttransplant lymphoproliferative disorder caused by Epstein-Barr virus can present several years after transplantation with fever, pancytopenia, generalized lymphadenopathy, and hepatosplenomegaly.

Bibliography
Petrara MR, Giunco S, Serraino D, Dolcetti R, De Rossi A. Post-transplant lymphoproliferative disorders: from epidemiology to pathogenesis-driven treatment. Cancer Lett. 2015;369:37-44. [PMID: 26279520] doi:10.1016/j.canlet.2015.08.007

Item 104   Answer: C

Educational Objective: Treat a patient with a moderate-severity purulent skin infection who is allergic to trimethoprim-sulfamethoxazole.

Empiric therapy with oral doxycycline is the most appropriate treatment for this patient after incision and drainage. Treatment of skin and soft tissue infections is guided by categorizing the infection as purulent or nonpurulent and by grading the severity of the infection as mild, moderate, or severe. The patient has a purulent skin infection (furuncle) of moderate severity (systemic signs of infection present, including fever and tachycardia). These infections are typically caused by methicillin-resistant *Staphylococcus aureus* (MRSA). Recommended treatment is incision and drainage and outpatient treatment with an oral agent active against MRSA. Oral trimethoprim-sulfamethoxazole or doxycycline is recommended by the Infectious Diseases Society of America (IDSA) for moderate-severity purulent skin infections; however, the patient has a known allergy to trimethoprim-sulfamethoxazole, eliminating it as an option.

Culture of the purulent material will allow for identification of the microbial agent and a reassessment of pathogen-directed therapy.

Mild (no evidence of systemic signs of infection), nonpurulent skin infections are typically caused by streptococci, and empiric outpatient treatment with an oral agent such as clindamycin, penicillin, cephalexin, or dicloxacillin would be appropriate according to recommendations from the IDSA.

Incision and drainage alone with clinical follow-up is recommended by the IDSA for patients with mild purulent infections. However, in a 2017 randomized clinical trial of patients with skin abscess measuring 5 cm or less who underwent incision and drainage, higher cure rates were observed among those who received antibiotic therapy than those who received placebo. Because this patient has systemic signs of infection, he would be considered to have at least a moderate purulent skin and soft tissue infection and would, therefore, require antibiotics in addition to incision and drainage.

KEY POINT

- Purulent skin infections with systemic signs of infection should be managed with incision and drainage followed by empiric oral therapy with trimethoprim-sulfamethoxazole or doxycycline.

Bibliography
Stevens DL, Bisno AL, Chambers HF, Dellinger EP, Goldstein EJ, Gorbach SL, et al. Practice guidelines for the diagnosis and management of skin and soft tissue infections: 2014 update by the Infectious Diseases Society of America. Clin Infect Dis. 2014;59:147-59. [PMID: 24947530] doi:10.1093/cid/ciu296

Item 105   Answer: E

Educational Objective: Evaluate the results of a tuberculin skin test.

This patient has a negative tuberculin skin test (TST), so no treatment or further management is recommended. The criteria for a positive reaction have been established by the Centers for Disease Control and Prevention (CDC) based on the patient's risks for tuberculosis. A TST reaction of 5 mm or greater should be considered positive in persons at high risk, including patients with HIV, patients with recent known contact with a person with active tuberculosis, persons with chronic fibrotic changes on chest radiography consistent with old tuberculosis, patients who have undergone solid organ transplantation, and other persons who are immunosuppressed (patients taking prednisone >15 mg/d or a tumor necrosis factor-α antagonist). A TST reaction of 10 mm or greater should be considered positive in recent (<5 years) arrivals from high-prevalence countries, injection drug users, residents or employees of high-risk congregate settings (prisons and jails, nursing homes, and other long-term facilities for older adults), hospitals and other health care facilities (which would include this patient), homeless shelters, mycobacteriology laboratory personnel, persons with clinical conditions that put them at high risk for active disease, and children younger than 4 years or those exposed to adults in high-risk categories. In patients with no risk factors for tuberculosis, 15 mm or greater should be considered a positive result.

Because latent and active tuberculosis were ruled out in this patient, a chest radiograph is unnecessary.

Sputum induction for culture is not indicated in the absence of clinical signs or symptoms of active infection and without testing results indicating tuberculosis infection.

Because the patient did not have evidence of latent tuberculosis, isoniazid treatment is not indicated. Isoniazid should not be initiated empirically without evidence of infection.

Because the TST is considered negative and the chest radiograph is normal, latent and active tuberculosis have been ruled out in this patient, and she does not need to be removed from her work area.

KEY POINT

- The criteria for a positive tuberculin skin test reaction have been established by the Centers for Disease Control and Prevention based on the patient's risks for tuberculosis; in patients with no risk factors for tuberculosis, 15 mm or greater should be considered a positive result.

Bibliography

Lewinsohn DM, Leonard MK, LoBue PA, Cohn DL, Daley CL, Desmond E, et al. Official American Thoracic Society/Infectious Diseases Society of America/Centers for Disease Control and Prevention clinical practice guidelines: diagnosis of tuberculosis in adults and children. Clin Infect Dis. 2017;64:111-115. [PMID: 28052967] doi:10.1093/cid/ciw778

Item 106 Answer: A

Educational Objective: Treat latent tuberculosis infection in a patient who is HIV positive.

The most appropriate management for this patient is daily isoniazid plus pyridoxine. He has HIV, and a tuberculin skin test (TST) produces a 5-mm induration, which is considered positive in patients who are immunocompromised. Because the chest radiograph was negative, he should be treated as having latent tuberculosis infection (LTBI) with 9 months of isoniazid therapy. Pyridoxine is added to LTBI treatment in patients at risk for peripheral neuropathy (such as patients with HIV, diabetes, uremia, alcoholism, malnutrition, and pregnancy). It cannot be determined if the patient's tuberculosis infection is newly acquired or long standing because the previous negative TST was performed when his CD4 cell count was extremely low.

Because this patient has no evidence of active infection, four-drug antituberculous therapy is not necessary.

Routine use of a TST and interferon-γ release assay (IGRA) is not recommended. In certain circumstances, however, using a second test when the result of the initial test is negative might be helpful when the risk of infection or progression is increased or risk for poor outcome exists, such

as in children younger than 5 years who have been exposed to a patient with active tuberculosis or in patients with HIV infection. Use of a second test for diagnosing infection when the result of the first test is negative can also be considered when the suspicion of tuberculosis is strong based on clinical presentation or radiographic imaging. Conversely, using both tests when the result of the initial test is positive might be helpful when a suspected false-positive result is obtained in a person at low risk for infection and progression to active disease. This patient is at high risk for tuberculosis and has a positive TST; therefore, additional testing with IGRA is not necessary.

Repeating the TST would not provide additional information. The Centers for Disease Control and Prevention recommends initiating antituberculous prophylaxis in patients who are HIV positive who have a TST induration of 5 mm or greater.

KEY POINT

- A 5-mm induration on tuberculin skin testing is considered positive in persons who are immunocompromised, including those with HIV; if no other signs of tuberculosis infection are present, treatment for latent tuberculosis infection should be initiated with isoniazid.

Bibliography

Lewinsohn DM, Leonard MK, LoBue PA, Cohn DL, Daley CL, Desmond E, et al. Official American Thoracic Society/Infectious Diseases Society of America/Centers for Disease Control and Prevention clinical practice guidelines: diagnosis of tuberculosis in adults and children. Clin Infect Dis. 2017;64:111-115. [PMID: 28052967] doi:10.1093/cid/ciw778

Item 107 Answer: E

Educational Objective: Treat recurrent cystitis in women.

The most appropriate management of this patient is urine culture plus ciprofloxacin. This young woman has a classic presentation and typical dipstick urinalysis findings of a lower urinary tract infection (UTI). Urine cultures are not generally necessary to confirm the diagnosis; however, culture and susceptibility testing are indicated when infection is recurrent. Recurrent UTI is defined as three episodes of UTI in the preceding 12 months or two episodes in the preceding 6 months. Recurrent UTI is common in women. A recurrent UTI may be a relapse or reinfection. Relapse is defined as an infection caused by the same strain (by repeat culture) as the initial UTI and occurs within 2 weeks of completing initial therapy. Reinfection is diagnosed if the UTI is caused by a different strain than that causing the initial infection or if a sterile urine culture was documented between episodes. Most recurrences are reinfections. While awaiting results, she should begin empiric treatment with ciprofloxacin twice daily for 7 days. Although fluoroquinolone antibiotics are no longer recommended as first-line agents for the treatment of cystitis because of increasing concerns for potential adverse effects and uropathogen antimicro-

CONT.

bial resistance development, ciprofloxacin and levofloxacin are the preferred antimicrobial agents when trimethoprim-sulfamethoxazole local resistance rates are high (>20%) or the patient has been treated with an antibiotic for a UTI within the previous 3 months. Having recently received antibiotics defines this patient's UTI as complicated, warranting 7 to 10 days of treatment with a fluoroquinolone antibiotic.

Nitrofurantoin, trimethoprim-sulfamethoxazole, fosfomycin, and oral β-lactams are not recommended as first-line empiric oral therapy in complicated cystitis because of concerns regarding resistance to these agents. In the case of culture-proven sensitivity, these agents can be used in the treatment of complicated UTI.

Ampicillin and amoxicillin are no longer acceptable UTI treatment options because more than one third of community-acquired *Escherichia coli* harbor resistance to this agent.

KEY POINT

- Ciprofloxacin and levofloxacin are the preferred antimicrobial agents for the treatment of recurrent cystis when trimethoprim-sulfamethoxazole local resistance rates are high or the patient has been treated with an antibiotic for a urinary tract infection within the previous 3 months.

Bibliography

Gupta K, Hooton TM, Naber KG, Wullt B, Colgan R, Miller LG, et al; Infectious Diseases Society of America. International clinical practice guidelines for the treatment of acute uncomplicated cystitis and pyelonephritis in women: A 2010 update by the Infectious Diseases Society of America and the European Society for Microbiology and Infectious Diseases. Clin Infect Dis. 2011;52:e103-20. [PMID: 21292654] doi:10.1093/cid/ciq257

Item 108   Answer: D

Educational Objective: Diagnose rhinocerebral mucormycosis.

This patient has mucormycosis (rhinocerebral form), which has a mortality rate of 60% to 80%. Various organisms are responsible for causing mucormycosis, with *Rhizopus* and *Mucor* species being the most common. Patients with uncontrolled diabetes or ketoacidosis have a unique susceptibility. Other risk factors include immunocompromise from hematologic malignancies, organ transplantation, and cancer chemotherapy. The most common presentation is rhinocerebral. This is a rapidly fatal infection that spreads from the sinuses retro-orbitally to the central nervous system. Symptoms and signs include headache, epistaxis, and ocular findings, including proptosis, periorbital edema, and

decreased vision. A pathognomonic finding on physical examination is the presence of a black eschar on the nose or palate. Mucormycosis is diagnosed by tissue biopsy and culture. The most important step in managing any form of mucormycosis is early, extensive, and repeated debridement of infected and necrotic tissue. The drug of choice is high-dose liposomal amphotericin B.

Cutaneous anthrax is the most common type of anthrax in the United States and results after causative microorganisms are introduced into a skin abrasion or open wound. Cutaneous lesions are initially pruritic and painless and subsequently progress to vesicular lesions surrounded by nonpitting edema. The lesions then become hemorrhagic or necrotic, and satellite lesions may form. Finally, a central black eschar can develop and usually resolves over 6 weeks. Anthrax does not cause rhinocerebral infection.

Rhinocerebral aspergillosis has a similar presentation to mucormycosis. A helpful clue to the correct diagnosis is the propensity of rhinocerebral aspergillosis to occur in patients with neutropenia, typically secondary to hematologic malignancy. In contrast, mucormycosis occurs most commonly in those with diabetes mellitus, especially with ketoacidosis, and typically is distinguished by the presence of the characteristic eschar. A biopsy is necessary to establish the correct diagnosis, which is important because treatment of the two conditions is different.

Lemierre syndrome (jugular vein suppurative thrombophlebitis) is a rare complication of acute pharyngitis that involves septic thrombosis of the internal jugular vein and bacteremia, typically involving *Fusobacterium necrophorum*. Lemierre syndrome should be considered in patients with antecedent pharyngitis and persistent fever despite antibiotic treatment. Soft-tissue CT of the neck with contrast typically shows a jugular vein thrombus with surrounding tissue enhancement. This disorder is not associated with necrotic involvement of the nose and sinuses.

KEY POINT

- Rhinocerebral mucormycosis is a rapidly fatal infection that spreads from the sinuses retro-orbitally to the central nervous system in immunocompromised patients, especially those with uncontrolled diabetes or ketoacidosis; a pathognomonic finding on physical examination of the nose or palate is the presence of a black eschar.

Bibliography

Farmakiotis D, Kontoyiannis DP. Mucormycoses. Infect Dis Clin North Am. 2016;30:143-63. [PMID: 26897065] doi:10.1016/j.idc.2015.10.011

Answers and Critiques

Index

Note: Page numbers followed by f and t indicate figures and tables respectively. Test questions are indicated by Q.

A — NAME AND ADDRESS (Please complete.)

Last Name   First Name   Middle Initial

Address

Address cont.

City   State   ZIP Code

Country

Email address

ACP®
American College of Physicians
Leading Internal Medicine, Improving Lives

Medical Knowledge Self-Assessment Program® 18

TO EARN *CME Credits and/or MOC Points* YOU MUST:

1. Answer all questions.
2. Score a minimum of 50% correct.

- -

TO EARN *FREE* INSTANTANEOUS *CME Credits and/or MOC Points* ONLINE:

1. Answer all of your questions.
2. Go to **mksap.acponline.org** and enter your ACP Online username and password to access an online answer sheet.
3. Enter your answers.
4. You can also enter your answers directly at **mksap.acponline.org** without first using this answer sheet.

To Submit Your Answer Sheet by Mail or FAX for a $20 Administrative Fee per Answer Sheet:

1. Answer all of your questions and calculate your score.
2. Complete boxes A-H.
3. Complete payment information.
4. Send the answer sheet and payment information to ACP, using the FAX number/address listed below.

B — Order Number

(Use the 10-digit Order Number on your MKSAP materials packing slip.)

C — ACP ID Number

(Refer to packing slip in your MKSAP materials for your 8-digit ACP ID Number.)

D — Required Submission Information if Applying for MOC

Birth Month and Day [ ][ ] [ ][ ]
M M D D

ABIM Candidate Number [ ][ ][ ][ ][ ][ ]

COMPLETE FORM BELOW ONLY IF YOU SUBMIT BY MAIL OR FAX

Last Name   First Name   MI

Payment Information. Must remit in US funds, drawn on a US bank.
The processing fee for each paper answer sheet is $20.

☐ Check, made payable to ACP, enclosed

Charge to ☐ **VISA** ☐ **MasterCard** ☐ **AMERICAN EXPRESS** ☐ **DISCOVER**

Card Number _____

Expiration Date _____ / _____   Security code (3 or 4 digit #s) _____
MM   YY

Signature _____

Fax to: 215-351-2799

Mail to:
Member and Customer Service
American College of Physicians
190 N. Independence Mall West
Philadelphia, PA 19106-1572

1 Ⓐ Ⓑ Ⓒ Ⓓ Ⓔ
2 Ⓐ Ⓑ Ⓒ Ⓓ Ⓔ
3 Ⓐ Ⓑ Ⓒ Ⓓ Ⓔ
4 Ⓐ Ⓑ Ⓒ Ⓓ Ⓔ
5 Ⓐ Ⓑ Ⓒ Ⓓ Ⓔ

6 Ⓐ Ⓑ Ⓒ Ⓓ Ⓔ
7 Ⓐ Ⓑ Ⓒ Ⓓ Ⓔ
8 Ⓐ Ⓑ Ⓒ Ⓓ Ⓔ
9 Ⓐ Ⓑ Ⓒ Ⓓ Ⓔ
10 Ⓐ Ⓑ Ⓒ Ⓓ Ⓔ

11 Ⓐ Ⓑ Ⓒ Ⓓ Ⓔ
12 Ⓐ Ⓑ Ⓒ Ⓓ Ⓔ
13 Ⓐ Ⓑ Ⓒ Ⓓ Ⓔ
14 Ⓐ Ⓑ Ⓒ Ⓓ Ⓔ
15 Ⓐ Ⓑ Ⓒ Ⓓ Ⓔ

16 Ⓐ Ⓑ Ⓒ Ⓓ Ⓔ
17 Ⓐ Ⓑ Ⓒ Ⓓ Ⓔ
18 Ⓐ Ⓑ Ⓒ Ⓓ Ⓔ
19 Ⓐ Ⓑ Ⓒ Ⓓ Ⓔ
20 Ⓐ Ⓑ Ⓒ Ⓓ Ⓔ

21 Ⓐ Ⓑ Ⓒ Ⓓ Ⓔ
22 Ⓐ Ⓑ Ⓒ Ⓓ Ⓔ
23 Ⓐ Ⓑ Ⓒ Ⓓ Ⓔ
24 Ⓐ Ⓑ Ⓒ Ⓓ Ⓔ
25 Ⓐ Ⓑ Ⓒ Ⓓ Ⓔ

26 Ⓐ Ⓑ Ⓒ Ⓓ Ⓔ
27 Ⓐ Ⓑ Ⓒ Ⓓ Ⓔ
28 Ⓐ Ⓑ Ⓒ Ⓓ Ⓔ
29 Ⓐ Ⓑ Ⓒ Ⓓ Ⓔ
30 Ⓐ Ⓑ Ⓒ Ⓓ Ⓔ

31 Ⓐ Ⓑ Ⓒ Ⓓ Ⓔ
32 Ⓐ Ⓑ Ⓒ Ⓓ Ⓔ
33 Ⓐ Ⓑ Ⓒ Ⓓ Ⓔ
34 Ⓐ Ⓑ Ⓒ Ⓓ Ⓔ
35 Ⓐ Ⓑ Ⓒ Ⓓ Ⓔ

36 Ⓐ Ⓑ Ⓒ Ⓓ Ⓔ
37 Ⓐ Ⓑ Ⓒ Ⓓ Ⓔ
38 Ⓐ Ⓑ Ⓒ Ⓓ Ⓔ
39 Ⓐ Ⓑ Ⓒ Ⓓ Ⓔ
40 Ⓐ Ⓑ Ⓒ Ⓓ Ⓔ

41 Ⓐ Ⓑ Ⓒ Ⓓ Ⓔ
42 Ⓐ Ⓑ Ⓒ Ⓓ Ⓔ
43 Ⓐ Ⓑ Ⓒ Ⓓ Ⓔ
44 Ⓐ Ⓑ Ⓒ Ⓓ Ⓔ
45 Ⓐ Ⓑ Ⓒ Ⓓ Ⓔ

46 Ⓐ Ⓑ Ⓒ Ⓓ Ⓔ
47 Ⓐ Ⓑ Ⓒ Ⓓ Ⓔ
48 Ⓐ Ⓑ Ⓒ Ⓓ Ⓔ
49 Ⓐ Ⓑ Ⓒ Ⓓ Ⓔ
50 Ⓐ Ⓑ Ⓒ Ⓓ Ⓔ

51 Ⓐ Ⓑ Ⓒ Ⓓ Ⓔ
52 Ⓐ Ⓑ Ⓒ Ⓓ Ⓔ
53 Ⓐ Ⓑ Ⓒ Ⓓ Ⓔ
54 Ⓐ Ⓑ Ⓒ Ⓓ Ⓔ
55 Ⓐ Ⓑ Ⓒ Ⓓ Ⓔ

56 Ⓐ Ⓑ Ⓒ Ⓓ Ⓔ
57 Ⓐ Ⓑ Ⓒ Ⓓ Ⓔ
58 Ⓐ Ⓑ Ⓒ Ⓓ Ⓔ
59 Ⓐ Ⓑ Ⓒ Ⓓ Ⓔ
60 Ⓐ Ⓑ Ⓒ Ⓓ Ⓔ

61 Ⓐ Ⓑ Ⓒ Ⓓ Ⓔ
62 Ⓐ Ⓑ Ⓒ Ⓓ Ⓔ
63 Ⓐ Ⓑ Ⓒ Ⓓ Ⓔ
64 Ⓐ Ⓑ Ⓒ Ⓓ Ⓔ
65 Ⓐ Ⓑ Ⓒ Ⓓ Ⓔ

66 Ⓐ Ⓑ Ⓒ Ⓓ Ⓔ
67 Ⓐ Ⓑ Ⓒ Ⓓ Ⓔ
68 Ⓐ Ⓑ Ⓒ Ⓓ Ⓔ
69 Ⓐ Ⓑ Ⓒ Ⓓ Ⓔ
70 Ⓐ Ⓑ Ⓒ Ⓓ Ⓔ

71 Ⓐ Ⓑ Ⓒ Ⓓ Ⓔ
72 Ⓐ Ⓑ Ⓒ Ⓓ Ⓔ
73 Ⓐ Ⓑ Ⓒ Ⓓ Ⓔ
74 Ⓐ Ⓑ Ⓒ Ⓓ Ⓔ
75 Ⓐ Ⓑ Ⓒ Ⓓ Ⓔ

76 Ⓐ Ⓑ Ⓒ Ⓓ Ⓔ
77 Ⓐ Ⓑ Ⓒ Ⓓ Ⓔ
78 Ⓐ Ⓑ Ⓒ Ⓓ Ⓔ
79 Ⓐ Ⓑ Ⓒ Ⓓ Ⓔ
80 Ⓐ Ⓑ Ⓒ Ⓓ Ⓔ

81 Ⓐ Ⓑ Ⓒ Ⓓ Ⓔ
82 Ⓐ Ⓑ Ⓒ Ⓓ Ⓔ
83 Ⓐ Ⓑ Ⓒ Ⓓ Ⓔ
84 Ⓐ Ⓑ Ⓒ Ⓓ Ⓔ
85 Ⓐ Ⓑ Ⓒ Ⓓ Ⓔ

86 Ⓐ Ⓑ Ⓒ Ⓓ Ⓔ
87 Ⓐ Ⓑ Ⓒ Ⓓ Ⓔ
88 Ⓐ Ⓑ Ⓒ Ⓓ Ⓔ
89 Ⓐ Ⓑ Ⓒ Ⓓ Ⓔ
90 Ⓐ Ⓑ Ⓒ Ⓓ Ⓔ

91 Ⓐ Ⓑ Ⓒ Ⓓ Ⓔ
92 Ⓐ Ⓑ Ⓒ Ⓓ Ⓔ
93 Ⓐ Ⓑ Ⓒ Ⓓ Ⓔ
94 Ⓐ Ⓑ Ⓒ Ⓓ Ⓔ
95 Ⓐ Ⓑ Ⓒ Ⓓ Ⓔ

96 Ⓐ Ⓑ Ⓒ Ⓓ Ⓔ
97 Ⓐ Ⓑ Ⓒ Ⓓ Ⓔ
98 Ⓐ Ⓑ Ⓒ Ⓓ Ⓔ
99 Ⓐ Ⓑ Ⓒ Ⓓ Ⓔ
100 Ⓐ Ⓑ Ⓒ Ⓓ Ⓔ

101 Ⓐ Ⓑ Ⓒ Ⓓ Ⓔ
102 Ⓐ Ⓑ Ⓒ Ⓓ Ⓔ
103 Ⓐ Ⓑ Ⓒ Ⓓ Ⓔ
104 Ⓐ Ⓑ Ⓒ Ⓓ Ⓔ
105 Ⓐ Ⓑ Ⓒ Ⓓ Ⓔ

106 Ⓐ Ⓑ Ⓒ Ⓓ Ⓔ
107 Ⓐ Ⓑ Ⓒ Ⓓ Ⓔ
108 Ⓐ Ⓑ Ⓒ Ⓓ Ⓔ
109 Ⓐ Ⓑ Ⓒ Ⓓ Ⓔ
110 Ⓐ Ⓑ Ⓒ Ⓓ Ⓔ

111 Ⓐ Ⓑ Ⓒ Ⓓ Ⓔ
112 Ⓐ Ⓑ Ⓒ Ⓓ Ⓔ
113 Ⓐ Ⓑ Ⓒ Ⓓ Ⓔ
114 Ⓐ Ⓑ Ⓒ Ⓓ Ⓔ
115 Ⓐ Ⓑ Ⓒ Ⓓ Ⓔ

116 Ⓐ Ⓑ Ⓒ Ⓓ Ⓔ
117 Ⓐ Ⓑ Ⓒ Ⓓ Ⓔ
118 Ⓐ Ⓑ Ⓒ Ⓓ Ⓔ
119 Ⓐ Ⓑ Ⓒ Ⓓ Ⓔ
120 Ⓐ Ⓑ Ⓒ Ⓓ Ⓔ

121 Ⓐ Ⓑ Ⓒ Ⓓ Ⓔ
122 Ⓐ Ⓑ Ⓒ Ⓓ Ⓔ
123 Ⓐ Ⓑ Ⓒ Ⓓ Ⓔ
124 Ⓐ Ⓑ Ⓒ Ⓓ Ⓔ
125 Ⓐ Ⓑ Ⓒ Ⓓ Ⓔ

126 Ⓐ Ⓑ Ⓒ Ⓓ Ⓔ
127 Ⓐ Ⓑ Ⓒ Ⓓ Ⓔ
128 Ⓐ Ⓑ Ⓒ Ⓓ Ⓔ
129 Ⓐ Ⓑ Ⓒ Ⓓ Ⓔ
130 Ⓐ Ⓑ Ⓒ Ⓓ Ⓔ

131 Ⓐ Ⓑ Ⓒ Ⓓ Ⓔ
132 Ⓐ Ⓑ Ⓒ Ⓓ Ⓔ
133 Ⓐ Ⓑ Ⓒ Ⓓ Ⓔ
134 Ⓐ Ⓑ Ⓒ Ⓓ Ⓔ
135 Ⓐ Ⓑ Ⓒ Ⓓ Ⓔ

136 Ⓐ Ⓑ Ⓒ Ⓓ Ⓔ
137 Ⓐ Ⓑ Ⓒ Ⓓ Ⓔ
138 Ⓐ Ⓑ Ⓒ Ⓓ Ⓔ
139 Ⓐ Ⓑ Ⓒ Ⓓ Ⓔ
140 Ⓐ Ⓑ Ⓒ Ⓓ Ⓔ

141 Ⓐ Ⓑ Ⓒ Ⓓ Ⓔ
142 Ⓐ Ⓑ Ⓒ Ⓓ Ⓔ
143 Ⓐ Ⓑ Ⓒ Ⓓ Ⓔ
144 Ⓐ Ⓑ Ⓒ Ⓓ Ⓔ
145 Ⓐ Ⓑ Ⓒ Ⓓ Ⓔ

146 Ⓐ Ⓑ Ⓒ Ⓓ Ⓔ
147 Ⓐ Ⓑ Ⓒ Ⓓ Ⓔ
148 Ⓐ Ⓑ Ⓒ Ⓓ Ⓔ
149 Ⓐ Ⓑ Ⓒ Ⓓ Ⓔ
150 Ⓐ Ⓑ Ⓒ Ⓓ Ⓔ

151 Ⓐ Ⓑ Ⓒ Ⓓ Ⓔ
152 Ⓐ Ⓑ Ⓒ Ⓓ Ⓔ
153 Ⓐ Ⓑ Ⓒ Ⓓ Ⓔ
154 Ⓐ Ⓑ Ⓒ Ⓓ Ⓔ
155 Ⓐ Ⓑ Ⓒ Ⓓ Ⓔ

156 Ⓐ Ⓑ Ⓒ Ⓓ Ⓔ
157 Ⓐ Ⓑ Ⓒ Ⓓ Ⓔ
158 Ⓐ Ⓑ Ⓒ Ⓓ Ⓔ
159 Ⓐ Ⓑ Ⓒ Ⓓ Ⓔ
160 Ⓐ Ⓑ Ⓒ Ⓓ Ⓔ

161 Ⓐ Ⓑ Ⓒ Ⓓ Ⓔ
162 Ⓐ Ⓑ Ⓒ Ⓓ Ⓔ
163 Ⓐ Ⓑ Ⓒ Ⓓ Ⓔ
164 Ⓐ Ⓑ Ⓒ Ⓓ Ⓔ
165 Ⓐ Ⓑ Ⓒ Ⓓ Ⓔ

166 Ⓐ Ⓑ Ⓒ Ⓓ Ⓔ
167 Ⓐ Ⓑ Ⓒ Ⓓ Ⓔ
168 Ⓐ Ⓑ Ⓒ Ⓓ Ⓔ
169 Ⓐ Ⓑ Ⓒ Ⓓ Ⓔ
170 Ⓐ Ⓑ Ⓒ Ⓓ Ⓔ

171 Ⓐ Ⓑ Ⓒ Ⓓ Ⓔ
172 Ⓐ Ⓑ Ⓒ Ⓓ Ⓔ
173 Ⓐ Ⓑ Ⓒ Ⓓ Ⓔ
174 Ⓐ Ⓑ Ⓒ Ⓓ Ⓔ
175 Ⓐ Ⓑ Ⓒ Ⓓ Ⓔ

176 Ⓐ Ⓑ Ⓒ Ⓓ Ⓔ
177 Ⓐ Ⓑ Ⓒ Ⓓ Ⓔ
178 Ⓐ Ⓑ Ⓒ Ⓓ Ⓔ
179 Ⓐ Ⓑ Ⓒ Ⓓ Ⓔ
180 Ⓐ Ⓑ Ⓒ Ⓓ Ⓔ